THE TRIUMPH OF MILITARY ZIONISM

THE TRIUMPH OF MILITARY ZIONISM

NATIONALISM AND THE ORIGINS OF THE ISRAELI RIGHT

COLIN SHINDLER

I.B. TAURIS

LONDON · NEW YORK

Published in 2006 by I.B.Tauris & Co Ltd
6 Salem Road, London W2 4BU
175 Fifth Avenue, New York NY 10010
www.ibtauris.com

In the United States of America and Canada distributed by
Palgrave Macmillan a division of St. Martin's Press
175 Fifth Avenue, New York NY 10010

International Library of Political Studies 9

ISBN 1 84511 030 7

EAN 978 1 84511 030 7

A full CIP record for this book is available from the British Library
A full CIP record for this book is available from the Library of Congress

Library of Congress catalog card: available

Printed and bound in Great Britain by MPG Books Ltd, Bodmin
camera-ready copy edited and supplied by the author

FOR

FELEK SCHARF 1914-2003

A SON OF JEWISH POLAND AND ADMIRER OF JABOTINSKY

'Hands off Czechoslovakia'
'For Your Freedom and Ours'

Slogans on banners at a dissident demonstration
Red Square, Moscow, August 1968

CONTENTS

ACKNOWLEDGMENTS

I would like to thank all those who have shown an interest in my work - my students, colleagues, family and friends. I apologize retroactively therefore if the most innocuous of chats has ended up in a discussion of Jabotinsky in the 1930s. Several libraries and archives in Tel Aviv, Jerusalem, New York, Washington, London and Oxford assisted me in my deliberations. In particular, I do wish to thank Amira Stern and her dedicated staff at Machon Jabotinsky in Israel where they devotedly look after the legacy of Jabotinsky. One member of the staff, Tanya Gruz, an immigrant from Kiev in the 1970s, passed away before the publication of this book. Not only was she extremely knowledgeable, but she was always considerate and insightful – and I am indebted to her. May her memory be for a blessing.

Jabotinsky spoke many languages fluently and I can testify that his letters in English were remarkably eloquent for someone born in Tsarist Russia as well as grammatically correct. It is a talent which my own generation despite the multi-cultural essence of our times has truly lost. Jabotinsky wrote in many languages and indeed often changed language in mid-letter. In addition, the publications of his movements were published in a plethora of languages in a multitude of countries where the Jewish Diaspora located itself. I would therefore like to thank the following for helping me to decipher material and often enlightening me as to its interpretation. They are Barry Davis, Misha Krutikov, Jenny Levin, Michael Sherbourne, Howard Spier and Lindsey Taylor-Guthartz. I am grateful to Paolo di Motoli who located some of Jabotinsky's student articles in *Avanti*. Yechiel Kadishai was able to read Menachem Begin's highly individualized handwriting and thereby to record his reconstructed speech relating to the Betar conference in Warsaw in 1938. Yitzhak Shamir shared his memory of pre-war Poland with me and particularly the ideological influences on him during his time in the Lehi underground. My students, Jill, Duchess of Hamilton, and Tancred Bradshaw helped to clarify individual points of British policy in Palestine during the inter-war years. I am also grateful to Barry Davis and Laurence Weinbaum for their comments in reading early drafts of the manuscript. I.B. Tauris have published my books previously and once again I thank them for their professionalism. I am indebted to Audrey Daly for her incisive copyediting. My son, Joshua, once again dealt with his father's inability to cope with the electronic wonders of the twenty-first century and formatted the manuscript.

The writing of this book came at a time of great stress when successive illnesses afflicted my family. The writing of this book certainly had a therapeutic function for myself therefore.

As in the past, I have used a transliteration system where familiarity has superseded convention. Any errors of fact or interpretation are mine alone.

Colin Shindler
London, September 2005

INTRODUCTION

Inevitably, therefore, the question must arise of 'transferring' those Arabs elsewhere so as to make at least some room for Jewish newcomers. But it must be hateful for any Jew to think that the rebirth of a Jewish State should ever be linked with such an odious suggestion as the removal of non-Jewish citizens.[1]

So wrote Vladimir Jabotinsky in his preparatory notes for his speech in Dublin on 12 January 1938. His mention of 'transfer' was made in the context of his opposition to the proposal in the Peel Commission Report to move nearly a quarter of a million Palestinian Arabs. Indeed, in a speech a few days earlier in Manchester, he told his audience that he was against both the compulsory and the non-compulsory transfer of Arabs. He commented that 'some Jews think that they can bamboozle the Arabs. They can't. You can only carry Zionism through straightforward methods.'[2] As early as the 1920s, Jabotinsky had disagreed with Israel Zangwill who suggested that half a million Arabs could be deported to Mesopotamia. He opposed Zangwill's belief that 'if you want to give a country to a homeless people, it is foolish to permit it to become a country with two peoples.'[3] Disagreeing with Zangwill, Jabotinsky remarked 'My generation grew up in the spiritual enthusiasm for freedom; you may attack it and call it all kinds of names – liberalism, anarchism, fatalism – but I prefer it.'

Such categorical responses would surprise many in Israel today – from the belligerent far Right who quote Jabotinsky at their rallies to those on the unthinking section of the Left who believe that Jabotinsky was a dyed-in-the-wool Fascist. As academics such as Joseph Heller and Sasson Sofer and loyal adherents as Shmuel Katz have shown, Vladimir Ze'ev Jabotinsky was a far more sophisticated and complex figure than such spitting imagery conveys. In part, the vision of Jabotinsky that comes down to us over sixty years after his death was constructed by both David Ben-Gurion and Menachem Begin. It was a product of the internecine war between the Right and the Left in Israel. But it was undoubtedly the product of Menachem Begin's determined attempt to seek and maintain the leadership of the national camp in Israel in 1948. It was also part of a wider desire to retroactively reinterpret Revisionist Zionism through the prism of the Irgun and its political successors.

This book is not a biography of Jabotinsky, but it does document Jabotinsky's identity as an authoritarian, secular, national liberal, someone who looked to Garibaldi, Mazzini and the early nineteenth century national revolutionary tradition - when nationalism was a progressive force. It primarily examines Jabotinsky's struggle against the Maximalists in his movement who often identified with the étatist interwar regimes such as the new Italy of Benito Mussolini. Jabotinsky inspired his followers to turn themselves into 'new Jews', no longer the downtrodden and despised of the ghetto. He taught them to see themselves as the spiritual heirs of King David who would break with history, demolish the ghetto walls and build the Jewish State. Such a philosophy urged a return to Zionist basics in which the figure of Herzl was selectively reclaimed. As Derek Penslar has commented, 'Every generation invents its own Herzl, from the stern and tragic visionary of classic Zionist ideology to the post-Zionist image of Herzl as the neurasthenic aesthete, a narcissist suffering from unrequited love.'[4] Herzl's pursuit of personal honour – transformed and integrated into a defence of Jewish honour – in his Zionist awakening became a foundation stone in Jabotinsky's promotion amongst his young disciples of hadar, a chivalrous, exalted self-dignity. Part of this education was to inculcate the ability to defend themselves – and especially when the British were unable either to protect the Jews of Palestine or to arm them.

There are some – often those who are not conversant with the struggle within the Revisionist movement – who apply the easy label of 'Fascist' to Jabotinsky. Walter Laqueur in his classic *History of Zionism* adopted a different stand. He wrote:

> In the leader of the Revisionist movement the similarities to Fascism were more apparent than real. The basic tenet of Fascism was the negation of liberalism whereas Jabotinsky to the end of his life remained a confirmed liberal, or, to be precise, a liberal anarchist....Jabotinsky, however much one may dislike some of his ideas and actions, was not a Fascist, and since a Fascist movement headed by a non-Fascist is clearly an impossibility, the Revisionist movement, for this reason if for no other, cannot be defined as Fascist in character.

> Within the movement there were however sections, some of them influential, which were less deeply imbued than Jabotinsky with the old fashioned principles

of liberalism or even actively opposed to them. Among them Fascist ideas had made considerable headway and, but for the rise of Hitler and Nazism, would no doubt have become even more pronounced.[5]

The exchange between Shlomo Avineri and Israel Eldad in the early 1980s was more typical of the polarized approach to the figure of Jabotinsky. The former understood him as an integral nationalist whilst the latter viewed him as the epitome of open liberalism. As Raphaella Bilski Ben-Hur and Joseph Heller have shown, Jabotinsky's 'Fascism' was intimately related to the context in which he expressed such views. For example, there is no doubt that Jabotinsky's views on national arbitration and corporativism are reflected in Italian Fascism. During the mid-1930s, Jabotinsky courted Mussolini's regime as Italian ambition to replace Britain in the Mediterranean became palpable. Such opportunism created pressure on the British and was facilitated by the fact that there was no state anti-Semitism in Italy. Many Italian Revisionists were sympathetic to Mussolini and such contacts enabled Betar to open a marine training school at Civitavecchia. Indeed, Eran Kaplan has pointed out that Italian members of Betar demonstrated with Italian soldiers in support of the military campaign in Abyssinia.[6] In his articles at this time, Jabotinsky denied any allegiance to Fascism, but was careful not to be critical of the Italian regime.[7] Ben-Hur writes 'Did he borrow elements from Fascism, or did he oppose Fascism and what it symbolized? Was he firmly rooted in the opposing camp of liberal democracy? For instance, Jabotinsky emphasized that his corporatist ideas did not derive from Italian Fascism but from Leon Blum's "Front Populaire" in France.'[8] It is clear that in the context of opposing the Maximalists in his movement – a context which many writers do not address – he condemned Fascism and spoke up unequivocally for liberalism and democracy. In December 1928, he privately referred to Abba Achimeir as 'talented, but too much a Fascist'[9] and condemned the political direction of Brit HaBiryonim after its formation two years later.[10]

In contrast, Jabotinsky also laid great emphasis on the acting out of ritual and the prominence of symbols. He invoked the heroism of the Jewish past rather than the interregnum of the despised ghetto. In his own movement, the focus was always on the leader. There were no elections for the head of Betar. No doubt, he became more authoritarian after the split in the Revisionist movement in 1933 – his enemies accused him of Bonapartism. Yet Jabotinsky seemed to imply that all this was a basic necessity during the breakthrough period to attaining the Jewish state.

It is, of course, notoriously difficult to define Fascism. Roger Griffin illustrated the labyrinthine complexities of doing so, but settled on the following definition:

> Fascism is a genus of political ideology whose mythic core in its various permutations is a palingenetic form of populist ultra-nationalism.[11]

Griffin places the Revisionists in the context of the irredentism of the IRA and the Basques as movements who struggle for liberal ends using illiberal means. Yet the Revisionists and their Maximalist offshoot, the Irgun Zvai Leumi were not one and the same. They, in fact, opposed the violence of the Irgun from Black Sunday in November 1937 until the establishment of the state of Israel in May 1948. Indeed, the Irgun, standing as the Herut movement competed with the official Revisionists in the first Israeli elections in 1949. The telescoping of the Revisionists with the inheritors of their Maximalist wing is all too common for those who are not acquainted with Jabotinsky's struggle against pro-Fascist and radical nationalist elements in the movements that he headed during the 1930s.

A more credible accusation is directed at Jabotinsky's inability to publicly condemn the Irgun's actions on and after Black Sunday in November 1937. His tortuous discussions with Eliahu Golomb, the lack of clarification in his article 'Amen' and his general approach towards the Maximalists suggest tactical manoeuvres rather than a dramatic change after a lifetime of following one path. Jabotinsky's plan for a symbolic uprising should be seen in this light. It was a suggestion which both puzzled and bemused the leaders of the Irgun – they regarded it as more public relations than public reality. As Sasson Sofer has remarked, 'The contention that had Jabotinsky survived he would have supported the revolt is the kind of speculation that history can never verify.'[12] Being the head of the Revisionists, Betar and the Irgun – organizations with very different political agendas – was in itself a contradiction, and Jabotinsky struggled in vain to bridge the ideological gap between his warring adherents.

The issues were too fundamental and led to future accusations of denial, ambivalence and indecision on the part of Jabotinsky's detractors. In riding the tiger, Jabotinsky clearly hoped that an amelioration of the political situation in both Europe and Palestine plus an intended integration of the Irgun into the Haganah would produce some space to outflank his adversaries. It was not to be. Ben-Gurion vetoed any re-entry of the Irgun which now attacked the British and war – unexpected by Jabotinsky – broke out. In August 1940, death claimed Jabotinsky at the age of 59.

Following his death, Ben-Zion Netanyahu eulogized Jabotinsky and characterized him grandiosely but symbolically in terms of the great figures of the ancient Jewish past.

> Jabotinsky was not made out of the same spiritual stuff as Herzl, Nordau and Zangwill. To best realize this, we should picture them as living in another epoch of Jewish history – that of two thousand years ago. Herzl, the majestic, statesmanlike leader, the dreamer of national grandeur, would perhaps have become an Alexander Yannai; Zangwill, the meticulous sharp-witted thinker – a Shammai; Nordau, the academic, encyclopaedic figure – a Rabban Gamliel. But Jabotinsky could have lived only as a Hezekiah ben Menachem, the founder of the Zealot sect or at least as a Yochanan of Gush Chalav.[13]

Perhaps it was this urge to zealotry which endeared him to his youthful followers. Yet whereas he was willing to speak of 'the conscience of the world' as late as 1938, Menachem Begin preferred the Maximalist ideal of stripping Zionism of its universalist aspects.

Some Jewish nationalists in Palestine saw Jabotinsky's defensive 'Iron Wall' as inadequate. They wished to utilize the 'Iron Wall' in an offensive sense and to retaliate against Arab attacks. Others wished to create an armed force which would ultimately oust the British from Palestine and thereafter declare a Jewish State. The desire to respond, however, grew exponentially during the period of the Arab Revolt in the late 1930s. The possibility of national redemption also provoked a sense of expectation amongst the youth in the areas of distress in Eastern Europe. After all, the question for young Jews who were second class citizens in the Poland of the 1930s was why remain the epitome of inaction and passivity? Why go to Palestine to experience attacks from enemies amidst a hand-wringing impotence to do anything about it? Why repeat the humiliation of Poland in Palestine?

Jabotinsky used all his political acumen, authority and charisma to find a way around this problem. He used the space behind his words to restrain those who challenged his political path. Clearly, the term 'Iron Wall' could be interpreted in different ways, but he fought for many years to circumvent his opponents and to control the arguments and the images that would win the hearts and minds of his followers. Initially in the early 1930s, he was successful in curtailing and marginalizing the activities of intellectuals such as Abba Achimeir and Yehoshua Heschel Yeivin. Unlike Jabotinsky, they found little to recommend in the western democracies and lauded Mussolini's Italy instead. Initially they even found some virtue in a strong resurgent Germany under Hitler. While Jabotinsky encouraged youth to be strong, proud Jews and to 'learn to shoot', at the same time he believed in England and diplomacy – as did his great rival Chaim Weizmann.

While both Jabotinsky and Achimeir attempted to clothe the coming state in the rhetoric of a secular religiosity and thereby to present the struggle to attain it as part of a living sacred history, unlike Achimeir, Jabotinsky believed in an evolutionary Zionism not a revolutionary one.

Many of his followers, however, did not perceive the difference. Jabotinsky's style of inspirational leadership certainly empowered his followers, but did not always move them to make rational compromises when deemed appropriate. The subtleties of Jabotinsky's arguments were often glossed over by admiring youth who seemed to prefer red-blooded rhetoric – and its extrapolation into action – to diminish their opponents. Indeed, Jabotinsky's transition from essentially a non-socialist position to an anti-socialist one in the late 1920s sharpened the political contrast with the Labour Zionist movement. He embraced the minimalist state and opposed the hegemony of the proletariat. He made a distinction between democracy and the rule of the majority. Every nation was 'a separate race' with its peculiar psychology. It thereby provided the basis for a bitter ideological clash with the Zionist Left. Jabotinsky was probably more attracted to the ideologues of anarchism such as Prince Kropotkin than to the certainty of socialist believers. All this permitted his young followers to treat the discipline of the Zionist Organization with a laissez-faire disdain. Jabotinsky's preference for a dissident individualism led inevitably to a fragmentation of his own Revisionists and a wider disunity in the Zionist movement itself. The formation of the New Zionist Organization in 1935 personified this, but it split the movement at a time when both the deteriorating situation in both Europe and Palestine demanded unity of purpose. Ironically, by the time war broke out, Jabotinsky was making strenuous efforts to reintegrate the New Zionist Organization into the Old Zionist Organization.

Jabotinsky's inner circle in the Revisionist movement in Paris were émigré Russian Jews. They often hailed from semi-assimilationist backgrounds and preferred to speak Russian rather than Yiddish. There was a distinctly different approach by the London office under the leadership of Meir Grossman. As Benjamin Akzin wrote in his autobiography:

> More practical minded than Jabo and the old Russian Zionists who surrounded him, impatient of their long-winded eloquence and their inefficiency when it came to deeds, Grossman had a much more pragmatic approach to Revisionism. To him, it was a zweckverband (an association with a specific limited purpose) rather than a weltanschauung (a general philosophy of life) as Jabo and his friends sometimes represented it. He was also more moderate on many points and sought to avoid too far-reaching a clash with other groups in Zionism.

This situation was further complicated by a personal factor: Grossman resented

Jabo's unique position within the movement. Unwilling to admit Jabo's charisma, he often organized majority decisions within the Revisionist Executive that went against Jabo's stand, and did not see why he couldn't do anything that Jabo did.[14]

These political and personal obstacles caused Jabotinsky to break with Grossman and his close colleagues in the Revisionist movement in 1933 over whether the organization should continue in its membership in the World Zionist Organization. It left him vulnerable to pressure from his Maximalist opponents and from a new generation of rapidly radicalizing impressionable youth. This exacerbated a tendency within the movement that already existed. Benjamin Akzin wrote that:

> Beside the analytical, rational considerations which brought people to espouse the Revisionist cause, it had also attracted many who were drawn to it by temperament, either because of their inclination to assume extremist positions or because they were nonconformists by nature. Jabotinsky's own personality, utilizing a first rate logical mind to the soul of a poet dissatisfied with daily humdrum, reflected these two aspects. Many of my Revisionist co-workers shared both characteristics.[15]

Menachem Begin had always been an adherent of the Maximalist wing of Betar in contrast to the founder of Betar, Aharon Propes, who was much more in the mould of a traditional youth leader. By the late 1930s, Begin was advocating the militarization of Betar and its effective transformation into a conduit for the Irgun in Palestine. In March 1939, Propes, who had conscripted Begin into the Betar, was finally displaced by his protégé – and a new approach began which mirrored Begin's worldview. The previous autumn, Begin had famously confronted Jabotinsky at the Third World Conference of Betar in Warsaw. Jabotinsky had uncharacteristically interrupted and savagely responded to Begin with a host of sarcastic and incisive remarks. Yet Begin carried the day amongst the youthful audience when a vote was taken – to change the Betar Oath and to embark on the third stage of Zionism: military Zionism. This well-known altercation symbolically marked the end of Jabotinsky's struggle. Up until his death less than two years later, he struggled – with considerable difficulty – to control his movement.

Menachem Begin was thus never a Revisionist, but a selective imbiber of Jabotinsky's broad political menu. Jabotinsky, the man and leader, was undoubtedly a figure of adulation and adoration for Begin. Menachem Begin recognized him – as did even his opponents – as a unique personality in the Zionist firmament, but this did not prevent him from opposing him on fundamental issues. In Begin's eyes, there was thus a distinction and a dislocation between 'the Revisionist movement' and 'the Jabotinsky movement'.

Begin indeed remained with Jabotinsky and the Betar, but there is no doubt that Abba Achimeir and the early Maximalists laid the ideological foundations for his world outlook.

Unlike Jabotinsky, Avraham Stern and David Raziel, Begin lived to realize his dream and to achieve his political goals. Menachem Begin's odyssey, both geographically and politically, until he was elected Prime Minister of Israel in 1977, is a fascinating journey for any student of history regardless of personal political views. Begin's arrival in the seat of power is certainly a testimony to his tenacity, political guile and indeed considerable luck over nearly three decades in the parliamentary wilderness. But Begin's ruthlessness in the hothouse of Israeli politics began in the pre-state era when he outflanked rivals to seize the mantle of leader of the national camp and thereby to be anointed the successor to Jabotinsky himself.

Many of those who had originally worked with Jabotinsky eventually distanced themselves from Begin – and many openly broke with him. In part, they did not recognize Begin as the inheritor and interpreter of Jabotinsky's teachings despite his repeated references to his 'father and teacher'. On one level, Begin probably believed this, on another, much of his commentary does not concur with the historical facts. Begin was sometimes at pains, particularly during the early years of his leadership of Herut, to telescope history and his own view of the past. Moreover, any political distance between Begin and Jabotinsky not only served to undermine his own standing in Herut, but provided political ammunition to his foes in the Labour Party. Thus, it is interesting to note that the confrontation with Jabotinsky in 1938 impelled Begin at a later date to reconstruct his speech – even though very little of the argument appeared in the official Revisionist press and what did appear was played down. Begin's reconstruction of his speech which was probably written many years later adds and subtracts from the official transcript and other versions of the speech. This hitherto unpublished manuscript seems to have been written after the Shoah and the destruction of Polish Jewry. Clearly, Begin had a psychological need to remember and reshape the past.

As others have remarked, Jabotinsky and Begin were the products of different times and different societies. Jabotinsky came from open, cosmopolitan Odessa. Like Trotsky, he came from an assimilationist background such that his Jewishness was incidental, a quirk of nature. It was a crisis of identity and expectation, as Michael Stanislawski has elegantly shown, that directed him along the path of Zionism. Begin, however, was a son of the shtetl, a scion of Briisk – the gateway of Brest-Litovsk – who grew up in the discriminatory

Poland of Marshal Pilsudski. The impoverishment of three million Polish Jews and the blatant anti-Semitism of the inter-war years led him to Jabotinsky's standard. Each man acted on different stages, according to the dictates of history, and this book in a sense looks at the overlap between their two epochs and the clashes between their different world outlooks.

PROLOGUE

On 18 January 1923, Vladimir Jabotinsky resigned from the Zionist Executive. In a letter to the Actions Committee, he wrote:

> (Our) policy is mainly characterized by the underlying assumption that a party which has no coercive powers at its disposal will therefore prove unable to defend before the British Government even its constitutional rights. I declare this assumption totally wrong. On the part of the English people and government he who stubbornly and systematically fights for a complete fulfilment will only meet with approval, respect and even though it be a long struggle – justice and satisfaction.[1]

An editorial in the London *Jewish Chronicle* supported his position and commended Jabotinsky on his refusal to submit himself 'to moral euthanasia for fear of being considered unamenable'. Jabotinsky responded:

> It must be a call to a fight, not a statement that everything is perfectly all right and there is nothing to fight against. What really poisons the Zionist willpower throughout the world is not only the attitude of the Administration in Palestine; it is the superfine docility of Zionist leadership.[2]

These comments defined Jabotinsky's past and predicted his future. Although he was known for being outspoken, the drama of this episode was all the more shocking because – for many Jews – he was the symbol of dynamism within the Zionist movement, the founder of the Jewish Legion, the brilliant orator, the cosmopolitan littérateur and the inspirer of downtrodden youth. *The New Palestine* likened him to a ' burning meteor in the Jewish firmament'.[3] But as a letter in the same issue of the *Jewish Chronicle* noted 'He seems to yearn for new and repeated sensations – the salt of life to Mr Jabotinsky.'[4]

THE PARTING OF THE WAYS

THE KING OF THE JEWS AND HIS SUBJECTS

When Sir Herbert Samuel arrived in Jerusalem in June 1920 as the first High Commissioner, his predecessor General Sir Louis Bols gave him a document to sign. It read: 'Received from the Chief Administrator of the Occupied Territory one Palestine, complete and in good order.' Samuel signed and added 'E and O.E' – 'Errors and Omissions Excepted.'

Samuel arrived just as the realization was dawning that nationalists throughout the Arab world, with rare exceptions, were irrevocably hostile to Zionism. Their hopes and expectations had been raised in March 1920 by the proclamation of the Emir Faisal as king of a Greater Syria which they had presumed included geographical Palestine. The Hashemites, however, did not speak for all Arabs. Nationalism was in its infancy and opinion in Palestine was divided about the future. Some pined for the good old days of the Ottoman Empire and others believed in a pan-Islamic entity. Many more embraced pan-Arabism in the shape of a unitary Arab state in the Middle East whose epicentre would indeed be a Greater Syria. Palestine, it was argued, was intrinsically part of Southern Syria. Few at that time were adherents of Palestine as a defined nation state. Thus the Syrian General Congress, meeting in Damascus in July 1919, presented a memorandum to the King-Crane Commission stating that 'there should be no separation of the southern part of Syria, known as Palestine, nor of the littoral western zone, which includes Lebanon, from the Syrian country.'[1] The Zionists were still under the impression that their good intentions to develop the land would be welcomed by all. The difficulties were attributed to a small minority of troublemakers. Chaim Weizmann, the Zionist leader, wrote to the Foreign Secretary, Lord Curzon, in April 1920:

> When I was in Northern Galilee, a number of sheikhs came in from the villages to tell me that they lived on the best of terms with the Jewish population and that they dissociated themselves from the anti-Zionist meetings that had recently taken place in the towns. It is indeed only in the towns that the movement exists, and there the numbers that have attended the meetings have not, as a rule, been considerable. There is no evidence of anything in the nature of a widespread and formidable national movement against Zionism.[2]

Yet Weizmann was aware of Curzon's views and the onset of change in British policy towards Palestine – the new Foreign Secretary had been distinctly unsympathetic to the Balfour Declaration which promised a Jewish national home in Palestine. He believed that the Arabs would be relegated to 'hewers of wood and drawers of water'.[3] In a private report to the Zionist Executive in November 1919, Weizmann had been severely critical of British officials, not simply for having no vision of the future, but also of presenting a polarized view of the situation. According to this version, the Jews were bound to displace the Arabs and thus there was no room for further immigration.

> The Arab is genuinely frightened of our immigration, not because he is anti-Jewish, but because he was told that we are coming to take away his land. The Mufti of Jerusalem, who is perhaps one of the most enlightened Arab gentlemen, who is honest and far from being fanatical, told me repeatedly that there was no room in Palestine for many more people to live. It was quite a revelation to him when I compared the density of population in Palestine with that of Lebanon. He was amazed to hear that with proper conditions of sanitation, irrigation and communication, the land could yield five, six or tenfold of what it is yielding now.[4]

Nationalism in Palestine was a relatively recent phenomenon which commenced in earnest after the Young Turks' Revolution of 1908. Their policy of Turkification both alienated and defined Arabs. The replacement of the Turks by the British, the synchronized emergence of other Arab nation-states in the Middle East – and the growing Zionist presence – all provoked resentment and protest in Palestine. In a nationalist demonstration during the Nebi Musa festivities in 1920, those protests spiralled out of control, ending in the killing and maiming of Jews in the Jewish Quarter of Jerusalem. Many victims ironically were members of the Old Yishuv, the community of ultra-orthodox Jews who had settled there long before the first Zionist wave of immigration in 1881. They not only differed from the newcomers in their piety, but also in that they were totally opposed to Zionism. Their anger against the secularized newcomers was located in the belief that God's hand should not be forced in bringing about the coming of the Messiah. Only with his arrival would a truly Jewish state be established.[5] Such Talmudic rationale was lost on the assailants who attacked the impoverished and docile ultra-orthodox.

Samuel's involvement in the future of Palestine had commenced when Turkey entered the war on the side of the Central Powers in early November 1914. It proved to be the cue for national movements within the Ottoman Empire to hasten its downfall and to prepare arguments for political independence. Palestine was also a subject of speculative discussion within the British Cabinet within a few days of Turkey's commitment to the Central Powers. Samuel, then President of the Local Government Board, intimated to Sir Edward Grey, the Foreign Secretary, that he believed that the likely outcome of the war would be the final collapse of the Ottoman Empire and it would suffer the fate of dissection amongst the European powers. And adding – almost as an afterthought – 'Perhaps the opportunity might arise for the fulfilment of the ancient aspiration of the Jewish people and the restoration there of a Jewish state.'[6] Grey concurred since 'the idea had always had a strong sentimental attachment for him.'[7] Samuel also mentioned this to Lloyd-George who replied that he was an enthusiastic advocate of the establishment of a Jewish state. Samuel viewed the Jewish state as the prime solution to the travails of East European Jewry. In a note on his talks, he raised the question of whether Russia would take the initiative:

> Her armies had been welcomed in Poland by the whole of the people except the Jews. She would, if she were wise, wish to gain the loyalty of her Jewish subjects, new and old, but for my part I doubted whether her own public opinion would allow her Government to grant them equal rights. If Russia took a leading part in the re-establishment of the Jewish State, the sentimental appeal to the Jews within her territories would be so strong that it could not fail to have an immediate and a powerful influence on their attitude.[8]

Both Chaim Weizmann and Vladimir Jabotinsky understood that the war offered an unprecedented opportunity for the Zionist movement. As Jabotinsky later wrote, 'Stone and iron can endure a fire; a wooden hut must burn and no miracle will save it.'[9] Indeed, until Turkey's entry into the war, Jabotinsky hoped for a stalemate between Britain and Germany and 'peace as soon as possible'.[10] The logical reaction, from Jabotinsky's point of view, to Turkey's entry into the war was therefore to initiate moves to create a Jewish Legion, under British or French auspices, which would participate in the invasion of Palestine.

Samuel's newly-found interest in Zionism coincided with Weizmann's conclusion that the time was opportune for an approach to the British Government. In a letter to C.P. Scott, the editor of the *Manchester Guardian*, Weizmann commented that any Jewish settlement in Palestine could become a British Dependency – 'an Asiatic Belgium in the hands of the Jews'.[11] He envisaged a community of a million Jews in Palestine within 25 to 30 years, a land of some 30,000 km^2 supporting a population of four million.[12] Samuel viewed the new Jewish state as literally a light unto the nations – 'a fountain of enlightenment and a source of a great literature and art and the development of science'.[13]

Through Scott, Weizmann eventually met Samuel who urged the Zionist leader to consider 'big things' in Palestine. This included the construction of railways, harbours and universities – and the building of the Third Temple.[14] Following a meeting with Lloyd-George and Weizmann, Samuel then placed a proposal, entitled 'The Future of Palestine', before the Cabinet in January 1915. Significantly, he had modified his original views and discarded the idea of an immediate state. Instead, he argued that any attempt to place half a million Arabs 'under a government based on the support of 80,000 or 90,000 Jews' would not command support and was a recipe for instability.

> The dream of a Jewish state, prosperous, progressive and the home of a brilliant civilization, might vanish in a series of squalid conflicts with the Arab civilization. And even if a state so constituted did succeed in avoiding or repressing internal disorder, it is doubtful whether it would be strong enough to protect it from external aggression from the turbulent elements around it. To attempt to realize the aspiration of a Jewish state one century too soon might throw back its actual realization for many centuries more.[15]

Instead, he proposed an annexation to the Empire. In March 1915, in a revised memorandum entitled 'Palestine', tailored to mollify French concerns, Samuel postulated five choices. Palestine could be annexed by France; it could remain Turkish; it could be internationalized; it could be annexed to Egypt and thereby become indirectly incorporated into the Empire. It could also be established as a British Protectorate which would encourage Jewish settlement. The latter idea emerged as the favoured choice of the British Cabinet since it coincided with British interests. Quoting Napoleon, Samuel believed that 'Palestine was the true defence of Egypt.'

Samuel's arrival in Jerusalem in 1920 was thus greeted by knowledgeable Arab nationalists with deep cynicism. In their eyes, Samuel was less than a neutral figure. It was known that after the war, he had continued with his advocacy of the Zionist cause. He had participated in a meeting on the second anniversary of the Balfour Declaration at the London Opera House and spoken of his hope that the Zionist experiment would be transformed into 'a self-governing commonwealth under the auspices of an established Jewish majority'.[16] He also inferred that the Jews would not obtain all that they wanted – 'delays' had been caused because of the strained relations between Britain, France and the Arabs. Samuel attended the Paris Peace Conference and then went to Palestine on behalf of the Foreign Office in order to investigate the prevailing financial and administrative conditions. In his report to Lord Curzon, he recommended a confederation of states, consisting of: an independent Syria under Faisal; western Syria under the French Mandate; an independent Hedjaz; Mesopotamia under an Arab monarch – and the British Mandate incorporating the Jewish National Home. In private, Samuel articulated the prospect of a Jewish state once a Jewish majority had been achieved. In a letter to his niece, he wrote that he thought that this would take at least fifty years.[17]

Samuel himself had wrestled with the decision whether to accept the post precisely because he was a Jew. Several British officials clearly did not like Jews. Others such as H. St. J. B. Philby, the Chief British Representative in Transjordan, felt that 'a Jewish High Commissioner responsible for the direct administration of Palestine could not adjudicate impartially on any matter in respect of which the interests of Palestine and Transjordan clash.'[18] But following the first outbreak of Arab nationalist violence, Weizmann and the other Zionist leaders convinced Samuel to accept office. Yet significantly, Samuel commented in his acceptance letter that the Zionists had to act gradually and be sensitive to Arab and Christian concerns.[19] Samuel's appointment drew protests from General Allenby, the Emir Faisal and a wide section of Arab opinion.[20] It was no wonder therefore that in contrast to the Arabs, the Jews therefore, were delighted that Samuel had been appointed. Jabotinsky even told *The Times* that Samuel would be impartial[21] and that 'no better choice could have been made'.[22]

SEARCHING FOR THE HOLY LAND

Herbert Samuel had been the first Jew to sit in a British cabinet and indeed served as Home Secretary in a Liberal Government. Although he was an acculturated Jewish Briton, he did not fit the normal stereotype of an assimilated Jew. On the contrary, he was unabashed in his openness to be recognized as a Jew and one who had associations with the Zionist cause. Yet this was not synonymous with membership of the Zionist Organization. Samuel was first and foremost a committed and long time adherent of the British Liberal Party. He had grown up in the shadow of the aging Gladstone – 'the greatest Englishman of that time'.[23] As early as 1902, he had written a book on Liberalism with an introduction by Asquith.[24] Moreover, he saw it as his duty to serve his country in an area important to the empire. Most Zionists, following Herzl's approach, did not see any conflict of loyalties arising. One observer commented that 'the new wine of liberalism was poured through the old bottles of the Military Administration.'[25] This adulation of Samuel was short-lived.

The British found it difficult to define Palestine – and such a lack of clarity in general produced a plethora of borders.[26] The *Encyclopaedia Britannica* in 1911 posited the view that Palestine was 'a geographical name of rather loose application'. It could be described as 'the strip of land extending along the eastern shore of the Mediterranean Sea... eastward there is no such definite border. The River Jordan, it is true, marks a line of delimitation between western and eastern Palestine; but it is practically impossible to say where the latter ends and the Arabian desert begins....Perhaps the line of the pilgrim road from Damascus to Mecca is the most convenient possible boundary.'[27]

Norman Bentwich, later the Attorney-General in Palestine, defined historic Palestine in 1916 as stretching between Dan in the north and Beersheba in the south, between the desert and the sea, 15,500 km^2 west of the Jordan and 10,400 km^2 to the east. Quoting Biblical sources, he suggested that the Jewish land might run 'from the Mediterranean to the Euphrates and from Lebanon to the river of Egypt'. He conceived that the Jewish inhabitants of cities such as Smyrna, Damascus, Aleppo and Baghdad might well return to cultivate the soil. Jews from Greece and the Balkans, from Persia, Georgia and Turkestan as well as the dispossessed of Russia and Poland could be attracted by this new venture. Bentwich in 1916 believed that despite the covetous claims of the Syrians to Palestine, it could still be possible to balance 'the claim of neighbourhood against the claim of ancient title' and that the children of Esau and the children of Jacob could live side by side in harmony. The Jew, he believed, had an important role to play between East and West.

> The Jew will be the ideal interpreter of the West to the East, and of the East to the West; for his history and his habit of mind make him kin on the one side to the Semitic peoples devoted to God, and on the other side to the Westerners devoted to human progress. He will be the reconciling element to bring the Semites into community of thought and action with the rest of the civilized world, and thus lay the foundation of a concord of the races.[28]

Arab nationalists did not exactly view things in the same fashion. Indeed, all attempts by Samuel to mollify the nationalist passions on the Arab side and seek a solution came to nought. Explanations of the meaning of the Balfour Declaration fell on deaf ears. The British partly viewed Zionist demands through historical claims – and Biblical history at that. Negotiations over the borders of Palestine were defined by one of the Biblical boundaries 'from Dan to Beersheba' [29] – essentially the central area where the Israelites settled – and ironically these parameters were invoked – not by the Zionists – but by the British and French.[30] Indeed the classic historical atlas of George Adam Smith[31] was consulted by Lloyd-George as to where exactly Dan was located. Sir Herbert Samuel even asked Smith if the Jordan had ever historically been the border of Eretz Israel. Smith said that it had never been the eastern boundary.[32]

Protestant advocacy for the return of the Jews had commenced with the revolt against Catholicism in sixteenth century Europe. As early as 1621, Sir Henry Finch published his work 'The World's Great Restauration or Calling of the Jews'. But the Protestant romance with the Holy Land started in earnest with Cromwell and the English Republic. Indeed, some Puritans even advocated a reversion to Saturday as the Christian Sabbath. The Barebones Parliament proposed that there should be 70 members of the Council of State – the same as the ancient Sanhedrin of the Jews. The Levellers often labelled themselves 'Jews' and their opponents 'Amalekites'.[33] A decade before the first Zionist settlers arrived, the Dean of Westminster, Arthur Stanley, declared that the Holy Land was 'a land more dear to us from our childhood even than England.'.[34]

Lloyd-George had been keen to keep the French out of Palestine and particularly out of the Holy Places. Moreover, he came from a strong Welsh Baptist background. The socialist Arthur Henderson, who was a Labour member of the government between 1915 and 1917, was a Methodist lay preacher. Moreover, Balfour's niece, Blanche Dugdale, noted that his 'interest in the Jews was lifelong. It originated in the Old Testament training of his mother and in his Scottish upbringing.'[35] Jan Smuts told South African Jews in November 1919 that a great Jewish state would arise and 'its glories will be greater than even those of the state of which we read in the Bible'.[36] In his memorandum to the British cabinet, Sir Herbert Samuel referred to the 'widespread and deep-rooted sympathy' within the Protestant world for 'the idea of restoring the Hebrew people to the land' and thereby redeeming 'the Christian Holy Places from the vulgarization to which they are now subject'.[37]

The historical connection 'from Dan to Beersheba' denoted the Victorian passion with the Holy Land, yet it related to the time when there was an Israelite presence in the country rather than to an earlier period when the ownership of the Land was no more than a divine promise. The delineation of the Land of Israel in the twentieth century was therefore grounded in an association with ancient history and the current political reality rather than in faith and God's promise to Abraham in Genesis. The Zionists went along with all this. They sought to blur the difference between the purely Biblical and the historical in order to achieve borders that were based on economic factors such as good agricultural land, access to water such as the Litani and the upper Jordan and efficient transportation facilities. This apparent acceptance of Biblical tradition was played out by Menachem Ussishkin when he impressed the Versailles Peace Conference by speaking in Hebrew – a hitherto dead and buried language – and sought 'the restoration to the Jews of the land that was promised to them four thousand years ago by the Power above'.[38]

The British, however, also pursued their interests – and these changed the moment the war ended. During the war, the Foreign Office had raised Lucien Wolf's memorandum with the British ambassador to the Tsarist court and advocated the immigration of Jews into Palestine until they could 'take the management of the internal affairs of Palestine (with the exception of Jerusalem and the Holy Places) into their own hands'.[39] While a preferred definition of a national home was left unsaid, the Foreign Office suggested that such an attractive offer would 'enable us to strike a bargain for Jewish support' in the war effort. The idea was mooted in Petrograd, but fell on stony ground. The Russian Foreign Minister said that he would welcome the departure of its Jews, but doubted whether many would actually wish to settle there.[40]

With the end of the war, government ministers who were neither Christian Zionists nor sympathetic to the national aspirations of the Jews began to see British interests in pulling back from the implications of the Balfour Declaration and an amelioration of Arab nationalism. The British significantly had made provision in the Mandate, granted by the League of Nations to them to control Palestine, for a last minute division of area. In part this was due to the desire of Lord Curzon, who had replaced Balfour at the end of 1919 at the Foreign Office, to inhibit the development of the Jewish National Home in Palestine and to channel British policy to these ends.[41] Curzon had opposed the Balfour Declaration and now after the war saw no need to further appease Zionist demands. He raised the issue of the East Bank's separation from the rest of Palestine even before the French had expelled Faisal from Damascus. France had always argued that it was the heir of the Crusaders, Guardian of the Holy Places and Protector of all Christians. During the war, it had been agreed that Syria and Lebanon would come under French jurisdiction – and so probably would Transjordan. With the war at an end and Palestine in British hands, Curzon's Foreign Office wished to redraw the map of the Middle East. Transjordan was therefore given to Abdullah and Iraq to Faisal to act as a bulwark against French intentions to extend their territory southwards. But it was also seen to be compensation for the Arab cause because of British support for Zionism. The logic of the change in British policy was to move from a Jewish national home in Palestine in the future to a bi-national state with an Arab majority. This, in turn, created charges of 'crude duplicity' from the emerging Labour movement in Britain. Following a visit to Palestine, the British Labour Party leader, Ramsay MacDonald commented:

> Mr Balfour made a declaration which meant to every Jew that Palestine was to revert to his government and that once again he was to take his place amongst the nations of the world. Probably Mr Balfour did not know what he was talking about, but the Government is now doing what it can to show that Mr Balfour's pledges to the Jews were of the same worthless character as Mr Bonar Law's to the miners.[42]

This was in line with a conference of socialist and Labour parties of the Allied countries which was held in London in February 1918. One clause in their memorandum on 'war aims' declared that in a Palestine liberated from the Turks 'a free state, under international guarantee' would be established where 'such of the Jewish people as desire to do so may return and work out their salvation free from interference by those of alien race or religion'.[43]

The British Labour party, however, was small and had not tasted power. In the meantime, the Liberals and the Conservatives held sway. Thus in the first draft of the Mandate in December 1920, Transjordan was included within the borders of Palestine. By August 1921, a new clause in the final draft suggested partition. In a letter to Churchill, Weizmann argued at length that this did not actually have to mean a fundamental change in British policy. He cited that parts of the historic Land of Israel had now been allocated to territory under the French Mandate and under Abdullah. Transjordan should still be open to Jewish colonization, he argued, since the Jews too would prove dependable against any French aggressive designs.[44] Samuel attempted to bolster such demands, but the Cairo Conference in March 1921 formally made the proposition to Abdullah.

In a letter to Churchill in 1920, Weizmann had evoked the biblical imagery of 'the fields of Gilead, Moab and Edom with the rivers Arnon and Jabbok, to say nothing of the Yarmuk' being historically, geographically and economically linked to Palestine.[45] Such exhortations in the end did little good when it came to the preference of British interests. Weizmann recognized this reality and eventually concentrated on western Palestine. Jabotinsky similarly opposed the proposed partition of Palestine and viewed it as 'an historical injustice'.[46] In several memoranda at the end of 1922, he called for the nullification of the exclusion of Transjordan from the Jewish National Home.[47] Transjordan, it was argued, had no tradition in Islamic thought. The important Muslim places of worship were located in Jerusalem and Hebron. Es-Salt (near Amman) did not have the same attraction as Jaffa and Acre. The intelligentsia lived on the West Bank – and according to Jabotinsky, 'they regard the handful of Bedouin across the street as primitives'.[48] Jabotinsky also argued that the East Bank ever since Roman times had been linked economically and politically with the West Bank when it supported a large population. Once again it could 'serve admirably for Jewish colonization on a large scale'.[49]

During the immigration from Poland between 1924 and 1926 and the impoverishment of the Jewish masses in eastern Europe, he argued that mass immigration to Transjordan was probably even more important than to Western Palestine.[50] Although Weizmann formally renounced any Zionist claims to Transjordan at the London Conference in early 1939, Jabotinsky made its retention a plank of Revisionist Zionist policy during the inter-war years. The old Zionists who claim 'from Dan to Beersheba', he proclaimed, 'were fearful of stating the case for Rabbat Ammon (Amman)'.[51]

The next outbreak of Arab nationalist fervour came on May Day 1921 when two rival demonstrations of the embryonic Communists, the Hebrew Socialist Workers' Party – its adherents known by the Hebrew acronym, the Mopsim[52] – and the Marxist Zionist Achdut Ha'avodah clashed in Tel Aviv. The Mopsim slogans boldly declared their support for the Leninist world order. 'All Power to the Workers and Peasants Council', 'Long Live the International Solidarity of the Jewish and Arab Proletariats.' An Arabic leaflet proclaimed 'Down with the British and French bayonets! Down with the Arab and foreign capitalists!'[53] Arab nationalists were astounded, if not mystified, by this short-lived ruckus where Jews fought one another. Their interpretation was altogether quite different. They took up the cry and mounted attacks on Jewish shops in Jaffa. The new outbreak of violence then spread to other parts of the country, aided by the transmission of rumour and counter-rumour and claiming the lives of almost a hundred Arabs and Jews including the Hebrew writer Yosef Chaim Brenner. The idea promoted by Churchill that the presence of Jews in Palestine would be a boon to the country was fast becoming an irrelevance. Nationalism was a far more potent force than the cause of economic amelioration and technological advance. The suggestion in *The Times* that a garrison could be formed from Arabs and Jews as a model of inter-communal co-operation by 'a league of Zionists and Arab notables who are sympathetic to Zionism' reflected only the hopes of the past.[54]

RE-READING THE BALFOUR DECLARATION

The killings worried Samuel, who temporarily suspended Jewish immigration. On 3 June 1921, he made a speech on the King's official birthday which was designed to soothe Arab nationalist sentiment – once again explaining that the Balfour Declaration was not intended to laud a Jewish government over the Arabs, only a home for the Jewish people in Palestine. Significantly the usual mention of the 'national home' on this occasion had been reduced to simply 'home'. He commented, 'If any measures are needed to convince the Muslim and Christian population that those principles will be observed in practice and that their rights are really safe, such measures will be taken.'[55] His remarks also focused on the fear of revolution by the Arab notables which had been underlined by the activities of the Mopsim and the May Day demonstrations. It also targeted the first immigrants of the Third Aliyah – many of whom had left Lenin's Russia before the descent into reaction and one-party rule and were therefore still sympathetic to the ideals of the October Revolution. Those infected by Bolshevism, Samuel explained, would be expelled.

Samuel also stipulated that immigration had to be tied to the economic absorptive capacity of Palestine – an issue which the Zionist Executive did not contest. Indeed, Samuel's figure of 16,500 families permitted to enter Palestine was reduced to 2,300 – such was the lack of preparedness on the part of the Zionists for this evolving situation. Control over immigration was withdrawn from the Zionist Organization and allocated to the Government Director of Immigration.[56]

The Zionists did not appreciate Samuel's rationale. On the contrary, they felt instantly betrayed by one of their own. In a letter to Churchill, never sent, Weizmann remarked that 'the Jewish National Home of the war-promise has now in peace-time been transformed into an Arab national home with such admixture of Jewish elements as the interests and prejudices of the Arabs will allow.'[57] Helen Bentwich, wife of the Attorney-General who was also Samuel's niece, confided to her diary the effect of the speech:

> H.E.'s speech which, to me personally, seemed very sad. Such a climb-down from the hopefulness of the last year's when he came. The Jews all felt as if they'd been at a funeral and received it without a sound. The moderate Arabs and the English were very pleased, but the ultra-Arabs were disappointed. I'm not a keen Zionist – but I did feel sorry for them.
> And it was a bitter moment to see the triumphant looks of the Arabs all around, and not least the expression on (Sir Ronald) Storr's face – the blackguard! Actually what he said wasn't too bad – but mentioning Bolshies by name and not the Arabs who had committed the murders, and the whole tone of apology about it, was most sad, from Britain's point of view too. I daresay he could do no more.[58]

Weizmann and Jabotinsky maintained a dignified silence in public, but gave vent to their frustrations privately. On reading the text of the speech, Jabotinsky intimated his negative opinion in a letter to his mother and sister.[59] In letters to his wife, he reflected the widespread pessimism of the Zionists,[60] proclaiming that 'Samuel has surrendered to the Arabs'.[61] Yet he refrained from criticizing Samuel publicly. Instead he drafted a rebuttal for Weizmann in a meeting with Lloyd-George, Balfour and Churchill in July 1921.[62]

Samuel's even-handedness was symptomatic of his liberalism. It also marked his choice of identity. Unlike Weizmann, he argued that the Arabs of Palestine had come to believe that 'Zionism means the overwhelming of themselves and their people by immigrant Jews, with the consequence that in the course of time they will lose their political predominance but also their lands and homes and their Holy Places.'[63] This, regardless of Weizmann's good intentions, was the hardening Arab perception, and nationalist revolt would diminish support for the Zionist enterprise and alienate British public opinion.

Samuel later noted that he would have considered it a tragedy if Jewish renewal would have been marked by 'hardship, expropriation, injustice of any kind for the people now in the land'.[64] He believed that Jews would win credit in the eyes of the world and satisfy the Mandatory Power by going along with British proposals. Samuel was looking for a traditionally liberal solution to a rapidly polarizing situation. The report of Sir Thomas Haycraft, the Chief Justice of Palestine, into the disturbances also blamed the Zionists, but significantly gave an indication of the shape of things to come. It argued that:

> ... only a greatly reduced Zionist programme be attempted by the Peace Conference and even that, only very gradually initiated. This would have to mean that Jewish immigration should be definitely limited, and that the project for making Palestine distinctly a Jewish commonwealth should be given up.[65]

Palestine should be included in 'a united Syrian state' and 'the extreme Zionist programme' greatly modified. The Commission pointed out that 'a national home for the Jewish people' was not the same as making Palestine into a Jewish state. Samuel further endorsed and commended the Commission's report to Churchill at the Colonial Office.[66] Weizmann, however, secured the support of Lloyd-George and Balfour against Samuel and Churchill. They explicitly stated that their understanding of the Balfour Declaration always meant 'an eventual Jewish State'.[67] Jabotinsky similarly opposed the Haycraft Report in a letter to the Zionist Executive.[68]

Even so, in May 1922, Samuel travelled to London to tell the government that its Palestine policy needed to be spelled out clearly so that no misconceptions could arise. This manifested itself in the Churchill White Paper the following month. Several attempts to come to a political arrangement with the representatives of Arab nationalism in Palestine always stumbled over the basic demand for the abandonment of the Balfour Declaration. Churchill's White Paper of June 1922 thus reflected Samuel's attempts at even-handedness and, by extension, views that he had held since 1915. In meetings with Weizmann, prior to the publication of the White Paper, Samuel proved impervious to persuasion and did not shift from his firmly-held convictions.

There was no question, the White Paper stated – in a clear rebuke to Weizmann – that Palestine would be as Jewish as England is English as the Zionist leader had suggested in his statement to the Peace Conference in 1919. 'His Majesty's Government,' it stated, 'regard any such expectation as impracticable and have no aim in view.' There would be no imposition of Jewish nationality on the inhabitants of Palestine, but simply the further development of the Jewish community. Jewish immigration would continue, but would not exceed the economic capacity of the country to absorb new arrivals.

This clearly differed from the original hopes of the Zionist leadership. At the Political Commission of the Zionist Conference in London in March 1919, proposals were suggested for submission to the forthcoming Paris Peace Conference.

> Palestine shall be placed under such political, administrative and economic conditions as will secure its reconstitution as the Jewish National Home which will ultimately develop into a Jewish Commonwealth, it being clearly understood that nothing shall be done which may prejudice the civil and religious rights of existing non-Jewish communities in Palestine or the rights and political status enjoyed by Jews in any other country.[69]

During the first half of 1922, Weizmann fought often futile rearguard battles against a watering-down of the principles of the Balfour Declaration. From the British point of view, the evolving ambiguity of the Declaration was to be exploited. A Jewish national home in Palestine did not mean a Jewish state, now or in the future. Jewish immigration into Palestine was not open-ended. Although the Mandate extended to Mesopotamia, Palestine and Transjordan, the latter was to be detached and given to the Emir Abdullah. Perhaps most important was the stated principle that the Jews did not enjoy special privileges denied to the Arabs.

The cumulative effect of all this turned Jabotinsky decidedly against Samuel. Starting with the Haycraft Report and concluding with the White Paper, Jabotinsky held Samuel responsible for all Zionist reverses and later accused him of bureaucratic tendencies and 'clumsy' endeavours:

> Although a clever man, Herbert Samuel has this strange shortcoming: he is organically a doctrinaire; he does not see things with his eyes as they really are, but through some sort of conception of his own.
> What he sees are not real men as God created them but some abstract human creatures, constructed or rather construed by himself in his own, Herbert Samuel's, image and likeness. Having mentally produced such a personage, he then submits to him his arguments and demands with results that should not be difficult to imagine. When he later became High Commissioner of Palestine, this characteristic of his caused considerable harm to ourselves, the Arabs and England's good name.[70]

The draft of the Churchill White Paper was shown to the Zionist Executive just hours before it was due to be released. It was accompanied by a nine-point questionnaire. Weizmann had been informed that unless the Zionists acquiesced in its contents, there would be wholesale revision of the draft of the Mandate and in particular paragraph four which recognized the Jewish Agency 'as a public body for the purpose of advising and co-operating with the administration of Palestine in such economic, social and other matters as may

affect the establishment of the Jewish national home'. At a hastily-called, late
night meeting, Jabotinsky proposed that the Executive's response should be
qualified in that while they would be unable to agree to the spirit of the
statement, they were prepared to 'conform in their activities' to the main
principles of the document in order not to complicate the issue for the British
Government. This was rejected by the majority out of fear that even a limited
display of independence would prove detrimental to their interests and counter-
productive to their mission. Yet the White Paper still confirmed that the Jews
were in Palestine as of right and not on sufferance. It further denied the Arab
claim that the British had promised them a state. In fact, the point was
reiterated that Palestine, west of the Jordan, had been excluded in the original
correspondence between Sir Henry MacMahon and Sherif Hussein.[71]

The acceptance of the White Paper was a necessary condition for the
confirmation of the British Mandate by the League of Nations. Weizmann
argued that the die was effectively cast and only when Jews would be present in
greater numbers, would there be future opportunities to reinterpret the
Mandate more favourably. It was, in effect, a declaration of how powerless the
Zionists were in reality. Jabotinsky voted against such unqualified acquiescence,
but assented to the majority viewpoint. Yet all in all, Jabotinsky was not unduly
concerned and later commented:

> As to the contents – it does not contain one line which, under strict legal analysis,
> would formally preclude the attainment of the aim of Zionism, which is the
> gradual formation of a Jewish majority in Palestine; and, as the statement does
> not preclude this, all the rest, though most unpleasant, is immaterial.[72]

In October 1922, the tide further turned with the replacement of Lloyd-George
by a Conservative government under Andrew Bonar Law who immediately
came under pressure to reappraise the Palestine question. The Conservative
press – Lord Northcliffe's *Times* and *Daily Mail* and Lord Beaverbrook's *Daily
Express*[73] – became increasingly critical of the entire Zionist enterprise.
Northcliffe had returned from a visit to Palestine with a sense of foreboding
about a pan-Islamic rising and a belief that many Zionists were in fact
Bolsheviks.[74] This had been stimulated in part through Northcliffe's meeting
with the Jerusalem representatives of Agudat Israel which represented
orthodox anti-Zionism in Palestine.[75] Numerous articles appeared in *The Times*
and in the *Daily Mail* and the Northcliffe press in general embarked upon a
vociferous campaign against 'the Palestine fallacy'.[76] During the election
campaign, the press barons attempted to bring pressure on the leader of the
opposition, Andrew Bonar Law and Conservative candidates, to commit
themselves to evacuate Palestine, but without success. As Jabotinsky pointed
out in a rejoinder, even if a newspaper magnate was called upon to form a

government, he would have to abide by the Balfour Declaration – it could not be withdrawn. And this was the fundamental obstacle which all future British governments – try as they might – would be unable to circumvent.[77]

THE ROAD TO RESIGNATION

NORDAU AND THE NEW ZIONISM

When the Mandate was officially ratified in August 1922, Jabotinsky regarded it as 'an almost idealistically elastic receptacle for our energies'. Only a few months before his resignation, he seemed to accept Weizmann's gradualism in promoting the Zionist cause. In a letter to Weizmann, he remarked that the Mandate would not exclude 'our most remote goal - even a Jewish state'.[1]

But Weizmann continued to have his misgivings about Samuel and bitterly castigated him in private.[2] Yet in public his approach was to 'understand' and to appreciate the delicate nature of Samuel's position. He reasoned that Samuel's presence was a better prospect than his absence. Any replacement might be far worse.

Jabotinsky found it difficult to hide his displeasure at the turn of events. He had originally greeted the first ten months of the new civil administration and commented later that there had been 'every opportunity for the most unlimited development for our economic activities'.[3] But it was the May Day disturbances in 1921 and his inability to prevent the killings that aroused his ire. In an interview a few days after the outbreak of the riots, he castigated the Mopsim, the embryonic Communist Party, for their 'unforgivable treachery' to the most elementary Jewish interests.[4] But the essential blame, in Jabotinsky's eyes, lay with the Zionist leadership and the British.

> The Zionist Commission must also be blamed (on the Jaffa riots) for not having been more explicit and insistent in its numerous representations to the Government. Reproach should also be levelled against the Zionist Executive in London for having failed to impress upon the Home Government the necessity for a better mandate. Finally, the Home Government itself is guilty of short-

sightedness, absence of a whole hearted programme, hesitation and attempts to please everyone without satisfying anyone in particular.[5]

Jabotinsky also expressed his dissatisfaction with the lack of funding for Zionist enterprises. He complained that if Jews worldwide did not pay the ma'aser (the tithe in Biblical times) and did not take the reconstruction of Palestine seriously, the British would soon distance themselves. The Jews were 'shouting and failing to pay, keeping up the sham of a world organization which in the nature of things can do nothing practical'.[6] Such disorganization in good practice in financial affairs and lack of accountability had led to a falling-out between Weizmann and Louis Brandeis. Eventually taking up Weizmann's invitation to work with Keren Hayesod, he duly noted that it was becoming increasing difficult to attract funding. This, he argued, in a memorandum to the Zionist Executive in November 1922, was due to the policies of the British administration and the inertia of the Zionist leadership about raising their voices.

> The success of the collection therefore depends on the energy or the Arbeitsfreude of these Zionist workers. Theirs is a hard and unpleasant task; they can only carry it out with the full weight of their enthusiasm if they know that the ultimate aim is still the same old Zionism – the creation of a Jewish Commonwealth in Palestine.[7]

Within this ringing criticism was a growing realization that Zionism had lost its way. There was a familiar 'old Zionism' with its anchored values, and a new more uncertain one, reflecting the times and fashioned in the image of Weizmann. The promise of a Jewish national home was fading and there was no cogent Zionist response to the crisis.

At this time, Jabotinsky began to reflect in part, on the views of the ageing Max Nordau who had been Herzl's comrade-in-arms and the intellectual impetus behind many early Zionist initiatives. He was regarded as the Zionist Aaron to Herzl's Moses.[8] Yet Nordau was kept at arm's length by the Zionist leadership. He did not age gracefully, but because of his pre-eminence in the birth of political Zionism, he was initially able to criticize Weizmann's diplomatic endeavours. At a meeting at the Albert Hall in London in July 1919 in the presence of Balfour, Lloyd-George, Robert Cecil, the Marquess of Crewe and others, Nordau was forthright in addressing the British Government.

> At a critical moment of the war, you decided that we Jews could be useful to your cause, and you approached us with promises which vague as they were, were nevertheless capable of a satisfactory interpretation. We fell in with your plans, and we have loyally carried out our undertakings. We are only asking to be allowed to continue to do so. We concluded an alliance with you. We are perfectly aware of the risks and obligations that it entails. We know perfectly well what you

require of us. We are to keep guard over the Suez Canal for you. We are to act as sentinel over your route to India and Asia. We are prepared to fulfil these onerous duties, but you must let us become strong enough to do so. Loyalty for loyalty. Fidelity for fidelity.[9]

Needless to say, Weizmann and Sokolov were less than pleased with Nordau, who did not care whom he attacked. He was critical of Herzl's predecessors who led the Hovevei Zion – the enthusiasts for Zion – of Russia and Eastern Europe and he was prepared now to openly condemn Herzl's successors. In particular, he was disparaging about those associated with these early efforts at immigration and colonization such as Ahad Ha'am, Weizmann's one-time mentor.

> Hovevei Zion was the title of a book followed by blank pages. Political Zionism provided the material for this title. The settlements of Hovevei Zion were nothing but exhibits in a museum which are arranged in a showcase in order to excite the admiration of visitors. Political Zionism set itself the task of turning them into instruments of daily life....to transfer the idea of the return to Zion from the plan of poetical dreaming and romantic dilettantism to that of direct national activity; to give it what it lacked, namely a wide political horizon, to link up with the realm of world politics.[10]

By 1919, the Balfour Declaration, in Nordau's eyes, remained no more than that – a theoretical statement of intent. 'For the moment, our "national home" has no more than a verbal existence. We are strangers in Palestine, just as in all other places where we have refused to assimilate.'[11] He argued passionately that 600,000 Jews should be brought immediately to Palestine from the Ukraine, Poland and Rumania following an outbreak of pogroms. As to the question of who would feed the mass immigration, he suggested that the Jews should wrestle with this difficulty by themselves.[12]

In contrast, as early as 1916, Weizmann had commented that it would be impossible to transplant millions of East European Jews 'by the wave of a wand'. Any such emigration would have to be counterbalanced by the natural population growth of the indigenous Jews. Most emancipated Jews would not leave the countries of their adoption. Only a minority, he argued, would depart 'in whom the Jewish consciousness will be sufficiently strong to draw them back to their own people'.[13]

This was in direct contrast to Nordau's views in 1905 when he stated that one sixth of the Jews were happy and would remain in the land of their birth, but ten million would emigrate.[14]

In 1920, in a series of articles for the Paris-based publication, *Le Peuple Juif*,

Nordau dissected the problems of Zionism. In one piece entitled 'Zionism: Causes of Failure and Conditions for Success', he accused Weizmann of being 'a dictator in the Zionist Organization' and responsible for introducing the methods of old Tsarist Russia.[15] Weizmann was 'heart and soul, a hovev zion...an irreconcilable opponent of Herzl and Wolffsohn... (some) believe blindly that Weizmann is the propounder of true Herzlian Zionism – something he has never claimed to be.'[16] The official Zionist press eventually retaliated by strongly attacking him – in Nordau's view unfairly – as 'a Bolshevik, a demagogue without conscience, a vain old man, greedy for publicity or plainly and simply, an imbecile'.[17]

As a student of the national revolutions of the nineteenth century, Nordau drew a parallel between the decline of Herzlian Zionism and the devaluing of the founding ideals of the French Republic. In the period before his death in 1923, he argued that the departure of young people from the 'contracted Zionism of today' was a positive event. Only a return to 'the complete Zionism, the pure Zionism, as it was promulgated in 1897' could bring about the emancipation of the Jewish people.[18]

Although Jabotinsky later propagated the hero worship of Nordau during the 1930s, he was actually highly critical of Nordau in the aftermath of World War I. Nordau had been sceptical about the formation of a Jewish Legion and indeed about siding with Britain. This emerged from Jabotinsky's discussion in Madrid with him on 3 November 1914 – shortly after the outbreak of war. Nordau was not as convinced as Jabotinsky that the Allies would win the war, and even dismissed the idea that the Zionist movement should move its headquarters from Berlin to a neutral country. Nordau asked who would serve in the Legion if Jews were already serving in the military units of their home countries. He also exuded a certain sympathy for the Turks – 'our cousin Ishmael'.[19] As an Austrian passport holder, he was unhappy to have been forced into exile by – of all regimes – the French Republic, the inheritor of the banner of Mirabeau, Robespierre and Bonaparte.[20] This apparent volte-face would not have encouraged him to look kindly on the Kaiser's enemies.

Jabotinsky had thus been irritated by the old man's iconoclasm as far back as 1914.[21] But it was Nordau's biting criticism following the Balfour Declaration and the self-evident success of the Legion that persuaded Jabotinsky to attack him in print on several occasions. In a congratulatory letter to an American Zionist gathering in Chicago in October 1919,[22] Nordau called for 'the gates of the Land to be opened to unrestricted immigration'.[23] Jabotinsky attacked the idea, saying that without an infrastructure, it was economically utopian. However, he argued that the flow of immigrants should be regulated by the Zionists and not by the British Administration. He therefore opposed Nordau's plan to bring hundreds of thousands of Jews in an unregulated fashion from areas of pogrom, persecution and mass deprivation in Eastern Europe. Ironically, this was similar to Herbert Samuel's stand which he enunciated during his speech at the London Opera House. Jabotinsky was even more caustic in his comments in recalling Nordau's opposition to his efforts to establish a Jewish fighting force during the First World War. Significantly, he singled out Weizmann for praise as the only one who had the foresight to work towards the formation of a Jewish Legion. Even so, despite his criticism, Jabotinsky praised Nordau for declining to expound 'moderate' opinions at the outset as any views would inevitably be watered down in future deliberations.[24]

Nordau had already suggested that a new political grouping should be established at the tenth Zionist Congress in 1911. Moreover, there were several prominent Zionists who looked to Nordau for symbolic leadership. Jacobus Kann, a Dutch banker, had published a critical book, *Eretz Israel: Le Pays Juif* as long ago as 1909. He now signed a criticism of the Zionist Executive.[25] A pamphlet was published, entitled 'Weakness in the Zionist Organization'[26] and an oppositionist conference mooted. In Palestine, the daily *Ha'aretz* lined up behind Weizmann and his supporters while *Doar Hayom* began to emerge as an organ of opposition to established policies.[27]

THE BREAK WITH WEIZMANN

In August 1920, Weizmann told English Zionists on the eve of the Jewish New Year that the past twelve months had been:

> the most momentous in the history of our galut (exile). The triumph of Zionism in San Remo has been followed quickly by the appointment of Sir Herbert Samuel as High Commissioner of Palestine, the doors of which country have already been opened to Jewish immigration.[28]

Jabotinsky did not perceive the situation in such rosy terms. Although in disagreement with Nordau, Jabotinsky also believed in the large scale immigration of Jews, but on a planned economic basis. In a letter to Weizmann in October 1920,[29] he laid out his demands for his full involvement in the Zionist Organization and acceptance of fundraising duties through the Keren Hayesod. This included demands to secure more influence in the appointments to posts in the British Administration including the High Commissioner; the retention and expansion of the Jewish Legion in Palestine; and the cementing of the linkage between the governance of the yishuv and the Asefat Ha'nivcharim (elected assembly of Jews). Weizmann agreed to all these demands for an effective reform of the Zionist Executive and the Zionist Commission in Palestine. Two months later, the British and the French agreed on the northern border of Palestine which was considerably to the south of the original Zionist map. In all areas, it was clear that it was British interests that really counted. But as Weizmann admitted privately, while Jabotinsky was 'a new broom...he was not too easy either'.[30] Weizmann admired Jabotinsky's energy and drive as well as his ability to grip an audience. But on stage in front of a crowd, as Weizmann confided to his diary, he regarded him as 'a prima donna'.[31] Just months after joining the Zionist Executive, Jabotinsky wrote to Weizmann, offering his resignation because of lack of communication about his efforts to establish a Jewish militia. Weizmann replied warmly recalling their solitary task in establishing the Jewish Legion:

> Our long standing friendship, our comradely joint work during the days of heavy responsibility and isolation, when we were both cut off from our Jewish world, must be a guarantee of future work and mutual confidence. We are all passing through a terrible time. God alone knows that I do not want to strain relations, least of all with you.[32]

Jabotinsky retracted his resignation, but the criticism remained, and within a short time, he had resigned again. On this occasion, he appeared on a platform of the oppositionist *Di Tribune* where its editor, Meir Grossman, called for Weizmann's dismissal.[33] Jabotinsky felt compromised and asked Weizmann whether he should go through with his resignation. Weizmann once more wanted Jabotinsky on board.[34]

At the 12th Zionist Congress in Carlsbad in 1922, Jabotinsky was strongly criticized at a closed meeting of the Zionist Executive because of his negotiations with Maksym Slavinsky, the representative of the Ukrainian nationalist movement which most Jews held responsible for the mass killings of Jews. Once more, he resigned only to withdraw it.[35] It was clear that fundamental differences and potential schisms were arising from the new situation. The Zionist Commission became the Palestine Zionist Executive, but it was the London branch which continued to exert real authority. A measure of dissent reflecting, almost by default, Nordau's outspokenness was beginning to take root. Weizmann's policy of reasonableness and gradualism seemed to be working against the Zionist experiment.

Weizmann believed that only a strategy based on flexibility and dealing with the reality of British power would advance the Zionist case. Yet the very term 'Jewish State' was placed in abeyance. Weizmann instead referred to it as 'shem hamforash' – the ineffable name of God. In a letter to his wife from Carlsbad, he commented that it was becoming impossible to work with Jabotinsky, but not to work with him and his friends would effectively mean creating a formal opposition.[36] In a private discussion with Weizmann at the Congress,

Jabotinsky told him that his approach had led to a dilution of the aims of the Zionist project and possibly its eventual oblivion. One compromise would lead to another, and therefore it was important to confront the British constructively. In conversation with a friend, Jabotinsky accused Weizmann of subconsciously acting the part of the Marrano[37] – a Jew who converted to Christianity under duress yet remained inwardly Jewish. In this context, Weizmann's desire to expand the Jewish Agency to include non-Zionist philanthropists was therefore more than merely pragmatic. It might indeed solve the financial problems in the short term, but for Jabotinsky it would further weaken the Zionist movement's determination not to distance itself from the ideals of the Balfour Declaration. Weizmann's public defence of Sir Herbert Samuel and the new direction of the High Commissioner's policies had coalesced into a docile acceptance of a new reality.

Jabotinsky's criticism of Weizmann later emerged as 'Ahad Ha'amism'. Asher Ginsburg, more commonly known by his nom de plume, Ahad Ha'am, had been the intellectual mentor of Weizmann, but he was also the dedicated opponent of Herzl whom he regarded as superficial, messianic and Jewishly illiterate. It was the difference between the Zionism of Eastern Europe which had evolved out of Jewish tradition and the Zionism of Central and Western Europe which had emerged as a reaction to anti-Semitism. The intellectual Ahad Ha'am was, in turn, characterized as a propagator of 'batlanut' – an academic unworldliness whereas Herzl was the powerful motor that fired the Zionist machine. A year after his final resignation, Jabotinsky wrote that in the early 1890s when 'Herzl was still a mere "feuilletonist" on a Viennese paper, the stern, joyless philosophy of Ahad Ha'am dominated the minds of the elite – but only of the elite.'[38] Weizmann as a young student had been a follower of Ahad Ha'am and compared his influence on young Jews to that of Mazzini on young Italians during the previous century.[39] For Jabotinsky, however, such teachings were interpreted as the source of the malaise which had afflicted the Zionist movement. In the 1930s, Jabotinsky classified the adherents of these different schools of thought as two 'psychological races' in Zionism.[40]

AN ALLIANCE WITH THE POGROMISTS?

At the meeting of the Actions Committee in Berlin on 16 and 17 January 1923, Jabotinsky argued once more against the worsening situation and the gradualist approach taken by Weizmann, who was not prepared to countenance direct criticism of Samuel. A resolution was also passed which laid the ground for a wider Jewish Agency. In response, Jabotinsky submitted three resolutions to the Committee:

1. To inform both the Home Government and the Palestine Administration that

the continuance of the present policy in Palestine threatens to ruin the Zionist movement financially, and to bring our enterprise in Palestine to bankruptcy.

2.To declare that the presence of anti-Zionists or anti-Semites in the British personnel of the Palestine Administration was contrary to the Mandate, and to instruct the Executive to insist on their withdrawal.

3.To proclaim, in view of the widespread assumption that Zionism has renounced its ideal, that the Movement stands on the basis of its historic aim and that our obligations vis-à-vis the Mandatory Power admit of no other interpretation.[41]

It was a cri de coeur from Jabotinsky – and it was ignored by the Actions Committee who refused even to put it to the vote.

Yet the basis of the opposition to Jabotinsky was not simply from those who believed that his proposals would actually be counter-productive, given the parlous state of the Zionist movement, but also from two other interconnected issues. One dealt with style and collective responsibility. The other, more fundamental, reason dealt with Jabotinsky's perceived irresponsibility in seeking to work with hostile, national movements.

In particular, the Labour Zionists represented by Achdut Ha'avodah at the meeting were aggrieved by Jabotinsky's agreement with Maksym Slavinsky, the representative of the Ukrainian nationalist forces. At the 12th Zionist Congress, Jabotinsky independently agreed that Jewish gendarmes would accompany Symon Petliura's army in a new invasion of the Ukraine the following spring. This would, Jabotinsky argued, prevent more atrocities from being perpetrated against the Jews. The accord itself did not commit the Jewish gendarmarie to participate in any military operations on behalf of Petliura's forces, and provided them with a great deal of independence and autonomy. This initiative followed the widespread pogroms in the Ukraine by nationalists in the continuing war against the Bolsheviks and for a reclaiming of national independence. The population of Jews in the Ukraine – including New Russia – was almost two million according to the 1897 census. Up to 150,000 Jews were massacred by the Ukrainians between 1918 and 1920. Clearly the very idea that Jews should work with reactionary pogromists was like a red rag to a bull for the socialists. It tarnished the good name of Zionism and called into question the affection of the socialist Zionists for the new-born Soviet Union which had managed to survive despite the best efforts of the Western Powers.

Many Jews regarded the leader of the Ukrainian nationalists, Symon Petliura, as 'a Jew hating leader of a Jew hating people'.[42] The English Zionist Federation even called for Jabotinsky's resignation over the issue.[43] Yet prominent Jewish participants in these events, such as Arnold Margolin and Solomon Goldelman, held opposite views in that Petliura and the Ukrainian government of the time actually attempted to combat the pogromists. Joseph Schechtman, later Jabotinsky's secretary and biographer, was a member of the Central Rada and the Small Rada, and he proposed the creation of self-defence units in November 1917. Petliura agreed in principle but the Jewish socialist parties deemed this idea to be overtly nationalist and counter-revolutionary and seemingly scuppered the idea, with terrible results for the Jewish population. Many delegates at a clandestine Zionist conference in Kiev in April 1922 had professed understanding of Jabotinsky's stand.[44] But for the overwhelming majority of Jews at the time, Petliura was, at best, indifferent to the fate of the Jews. At worst, he was responsible for the mass killings.

Jabotinsky himself had good memories of Ukrainian nationalism – memories which stemmed from an earlier period.[45] Indeed, his interest in the Ukrainian national question was first noted in an article as early as 1904,[46] shortly after his espousal of Zionism. He suggested that the Jewish national movement should 'find and unite with allies whose interests overlap to some extent with ours. Herein lie our tasks in the general political area'. As a new adherent of Zionism, he drew deeply on the co-operative model of different national movements in the nineteenth century.

Moreover, Jabotinsky understood that as the Jews were themselves a national minority within other national minorities in the Tsarist Empire, they were especially vulnerable to accusations of being unwitting agents of Russification in an attempt to undermine the Ukrainian national movement. Indeed, this is how many Ukrainians perceived such assimilated Russified Jews – a view Jabotinsky attempted to combat. Russia's tactic of playing one nationality against another was by no means novel. Russia had been instrumental in bringing about the defeat, partition and disappearance of Poland in its sweep westwards in the eighteenth century. St Petersburg did not recognize the Ukraine, only 'Little Russia'. It was only in 1905 that the St Petersburg Academy of Sciences acknowledged Ukrainian as the distinct tongue of a distinct people. In 1897 almost three million Jews inhabited Ukrainian ethnic territories – some 28 per cent of world Jewry. Jabotinsky argued that it therefore made sense to work with the nascent Ukrainian national movement and identify common goals and aspirations. In addition, his support for Ukrainian nationalism and other minority national movements between 1904 and 1914 must be understood in the context of his struggle against Jewish assimilationism and rival ideologies such as those advocating national-cultural autonomy in the Jewish diaspora.[47] This manifested itself in a defence of the Ukrainian language and culture. In an article in 1911 on Taras Shevchenko, the Ukrainian national poet, Jabotinsky drew comparisons with the Italian poet, Giuseppe Gioacchino Belli, who composed sonatas in Romanesco dialect rather than normative Italian.[48] Thus Jabotinsky began to contribute articles to the nationalist publications *Ukrainskii vestnik* (in 1906) and *Ukrainskaia zhizn'* (in 1912). The *Vestnik's* editor was Mykhail Hrushevsky, who became president of the Ukrainian People's Republic in 1918; the editor of the *zhizn'* was ironically Symon Petliura.

Jabotinsky's opposition to the Russian melting pot philosophy took place within an exchange with the Russian liberal Pyotr Struve. Jabotinsky took issue with the overt nationalism and latent assimilationist approach which characterized Russian liberalism. He argued in a series of articles that democratization and a liberal Russia would not automatically solve the nationalities question. For his part, Struve contended that the Ukrainians were part of the Russian nation while the Jews were unable to progress from their narrow societal base to create an evolving culture.

Jabotinsky thus saw close similarities between the goals of the Ukrainian and Jewish national movements. Both peoples lacked independence, but had attempted to keep alive their national and cultural identities. Both were systematically discriminated against by the empires in which they lived, though for different reasons and to differing degrees. Both suffered from reactionary enemies – the Black Hundreds in Russia and the Polonizers in the Russian and Austrian areas of Poland. National liberation for Ukrainians and Jews alike could come about only through democratization. The fact that before the First World War the Ukrainian national movement adopted a positive attitude towards the Jewish national movement impressed Jabotinsky. Perhaps most important of all, the concept of co-operation between the two national movements was symbolic of an emerging independent Jewish national policy and a pragmatic understanding of Zionist aims. It also appealed to Jabotinsky's understanding of the national movements of small peoples during the nineteenth century.

From Jabotinsky's point of view, this was the background to his formal meeting with Petliura's representative Maksym Slavinsky during the 12th Zionist Congress in Carlsbad in 1921. Slavinsky, a minister in Petliura's government, was an old friend of Jabotinsky from Odessa. His wife was Jewish and his stance had been an espousal of moderation and as a known friend of the Jews. In the elections for the Second Duma in 1907, both Slavinsky and Jabotinsky ran for office in the same constituency which boasted a large Jewish population. Slavinsky was elected and Jabotinsky was not. Even so, Slavinsky, perceived as a pro-Jewish candidate, was blocked by reactionary and anti-Semitic groups from reaching the Duma. Jabotinsky and Slavinsky subsequently worked together on the same publications, *Ukrainskaia zhizn'* and *Russkie vedomosti.*

Therefore, in his message to the Zionist Congress which was read out by

Jabotinsky, Slavinsky condemned the attacks against Jews, but distanced the Ukrainian people as a whole from them and concluded with an appeal for brotherhood between Ukrainians and Jews. But all this did not go down at all well with the delegates – particularly, the East Europeans and the Anglo-Americans who forcefully laid the blame on the Ukrainian nationalists. Jabotinsky was characterized as an apologist who downgraded and glossed over the mass killings. The pogroms in the Ukraine had deeply distressed the Jewish world although both sides had an interest in preventing further atrocities. Jabotinsky also understood the iconic value of a Jewish army. This had been his raison d'être in his struggle to create the Jewish Legion. With its disbandment, resurrecting this symbol of the Jewish national movement in military guise had considerable inspirational value. Although the planned Ukrainian incursion for 1922 never took place, the vehemence of the reaction of the Jewish world surprised him. In a letter from New York to Yona Machover[49] several months after the agreement, the Slavinsky affair. which he considered to be a serious matter, still bothered him. Clearly, Jabotinsky felt that the criticism was unfair and that he had been misjudged. Significantly, he returned to the subject on several occasions during the next twenty years and never renounced his original analysis.[50]

Yet the Slavinsky affair convinced the Zionist Left[51] that he was a rabid anti-Communist and heartless reactionary. For others, he was plainly irresponsible. The incident evoked a more general principle which fomented bitterness and heated discussion on the Left – and indeed not only on the Left. Was it morally right to work with those who may have been the propagators of anti-Semitism and whose hands, in all likelihood, were stained with Jewish blood? Although anti-Semites and reactionaries had different motives for co-operating with Zionists, did logic dictate that even for a powerless people such as the Jews, such a direction was justified? Herzl had made a similar decision in seeking an interview in August 1903 with Vyacheslav von Plehve, the Tsarist Minister of the Interior in the aftermath of the Kishinev pogrom. Herzl had hoped that an intervention would convince von Plehve to suppress the activities of the anti-Semitic Black Hundreds. All this came on the eve of the 6th Zionist Congress. Zionist opinion was totally divided. As Weizmann recalled a half a century later:

> There were some who believed that the Jewish leader could not pick and choose his contacts, but had to negotiate even with a murderer if some practical good would come of it. Others could not tolerate the thought of this final humiliation. But there were still others – I was amongst them – who believed that the step was not only humiliating, but utterly pointless.[52]

Herzl had hoped not only to stop anti-Semitism, but also to persuade the Russians to place pressure on the Sultan to open the gates of Palestine. Weizmann was biting in his criticism:

Unreality could go not further; anti-Semites are incapable of aiding in the creation of a Jewish homeland; their attitude forbids them to do anything which might really help the Jewish people. Pogroms, yes; repressions, yes; emigration, yes; but nothing that might be conducive to the freedom of the Jews.[53]

For many, Jabotinsky had simply repeated Herzl's mistakes. This dovetailed with the irritation of those attending the Actions Committee who felt that Jabotinsky had no concept of the red lines beyond which he should not step. His adversaries had come to believe that his every action was predicated on his impulsiveness.[54] For Jabotinsky, there was a sense of the prophet outcast, a desire to preach the truth from the desert to his misguided people. Herzl proved to be the exemplar. For a man who had suddenly embraced Zionism, its lesson was now being unlearned. Shortly after Herzl's death in 1904, Jabotinsky majestically wrote:

> Then he (Herzl) appeared and, responding to the vague impulsive yearning of our souls, spoke to us: 'Create your own history; step out on the arena and see to it that from now on your destiny shall be created by you only.' Never did an echo on earth bear such resemblance to the voice that caused it as did his response to our expectations. And hence, never did mortal words have such a regenerating influence upon a generation.[55]

Many years later, Jabotinsky pondered on the nature of leadership and recalled that he had not heard the term 'leader' in daily use during Herzl's time. Jabotinsky concluded that it was only in England that the word had taken on the interpretation of being an elected official who is soon discovered to be no superman. Jabotinsky saw a profound difference in the role of the leader who was defined in an intellectual context rather than in a managerial one:

> The true meaning of the word, leader, is far from the meaning attached to the English word of the same name. An English 'leader' is virtually, the slave of his party; a real 'leader' in the true sense of the word, is something quite different. He must be a man who instead of the whole party doing the thinking has been given official authority to be the only 'thinker'.[56]

Such views did not endear him to those who believed in devolved leadership and democratic representation. His frequent criticisms of the movement and its leadership in the pages of the Jewish press betrayed the principle of collective responsibility. If he was a member of the Executive, his colleagues argued, then he should keep to the line of the majority. This was voiced even by those who were close to his views. His numerous resignations and subsequent withdrawals of them did not suggest a figure who could work to ensure unity and stability in difficult times. Yet many also joined Jabotinsky in voicing their genuine sense of stagnation. Weizmann heeded this background criticism and indeed contemplated stepping down, viewing Jabotinsky as his possible successor.[57] Yet by 1923, Jabotinsky was isolated amidst calls from Executive members for his resignation. How serious were such calls or whether they were made in the heat of the argument is an open question, but clearly many gave vent to pent-up feelings. In particular, the General Zionist, Yitzhak Gruenbaum, attacked Jabotinsky for his theatrical manner of handling even the mundane. At the meeting of the Actions Committee, Jabotinsky stated that he would not resign, but would continue to fight from within.[58] He reiterated that he was determined to remain on the Executive. But he changed his mind once more, probably after spending a sleepless night thinking about the issue. In his letter of resignation to the President of the Actions Committee, he remarked that he had taken 'consultation with some of my political friends'.[59] In all likelihood, Jabotinsky took this decision alone, and based it on his sense of frustration, his growing isolation, the hostility to his views and his disregard for a united front – and perhaps, deep down, a sense of humiliation that he was not appreciated by lesser figures.

A STRANGE ODYSSEY

THE PATH TAKEN

Trotsky once commented that those who desired a quiet life were unfortunate to have been born into the twentieth century. Jabotinsky would have sympathized with the sentiment. Yet following his resignation from the Zionist Executive in January 1923, Jabotinsky decided to forsake public life and to retire to his literary activities. In a letter to his family, he spoke of a stone being lifted from his heart; of his lack of obligations and his happiness in that he didn't have to support policies in which he did not believe.[1]

His commitment to the Zionist cause was now limited to saving the expiring Russian language weekly *Rassvet* which had moved to Berlin and to forging an association with the Hasefer publishing house. To save the periodical from extinction, brought on by the instability of Weimar Germany, Jabotinsky agreed to undertake a speaking tour of the Baltic States.

It was a visit to Riga in November 1923 that proved to be a turning point in Jabotinsky's career. Only two states in Eastern Europe, according to him, showed any real semblance of tolerance towards the Jews. One was Czechoslovakia, the other Latvia. For Jabotinsky, Czechoslovakia was the liberal republic of Masaryk and Benes which had turned its face against anti-Semitic nationalists and ensured that the Jews were recognized as a nationality.[2] Masaryk also expressed sympathy for Zionism. Jabotinsky admired the Czech Sokol movement – a youth movement based on patriotism and the gymnasium[3] which became the model for Betar. At that point in time, the early 1920s, the Latvians, Jabotinsky similarly reasoned, were 'a serious people with an efficient government' and they were not subject to 'a hysterical national zealotry' about ethnic minorities and foreigners.[4] Despite this positive appreciation, Jabotinsky also warned about the developing economic exclusion of Jews in Latvia and that there would be an inevitable clash between a rising Latvian entrepreneurial class and Jewish economic interests. In this context, he mentioned that he had witnessed a demonstration of thousands of people in Vilna. They were, he noted, smartly dressed and well-turned-out, but they still shouted 'Juden Raus'.[5]

Jabotinsky's charisma and mesmerizing rhetoric enchanted his audience in Riga, the student group Hasmonea, with an address 'Activism and Zionism'. In an article written a couple of years later, he recalled that they had reproached him for not consummating the affair. 'And what now? How can you propagate such views and stir up young people if you don't intend to call them to action. Either shut up or set up a movement.'[6] According to Jabotinsky's account, following an indulgence in drink and song, the students took a sword and tapped it on the table three times to confirm their pledge that together with Jabotinsky they would 'roll up their sleeves and straighten out the Zionist movement'. Hasmonea boasted a selected membership of eighty with its eldest member being just twenty-two years of age. In Riga, the Jewish intelligentsia looked more towards Germany than to Russia. Yet Jabotinsky believed that for these students all this was little more than a cultural veneer. 'Now,' he wrote, 'there is more space for Bialik and Peretz than Chekhov and Hauptmann.'[7]

In addition to the student group, Jabotinsky met a group of high school students and spoke to them about Eliezer Ben-Yehuda, the father of the Hebrew language and his old comrade-in-arms, Joseph Trumpeldor. This led to the establishment of the Joseph Trumpeldor group of Zionist Activist Youth, which evolved into Betar, the acronym for Brit Yosef Trumpeldor (the covenant of Joseph Trumpeldor).[8] In Hebrew, Betar was spelled with the letter 'tav' rather than 'tet' to symbolize a link with the fortress of Betar, the last stronghold of the Jews in their war against the Romans. Aaron Propes, the chairman of the Riga group, became the first member of Betar.[9]

On his return to Berlin, Jabotinsky wrote that the experience had 'sealed his fate'. He thereby made the decision to turn aside from writing and literary pursuits in order to create a new Zionist movement.[10] After Riga, he concluded that he could no longer play the part of the talented functionary. Many years later, Zalman Shazar, a Labour Zionist opponent, incisively commented that 'Jabotinsky always thought of himself as being a beloved child destined to be the first violinist, not needing any orchestra and not needing to be bound by one.'[11] In the early 1930s, in the midst of his quarrels with the Labour movement, Jabotinsky interpreted his path in life as personifying that of the solitary outsider, seemingly bearing the harsh message of unvarnished truth. In an article in 1932 which depicts a conversation between Jabotinsky and his trusted typewriter, the machine tells its owner:

At birth every individual receives a special dowry which lasts him during the entire span of his life. This, in all probability, is your dowry, and it is useless to struggle, because you will never be rid of it. Your lot is to be a perpetual sinner, replete with evil, always to be hated and whose name will be used as a blasphemy.[12]

Benjamin Akzin, for many years one of Jabotinsky's closest associates in the Revisionist Zionist movement, described him as someone who united 'a first-rate logical mind with the soul of a poet dissatisfied with the humdrum of daily life'.[13] No doubt the necessary respectability of diplomatic endeavour was vital, as was the boredom of meetings and the vulgarity of fundraising, but such a lifestyle as an official representative of the Zionist movement also created a perpetual restlessness in Jabotinsky. In addition, the increasing ambivalence of the British and the growing sense of hopes dashed pervaded Zionist activity. This provided the stage upon which Jabotinsky decided to act. He thus began belatedly to move towards Nordau's position that Herzlian Zionism had indeed been marginalized and essentially betrayed. But, equally importantly, he also identified with Nordau's manner of opposition. Jabotinsky viewed him as an Ibsenesque figure – one of an array of nineteenth century intellectuals – Nietzsche, Bjoernson, Pisarev, Curie – who formidably challenged the conformity and complacency of their epoch. It did not actually matter that Nordau disliked Ibsen and Nietzsche. It was Nordau as Zionist symbol and European thinker that was resurrected. On the tenth anniversary of Nordau's death in 1933, Jabotinsky drew an uncomfortable comparison between the assimilationism of Jews in the German-speaking world in the latter part of the nineteenth century with their deteriorating situation at the inauguration of the Nazi regime. Jabotinsky resurrected Nordau as a premature anti-assimilationist, 'a reformer of our national life, one of the children of the prophets'. In February 1933, he wrote:

A Dr Stockman is always disliked. Even though he be popular for a time, people soon begin to shout that he is an 'enemy', that he hates everything in the world, that nothing is sacred to him, that he is a soul who cannot witness things with a positive enthusiasm, who sees in every accomplishment only its disadvantages, whose only joy is to minimize everything, whom the Almighty, at his birth, forgot to bless with the sweetest of gifts – the talent to feel and love creative phenomena. It was an undeserved, empty accusation – even with the other Nordau, anger against the world's lies was due to a real love for humanity; but the clearest answer to this calumny he gave us his own nation.[14]

Jabotinsky saw himself in these words. Nordau whom he had severely condemned now became the exemplar and the teacher, a man of character who knew how to act. Nordau was seen as the great popularizer – someone who was far more adept than either Ibsen or Nietzsche in the ability to communicate a message:

The genuine, the specific art of a 'publicist' is the power to reach with his word the deepest depths and darkest corners of the reading public, to gain the attention of the most indifferent mind, to influence even a sleepy-head, even a watery soul.[15]

Jabotinsky viewed himself differently from other Zionist leaders. When asked if he regarded himself as a revolutionary, he had no qualms about replying in the affirmative, citing his desire to 'uproot all that is rotten'.[16] On his death, one of his followers attempted to locate a historical model on which to base his image of Jabotinsky.

Nor was he made of the same spiritual stuff as Herzl, Nordau and Zangwill. To best realize this, we should picture them as living in another epoch of Jewish history – that of two thousand years ago. Herzl, the majestic, statesmanly leader, the dreamer of national grandeur, would perhaps have become Alexander Yannai; Zangwill, the meticulous, sharp-witted thinker – a Shammai; Nordau, the academic, encyclopaedic figure – a Rabban Gamliel. But Jabotinsky could have lived only as a Hezekiah ben Menachem, the founder of the Zealot sect, or at least as a Yochanan of Gush Chalav.[17]

LEGITIMIZING THE MARGINS

For Jabotinsky and his more intellectual followers, Nordau in death now epitomized 'a red-blooded Zionism',[18] not simply maximalist in political terms, but maximalist in terms of the spirit. A liberating Zionism without frontiers. Jabotinsky often recalled his famous discussion with Nordau in November 1914 where the old man pointed out to his young friend that:

Those are words of logic, but logic is a Greek form of wisdom which our people detest. A Jew learns not from reason but from catastrophes. He will not buy an umbrella just because clouds have appeared in the sky. He will wait until he is thoroughly soaked through and contracts pneumonia.[19]

This quote, included in his autobiography was widely reproduced in Revisionist Zionist publications in many languages in the 1930s.[20] The objective of this exercise was to urge young Jews to be pro-active, to take matters into their own hands before it was too late. A sentiment which clearly resonated in the Europe of the Dictators. Many inferences can be made from this comment, but one which seems marginal – but is actually central to – is that Jews should embrace an essentially non-Jewish philosophy rather than continue the age-old tradition of passive acceptance of fate's decree. Of course, this was the same argument of the religious proto-Zionists, Alkalai and Kalischer, who effectively argued the case for human intervention in the return to Zion, in contrast to other ultra-orthodox figures who believed that God's hand should not be forced. Rather than go to the orthodox Judaism of Alkalai and Kalischer, Nordau, however, placed the example in the context of Hellenism, the philosophy of the ancient enemy of the Jewish struggle for independence. And Jabotinsky gladly embraced it in identifying with the narrative of nineteenth century European nationalism. It suggested a common language between Nordau and Jabotinsky and a common experience shared with Herzl. Moulded by nineteenth century Europe, Nordau and Herzl epitomized almost classical Jewish stereotypes whose 'Jewishness' was initially defined by escaping from it.

Yet Nordau had come to understand that the textbook emancipation of the Jews was the God that failed. In his speech to the first Zionist Congress in 1897, Nordau argued that the men of the French Revolution emancipated the Jews 'only for the sake of logic'. It had more to do with theory than with practice:

> The philosophy of Rousseau and the encyclopaedists had led to a declaration of human rights. Then this declaration, the strict logic of men of the Great Revolution, deduced Jewish emancipation. They formulated a regular equation: Every man is born with certain rights; the Jews are human beings, consequently the Jews are born to all the rights of man. In this manner the emancipation of the Jews was pronounced, not through a fraternal feeling for the Jews, but because logic demanded it. Popular sentiment rebelled, but the philosophy of the Revolution decreed that principles must be placed higher than sentiments. Allow me an expression which implies no ingratitude. The men of 1792 emancipated us only for the sake of principle.[21]

In Nordau's view, the nations which had emancipated the Jews had, in fact, deluded both themselves and their Jews. Throughout the nineteenth century, hosts of puzzled and insecure Jews had engaged in a collective mimicry in an attempt to be someone else – Prussians, Russians, Frenchmen, Italians. Their awakening, Nordau suggested, had been rude, unexpected and anti-Semitic. As Herzl later wrote, it was this 'secret psychic torment' which had the effect of leading him to Zionism.[22]

The Berlin Haskalah (Enlightenment) however, had symbolized the disintegrative approach to modernity which affected several generations of Jews in German-speaking lands. The leading exponent of the German Enlightenment, Moses Mendelssohn, simply believed that the Jews were incapable of arousing themselves from the spiritual sleep of centuries and embarking on such a national venture as the creation of a Jewish state in Palestine. The natural instinct for freedom, he argued, had been snuffed out through living on the margins of history – it had been transformed into 'a monkish piety'.[23] In Budapest, Herzl similarly represented the Jew brought up within the German cultural milieu and adhering lightly to a scanty religious background. Reaching adulthood, the loose religious moorings were progressively detached within the search for other means of identification – for Herzl, this meant Prussian nationalism and Christianity amongst them. In another model of 'Jewishness', Nordau rejected his traditional background and the outlook of his father, a rabbi and 'a Hebrew grammarian and scholar' [24] who rejected the minutiae of the life of a religious official. Instead, he tutored the children of the Talmudic scholar, the Hatam Sofer, and wrote poetry and plays in German. This duality was too difficult for his son, who rejected both Judaism and Jewishness at the age of fifteen. His odyssey led him to obfuscate his background by changing his name from Simon Sudfeld to Max Nordau – from a southern field to a northern meadow.[25]

It was only the outbreak of anti-Semitism that upset his persona of a German writer. Thus, whereas Nordau had some knowledge of Judaism, Herzl was wonderfully oblivious of much of it. In a letter to his family on arriving in Basle for the first Zionist Congress in 1897, Nordau wrote:

> As soon as I arrived this morning, I went looking for Herzl. I hired a carriage and drove to the synagogue where I found him. I had quite forgotten that it was Saturday. There I found myself in the midst of the service. And there was Herzl draped in a talit (a prayer shawl). They wanted to honour me with an aliyah (a calling up to the reading of the weekly portion from the five books of Moses), but I refused and fled in confusion. [26]

Nordau believed that civilization had developed, not 'thanks to religion, but in spite of it'.[27] He also recognized that faith in general was not central to governance.

> With the exception of the Jews and perhaps the Tibetans, the state, even when ruling with the help of faith, has never relied upon religion alone. It has never trusted to the fear of God to induce the subject to pay his taxes, shed his blood or obey his superiors. [28]

HERZL THE ASSYRIAN EMPEROR

If Nordau was selectively quoted, Herzl was exalted by Jabotinsky as the one true Zionist from whom all others deviated. In the 1930s, Revisionist Zionists, and especially the youth of Betar, anointed Jabotinsky as Herzl's one true heir rather than Weizmann. Moreover, Jabotinsky did not discourage this. Herzl's deep dislike of any hint of revolutionary activity and his advocacy of different forms of co-operativism were expunged from the Revisionist vocabulary. Moreover, Weizmann was portrayed as the very antithesis of authentic Zionism despite the fact that he spent his entire life in treading the same corridors of power as Herzl. Thus, Herzl was selectively quoted to confirm the prevailing wisdom. Indeed, even in death it was noted that both Herzl and Jabotinsky died young of heart failure in the same Jewish month of Tammuz.[29] One South African acolyte discovered that the initials of the Hebrew names of Jabotinsky, Herzl and Bialik spelled 'zahav' (gold) – 'and these three were the golden triumvirate of the Jewish renaissance.'[30]

After his demise in 1904, Herzl was raised to the statuesque level of a Biblical prophet by the Zionist movement. For the Revisionists, this was integrated into the figure of a romantic nationalist. Herzl was thus the heir of Moses and Bar-Kochba. Jabotinsky, in turn, was proclaimed the true successor of Herzl:

> Moses the prophet, who came to a people of slaves in the dawn of history to preach to them the hard lesson of freedom, was the first one in this long line. The Bible tells us of the great tragedy of his struggle: not Egypt nor the Canaanites nor the desert formed his main difficulty. His principal obstacles were the men whose souls were already stained by the mental shackles of slavery. Gideon, Samson, the Hasmoneans, Akiva, Bar-Kochba, were among the men who undertook the same task: some with success, others, without. In modern times, the lamp of freedom in Jewish life was lighted by Herzl.
>
> But in the stale and vitiated moral atmosphere of a warped community, the fire soon dies out. It flickers weakly, powerless to penetrate the darkness. Another torch-bearer has to come then, open doors and windows, relight the lamp, and revive in the wavering crowd the will for freedom, the determination to fight for it, clear thinking and an undistorted sense of values. In this generation, the torch-bearer of our people, the successor of Herzl and of the earlier prophets of freedom, is Vladimir Jabotinsky. [31]

Herzl's death in 1904 coincidentally occurred at a moment when Jabotinsky – in his quest for an intellectual meaning to life – discovered Zionism. The previous year, in August 1903, he had attended the 6th Zionist Congress at Basle as an outsider exploring a new political phenomenon which intrigued him.[32] As a journalist for *Odesskie novosti*, he had the option of remaining an interested but detached outsider. After hearing Herzl, he understood that he was at an ideological crossroads in his life.

> He has the most interesting looks of anyone I've ever seen, at once extraordinarily masculine, hard and graceful. A profile of an Assyrian Emperor like those engraved on ancient marble slabs: the manner of a man confident in his next ten years, if not accustomed to ruling then prepared immediately to do so. I listened and thought a great deal about this man: the Zionist movement has deep roots and does not depend on one man, but its entire leadership, its entire direction, its entire responsibility falls on Theodor Herzl.[33]

Herzl, in a sense, filled a growing spiritual and ideological vacuum in his life, nourished by a feeling of not having achieved his literary potential.[34] Almost a decade later, he coloured his former understanding in national hues, commenting that he was 'doomed to be considered an inauthentic and less than fully fledged Russian, a probationary Russian, an apprentice in the Russian cultural workshop'.[35] From Basle, Jabotinsky returned to Rome, the capital of his 'spiritual homeland'[36] where he had spent his student days – and thought deeply about his recent experience and the meaning of 'Jewishness'. He returned to Odessa as a convert – a convert not only to Zionism, but to a rationalized 'Jewishness'. As Herzl had remarked during his opening address to the first Zionist Congress, 'Zionism is a return to Jewishness even before there is a return to the Jewish land.'[37] Like Herzl, it was a 'Jewishness' moulded by the historic failure of the Enlightenment to truly emancipate the Jews. It was not a 'Jewishness' moulded by Judaism.

Indeed, for the ultra-orthodox, Herzl's pronunciations were heretical. The Kamenitzer Maggid, a known preacher at the Federation of Synagogues in England, regarded him as a second Shabbetai Zvi – the false messiah of the seventeenth century.[38] But for Jabotinsky, Herzl was transformed into an almost supernatural figure of hero-worship. He later wrote about Herzl's call for 'the assertion of our historic creative power' and his invocation to take the destiny of the Jews into their own hands. The figure of Herzl, the Assyrian Emperor, and the dreams of Zionism provided the young Jabotinsky with the means to fill a spiritual void – and he was not shy in writing passionately about this. The most striking example of this excavation of Jabotinsky's soul was revealed in his article 'Shiva' which was published shortly after Herzl's unexpected death:

> We were sitting at the time in the gutter, at the end of the great highway of life, and on this road we watched the majestic procession of nations on their way to their historic destinies. And we were sitting aside, like beggars with outstretched hands, begging for alms and swearing in different languages that we merited the charitable offering. Sometimes it was given to us, and then it appeared that we were pleased and contented because the master was in a good mood and had thrown us a gnawed bone. So it only appeared, for deep in our souls was growing a repulsive disgust for the beggar's spot in the gutter and for the outstretched hand, and we felt a confused attraction for the great highway, a desire to walk upon it like others, not to beg but to build our own happiness. [39]

Jabotinsky's powerful ode to this quasi-messiah not only lauded Herzl, but it was also a confession of his own salvation. Before he was lost, but now he was found:

> We changed; we were brought to life by touching the earth upon which he moved. It is only recently that I felt that earth and it is only from that moment that I understood what it meant to live and breathe – and if on the morrow I should have awakened to learn that this was merely a dream, that I am what I had been, and that ground is not and cannot be under my feet, I would have killed

myself, for it is impossible for one who has breathed the mountain air to return and be reconciled to sprawl once more in the gutter. [40]

Kornei Chukovsky, the Soviet literary critic and author of children's books, who knew Jabotinsky in his Odessa days, noted the dramatic change in his friend and mentor when he embraced Zionism. He was transformed from someone who was 'intoxicated by life itself' to 'an intense, dour individual'.[41]

Jabotinsky argued that the cure for personal sorrow was working for the cause of Zion. 'On earth, there should be no other idols, but this goddess. There was the legend of the living water, and I did not believe it, but now I do, because the living water is work.' This utilization of 'living water' significantly transferred the religious imperative in Judaism of spiritual cleansing through immersion in water to that of his conversion to Zionism. In Jabotinsky's eyes, Zionism had propagated a profound soul-searching and the death of Herzl, perhaps a father figure, doused a glowing light. Out of this came a sense of mission and purpose:

> In days of mourning, it is impossible not to look into one's soul and talk about it to your friends, and therefore it should not be held against me if I speak of what is going on in my soul, and what is concealed in that word – work. Believe me; no song possesses so much depth and beauty for me as that word.

> Since I began to think, different problems nestled in my brain, problems I could not solve and which were wearing me out and filling my soul with anguish and distress. But now I have found the solution to all these problems in one powerful word – work. And no matter into what labyrinth my rambling thoughts will sometimes cast me, and I wander there without Ariadne, without light – in the word, work, I find an inconsumable, fireproof, unalterable thread.

> Just as I realize that our ego exists, that even were everything else to be proved an unjust illusion and I would still be powerless to deny the existence of our ego, so I feel that it is in the word 'work' that we find the purpose, the justification and the reward of life. Are we striving for the significance of life? Do we want happiness? Do we want salvation? Work! [42]

In addition, Jabotinsky published 'Dr Herzl' in 1905[43] and wrote a poem 'Hesped' (Eulogy)[44]. Indeed, he continued to refer to Herzl's example and legacy throughout his life. Herzl, for Jabotinsky, represented the paradigm of the Jew, created by rationalism and the Enlightenment. The Jew was no longer the suffering believer of the ghetto. Thus Herzl's correspondence and discussions with Dr Moritz Güdemann, the Chief Rabbi of Vienna, revealed a concept of God that was a 'historical god' and a 'will to good'. Herzl's God was defined by reference to Spinoza and to the natural philosophy of the Monists.[45] Herzl admired such rationalists such as Montesquieu, Heine and Voltaire – and this ran through all his writings. Asked by the editor of the London *Jewish*

Chronicle about his beliefs in November 1895, he replied that he was a freethinker and that the guiding principle in the future Jewish state would be, 'Let everyone seek salvation in his own way.' [46]

Jabotinsky thus could identify not only with Herzl's approach, but also with his persona and his background. But there was a difference. If Herzl was at least able to retain a modicum of identification from a minimalist Jewish background, Jabotinsky had virtually no Jewish sources to call upon. Writing in 1939, a year before his death, he commented that he had no common past with the leaders of traditional Jewry and that in itself had induced a spiritual deficiency:

> The atmosphere of my upbringing in old Russia, as later in old Italy, was permeated with a rationalist outlook. In the end, it led me almost unconsciously to the conviction that rationalism is unable to reveal to me the one truth worth knowing – where I come from and whither I go and what the meaning is of my soul's hunger – but so it has remained, an empty space in my mind and an unanswered question – too late for me and my generation to fill up with content; but together with the consciousness of my own incompleteness the belief remained in my heart that the educated man in the Jewish future, the elite of the state – people of Israel in the year 1960, will be a spirit completely in harmony with itself, intangibly linked with the pulse of the hidden secrets within us which have now begun to reveal themselves.[47]

For Herzl, this 'incompleteness' manifested itself in many ways. For example, Herzl erected Christmas trees for his children at home and did not bother to have his son circumcised.[48] He had no understanding of kosher dietary laws and was happy to infringe the Sabbath laws by lighting a cigarette. For Herzl, as for Jabotinsky later, imbibing 'Jewishness' in the cause of Zion was a learning curve. Herzl was adept in utilizing religious symbols, such as the menorah, which related to the Jewish past for the political purpose of regenerating a sense of Jewish nationhood and national self-esteem. Although unfamiliar with religious culture, Herzl employed well-known phrases from traditional Jewish sources to convey a sense of familiarity to his audience. Thus at his last Zionist Conference, Herzl proclaimed the traditional oath, 'If I forget thee, O Jerusalem, let my right hand wither' from the Book of Psalms. This had been uttered by generations of Jews – sometimes in the most adverse of situations – but in this instance it was remembered long after by religious delegates as an oath taken 'with holy fervour in Hebrew'.[49] From the very beginning of his Zionist activities, Herzl had understood the importance of communication:

> You must convert the algebraic to the numerical. There are people who do not understand that $(a + b)^2 = a^2 + 2ab + b^2$. For them, you must calculate it in familiar terms.[50]

Herzl's search for a new identity was undoubtedly also connected with the disappearing middle ground of European liberalism and its hardening and polarization into populist and ideological movements. In particular, it was the election of the Christian Socials' anti-Semitic leader, Dr Karl Lueger, in April 1895 which had prompted the writing of 'The Jewish State' a few weeks later. Herzl remained a believer in the triumph of reason and the exercise of rationality. A Jewish migration from Europe, Herzl argued, would not only decrease the pressure on the Jews, but also allow liberals time to regroup and regenerate themselves. Liberalism was the only approach to the future – and it was a rationale which Jabotinsky attempted to apply himself.

Herzl's embrace of Prussian nationalism during his student days never left him during the years of his advocacy of Zionism. He had reacted strongly to the publication of Eugen Dühring's book *The Jewish Question as a Racial, Moral & Cultural Question* in 1881 which sanitized anti-Semitism amongst the intelligentsia. The growing cosmopolitan nature of the multi-national Austro-Hungarian empire provoked a Viennese reaction against both liberalism and social democracy. In March 1883, Herzl resigned from his student fraternity because of growing anti-Semitism, yet his delight in Prussian nationalism remained. Its style rather than its political intent served as a template for Herzl's new Jewish nationalism. It was not the social Darwinism of the Germanophile anti-Semites, but 'an image of politics as an arena of heroic deeds, courage, manly discipline, self-sacrifice, decisive leadership and self-effacing obedience'.[51] Bismarck was elevated as the archetypal nation-builder. While Jabotinsky built upon this through importing recent heroes such as Garibaldi, both understood Jewish nationalism as a means of transcending their perception of normative Jewish traits. While Herzl distanced himself from East European Jewry, Jabotinsky raged against the ghetto. Herzl idealized the duel and fantasized challenging and killing Lueger in a contest. In the dock, he would denounce the anti-Semites and passionately expound on the Jewish problem which would earn him an acquittal.[52] For Herzl – as for Jabotinsky later – the question of Jewish honour and self-dignity became central, politically and psychologically – and even more so for their followers.

Herzl's Zionism was also framed by his deep-seated Austro-Hungarian liberalism despite the desertion of the official liberals from overtly condemning the rise of anti-Semitism. One scholar explained that Herzl's omission of any real mention of the Arabs in his diary and his desire that the Jewish state should transcend great power rivalries was 'the liberal recoiling from the facts of irreducible conflict and from the spectre of force as the ultimate decisive factor in politics'.[53] Herzl, although living through the twilight years of Hapsburg rule, occasionally entertained less than liberal thoughts. In unpublished notes, he argued that if Jews believed that they were being marginalized and ejected from participating in society, they should join revolutionary groups and retaliate. They should respond with 'pistol bullets when their window panes were broken'.[54] Yet on more public occasions, such as a discussion with the Grand Duke of Baden in 1898, Herzl promoted Zionism as a means of converting Russian socialists and anarchists in the hope of securing a German protectorate over Palestine. For Herzl, the Grand Duke represented the old Prussia in the spirit of the founder of the German empire, Kaiser Frederick.[55] In a letter to Baroness von Suttner in 1899, Herzl wrote about Zionists being 'everywhere engaged in battle with the revolutionaries'.[56] Like Jabotinsky, he had admired the style of socialist politics prior to his conversion to Zionism. But both men came to view socialism both as a distraction from the national struggle and in opposition to their own liberal capitalist views. Both incurred the wrath of socialist Zionists. Nachman Syrkin attacked Herzl at the second Zionist Congress while Ben-Gurion berated Jabotinsky and the Revisionists throughout the 1930s. Herzl even condemned Nordau for 'quite uncalled-for advances to socialism'.[57] Unlike Jabotinsky, Herzl did not speak of a 'break-through period' where the Jews would act like cogs in a machine to achieve a Jewish state, but he certainly envisaged a disciplined approach where all would perform in unison for a common goal. In an early letter to Baron Hirsch in June 1895, Herzl envisaged the emerging Zionist movement as an army about to move – for which 'moral training' was necessary for its march.[58] In depicting Zionism as a nationalist crusade, he wrote:

> For a flag men will live and die; it is indeed the only thing for which they are ready to die in masses, if one trains them for it; believe me, the policy of an entire people – particularly when it is scattered all over the earth – can only be carried out only with imponderables that float in thin air. Do you know what went into the making of the German Empire? Dreams, songs, fantasies, and black, red and gold ribbons – and in short order. Bismarck merely shook the tree which the visionaries had planted.[59]

Herzl further argued that that the young Jews of his generation whose personal and professional dreams had been shattered would now rally to Zionism. 'Out of this proletariat of intellectuals, I shall form the general staff and the cadres of the army which is to seek, discover and take over the land.'[60] Zionist officials would be 'in uniform, trim, with military bearing, but not ludicrously so'.[61] Herzl occasionally invoked Napoleon and the Grande Armée as a means of depicting both his own youth and the possibilities open to all in the new Jewish homeland. He believed that Jews would fight for their country of birth in 'the next European war' and would then be received with all honours in the Jewish state as 'experienced warriors who have faced death and will enhance the prestige of our army'.[62]

Herzl's espousal of various forms of co-operativism distinguished his approach from Jabotinsky's promotion of the individual and individualism. It also reflected to some extent, Jabotinsky's reaction to the changed political circumstances of the inter-war years. Herzl lived before the great slaughter of World War I and the October Revolution while Jabotinsky inhabited an epoch when world outlooks and political identities had been forged by such events. Both men attempted to educate youth and to create the 'new Jew' by similar imperatives, but different methods, in vastly different times.

WHO WAS VLADIMIR JABOTINSKY?

The decision to resign from the Zionist Executive and withdraw from public life to devote himself to his literary activities in 1923 was related to his attempts to rationalize his dual identities as a Russian man of letters and a Zionist activist. Indeed, his lack of Jewishness surmounted obstacles – the Polish colonels, normally cold towards Jews, warmed to him in the late 1930s. Although an East European, Jabotinsky was incapable of acting the part of the son of the shtetl. For many, he remained the quintessential Russian intellectual. Yet the path which he mapped out for himself traversed the contours of both self-definition and ideology. His reports on the 6th Zionist Congress in Basle in 1903 – his essential introduction to Zionist activism – for the Odessa press indicated that he had little idea of the issues at stake.

The intellectual elite of Russian Jews had attempted to synthesize a fusion of Jewish national sentiment and Jewish tradition. It was against the world of piety and its innate subservience that the early Zionists, Ahad Ha'am, Bialik, Smolenskin, Lilienblum and even Weizmann all reacted and attempted to transcend. These East Europeans were essentially transitional figures who were too intellectually curious to fit into the world of the yeshiva, yet too traditional to contemplate leaving its cultural milieu. They embraced national regeneration and venerated the Jewish intellectual heritage.[63] The Central Europeans, Herzl and Nordau, however, were further removed from Jewish tradition. As Westerners, they were culturally and religiously distant from the East European experience. Nordau had consciously renounced his background while Herzl was profoundly ignorant of Jewish ritual. Jabotinsky, on the margins, was even further removed from the acculturated lifestyle of even Western Jewry.

In one sense, this was not surprising. Jabotinsky was the product of the great wave of Jews who had emigrated to 'New Russia' in the middle of the nineteenth century where Tsarist authoritarianism was more relaxed. Jabotinsky's father was such a Russified Jew, born in the 'New Russia', educated during the liberalism of the 1860s, distant from the Jewishness of his forebears – and his son even more so. A beacon of this new openness was cosmopolitan, freethinking Odessa. It had been declared a free port in 1817 and thereby a thoroughfare for duty-free goods. Powered by the expansion of markets and the drive for industrialization, the population increased from just over 2000 in 1795 to 400,000 a century later. By the time Herzl launched political Zionism, nearly 35 per cent of Odessa's population were Jews.[64] Odessa, less controlled by both Tsars and rabbis, proved a rival attraction to those Jews who contemplated emigration to Europe or the United States. Although ostensibly within the Ukraine, Odessa was an anomaly. Only ten per cent of its population, according to the 1897 census, were actually Ukrainian. Jabotinsky credited Catherine the Great for geographically locating the city, the Duc de Richelieu for building it, the Italians for settling it – as well as their expertise in smuggling and giving it 'their language, their architecture, their love of music – and wealth'.[65] Indeed, the street signs were originally in both Russian and Italian. There was a French newspaper and an Italian theatre, a Persian bazaar and a Tartar settlement, an Armenian alley and a Bulgarian street. It was in Odessa where the Greeks planned the war of liberation of their homeland in 1821 and where the Poles hatched their conspiracy for revolt in 1863. The Ukrainians, noted Jabotinsky, provided the sailors, masons and tramps – 'the salt of the earth'. He later recalled that of the twenty pupils in his class at school, some thirteen nations were represented.[66] After the Bolshevik Revolution, Jabotinsky nostalgically idealized the Odessa of his youth. In a light-hearted note to Ida Kremer, an internationally renowned songstress, Jabotinsky rebuked her for distancing herself from 'the wonderful city you don't love. Yet you are yourself an inspiration of all the fun, devilment and melancholy; and I did meet you under its acacias and lilacs and rowed with you in the sea.'[67]

Odessa was undoubtedly important for Jabotinsky not only as a place strong on nostalgia and good memories, but also where he was shunned and criticized by Bundists, Russifiers and indeed Zionists at different stages in his lifetime and in particular because of his advocacy of establishing a Jewish Legion.[68] Indeed in 1936, in proposing his plan for a mass evacuation of Jews from Poland, Jabotinsky spoke about his love for Odessa, 'my beautiful toy of a city', which he had personally 'evacuated', following the call of national conscience. One of his contemporaries from Odessa later commented that he could not imagine that people such as Pinsker or Jabotinsky could have grown up in Vilna or Warsaw, 'only Odessa could provide (them) with the necessary stimulus.' [69]

In his autobiography, significantly Jabotinsky recalled that his jailer in the Odessa prison in 1902 gave him the codename of 'Lavrov' after the positivist, Pyotr Lavrov, a leading theorist of Russian populism who influenced the Zemlya I Volya (Land and Liberty movement). Lavrov argued that progress came about through the focused actions of 'critically minded individuals'[70] who owed their education and subsequent status to the sacrifice of the masses.

This line of thinking resonated amongst many young Russians. Thus, Jabotinsky inhabited an ethereal world, an identity in abeyance – not able to gain admittance to the Russian people because of an accident of birth, but too Russified and detached to qualify as a nationally conscious Jew. This ambivalence accompanied Jabotinsky throughout his life and fashioned his relationship to Judaism. A long-time colleague in the Revisionist movement wrote that Jabotinsky 'well remembered (Comte de) Laplace's remark to Napoleon that, in writing his Mécanique Céleste, he found no need to assume the existence of God. Jabotinsky did not attend religious services and did not observe the Sabbath and the Jewish dietary laws.'[71] Indeed, in the late 1920s, he happily summoned his colleagues in the Revisionist movement to meet him on the afternoon of Yom Kippur.[72]

Jabotinsky's disdain for organized Judaism evolved into a questioning of the meaning of ritual – even though Jabotinsky was unable to embrace religious ritual itself. Indeed, the framework of his movement and particularly the Betar youth group was constructed around an admixture of ritual, ideological belief and chivalry. This evolved towards the end of his life into an appreciation of the survivalist instincts which Judaism had endowed:

> At first I was annoyed that people who are able to touch the realms of sanctity should at the same time concern themselves with such pragmatic, anthropomorphic bagatelles in, for example, a ritual. But then there came a time when I made a great discovery that perhaps three quarters of true culture consists of ritual and ceremonial, justice and political freedom stand and fall with the ritual of the court and parliamentary procedure, and the whole of social life would sink into barbarism if it were not for our being held in the iron harness of the ancient ceremonials of conventions and customs. It was only after this 'discovery' that it became clear to me that a wreath of holy stubbornness must be possessed by a minority in order to maintain and publicly demonstrate a complex of ritual which is so different from the ritual of its environment; and it became clear to me what it was that drew me to traditional Jewry; it was the courage of swimming against the stream, the magic spirit of 'in spite of everything'. [73]

Jabotinsky's realization was reflected in the parallel between the rituals of his own movement and traditional Judaism, united by the 'wreath of holy stubbornness'. In one sense, this was not unexpected because of his belief in the rationalism of the French revolution – a revolution which replaced faith in God by faith in the nation. As he wrote in 'The Idea of Betar': 'there is only one God, one ideal, to rebuild the Jewish state'.[74]

Jabotinsky wanted to create a new Jew – a Jew rooted in the heroic nationalism of the distant past, a modern day Bar-Kochba. In reality, such a regeneration stemmed more from non-Jewish roots. The diplomatic Zionism of Herzl and later Weizmann grew, to some extent, out of the traditional Jewish norms of barter and compromise. Although Jabotinsky followed this path, he placed emphasis on demanding rather than requesting. Similarly, the concept of learning how to shoot[75] and an exhortation to Jewish youth to be familiar with the ways of the military imitated nineteenth century European examples. This was rationalized as going back to the roots of the nation when the Jews lived a normalized existence in their own state. The intervening two thousand years were depicted as a rabbinic safeguard designed to protect the people – this had ended with the advent of the European nation-state. Indeed, as early as 1905, Jabotinsky had argued for a Jewish civil guard which would operate within the framework of a national autonomy for the Jews in the Tsarist Empire.[76] Thus the example of Bar-Kochba was exalted[77] – and Jabotinsky himself was compared to him. The immediate past conjured up a world of humiliation and shame. Even before Jabotinsky had founded the Revisionist Zionist movement, he wrote disparagingly of the world of the ghetto:

> The ghetto despised physical manhood, the principle of male power as understood and worshipped by all free peoples in history. Physical courage and physical force were of no use, prowess of the body rather an object of ridicule. The only true heroism of the ghetto acknowledged was that of self-suppression and dogged obedience to the Will above.[78]

One reason why the Judaic world rejected the secularism of the new European nation-state was that it did not have sufficient confidence in a system which based itself on human rationality to attain absolute truth. In the view of the orthodox, earthly opinion and judgement was relative and could change. Moreover, there could be more than one interpretation and the absence of a Jewish Pope suggested the acceptability of a plethora of opinions. Yet this ran counter to the Revisionists' ethos. Jabotinsky demanded discipline within and in contrast, he also advocated a disciplined synchronization of Jewish youth which would produce the breakthrough to Zion. He believed in a centralized machine concentrated on one goal during the breakthrough period to the state.

> Many asked me: 'Do you really want to turn people into machines? Modern culture strives for the freedom of the individual and fights against mechanization.' But there is a difference: If in the days of Tsar Nicholas we were forced to do things – that was bad. But today, when our youth realized the necessity to organize by itself, and 10,000 people execute a simple move as if they were one – yes, that too is a machine. But if a people does not know how to be a machine by itself – it is not a nation….a nation knows how to act in unison born of a single desire.[79]

Jabotinsky's remoteness and unawareness of Jewish life can only be compared to that of Trotsky who similarly came from a bourgeois background and also went to school in Odessa. Both came from the acculturated milieu that the Jews of Odessa inhabited to varying degrees of Russification. Both Trotsky and Jabotinsky sought a clarification of identity and an intellectual anchorage. Both attended the 6th Zionist Conference in Basle in 1903.[80] Jabotinsky chose particularist Zionism. Trotsky chose universalist socialism and permanent revolution. It is therefore understandable why Jabotinsky leaned towards Herzl and Nordau rather than Ahad Ha'am and Chaim Weizmann. The Haskalah – the Jewish Enlightenment – did not impinge on his psyche or intellectual development. The legacy of the maskilim was foreign to him. It was an alienation from which he could never escape – and nor did he wish to. Weizmann commented in his autobiography:

> Jabotinsky, the passionate Zionist, was utterly un-Jewish in manner, approach and deportment. He came from Odessa, Ahad Ha'am's home town, but the inner life of Jewry had left no trace on him. When I became intimate with him in later years, I observed at closer hand what seemed to be a confirmation of this dual streak: he was rather ugly, immensely attractive, well spoken, warm-hearted, generous, always ready to help a comrade in distress; all of those qualities were however overlaid with a certain touch of the rather theatrically chivalresque, a certain queer and irrelevant knightliness which was not at all Jewish.'[81]

Following Herzl's death, Jabotinsky, armed with the new awareness about himself, significantly engaged in polemics with assimilationists and with the supporters of other Jewish ideologies. In an article in 1905, he attacked those Jews who immersed themselves solely within the Russian educational system in order 'to remove the spirit of fanaticism and narrow-mindedness'. This, he argued, stripped the individual of his knowledge about himself:

> Had he but known the immense wealth of Jewish grandeur, he might have perceived how many and how noble are the forces hidden in this small people, this undefeated people; he would have felt the pride, and would have rejoiced in the knowledge that he is a Jew; all the stigmas of Jewish distress would have appeared to him less serious.
> For it is much easier to suffer for something beloved than for something hated or almost-hated.[82]

Jabotinsky was acting out his own resolution of his Jewish and intellectual challenges. In the early years of his career, he began to seek an answer for his puzzlement in converting to Zionism. He believed first of all that education was the link to a sense of belonging. However, there were those who never had a Jewish education and possessed no national consciousness before the unexpected blow of anti-Semitism turned them towards Zionism. He also recalled that children rebel against the lifestyle, beliefs and traditions of their family – against their education. For Jabotinsky, it was something which preceded education. 'I studied this question deeply and answered it myself. The blood. This point I now uphold to be the truth.'[83]

Jabotinsky later spoke of every nation as 'a separate race' each with its own psychological outlook. This permitted him to lift the image of the Jew in the eyes of his followers. Undeniably, he associated the East with backwardness and at a time when race and nation were often interchangeable terms, reflected the Eurocentric views of the inter-war years. This rejection of the East and promotion of the West applied to both Jews as well as to Arabs. Moreover, such backwardness was equated with religion. Such 'savage Eastern customs', he argued, characterized a disdain of free inquiry, religious intrusion in every corner of Jewish life, the fettered situation of a woman who sported a sheitl (wig) and would not shake hands with men.[84] In his autobiography, Jabotinsky freely quoted Nordau that 'the Jews came to the Land of Israel to push the moral frontiers of Europe up to the Euphrates'[85] and that the Palestinian Arabs, he said, were culturally '500 years behind us'.[86] And yet, unlike other Zionist leaders, he was brutally realistic about the consequences of this clash of nationalisms. While Jabotinsky opposed any notion of transfer and maintained that there would always be two nations in Palestine, he commented:

> They (the Palestinian Arabs) feel at least the same instinctive jealous love of Palestine as the Aztecs of old felt for ancient Mexico and the Sioux for their rolling prairies. To imagine as our Arabophiles do that they will voluntarily consent to the realization of Zionism in return for the moral and material conveniences which the Jewish colonist brings with him, is a childish notion which has at bottom a kind of contempt for the Arab people. It means that they despise the Arab race which they regard as a corrupt mob that can be bought and sold, and are willing to give their homeland a good railway system.[87]

Jabotinsky's writings before World War I focus on the questions of race, nation and state. He spent the year 1907-1908 studying such questions in Vienna. He was clearly influenced by the writings of Karl Renner[88] and Rudolf Herrmann von Herrnritt[89] on the national question in the Austro-Hungarian empire. Jabotinsky had written an introduction to the Russian edition of Renner's *State and Nation*.[90] Renner's central contribution was the separation of nationality and citizenship — a divorce between the idea of nationality and its attachment to territorial space.[91]

In 'An Exchange of Compliments' which was published in 1911, Jabotinsky depicts a philosophical discussion between a Russian and a Jew about Stolypin's controversial article 'An Inferior Race'. The Jew commences with the statement;

> There are no superior or inferior races. Each race has its qualities, its own features, a certain composition of its talents. I am sure that if it would be possible to find an absolute scale and to evaluate exactly the special talents and qualities of each race, we would discover that all races are almost equal in their value.[92]

While Jabotinsky did not explain the meaning of 'almost', in his essay 'Race', he made the distinction between race and racial purity. While disparaging the very idea of a pure race, he suggested that 'when all other conditions are identical, two persons who differ physiologically will differ in their psychic response to an entirely identical stimulus. The physical differences are always accompanied by psychic differences.'[93] He took issue with the Marxist understanding of historical materialism in that the determining factor on the evolution of humankind is the state of the means of production in a given community at a given moment. Marx did not include natural factors such as soil, water or the climate. Jabotinsky agreed with Engels that the process was more complex. He argued that the prime factor influencing the means of production was the intellect.[94]

> The most important thing, therefore is the 'thought'. From among all the means of production, the supreme, first and most important one is our spiritual mechanism. But each race has a different spiritual mechanism. This has nothing to do with the question whether there exist 'pure' races. Certainly each race is mixed and this applies to us Jews too – but the mixture is different.

> The quality of the 'spiritual mechanism' depends on the 'race', the strength of the intellect, a stronger or weaker leaning to search for new ways, the preparedness to be resigned to the prevailing situation or the daring which urges to invent; the stubbornness or on the contrary the character that gets tired with the first failure. The supreme means of production is in itself a product of race. This is why each race has an explicit uniqueness, and aspires to become a nation.[95]

THE NATIONAL REVOLUTIONARY
LEGACY

Rationalism and Religion

Jabotinsky reflected his positivist philosophy in his personal life by rejecting rabbinic Judaism. In an early writing, he asserted through the vehicle of Cervantes's *Don Quixote* that there was a human need to worship an abstraction, to create a personal living God – 'and to commit acts of heroism in His name'.[1] In a response to an article by Joseph Klausner in 1926, he condemned 'organized religion'.[2] In his reply – aptly titled 'The East' – Jabotinsky interpreted certain facets of Judaism as part of Eastern civilization which he regarded as incompatible with the liberal traditions of European – and specifically liberal Russian – culture. In the orientalist genre that fashioned Nordau, Buber and Weizmann as well as Marx,[3] Jabotinsky vehemently characterized 'Easterness' in negative terms, but he made a distinction between it and the 'East' as a geographical locality. Thus Baghdad could be more 'Western' than Rome at one point in its history.[4] Moreover, Jabotinsky blamed 'Easterness' for the intrusion of religion into everyday life. The cultured peoples of the West, he wrote, did not permit religion to enter into 'the legislature of the land, into philosophy, into science, into the diet'.[5] Jabotinsky criticized the customs of both Jews and Arabs. In the1920s, he referred to 'the 700,000 Arabs of Palestine' as 'primitive and polygamous'.[6] Jabotinsky's attacks on issues such as kashrut – keeping the dietary laws – or the status of women within Judaism were fashioned by his belief that many traditions were an unwelcome reminder that the Jews had retained a measure of 'Easterness' in their customs despite eighteen centuries in Europe. His short story 'Edmee', about a German Jewish academic's visit to Turkey, begins 'The East? It is entirely foreign to me. Here you have a living repudiation of your theories about race and the call of blood. I was born a westerner in spite of the shape of my nose.'[7] European Jews, in Jabotinsky's view, should overcome the remnants of Eastern backwardness as typified by many Jewish traditions. The Haskalah, he argued, had arisen to distil traditions and laws of the past from the national essence.[8] Later he seemed to modify his views – at least in public. During the founding conference of the New Zionist Organization in Vienna in September 1935, Jabotinsky insisted that the constitution include a reference that one of the aims of Zionism was 'the inculcation of the teachings of the Torah'.[9] No doubt he was appealing to the national religious, the ultra-orthodox and the simply observant who could not identify with the secularism of the Labour movement in the hope that they would join him. In a letter to his son shortly after the conference, he remarked that he saw no holiness in the religious ritual, but that 'one could establish a system of ethics without divine connection. This I have maintained throughout my entire life. But at this moment, I am certain that it would be more appropriate to inculcate these moral principles which are connected with that mysterious unknown over and above the realm of human reach.'[10]

Nineteenth century historians such as Macaulay and Dubnov had referred to an inner spiritual, intellectual and social universe which constituted history. 'Politics and occasional wars are but its husk.'[11] Jabotinsky questioned the Jewish understanding of this interior and effectively reversed its accepted interpretation. Contemporary Judaism was thus not the inner treasure, but merely a watchman over the national essence.

> If the people voluntarily encased their religious consciousness within an iron frame, dried it out to the point of fossilization, and turned a living religion into something like a mummified corpse of religion – it is clear that the holy treasure is not the religion, but something else, something for which this mummified corpse was supposed to serve as shell and protection.[12]

This rejection of the meaning of Judaism in Jewish history stems partly from Hegel's view of the Jews. Hegelian philosophy relates that the Oriental world was static and unchanging. Although Hegel believed that the Jews were primarily a national group, true history begins with the emergence of Europe. The Jews, according to Hegel, were intellectually isolated in the Orient and therefore did not have a true historical tradition. They were ossified by their religion and rendered incapable of imbibing the Christian message which could have moved them onto the next plain of human development. While it was true that Judaism had introduced monotheism to the world, Jesus had transcended the borders of the House of Israel and universalized its message for all humanity. However, the triumph of Christianity should have borne witness to the disappearance of the Jews as in the case of other ancient civilizations. Why then had the Jews survived? This was a question which Hegel was unable to answer.

The Enlightenment thinker, Nachman Krochmal, argued that the Jews were unique simply because they were structurally eternal and not transitory. This derived from the Jewish people's relationship with 'the Absolute Spirit' – in religious terms, God. This relationship skirted conventional understanding of time and space, therefore the Jewish contribution to history assumed a universalist character whereas those of Assyrians, Greeks and Romans had been particularist.[13] This inversion of Hegelian and Marxist approaches to the Jews suggested that Jewish history was somewhat different from normative history. Hegel argued that all nations followed the course of evolutionary history as postulated by Vico and Herder. Krochmal suggested that the eternal destiny of the Jews was conditioned by its relationship to God which led to a revival and renewal in succeeding epochs of history. The cycle of growth, blossoming and decline that afflicted great empires and civilizations was actually repeated in the case of the Jews. The Chimelnitski pogrom in 1648, Krochmal argued, had characterized the end of the last cycle, but the Haskalah and the emancipatory legacy of the French Revolution symbolized national renaissance in the new cycle. Other Jewish thinkers similarly tried to understand why Jewish history did not conform to the accepted theories of the times. Thus, Simon Dubnov depicted the Jews as dually national and universal:

> If the history of the world be conceived as a circle, then Jewish history occupies the position of the diameter, the line passing through its centre, and the history of every other nation is represented by a chord marking off a smaller segment of the circle. The history of the Jewish people is like an axis crossing the history of mankind from one of its poles to the other. [14]

Hegel's views were also challenged by Moses Hess, a one-time colleague of Marx and a socialist proto-Zionist. The Jews, he proposed, were an intermediary between East and West. Their land was indeed in Asia, but the people were in exile in Europe. Unlike Jabotinsky, Hess's traditional background reinforced his political reasoning and he envisaged a regenerated Jewishness. In his book, *Rome and Jerusalem*, Hess wrote:

> The rigid forms of orthodoxy, the existence of which was justified before the century of rebirth, will naturally, through the productive power of the national idea and the historical cult, relax and become fertile. It is only with the national rebirth that the religious genius of the Jews, like the giant of legend touching mother earth, will be endowed with new strength and again be reinspired with the prophetic spirit. No aspirant for enlightenment, not even a Mendelssohn, has so far succeeded in crushing the hard shell with which Rabbinism has encrusted Judaism without, at the same time, destroying the national ideal in its innermost essence.[15]

Although Hess was regarded initially as a radical young Hegelian, he actually described himself as a disciple of Spinoza. In his Zionist phase, Hess looked to

Spinoza rather than Hegel in understanding the Jewish national spirit. Indeed, in his *Tractatus Theologico-Politicus* in 1670, Spinoza contemplated the establishment of a future Jewish state. For Hess, Spinoza was the true prophet of the new age who philosophically made possible the French Revolution. Hess saw the changing direction of the Jews as a signpost on the road to universal redemption. Unlike Marx, he did not believe that the social evolution of humankind as rational beings could be determined precisely and predicted scientifically. Vico and Herder believed that history clearly did not move in straight lines. Herder, in particular, influenced the Jews because as an early anti-colonialist, he was the first to identify the need to belong. As Isaiah Berlin remarked, Hess believed that 'social equality was desirable because it was just, not because it was inevitable.'[16] Much to the disgust of Marx, Hess's socialism and emphasis on morality owed more to Spinoza and his Jewish background than to Hegelian historicism. He stood clearly against radical determinism and this separated him from the Hegelians and the Marxists. The schism was consecrated by Hess's understanding for the progressive nature of nationalism from which Marx had auto-emancipated himself. Such thinking led to a profound understanding and respect for the Italian Risorgimento and Mazzini's activities.

Although Jabotinsky distanced himself from Hegel's understanding of the Jews, he also did not agree with the arguments of Hess and Dubnov which upheld the intellectual value of Judaism during the millennia of exile.[17] Jabotinsky rarely mentioned Spinoza, Hess or Krochmal. He preferred the logic of geographical and historical determinism, drawn from the minds of nineteenth century philosophers rather than from the Haskalah. Jabotinsky often argued that the imprint of national independence on the Jewish psyche had become almost genetic as it was passed down the generations. However, as several writers have acknowledged, the work of the nineteenth century English historian Henry Thomas Buckle also influenced Jabotinsky. Buckle's ideas connected the Jews powerfully to the religious, historical and national space of the Land of Israel. Moreover, Jabotinsky's views on race cemented such determinism.[18] Jabotinsky's answer to the question 'why had the Jews survived?' was therefore not formulated on the basis of inner Jewish sources. There was no echo of the intense debates invoking Spinoza, Mendelssohn and Friedlander, but rather on broader theories emanating from European thinkers such as Comte, Buckle and John Stuart Mill.

Jabotinsky recognized this and even made a virtue out of it. In an article in 1934, commemorating Joseph Klausner's sixtieth birthday, Jabotinsky argued that Zionism did not have to be fortified through 'only Jewish sources with all accompanying pilpul (Talmudic argumentation) for and against'.[19] Interestingly enough, it was Ferdinand Lassalle, a founding father of German social democracy, who impressed Jabotinsky – 'a talented publicist'.[20] A man reknowned for his intellectual brilliance and passionate commitment, Lassalle saw his Judaism and Jewishness as an impediment. For him, the Jewish presence in the development of history had to be overcome, transcended and ultimately extinguished. Unlike Hess, Lassalle neither returned to his Jewishness nor attempted to integrate it into his socialism. In a letter in September 1860 to a woman whom he wished to marry, Lassalle proclaimed that he was 'no more a Jew than you are'[21] and commented:

> I do not like the Jews at all; indeed in general I abhor them. I see in them only degenerate sons of a great, but long past, age. In the course of centuries of bondage those people acquired the characteristics of slaves, and this is why I am extremely unfavourable to them. [22]

He would have left Judaism behind, he argued, but to do so for a public figure such as himself and the leader of a political party would pander to prejudice and be regarded as a cowardly act. Eduard Bernstein later commented that as Lassalle adopted more radical views, 'there grew an ever stronger longing to shake off the Jew in him'.[23] Yet for Jabotinsky, it was Lassalle, the advocate of Jewish self-deprecation, that was quoted and admired rather than Hess the Zionist. His long-term secretary, Joseph Schechtman, wrote:

> Certain striking similarities between Herzl and Lassalle, the German socialist leader of Jewish origin, have been noted. Jabotinsky, too, seems to have been fascinated by Lassalle. It cannot be mere coincidence that he knew Lassalle's literary writings by heart. These had never thought to have great merit and none but a few German experts in the history of socialism knew of them. In a conversation in the 1930s with a Polish Foreign Ministry official, the question came up whether reason or the sword ruled human destiny. Jabotinsky quoted Lassalle's *Franz von Sickingen* to the effect that all that is great owes in the end its triumph to the sword. It was the flamboyant, romantic, sentimental element in Lassalle and in Jabotinsky that influenced their political style and led them beyond liberalism: the one towards socialism, the other towards Zionist activism.[24]

In common with other German Jewish intellectuals of his time such as Heine, Borne and Hess, Lassalle struggled with his Jewish identity as a bi-product of Prussia's concerted effort to eradicate the emancipatory effects of French rule. In his diary, the young Lassalle wrote about leading the Jews 'sword in hand along the path to independence'.[25] In confronting the reactionary policies which forced Jews to convert and assimilate, in another diary entry, he also railed at the passivity of the Jews in accepting this situation:

> Nation of cowards, you deserve no better fate. The trampled worm will turn, yet do you but bow the head more deeply. You cannot die or wreak destruction; you

know not the meaning of righteous vengeance. You cannot bury yourself with your foes and mangle them even in the agony of death. You are born to servitude.[26]

No doubt such sentiments and the difficulty of identity struck a chord with Jabotinsky. But it was Lassalle's publication of *Franz von Sickingen* in 1859, a five-act drama based on a revolt against the Papacy during the Thirty Years War, with which Jabotinsky identified. The play illustrated the struggle to unify the Germans and overcome the petty rivalries of minor nobles. Sickingen was depicted as 'towering above others of his class by his moral and intellectual qualities, his military capacity, his broad views and his readiness to succour the oppressed'.[27] Sickingen and his compatriot Ulrich von Hutten – a close associate of Martin Luther – ultimately failed in their attempt to outwit their princely opponents. Yet they were modelled on Garibaldi and Cavour in their contemporary struggle to unite Italy and, by extension, were potent symbols for German reunification. Moreover, it was no coincidence that Lassalle published *The Italian War and Prussia's Duty: Democracy's Call* at the same time.

The drama and its central characters served as a paradigm for Jabotinsky personally and for the Zionism that he wished to project. Lassalle's views on Jews were secondary – what mattered was the romanticism of the cause, the call to rebellion and the need for self-sacrifice – and Jabotinsky understood this well. In addition, Lassalle attracted the ire of Marx who questioned the making of Franconian noblemen into the central characters in this drama and criticized a general drift from Hegelian truths. In reality, Sickingen was not based on the dialectical understanding of history. 'If events are determined by leaders and not by laws, by arbitrary will and not by historical necessity, then the "hero" has been reborn.' [28]

Franz von Sickingen placed both Hegel and Marx at a distance.[29] To Jabotinsky's delight, it also lauded the importance of military might:

It was the sword, the sword of Charlemagne
That brought the faith of God to German hearts
It was the sword that struck paganism low
The sword that freed the Holy Sepulchre
The sword that drove Tarquinius out of Rome
The sword that pressed Xerxes out of Greece
And freed the land for learning and the arts[30]

THE REVOLUTIONARY TRADITION

Jabotinsky, like all his older contemporaries Hess, Pinsker, Herzl and Nordau, believed that the modern Zionist movement emerged out of the legacy of the French Revolution rather than the Bible. It involved the replacement of the centrality of God by 'the religion of liberty'. Benedetto Croce whose writings highly influenced Jabotinsky wrote:

> The concept of personal dignity was revived, and with it the feeling of true aristocracy, with its code, its rigidity and its exclusiveness, an aristocracy that had now become liberal and therefore wholly spiritual. The heroic figure that appealed to all hearts was the poet militant, the intellectual man who can fight and die for his ideas – a figure that was not confined to the ecstasies of the imagination and pedagogical illustrations, but appeared in flesh and blood on battlefields and barricades in every part of Europe. The 'missionaries' of liberty had as companions the 'crusaders' of liberty.[31]

The idea of the nation-state evolved from the Protestant Reformation. Luther's belief that salvation could be attained through faith alone and 'the priesthood of all believers' set in train the fragmentation of a Europe dominated by the papacy. The influence of national revolutionary movements in the remnant of Catholic Europe in the first half of the nineteenth century formed the ideological inspiration for modern Zionism. But it was also the Church's willingness to promote covert anti-Jewish feeling and to support the forces of reaction in a futile attempt to hold back liberalism that additionally contributed to the development of Zionism. Max Nordau inveighed against Catholicism even before he became a Zionist. The Dreyfus Affair confirmed his belief that the Church was engaged in a broad attempt to reclaim its former prestige and rewind the political clock to the pre-revolutionary era. Nordau did not mince his words: the Church had invented the Dreyfus Affair and manipulated anti-Semitism 'with that adroitness acquired by 1,500 years of practice'.[32] For Croce, the Catholicism of the Church of Rome was 'the most direct and logical negation of the liberal idea'.[33] Yet the intellectual inheritance of the Revolution also contained the seeds of assimilationism in banishing the idea of a separate Jewish nationality. Revolutionary France did not believe in the idea of a multi-national state and favoured the idea that the Jews no longer constituted a nation. The logical conclusion was that Jews should essentially be denationalized. Nationality and the state should be synonymous. As Clermont-Tonnerre famously remarked in 1789:

> Everything must be refused to the Jews as a nation; everything must be granted to them as individuals. They must be citizens. It is claimed that they do not wish to be citizens. Let them say so and let them be banished; there cannot be a nation

within a nation.[34]

Adrien Du Port, a leader of the Left in the National Assembly, spoke of the Jews as 'wishing to assimilate in our midst'. Robespierre similarly espoused such views even though he was a powerful champion of Jewish rights. Even when the Revolution passed into its most radical phase, the Jacobins while initiating the principle of equality of rights for Jews refused to acknowledge the Jews as a separate community. The enfranchisement of the Jews depended on their willingness to renounce their claims to autonomy in the new France. Mirabeau placed the revolutionary offer in front of the Jews.

> Gentlemen! Are our laws your laws? Are our courts of justice yours too? Are you legally our fellow citizens, our brethren? Will you be able to take the civic oath in your hearts as well as by word of mouth? If such be the case, excellent! Then you are good Frenchmen, then you will be active citizens. If not, then remain passive citizens and wait until your city, Jerusalem, is rebuilt and there you can be active or passive as you choose.[35]

There were many Jews who accepted Mirabeau's well-intentioned offer and embraced the emancipatory possibility – and its invisible progeny – assimilation, acculturation and conversion. The emancipation of the Jews emerged because it met the needs of the Enlightenment. As Nordau later proclaimed, it met the demands of logic. It was an emancipation according to the textbook, an offer made on the basis of 'universal propriety and justice, but not justice long denied to the Jews specifically'.[36] A change in society, it was argued, would induce a change in the Jews. The Jews, however, wanted an end to discrimination and access to civic equality in French society, but they also wished to retain their particularist affiliations. Indeed, many Jews were attracted and then seduced by the possibility of entry into the host society. Some did not wish to be different or to be considered different. Many others opted for the more difficult choice, neither to rebuild the ghetto walls nor to assimilate: to be Jewish by nationality as a loyal citizen of the state. The revolution certainly divided Jewish communities between those who wished to maintain the status quo and those who wished to take advantage of the new freedoms. In Holland, for example, the rabbis and the communal leaders looked back in favour upon the ancient regime while Jewish liberals supported the Batavian Republic and 'Felix Libertate'. The future was indeed bright and they wanted to be in tune with the spirit of the times. As Alexis de Tocqueville – who shared the early Zionists' suspicion about the power of human rationale – later remarked, 'Never had humanity been prouder of itself nor had it ever so much faith in its own omnipotence. And joined with exaggerated self-confidence was a universal thirst for change which came unbidden to every mind.' [37]

But revolution came at a price. Rousseau, who provided the inspiration for the revolutionary tradition, actually opposed the idea of bloody insurrection.[38] Although Jews welcomed the Revolution with open arms and even joined the National Guard, few were involved at this stage of the emancipatory process in the upper echelons of revolutionary action. In Metz, Jews sang the 'Marseillaise' in Hebrew. When Jacobinism erected the Temple of Reason, a few Jacobin Jews initiated the closing of synagogues and the burning of the Torah. Some paid the price and were guillotined during the Great Terror. Altering the status of the Jews in France at that time was symbolic of the new thinking, regardless of the Jewish reality – and it was strongly opposed by representatives of the old order, the aristocracy and the Church. Significantly the theory that the Revolution was the result of a conspiracy integrating the Philosophes, Masons and Jews first appeared as early as 1799 when the Abbé Augustin Barruel published his *Memoires: Pour Servir a l'histoire du Jacobinism (1797-1799)*.[39] Thus this occurred well before disproportionate numbers of Jews became involved in movements of social change in Europe after 1815. Later writers such as Alexandre Weill and Joseph Salvador interpreted the Revolution retrospectively in terms of the vision of the Hebrew Prophets. Thus Salvador's *Paris, Rome and Jerusalem* in 1860 postulated that the French Revolution had been inspired by the values of the old Jerusalem and would in turn inspire the building of the new Jerusalem.

Yet the Jacobins erected the standard of the nation-state – and backed it with a militant religiosity of ideology and violence. Jacobinism stood in direct contradiction to the overarching idea of multi-national empires such those of the Hapsburgs and the Ottomans – united by a king above nationality. By the middle of the nineteenth century, the national revolutionary ideal had begun to fade and was replaced by sentiments of national superiority and imperial rivalry. Indeed, although the French Revolution was a nationalist revolution, after 1848, the Year of Revolutions, it became the status quo rather than a model for change. The elites co-opted the legend and its political legacy moved from the political Left to the political Right. In the age of imperialism, Jews were consequently defined to be outside the nation regardless of whether they accepted Mirabeau's proposition or not. Mirabeau's throwaway conclusion to await a rebuilt Jerusalem and to go and settle there thus became uncannily prophetic. For Jews, especially those living in central and Eastern Europe, it predicted the shape of things to come. Yet the French Revolution was recalled fondly both by those who embraced it as a means of transcending Jewishness and those who viewed it as a means of transforming Jewishness. As early as the 1820s, Orly Terquem, the author of *Lettres Zarfatiques* suggested that the second day of Passover should be celebrated on the anniversary of emancipation and devoted to recalling the Comte de Mirabeau and the Abbé Gregoire rather than Rabbi Eliezer and Rabbi Tarfon.[40] This admiration for romantic nationalism spawned by the French Revolution united the thinking of Jews who were distant or alienated from Jewishness such as Herzl and Nordau. Indeed even when describing the tasks of Betar in the 1930s, Jabotinsky significantly noted that: 'The French nation carried out its "mission" of instructing the world in the teachings of liberty and equality which it accepted during the great French Revolution.'[41] Moreover Jabotinsky later argued that any flaws in the Revolution should not dissuade a potential adherent. Thus the Terror, Bonapartism or even the false dawn of emancipation should not detract from an appreciation of an ethical revolution as a paradigm for Zionism:

> A great thing has a character – 'features'. Whatever is expressive of those features is part of the truth; whatever is in contradiction of that character is an accident, a scar, a rash.
> The most beautiful epochs of world history had their ugly stains. There are a thousand and one repulsive incidents that one can relate of the French Revolution, of Lincoln's civil war, of Garibaldi's battles; and perhaps they should be related – in a scientific history volume. But when one wishes to relate the essence of an episode, the beauty of which must today be universally affirmed, it is puerile to examine the mud – even though mud often gathers where people gather. It is puerile to mention, in a short survey of the French Revolution, that during the attack on the Bastille, pickpockets were busily at work – even though it may be a fact. A healthy mind regards only what is important and what is important is that which is expressive of the 'features'.[42]

Jabotinsky preferred to recall Napoleon's appeal to the Jews during his Holy Land campaign in 1799. The Jews, Napoleon proclaimed, were the rightful heirs of Palestine. They should rise up and show that the Ottomans had not extinguished 'the courage of the descendants of those heroes whose brotherly alliance did honour to Sparta and Rome'.[43] Indeed as early as 1902, Jabotinsky had written a poem about Charlotte Corday, the Girondist who had murdered Marat in his bath. 'Poor Charlotte' was banned from publication by the Russian censor. But the internationalism of the national revolutionary ideal, linking the Irish with the Italians, the Poles with the French, the Hungarians with the Americans was an inspiring rallying cry. The Polish revolutionary slogan 'For your freedom and ours' was still being utilized by Jabotinsky as late as a month before his death in 1940.[44] Rousseau spoke about such internationalism as a jump of the imagination – from what is to what could be. It was the national messianism – particularly from the devoutly Catholic nations of Poland and Italy which highly influenced Jabotinsky. This reinforced the sense of separation of Odessa from tsarist autocracy. Indeed, Jabotinsky recalled that during his youth in Odessa his schoolmates had dreamed of running away to fight for the Boers against the British. He related that the Boer war and the Dreyfus affair 'taught us the lesson that it is correct to fight for right and justice even if you are weak and your opponent is powerful'.[45] National regeneration was an integral part of the desire to fight in other causes. Jabotinsky also drew on the fact that there were other nations who were also moving away from an 'epoch of assimilation' and which, at one point, had seemed to be on the point of extinction. In particular he cited the Indians who, not long ago, would ridicule their own culture and sing only English songs and the Czechs who seemed more German than the Germans.[46]

Above all, the idea of a Jewish army – the Jewish Legion – sprang out of the context of revolutionary nationalism inspired by the French Revolution. As early as 1792, national Legions – the Belgian, the Batavian, the German - were established on French soil. The army which defeated the Prussians at Valmy and Jemappes in the autumn of 1792 was heavily internationalist.[47] Revolutionary France was the inspiration for Poles whose own country had disappeared by 1795, trisected and devoured by three empires. Thus seven thousand Poles were serving under the tricolour by 1797. The figure of Napoleon and the revolutionary heritage mesmerized Poles throughout the nineteenth century despite the fact that France distanced herself from Polish aspirations. The Poles and the Italians utilized their deeply-held Catholicism as a cultural, motivating force in securing independence. Exiled Poles looked upon their country as the Christ of the nations. Humiliated, persecuted, defeated, but it would rise again. The French historian Jules Michelet understood 1789 as the second coming.[48] As with the Irish and the Italians, the religion of revolutionary nationalism demanded its priests as interpreters and communicators. In the age of romantic nationalism, this became the task of poets. Thus Coleridge bemoaned the crushing of the Kosciuszko revolt in 1794 while Wordsworth extolled 'France standing on the top of golden hours / And human nature seemingly born again.'[49]

In the Polish case, this became the raison d'existence for Adam Mickiewicz who often drew allusions from the Catholic liturgy. Mickiewicz's son of God was Napoleon, condemned to die for his faith on St. Helena. Indeed, Heine had suggested that Waterloo was the first station of the cross.

The inevitable step was to connect nineteenth century Poland to ancient Israel. Following the Polish defeat of 1831, Heine wrote that Poland's 'real existence has in no sense ended with her political substance. Like Israel after the fall of Jerusalem, so perhaps after the fall of Warsaw, Poland will rise, called to the highest destiny.'[50] As France retreated from its commitment to Poland, Mickiewicz distinguished between the real France and the opportunism of Louis Philippe and Louis Napoleon – an allegory to the distinction between the heavenly Jerusalem and the earthly one. The three Israelite nations – the Jews, the French and the Poles – would eventually redeem humankind.[51]

Moreover, Jews increasingly participated in these uprisings against the old order.

It became logical therefore to include the Jews amongst the nations. Thus Lafayette founded a committee for the emancipation for the Jews in Paris in 1831 which attempted to form battalions led by Polish officers. In 1851, Benedetto Musolino, a member of Figlinoli della Giovine Italia (Young Italy) proposed a programme for the national and religious rehabilitation of the Jews in their own homeland in Palestine.[52] During the Crimean War, Armand Lévy – on the Republican Left in France – and Mickiewicz proposed the formation of a Jewish Legion which would liberate Palestine.[53]

THE SPIRITUAL HOMELAND

Jabotinsky famously praised Italy in his autobiography. 'If I have a spiritual homeland, then it is Italy more than Russia.'[54] The model of the Italian struggle for reunification and independence both directly and indirectly played a central role in Jabotinsky's world outlook – and thus in the reunification of the Jews in their own homeland. Mazzini personified the merging of romantic nationalism and patriotic internationalism, the national liberal connection between particularism and universalism. Hence his slogan 'noi faramo l'Italia anche uniti col Diavolo' (for Italy we would even unite with the Devil). He condemned 'the Catholic dogma of absolute passivity that poisoned the sources of liberty and placed despotism at the summit of the social edifice.'[55] Croce characterized his 'moral greatness, the greatness of an apostle who lives and operates equally with the illuminating and inflaming word and with his example, and advises and urges to similar conduct those whom he addresses and whom he gathers about himself. All the rest, in the complex of his ideas, is either not his own or else is secondary or vague or erroneous.'[56] Again the importance of poetry suffused the politics of Italian nationalism. Four years after founding Giovine Italia, Mazzini wrote:

> Poetry, the flower of the angels, nourished by the blood of martyrs, and watered by the tears of mothers, blossoming often among ruins, but ever coloured by the rays of dawn; poetry, a language prophetic of humanity, European in essence and national in form, will make known to us the fatherland of all the nations...
> Poetry will teach the young the nobleness of sacrifice, of constancy, and silence; of feeling oneself alone without despairing; in an existence of suffering unknown or misunderstood; in long years of bitterness, wounds, and delusion, endured without murmur or lament; it will teach them to have faith in things to come, and to labour unceasingly to hasten their coming, even though without hope of living to witness their triumph.[57]

In contrast, Jabotinsky also appreciated the Conte di Cavour, the diplomat and political facilitator who was 'incredulous of the virtues of dictatorships, nourished equal incredulity of the miraculous virtues of the masses in politics, and detested in Mazzini the dictator and demagogue combined.'[58]

Jabotinsky's teenage years were passed in Rome where he wrote for the Odessa press and immersed himself in Italian culture. It was also a time when Rome was still bathing in the warm waters of the Risorgimento. Garibaldi, himself, had died but twenty years before and was promoted to epic proportions by European liberals. On the centenary of his birth, George Meredith published a poem in *The Times* to commemorate the event:

> We who have seen Italia in the throes
> Half risen but to be hurled to the ground, and now.
> Like a ripe field of wheat where once drove plough,
> All bounteous as she is fair, we think of those
> Who blew the breath of life into her frame:
> Cavour, Mazzini, Garibaldi: Three:
> Her brain, her Soul, her Sword; and set her free
> From ruinous discords, with lustrous aim.[59]

Yet as recent research from the newly opened Soviet archives suggest, at that time of his life, Jabotinsky exhibited the anti-nationalist worldview of many young Russians. He was 'radically individualistic, anti-nationalist, quasi-nihilistic and aestheticist'.[60] Kornei Chukovsky remarked sixty years later that 'he voiced youthful, free and outrageous ideas about conventional morality, about marriage, about rebelling against established traditions'.[61] A contemporary who read his articles under his pen-name Altalena later recalled that:

> nothing in them could be taken as indication of his future as a Zionist leader. Altalena's articles were light, witty, a bit Heinesque – about everything and nothing.
> From time to time, he would forsake his feuilletons for poetry, as light and pleasant as his prose. The general impression was that the writer possessed two great qualities: an undeniable literary gift and the delightful intoxication of carefree youth.' [62]

Significantly, there was also no mention of the Risorgimento in his articles for *Odesskii listok*, no hero worship of Garibaldi, Mazzini and Cavour. Neither was there any mention in letters to friends in Italy in later years. The first adulation of the heroes of the Risorgimento appeared in an article [63] in 1912 where he strongly defended Garibaldi and the purity of Italian nationalism against contemporary radical critics. Garibaldi was scarcely mentioned in letters and articles even during World War I. Yet, significantly, in the bitter disagreement with the Zionist Executive over the formation of the Jewish Legion, Jabotinsky put forward the model of 'friendly separation in tactics' between the diplomat Cavour and the hero-liberator, Garibaldi.[64]

One explanation for his earlier omissions might have been a cautious approach to the Russian censor or simply that he marginalized Garibaldi's nationalism at that point in his ideological development. The worship of Garibaldi was certainly more pronounced during the 1930s when Betar began to grow in numbers. The heroes of the Risorgimento also featured in his autobiography – which was written during this period. But as he inferred on its publication – 'memoirs are literary works' rather than works of history.[65] His secretary, Joseph Schechtman, commented many years later that they were 'strangely impersonal', 'scant and carefully selected and censored than is generally supposed'.[66] Yet after his return to Odessa, it is clear that his appreciation for the progressive phase of the national revolutions of the first half of the nineteenth century began to surface as early as 1902. In his article 'On Zionism'[67] there was condemnation of both the advocates of reactionary nationalism and the Left's belief that this was the only form of nationalism. The confusion between the earlier pre-1848 national revolutions with the later period of national superiority and imperialism afflicted both Left and Right. In another article in 1903, he once more promoted the internationalism of the national struggles of the earlier period.[68] At this stage in his life; Jabotinsky neither advocated Zionism nor embraced Garibaldi.

Jabotinsky registered at the University of Rome in 1898 where he attended two lecture series 'Philosophy and History' and 'Moral Philosophy' by Antonio Labriola who had taught the first course on Marxism in Italy. Labriola had translated the Communist Manifesto into Italian and written three works on historical materialism in the 1890s. He was the representative of a non-dogmatic 'Latin' Marxism and interpreted historical materialism as 'a philosophy of praxis', based on non-economic factors.[69]

Labriola was a student of the Hegelian 'idealist realism' philosopher and former priest Bertrando Spaventa and was frequently involved in the debates with the proponents of Darwinism, Positivism and neo-Kantism. He fashioned his views when the reunification of Italy had been accomplished according to the Hegelian thesis of the nation making the state. Yet once the 'heroic age' had passed, there was a realization that there was a need to create a cultural tradition out of the ethnic mixture that constituted the new Italy.[70] Thus Jabotinsky was exposed to the twin legacies of making both Italy and Italians – the Hegelian thesis and its converse. Moreover, in his youth Labriola was attracted by the writings of Spinoza which he knew 'by heart and with loving understanding'.[71] Indeed he had published a study of Spinoza's theory of affections in 1867.

Labriola, like Moses Hess, was clearly attracted to the new rationalism announced by Spinoza:

> Until the heroism of Baruch Spinoza shall become the matter-of-fact virtue of everyday life in the higher developed humanity of the future, and until myths,

poetry, metaphysics and religion shall no longer overshadow the field of consciousness, let us be content that up to now, and for the present, philosophy in its differentiated and its improved sense has served, and serves, as a critical instrument and helps science to keep its formal methods and logical processes clear: that it helps us in our lives to reduce the obstacles which the fantastic projections of the emotions, passions, fears and hopes pile in the way of free thought; that it helps and serves, as Spinoza himself would say, to vanquish 'imaginationem et ignorantiam'.[72]

Yet Labriola was no absolutist. Indeed, he criticized determinist theories and propounded Marxism as a practical philosophy. There were no 'immanent laws of historical development'.[73] In a letter in 1897 to Georges Sorel, he argued that socialism was not 'a church, not a sect, that must have a fixed dogma or formula'.[74] He broke with Sorel who went on to advocate that socialism would only be achieved through violent confrontation. Labriola argued that historical materialism should take account of the social and historical nature of human beings – a process which leads 'from life to thought, not from thought to life'.[75] Indeed, Labriola was a critical admirer of Masaryk who, although not a socialist, possessed an extensive knowledge of socialist literature which he placed 'on high in the name of science'.[76] Yet there was a clash on Masaryk's idea of moral consciousness which went far beyond Labriola's defined limits of historical materialism. In discussions with his students, Labriola never raised the Jewish question. Even a severe criticism of Nordau's controversial book *Degeneration* did not touch upon it.[77]

Unlike other European states, fin-de-siècle Italy did not have a heritage of anti-Semitism or dislike of Jews. Herzl visited Rome in 1904 and met King Victor Emmanuel III. Herzl subsequently quoted the monarch in his diary as saying that 'In our country there is no distinction between Jews and Christians. Jews can become anything, and they do. The army, the civil service, even the diplomatic corps – everything everywhere is open to them.'[78]

Antonio Labriola rejected liberalism as early as the 1870s when he began to discover a new intellectual belief in socialism. He was said to be an excellent teacher, inducing his students to reach their conclusions independently. Jabotinsky probably appreciated Labriola's ideological openness which must have contrasted dramatically with Tsarist society. As a Zionist leader, Jabotinsky later argued that Marxism should still be utilized as a diagnostic tool rather than a dogma to be obeyed. Indeed, in 1933, he was still arguing that a central cause of historical phenomena was the condition of the means of production.[79] Labriola's studies were popularized through a small band of his students who disseminated them throughout the wider socialist movement. Indeed, Jabotinsky was even critical of Italy's colonial dreams in his dispatches for the Odessa press.[80] This certainly echoed Labriola who commented on 'the craze for founding colonies in places where it is almost impossible to do so'.[81]

In his autobiography written in the 1930s, Jabotinsky proclaims that as a young man he did not know whether he was a socialist.[82] But following his sojourn in Italy, he states that he learned to have faith in socialism from Labriola and Enrico Ferri. He contributed several articles in April 1901 to the socialist journal, *Avanti*, on public opinion in Russia and on the views of progressive youth.[83] Indeed, according to his later writings, four issues of this journal,[84] which contained his defence of progressive youth, were located in his home prior to his arrest on 1902. He also states that he tackled *Das Kapital* in the Odessa prison.[85] All this seemed to reflect a broad sympathy for change in Russia, rather than the rigidity of an ideological position, bound by rules and regulations.

Individualism, Jabotinsky always argued, must reign supreme. Hence his famous comment that 'in the beginning God created the individual'.[86] He therefore rejected a central feature of Labriola's 'abstract socialism' – his opposition to individualism. Following his conversion to Zionism, Jabotinsky in a sense reacted to his past by engaging in polemics with the Bund and Jewish members of the Kadet Party such as Maxim Vinaver[87] and indeed became openly critical of Jewish involvement in revolutionary activity in Russia. He condemned the propagators of revolution who would use sympathetic Jews as 'an easily inflammable material'. They were 'the yeast in the dough and it is their destiny to excite fermentation in immense and clumsy Russia'.[88] An interview with Georgy Plekhanov 'the Father of Russian Marxism' in 1905 provided another opportunity to question his past and to clarify the present. At this time of transition, he still advocated the class struggle, because as he pointed out he was 'unable to do otherwise'.[89]

Like Herzl, Jabotinsky began to confront the difficulties of the broad Left in viewing the Jews with national characteristics. But in contrast Herzl had never harboured any socialist sympathies – indeed he was at pains to reject the 'social democratic' label for Zionism.[90] Herzl excoriated social democrats in Central Europe for whom 'the Jewish question has become a source of embarrassment'.[91]

Many Jews, after being disappointed by the liberals and barred by the nationalists, turned to socialism. This, argued Herzl, had 'judaized socialism' and socialism would seek to purify itself by anti-Semitic means.

The lack of understanding for Jewish nationalism and the success of the Bolsheviks in Russia in 1917 later put paid to any lingering sympathies that

Jabotinsky exhibited for socialism. But at the end of his life, he still spoke highly of what he termed 'nineteenth century Italian liberalism'.

> A dream of order and justice, lacking any vestige of violence, a universal humanitarian vision embroidered with compassion, tolerance and conviction of the fundamental goodness and honesty of the human being.[92]

In addition to Antonio Labriola and Enrico Ferri, other Italian philosophers such as Maffeo Pantaleoni [93] were also mentioned in articles in the 1930s when Jabotinsky was attempting to steer an ideological pathway between Communism and Fascism. Benedetto Croce, a one-time student of Labriola, was regarded by Jabotinsky as 'the first who taught me to discern the vibrations of the aesthetic nervous system which underlines the clockwork which drives the wheels of history.' [94] This probably related to Croce's radical idealist period which saw the publication of his *Aesthetic* in 1902. Croce certainly emphasized spiritual values in the unfurling of history and probably induced Jabotinsky to expound his views on psycho-Marxism in several articles during the first half of the 1930s. However, Croce's later theories on liberalism – as a means of undermining Mussolini's Fascism – and his historical works probably attracted Jabotinsky not only ideologically but also as a means of replying to the charge that he had espoused Fascism. Indeed, as Croce inferred in 1925, 'to be a liberal was not simply to espouse individualism, but also to locate it within the customs and beliefs of a particular historical heritage.'[95] In his article, 'The Revolt of the Old Men' in 1937, Jabotinsky bemoaned the marginalization of the love of freedom and 'the leadership plague' of the Communists and the Fascists during the inter-war years. He contrasted this with the nineteenth century:

> It is possible to define the state ideal of the nineteenth century as follows: A 'minimum' state or a more extreme definition 'moderate anarchy'. I am not sure whether in the nineteenth century the term 'proletarian regime' was ever heard. Nevertheless, in my youth, I never heard of it. A person of the nineteenth century could not even picture to himself the smell of the state in every phase of his life like the smell of burning meat permeating from the kitchen. The idea of pure police states is like a dense forest from which man cannot extricate himself.[96]

THE CHALLENGE OF THE
REVISIONISTS

THE BIRTH OF A MOVEMENT

The Union of Zionists-Revisionists was established by Jabotinsky in April 1925 as a movement which advocated a return to Zionist basic principles. It did not see itself as revolutionary or indeed even as adhering to the Right. Instead, it projected itself in the role of redeemer – a movement which would reclaim the clarity and dynamism of Herzl. In a speech in Paris in January 1925, Jabotinsky pointedly embraced the legacy of Max Nordau.[1] Indeed, in their early programmes, the Revisionists even welcomed the class struggle in Palestine as 'an unavoidable and even healthy phenomenon' – albeit without taking sides.[2] But the prevailing ethos also suggested that concessions and compromise would clearly not be part of the Revisionist agenda. It was Weizmann and his allies who were the real revisionists, they claimed, not the followers of Herzl and Jabotinsky.

Jabotinsky himself defined Revisionism in the context of British support for Zionist colonization. In explaining his stand to the Shaw Commission in early 1930, Jabotinsky commented:

> When we started our movement in 1925, the official point of view, as expressed by Dr Weizmann and his associates, was this: the business of Zionism can be completed and achieved simply by the process of the Jews pouring into Palestine money and energy and it ought not to matter at all what the attitude of the Government was, provided that the Government was a decent European administration. We demanded the revision of this point of view, saying that a large scale colonization cannot be conducted independently of a government, that it is government enterprise by nature and can only be completed by legislative and administrative action if the government supports the colonization.[3]

85

In a letter to *The Times* in September 1929,[4] Jabotinsky spelled out what he expected from such a 'colonization regime':

1. the opening up of Transjordan for Jewish colonization – 'the country east of the Jordan possessing better soil, more water and fewer inhabitants than the western half of the Holy Land';

2. a series of land acts – 'bringing all the waste lands of the country under the state's control as a land reserve for colonization and preventing speculation in land values';

3. customs tariffs, transport rates and taxation facilities – 'to give full support to local industries and inclusion of Palestine in any scheme bearing the character of Imperial preference or Imperial co-operation';

4. protection of Jewish settlements or neighbourhoods – 'by means of Jewish units, military and constabulary under government control';

5. 'no parliamentary or semi-parliamentary institutions until both nationalities, Jews and Arabs, jointly demand their introduction'.

The Revisionist movement arose at a time of severe disillusionment with the development of the Zionist programme. In the eyes of many, Weizmann's diplomacy had borne no fruit and the British Government seemed to be continually backtracking and thus watering down the hopes raised by the Balfour Declaration. Indeed, in the same month as the Revisionists announced their existence to the world, the Secretary of State for the Colonies, L. S. Amery, defined the current British understanding:

> The expression 'a national home for the Jews' means nothing more than that the present existing Jewish communities should be allowed to fulfil their desire to live their own cultural life, to have an opportunity of development and that this should be recognized as a matter of right, not merely of sufferance.[5]

Amery's unfortunate slip of the tongue in substituting the Balfour Declaration's 'a national home for the Jewish people' with one simply for Jews seemed an accurate reflection of the downgrading of the nation to the status of a cultural and religious community. The hopes that Sir Herbert Samuel had brought with him to Palestine in 1921 had not materialized on his departure in June 1925. An editorial in the *Jewish Chronicle* described him as 'an abject failure and a faithlessness that has been manifest throughout'.[6] He arrived, the critics argued, as a second Nechemiah, but he left a second Sanbalat (Jewish governor of Samaria during the Persian Empire). Not surprisingly, the general atmosphere of disillusionment contributed to the resignation of Robert Stricker in Austria, Nechemiah de Lieme in Holland and Yitzhak Gruenbaum in Poland from the leadership of their national federations at the beginning of 1925.

The founding conference of the new movement at the Café de Pantheon in

Paris therefore took place at a propitious time for Jabotinsky's ambitions. The first paragraph of the Revisionist programme stated that the movement was a part of the World Zionist Organization, but it was also not a party in the conventional sense such as the Labour Zionist party, Poale Zion. Indeed, members of its central committee retained their membership in other Zionist parties such as Mizrachi and Zeire Zion. This, in itself, was a contradiction and symbolized a division in the movement as to the understanding of its identity from the very inception. Leading members of the Executive such as Meir Grossman were assertive in their desire to remain within the Zionist Organization, participate in its deliberations and eventually oust Weizmann and his supporters in a future Congress. Jabotinsky saw things differently. He was ambivalent about the overarching importance of the centrality of the Zionist Organization. He would have preferred to have remained outside or on the sidelines as part of a rival umbrella organization which would operate according to the Revisionist programme. This new group would revitalize and redirect the Zionist movement. Indeed, on the eve of the founding conference of the Revisionist movement, Jabotinsky expressed his ambivalence in an article which laid out the options.[7]

Significantly the conference voted to ignore his advice and to remain within the Zionist Organization while retaining the right of independent action to present their case. Jabotinsky, however, operated within the context of his ambivalence, referring to the Revisionists as a movement to his followers and as a party to the French politician, Anatole de Monzie.[8] His fatigue with party politics was symbolized by his reticence to participate in the 14th Zionist Congress. In a letter to Joseph Schechtman, he proclaimed his unwillingness to speak at the Congress in the summer of 1925 and was adamant that if the Revisionist movement attracted an increasing number of adherents, then his hands would inevitably be tied. He further did not wish to 'perform' without any political benefit and disparaged his potential audience as 'five hundred heads of *stimmvieh*' (unthinking herd of voters).[9] Jabotinsky was more interested in publicizing the Revisionist agenda through articles and speeches. Indeed, *Rassvet* had been revamped and was now published in Paris as a vehicle for Revisionist ideas. Jabotinsky was seemingly far more enthusiastic about the published word than the mechanics of the organization.[10]

In addition to his expectations of the British, he diverged from Weizmann's interpretation of Zionist priorities and indeed on where the very borders should be. Jabotinsky defined the first aim of Zionism as 'the creation of a Jewish majority on both sides of the Jordan'.[11] He also argued that the Zionists should not remain silent on their aims or use coded language. He pointed out that the 'spiritual centre' of the cultural Zionists did not actually require a Jewish majority and logic therefore dictated that there was no need to promote

Jewish immigration to Palestine. Jabotinsky calculated that it would require an annual influx of 40,000 Jews over a period of 25 years to achieve parity with the Arab population plus an additional 50,000 per annum after that to cement that majority.[12] This, thereby, formed the basis of the Revisionist claim to Transjordan whose separation from the rest of Palestine was termed a 'practical and historical injustice'.[13] The Revisionist Programme further defined the specific aim of Zionism as 'the gradual transformation of Palestine into a Jewish commonwealth – a self-governing Jewish commonwealth under the auspices of a Jewish majority'.[14]

The term 'Jewish commonwealth' was actually based on Sir Herbert Samuel's speech to a Zionist gathering in November 1919 at the London Opera House. The US Congress had also passed a resolution in December 1918 that the Jewish National Home would eventually lead to an autonomous commonwealth. The meaning of a 'Jewish National Home' had been continually reinterpreted by the British and accepted by Weizmann since the halcyon days of the Balfour Declaration. In his address to the first Revisionist Conference, Jabotinsky attempted to demystify the meaning of 'a national homeland for the Jewish people'. The definition of 'oeffentlich-rechtlich gesicherte Heimstaette' at the first Zionist Congress in Basle which became the basis of the Balfour Declaration, he argued, was not always understood as a Jewish state. The concept of a 'state' was a flexible one and could be applied to both France and Kentucky. The meaning of a Jewish state, he explained, would initially be defined through the vehicle of a Jewish majority and then autonomy.[15] Jabotinsky was happy to quote the memorandum of Sir George Buchanan, the British Ambassador in Petrograd, to S. D. Sazonov, the Russian Foreign Minister in 1916 which had been deliberately published by the Soviets to embarrass the British:

> The only aim of His Majesty's Government is to find an arrangement which, by being sufficiently attractive for the majority of Jews, would secure Jewish support. In view of this consideration, it appears to His Majesty's Government that, should the scheme foreshadow an authorization for the Jews (as soon as their colonists in Palestine become strong enough to hold their own vis-à-vis the Arab population) to take into their own hands the administration of the inner affairs of that region (except Jerusalem and the Holy Places), the arrangement would be extremely attractive for the majority of Jews.[16]

Yet even the advocacy of a majority of Jews was not the same as the automatic establishment of a state. Jabotinsky commented that 'the name of the disease is minority. The name of the cure is majority. Whether "a country with a Jewish majority" is tantamount to "a Jewish state" is a speculation in words.'[17] Jabotinsky further argued that if a Jewish majority was attained after 25 years of immigration, then it could merit inclusion within the British Empire or another 'civilized commonwealth of nations' or even within 'a real League of Nations'. All, Jabotinsky claimed, would be equally satisfactory. In his speeches, Jabotinsky argued that the term 'national home' had no fixed meaning and could be interpreted to mean the equivalent of a new ghetto.

> A Jewish majority does not mean that we intend to 'rule' over our neighbours; but we want Zion to become a country where the Jew can no longer be overruled. The main characteristic of the Galut (exile) is precisely the fact that everywhere in the Diaspora the Jew can be, and always is, overruled – because the Jews are everywhere in a minority. Zionism would be meaningless if, after all our efforts, we were to face ultimately the same condition in Palestine.[18]

Meir Grossman further suggested that through acquiescence, the notion of the Jewish national home in the fashion that it was understood and intended by Balfour in 1917, had been sacrificed by the Zionist leadership.[19] Jabotinsky drew upon contemporary examples to illustrate the weakness of a minority, no matter how long it had dwelled in an area:

> Thus, for example, the Germans, in the course of 500 years, established a rich German culture in Estonia and Latvia, remaining nevertheless in a minority; we now see what has become of it all. Riga is a Latvian city and the Dorpat University an Estonian high school. Similarly Greek culture dominated Asia Minor for 3000 years and more, and in the end the Turkish majority not only destroyed the whole of that great civilization, but also expelled practically all the Greeks.' [20]

He was acutely aware that Arab public opinion was vehemently opposed to the creation of a Jewish majority in Palestine. They would fight it 'for a long time' and only the eventual realization of the power of a Jewish majority would lead to the path of reconciliation. In a future state, he argued, there would be 'absolute equality' between both peoples. 'The political, economic and cultural welfare of the Arabs will remain one of the main conditions for the well-being of the Land of Israel.' All opposition to this transformation of Palestine was simply 'unjust'.

> One may neither come to terms with injustice nor make any concessions to it. In this case, especially, namely, the question of the formation of a majority, there is, from our side, no possibility to concede anything.
> One can only struggle against injustice with peaceful means as long as it is not expressed in acts of violence, and with other means when it assumes the form of violence.' [21]

The raison d'être for the establishment of Revisionist-Zionism was above all a move to revive the Zionist movement. For Jabotinsky, it was as if the passion and melodrama of the Herzlian legacy had drained away. He criticized those who preferred not to think aloud. 'Toujours y penser, jamais en parler.' If the

British government was not persuaded:

> Revise with a critical eye that pusillanimous superstition popular among some
> Jews (no Gentile shares it) which says that we are, oh, such a weak people, utterly
> defenceless, condemned, poor wretches to bear any blow and deprived of all
> means of effective resistance. But I emphatically refuse to discuss the question of
> our poor wretchedness or otherwise when it is a question, first of all, of
> appealing to reason and sense. And the first step in this direction is a frank
> statement of our real objectives; satisfy yourself first as to whether your demands
> have ever been authoritatively presented. [22]

Weizmann, according to Jabotinsky, had replaced the Herzlian determination by
'a gospel of drives for money'.[23] Weizmann had engineered the expansion of
the Jewish Agency to include a 50 per cent representation of non-Zionists in
order to create the Palestine Economic Corporation which would promote
trade and industry.[24] The idea of opposing 'philanthropic colonization'[25]
catalysed the formation of a radical Zionist coalition from a conference of
oppositionists in Berlin in June 1925. A manifesto published at the beginning
of July inferred that the inclusion of wealthy non-Zionists meant a loss of soul
of the movement, an erosion of ideals and an obstacle in initiating a
fundamental change in Jewish life. For Jabotinsky, Zionism meant transforming
and reinventing the Jew. All this characterized the run-up to the 14th Zionist
Congress in July 1925.

For the first time, an opposition to Weizmann in Congress was emerging.
Weizmann was clearly uncomfortable with the return of his former Chelsea
flatmate to Zionist public life. On the eve of the conference, he had told the
English Zionist Federation that a return to ideals was, of course, a necessity, but
that rivals had to pull in the same direction. Weizmann considered the
Revisionists to be as 'harmful as the Mopsim' – the Jewish Communists in
Palestine.[26] Jabotinsky, although reluctant to attend, critically analysed the
situation and repeated the Revisionist panacea at the Congress and was loudly
applauded. He spoke of the political passivity of the Executive and accused
them of weakening and, indeed, of shattering the Zionist case in England and
at the League of Nations.

Weizmann responded by reiterating his belief that only a cautious approach
would pay off. In particular, he believed that sensitivity towards the Arab world
was a paramount necessity. He replied to Jabotinsky's speech at the Congress by
stating that Revisionist policies would certainly work if the Zionists were
colonizing Rhodesia instead of Palestine. The latter, he reminded his audience,
was 'a sensitive world nerve....our mission is to open up the Near East to
Jewish initiative by way of Palestine and a policy of justice is therefore
essential.'[27] He also opposed Jabotinsky's desire to re-establish the Jewish

Legion whose formation he had ardently supported. Its resurrection at this time would be counter-productive.

> Any don quixotic attempt to get the government or the Jewish people to spend money on Jewish armies is tomfoolery. And what would a Jewish unit do in case of a rising? It would be hopelessly outnumbered; it would serve as a constant irritant. I fail to see how it could be seriously discussed. Jabo is not satisfied with a militia – he wants an army.' [28]

Weizmann was genuinely perplexed by Jabotinsky's demands and the rise of Revisionist Zionism. In a letter to the American Zionist leader, Stephen Wise, in April 1926, he commented:

> Palestine is quiet and peaceful, and for the present at any rate, there is not the slightest fear of any trouble arising. Transjordania is much more peaceful than it ever was before. Why raise a bogey? Why arouse our enemies? All our opponents? It is midsummer madness. Nobody except a few partisans of Jabo want it. And I don't think that even Jabo in his heart believes in the scheme. I am sure that in a few years, say three years, the formation of a Jewish militia may follow as a matter of course and the point at present is to increase the population. We are 17 per cent now. If the immigration continues at the present rate, we shall be 35 per cent or so in another five years. Much will change then. Any unwise step which we might take now, likely to retard the development, is a criminal offence against the National Home.[29]

Indeed, in a letter to his wife, Weizmann portrayed the Revisionists as busying themselves with 'parades, protests and playing at soldiers'.[30] But the times were against Weizmann. A barrage of criticisms led by Jabotinsky induced Weizmann to call for a vote of confidence. Although he won this by the overwhelming margin of 136 to 17, even more refused to cast their ballot papers. Weizmann and his colleagues initially announced that they would be unable to serve, but eventually they were persuaded to return to their duties.

The core of the Revisionist movement outside Palestine consisted of mainly Jewish émigrés from Russia. In Palestine, the situation was the same. Many were semi-assimilated Russian Jews who preferred to speak Russian rather than Yiddish. The second biggest group of supporters were Sephardi Jews. Three out of the four Revisionist delegates at the 1925 Zionist Congress were elected by Sephardi communities.[31] By 1926, the Revisionist movement could boast of branches in 18 countries, headed by a 14 person executive. The office in Paris published a weekly in Russian (*Rassvet*) and a monthly in Yiddish (*Der Neuer Veg*). A German language monthly was published in Basle and *The Zionist* appeared in New York in May 1926.

The British differentiated Jabotinsky's followers from those of Weizmann at an early stage and soon began to label the Revisionists as 'extremist'.[32] On his departure from Palestine in the autumn of 1925, Sir Herbert Samuel pointedly referred to his hope that the leadership of Zionism would remain in moderate hands.[33] Zionist opponents responded to Jabotinsky's stream of criticisms and termed him 'Cassandra' after the mythical princess of Troy who obsessively prophesied only defeat and was never believed. He, in turn, referred to 'the blindness of the ignorance or perhaps the light-mindedness of our opponents'.[34]

Yet Jabotinsky significantly continued to promote 'the honesty of England' within the Revisionist movement. Indeed, he supported Josiah Wedgwood's contention that the Jewish National Home could become the 'seventh dominion'.

> Palestine is the Clapham Junction of the British Empire. It will become the Jewish Dominion of the Empire in the same sense as South Africa is a Dutch dominion and Canada is French. It seems clear that Palestine must remain attached to the British Empire since it needs protection from other peoples to a greater extent than do other parts of the Empire.[35]

The two subsequent Revisionist Conferences, Paris 1926 and Vienna 1928, indicated a growing schism on the question of the right of independent action outside Congress and of the demand of the Palestine branch, in particular, to act independently. Although papered over in the Paris Conference in 1926, the issue began to assume an increasing importance in the succeeding conference. While Grossman and Lichtheim questioned the right of the Palestinian branch for wider autonomy, the younger delegates together with those from Palestine tended towards more radical views. Jabotinsky, believing in a broader framework, sided with the latter rather than with his colleagues on the Revisionist Executive and advocated independent political action. Clearly, he wished to continue to pursue his diplomatic forays and not to be hamstrung by the official Zionist movement. Yet at the same time, he attempted to prevent a split by calls for patriotism and idealism – thereby avoiding a vote on the matter. Jabotinsky's position thus became that of pacifier and conciliator in a Revisionist movement where an ongoing polarization was a reflection of both the deterioration of Jewish-Arab relations and the stagnation of the Zionist raison d'être in Palestine.

THE POLITICS OF BELONGING

With the rise of the Labour movement under Ben-Gurion, Jabotinsky seemingly moved from a non-socialist position to an anti-socialist one. In part, this was a reaction to news of continuing repression in the USSR and the consolidation of the Stalinist regime. It was also an opportunity to attract the Polish Jewish middle class which had emigrated during the fourth aliyah (1924-1926). They had imbibed both the ideological and nationalist disdain for the Marxism-Leninism of their former geographical neighbour and imported it into the Middle East. Hence Jabotinsky's article 'We, the Bourgeousie'[36] made its appearance in April 1927.

One area where Jabotinsky invested considerable time and energy was in the attraction of youth to his ideological banner. Betar was no ordinary youth group, but, for Jabotinsky, the very means of transforming the Jewish psyche – no longer the passive submissive ghetto Jew, but the indefatigable fighter for Jewish statehood. The idea of rebellion – whether it be against their parents' docility, the followers of Chaim Weizmann, the British Administration or the nationalist aspirations of the Palestinian Arabs – was an attractive proposition to any young person. Jabotinsky fuelled this with an undiluted faith in the Jewish future. In December 1928, he signed a two year contract to edit the daily *Doar Hayom*. This provided him with a prime vehicle to propagate his views in Palestine. It would be a 'European' newspaper, he proclaimed. Grossman had previously described it as 'lively, sensational, always pursuing a campaign and making sensational discoveries'.[37] Jabotinsky's first contribution was appropriately titled 'Ani Ma'amin' (I Believe).[38] The proprietor of the daily, Zalman White, wanted to build an alternative outlet to the Weizmann – Ben-Gurion approach and believed that Jabotinsky could provide it. Yet Jabotinsky already had a job working for the Judea Insurance Company. He was therefore more of a nominal editor who essentially left the organization and production side of the newspaper to Shlomo Gepstein, the deputy editor. Circulation increased dramatically and it soon boasted contributions by writers such as Arthur Koestler and Joseph Klausner. In a letter to Meir Grossman[39] on the eve of his appointment, Jabotinsky appraised his potential contributors from the youth of Palestine. From the first rank, he pointed to Yehoshua Heschel Yeivin, Avigdor Hameiri and Uri Zvi Greenberg. Yeivin, who had defected from *Davar*, was viewed as a rising star by Jabotinsky. Other less prominent contributors such as Shalom Schwartz and Baruch Weinstein were singled out, as was Abba Achimeir whom he described as 'talented, but too much a Fascist'. He was thus specific in his appointment of the editorial board.[40]

Teenage Jews delighted in the theatre which the fifty year old Jabotinsky offered them. The forensic dissection of the old guard's position and the biting criticism of its leaders made Jabotinsky as much loved by the nationalist youth as he was loathed by his opponents amongst the General Zionists and within the Labour movement. His leadership was exciting, clear and purposeful. Young Jews could not only change themselves but also change history. And in Eastern Europe where Jews were effectively second class citizens who were discriminated against, even more so.

Weizmann's decision to expand the Jewish Agency with well-to-do non-Zionists went against the grain for many young people. It injected a dose of impurity into Zionist ideals. Indeed, Jabotinsky was quite willing to openly condemn Jewish philanthropists even if it meant cutting off access to potential funding.

'I do not doubt that Mr Warburg's friends are rich; but money for Zionist work does not come from bank deposits only, it comes from the heart.'[41] Jabotinsky argued that Jewry could not be transformed by offering seats on the Jewish Agency Board to the wealthy. His rhetorical assault on unelected philanthropists and the Zionists who had involved them was received with great enthusiasm by the youth, the Revisionists and beyond. On the eve of the 16th Zionist Congress in 1929, he commented:

> What has happened to the present Zionist generation is precisely what happened to the generation of Hebrews who left Egypt four thousand years ago. They had just enough spirit to rebel against their conditions and start on the big trail. Once on the trail, however, they carried most of the slave's moral toxins in their blood. One is the inveterate worship of the wealthy – 'geverim' is the name. For centuries our forebears have been accustomed to entrust the 'geverim' with all public business.
> The leaders of the present Zionist Executive, themselves little more than a refurbished and ornamented edition of this spirit, have most naturally exploited this inborn tendency in the Jew.[42]

Jabotinsky also viewed the youth of Betar as the kernel for a future defence force which would protect Jews from attack by Arab nationalists. In the absence of adequate British protection, such a pool would form the nucleus for a revived Jewish Legion. Jabotinsky's concept of an Iron Wall[43] was thus a defensive measure and not an offensive one. In a meeting in Vienna in 1927, a student group told Jabotinsky that they would reform themselves and do away with the traditional associations of a student fraternity. To which he replied:

> You can abolish everything – the cap, the ribbons, the colours, heavy drinking, the songs, everything, but not the sword. You are going to keep the sword. Sword-fighting is not a German invention, it belonged to our forefathers. The Torah and the sword were both handed down to us from heaven.[44]

In a letter to the youth of the town of Wloclawek in Poland in March 1927, he told them that every Jewish boy or girl was 'a soldier of the people'.[45] Judaism was invoked as a nationalist symbol, often tinged with military authentication, but not as religion per se. The writings of the founders of Zionism – Pinsker, Ahad Ha'am, Herzl and Nordau – were important since they instilled 'European culture in place of obscurantist orthodoxy'.[46]

And yet it was the confluence of nationalism and religion in Palestine which provided the excuse for Arab violence against Jews in 1929. The crossroads of nationalism and religion for both Judaism and Islam coincided at the Kotel – the outer Western Wall of the Jewish Temple – and above it – at the Haram as Sherif. The former was a traditional site of Jewish worship throughout the centuries. The latter was regarded as the location where the Prophet ascended to heaven.

The Western or Wailing Wall was regarded by Muslims as religious territory since here the Prophet's horse, Buraq, had been tethered. Moreover, it was regarded as legally Muslim property. The Ottomans had allowed the Jews access to the Wall and the Mandate continued this custom. The Wall resonated with Jewish history and the loss of nationhood. Edmund de Rothschild had attempted to purchase it before World War I and *Doar Hayom* had been campaigning for the establishment of a worldwide fund to buy the area throughout the 1920s.[47] However, the post-World War I period bore witness to the growth of both Jewish and Arab nationalism. The Mufti of Jerusalem was both an Islamic leader and a radical Palestinian Arab nationalist. As head of the Supreme Muslim Council, the Mufti embarked on a fundraising campaign to repair the al-Aqsa mosque and the Dome of the Rock, which were both situated on the Haram. The campaign in Muslim countries simultaneously constructed a network of political support for the Palestinian Arab cause. The Mufti's followers argued that the Jews wished to appropriate the Haram as well as the Wall and to construct the Third Temple on its site. Despite repeated explanations that the Jews only wished to gain access to the Wall and had no designs on the Haram, the claim was made time and again to exacerbate hostility towards the Zionists. The rise of Palestinian Arab nationalism catalyzed a determination to undermine the historical right of Jews to worship unhindered at the Wall. Thus both in 1922 and 1925, the Muslim authorities complained when benches were brought to the Wall by the Jews, and they were subsequently removed. The Jews again brought in benches and screens for the Yom Kippur service in 1928 so as to construct a mechitza, a barrier designed to separate the prayer areas for men and women. The British Deputy District Commissioner of Jerusalem, Edward Keith-Roach, responded to Muslim protests and ordered the removal of the offending benches. By the following day, Yom Kippur, this had still not been carried out and the British forcibly intervened and removed the benches amidst a scuffle with the attendant Jews. This was considered to be not only an insensitive affront to religious Jews, but was also viewed by the Zionists as further backtracking on the question of Jewish status on the part of the British. In the Colonial Secretary's White Paper in November 1928 on the incident, the Jews were accused of being less than tactful and of turning a purely religious question into a political and racial one.[48]

During the following year, the Mufti encouraged a campaign of harassment of Jewish worshippers through a cacophony of music and noise. New building works were constructed to this end and the narrow walkway in front of the Wall was transformed into a thoroughfare for the local Arab inhabitants. All this was perceived as legal under the law since the pavement in front of the wall, the surrounding courtyard and its dilapidated dwellings all formed part of the property of the al-Ghuth Abu Madian Waqf, a religious and charitable trust said to have been founded during the time of Saladin. Although the Jews were formally informed that they had no rights regarding the Wall in 1840 and in 1911, the deteriorating situation represented a reversal of the accepted norms under the Ottomans and thereby a violation of the status quo. The Mufti's campaign of harassment catalysed a potent alliance of religious and nationalist forces amongst the Jews, who became increasingly aggrieved at the perceived insults. The secular socialists of the Labour Zionist movement were less moved by the continuing problem of the Wall. The British realized the explosive potential for such an inherently difficult situation and had asked the Zionist Executive to calm the situation by playing down the Mufti's provocations. The leaders of the Yishuv concurred and advocated self-restraint and the avoidance of retaliatory protest.

KLAUSNER AND THE CAMPAIGN FOR THE WALL

The policy of 'havlagah' or self-restraint was followed by *Davar* and *Ha'aretz*, but not by Jabotinsky's *Doar Hayom*. The latter reflected the growing agitation of many nationalist and religious Zionists. A central figure in this campaign to actively protest against these developments was Professor Joseph Klausner who held the chair in Modern Hebrew Literature at the Hebrew University in Jerusalem. He was also a historian whose expertize was in the Second Temple period. Klausner was a long-time Zionist intellectual who had heard Herzl at the first Zionist Congress. Indeed, he had succeeded Ahad Ha'am as editor of *Hashiloah*. But he was also part of the Odessa circle which included Jabotinsky and Ussishkin and very much a fellow traveller with Revisionism although not a party member.[49] Jabotinsky recognized him as such – 'not a party man'[50] – but there is no doubt that he contributed extensively to the 'Zionist education' of Betar and nationalist youth in general. Klausner was unusual in that he was an independent academic who was active in Zionist polemics – and rarely on the side of the Zionist leadership. In questions of religion, he was a traditionalist who accepted the logic of Biblical criticism. Such endeavours propelled him to the forefront of the rising anger at the lack of resolution of the Wall controversy.

Klausner established his 'Pro-Wailing Wall Committee' on the eve of a minor fast day in the Jewish calendar – sheva asar b'Tammuz – the seventeenth day of the month of Tammuz. This commemorates the first breach in the outer wall of the Second Temple by the Romans in the year 70. It is followed by a period of three weeks, leading up to the obligatory fast of Tisha B'Av – the ninth day of the month of Av – when Jerusalem was finally conquered and the Temple destroyed. The three weeks resonate with a sense of increasing grief and impending catastrophe where no public rejoicing takes place and no marriages are solemnized. Orthodox Jews refrain from eating meat and drinking wine. In Hebrew, the period is known as 'bein hametzarim' – between the straits – and in Aramaic as 'telata d'puronata' – the three weeks of rebuke. The mood deepens during the last nine days and reaches its crescendo on Tisha B'Av, a day of mourning and remembrance which evolved over the centuries into a day to commemorate numerous tragedies in Jewish history where Jews died for their faith.

For Klausner personally as an expert in this period of history – and for the nationalist and religious in general – the three weeks in July and August 1929 exuded great symbolic meaning in terms of the controversy over the Wall and the right of Jews to worship there. The establishment of the Pro-Wailing Wall Committee spawned satellite groups in different parts of the country. The Committee created a programme of political activities which were organized and promoted by a loose coalition of Revisionists, religious Zionists and young people.

Another spark which ignited Jewish anger was the permission given to the Muslim authorities to build a fence by the Wall. This was only communicated to Chief Rabbi Kook by the British on 20 July, but the Zionist Executive had seemingly been notified as early as 13 June. *Doar Hayom*, the daily newspaper allied with the Revisionists and under the editorship of Jabotinsky began a daily coverage of the controversy. Thus leading articles took the Zionist leadership to task for their inaction on such a crucial matter.[51]

But a central issue in terms of Jewish response was that the Zionist leadership, including Jabotinsky, had already left the country for the 16th Zionist Congress in Zurich. In addition, the British High Commissioner, Sir John Chancellor, was out of the country. The political vacuum created thus allowed *Doar Hayom* and the Pro-Wailing Wall Committees to pursue a more radical agenda in the run-up to Tisha B'Av. Articles appeared under headings such as 'The Word of Pilate 5689' and 'The Pacifiers at Work'. The issue of 6 August included a piece entitled 'Cheer Up!' which praised the efforts of Klausner's Committee. It commented:

> Even when the official leadership has ceased to exist, there are honest people who feel the pain of the nation. Israel is not an orphan – a nation of 17 million

is not a slave who can be spit at by all its enemies and can be cynically handled by petty governors.

One thing is necessary: that we rise and take action; that we believe in ourselves and in that great mission which we imposed upon ourselves; that we raise our voices and release ourselves from the chains of depression, degradation and defeatism.[52]

The Labour movement attempted to respond to the crisis as best it could. On the one hand, it recognized that the Zionist leadership had given an ineffectual response to the issue of the Wall and had failed to quench the rising anger in nationalist and religious circles. On the other hand, to allow Klausner's Committee and the Revisionists to exploit a sensitive issue could have unseen results. In article entitled 'Responsibility', Meir Dizengoff, the founding mayor of Tel Aviv, commented that 'this movement of protest must be worthy of the nation. It must bring us a blessing and help and not injury and ruin. It must be a movement of a well organized Yishuv and not that of isolated groups and individuals, each one of whom acts on his own responsibility.'[53] *Doar Hayom* replied by widening the attack in criticizing its rival dailies for their less than militant stand. But they too were criticizing the Zionist Executive for 'not fully appreciating the importance of the Wall and the bitterness.....over the infringement of the status quo'.[54] The Labour movement's *Davar* which was no friend of the Revisionists accused the Zionist Executive of concealing the truth and of effectively giving up any struggle for the Wall. It considered that the resolutions at the Congress and the general condemnations were insufficient in the circumstances. It warned that 'we dare not begin our joint life with our Arab neighbours with quarrels and disputes and we must do everything in our power to avoid a misunderstanding of a religious nature.'[55] *Ha'aretz* openly confronted the Revisionists and warned about the daily dose of 'the propaganda of poison' from the columns of *Doar Hayom*.[56]

In another edition, *Davar* urged the Yishuv to take action over the question of the Wall and warned against allowing 'a group of lunatics' who published daily 'words of incitement' to fill the vacuum vacated by the leadership.[57] Siegfried Hoofien, the General Manager of the Anglo-Palestine Company, sent a telegram to Jabotinsky at the Zionist Congress in Zurich.

> *Doar Hayom* ignores all action of Congress relating to Kotel and calls for insubordination although the public is not influenced thereby yet there is incitement among the youth which might lead to accidents without being of any practical utility. I ask that you cable them to change their attitude...[58]

Jabotinsky responded to Hoofien straight away that he would contact *Doar Hayom*. The outcome, however, was not a cooling of the temperature. *Doar Hayom* reacted to the critical comment emanating from Zurich with considerable irritation. In an article entitled 'Libel', it condemned rumours that the newspaper was 'stirring up the people to violent acts'.[59] Indeed, it claimed instead to be 'radical opponents of violence', but was vehemently opposed to 'the diplomacy of silence, the diplomacy of the ostrich'. Thus it was necessary to speak up in order to influence 'Jewish, English and world opinion'. Klausner's Committee also felt obliged to publicly explain its raison d'être. in the pages of *Doar Hayom*. It argued that it should not have had to establish itself if the Zionist leadership had responded in the appropriate manner. 'We cannot trust any more the action of the existing institutions in this matter and it was decided to take separate action.'[60] The Committee condemned the 'narrow blurring sectarianism' of the current leadership and bemoaned the fact that there was no 'national supreme leadership in the country'. Yet Klausner in an article in *The Palestine Weekly* on the same day wrote, 'But what about the Jews, cannot they too throw stones, have they not hands and even fists? What did Shakespeare say through his Shylock "Hath not a Jew eyes .....if you wrong us, shall we not revenge..."' [61]

The struggle to retain access to the Wall and to stop Arab harassment was, of course, more central to the concerns of the broad Revisionist-National Religious camp than to the General Zionist-Labour bloc of Weizmann and Ben-Gurion. The Committee further published an appeal to the Jewish Diaspora in *Doar Hayom* during 'the nine days of mourning'[62] and called upon Jews to protest and demonstrate outside British consulates around the world. It reiterated many of the issues raised in previous statements, but it also unreservedly attacked the political use of an Islamic holy site by the Arabs. It pointedly asked that if the area was so sacred why had it been kept in a state of neglect and relegated to the status of a market thoroughfare?

The Committee's appeal was followed by a notification that a protest meeting by the World Federation of Hebrew Youth would be held on the eve of Tisha B'Av in Tel Aviv. According to British intelligence who monitored the meeting, 6000 people attended the gathering at Beit Ha'am in Tel Aviv.[63] Significantly the speakers were Israel Habbas of Mizrachi, the religious Zionists, Baruch Weinstein for the Revisionists and Itamar Ben-Avi, Jabotinsky's predecessor as editor of *Doar Hayom*.[64] The meeting adopted four resolutions in support of the campaign for the Wall.[65] Detailing Tel Aviv's 'sharp and expressive protest', it requested the British government to restore the rights of the Jews to the Wall and called for the dismissal of those officials in the Palestine Administration whose aim was to negate 'the building of the Jewish State in Palestine in opposition to the Mandate'. It further demanded that the Colonial Office appoint a parliamentary commission to investigate the situation. Finally it 'instructed' the Chief Rabbinate and Joseph Klausner's committee to continue the political struggle for the Wall. The meeting was followed by a march through central Tel Aviv in which black-edged Zionist flags were carried.

On the evening of 14 August 1929, to mark the commencement of Tisha B'Av, Klausner, together with a Mizrachi representative, spoke at a meeting attended by several thousand people at the Yeshurun synagogue in Jerusalem. At the end of the service, the entire congregation walked down to the Wall. On the following day, scores of youths from Tel Aviv made their way to Jerusalem and gathered at the Lemel School. Two Jewish administration officials were deputed to speak to the youths who were from a number of groups including Betar, Maccabi and the Scouts, and to dissuade them from carrying out any protest. It was to no avail and the officials concluded that the young people were adamant that they would proceed with their intention to march to the Wall. They were going to hand in the resolutions from the Tel Aviv meeting to the acting High Commissioner, march past the offices of the Zionist Executive and raise a black-edged Zionist flag at the Wall. The two officials came away from the meeting of the opinion that 'it would be inadvisable to prevent the Jewish youths from proceeding to the Wall even if they went in a body'.[66] Harry Luke, who had been appointed Chief Secretary in July 1928, found himself deputizing as High Commissioner in Sir John Chancellor's absence. He had been an Assistant District Governor of Jerusalem and served on the Haycraft Commission in 1921 which had produced a less than sympathetic attitude to Zionist endeavours. On advice from his associates and clearly fearing a repetition of the incident on Yom Kippur, Luke decided that the best course of action was to permit the procession but to instruct that the young people should not demonstrate, produce flags, shout slogans, march in military formation or raise the Zionist flag at the wall. The youths agreed to the conditions – except for the raising of the flag – and proceeded to march off without any interference from the dozen or so British policemen who seemed to have been oblivious of Luke's orders. The demonstration of 300 was quiet and orderly. The resolutions were handed in, the flag raised, and the Zionist anthem sung, then the crowd quickly dispersed at the end. The Chief Rabbi, Avraham Yitzhak Kook, later received the chairman of the World Federation of Hebrew Youth and expressed his deep gratitude to the marchers which 'testified to the national pride and the Maccabean zeal'.[67] He said that the Wall was 'more venerated than all the synagogues and majestic temples'. But Kook also defined the purpose of the campaign 'to clear all those ugly shacks (next to the Wall) and to create there the meeting place of the nation of Israel as a whole'. The Palestinian Arabs, needless to say, did not see it in such terms.

The following day, after Friday prayers, a Muslim demonstration was permitted by Luke. They turned on the few Jewish worshippers present and chased them from the Wall. Prayer books and prayer petitions were burned amidst a general atmosphere of mayhem while an understaffed police force did little. *Doar*

Hayom swiftly brought out a special supplement, entitled 'Arabs attack congregants at the Wall' by Wolfgang Von Weisl, a Revisionist and the correspondent for the *Vossiche Zeitung* of Berlin.[68] In a confidential dispatch to Lord Passfield, the Colonial Secretary, a few days later, Luke described it as ' a special supplement of excited and exciting news of misleading and false character'.[69] Von Weisl further testified to the Shaw Commission that the supplement had been brought out in great haste and against his advice.[70] Moreover, the effect of Von Weisl's article was all the greater in the absence of the rest of the Hebrew press due to the onset of the Jewish Sabbath. In an attempt to calm the situation, Luke agreed to meet Klausner, Isaiah Braude, the representative of the Zionist Executive in the absence of the leadership in Zurich, the deputy mayor of Jerusalem and a leading figure in the Anglo-Israel Bank. In testimony in camera to the Shaw Commission several months later, Luke described Klausner as someone who would not listen to reason and preferred emotional rather than intellectual arguments.[71] Klausner, in a letter to Pinchas Rutenberg in London, in turn, complained that Luke only gave one answer 'non possumus' and did not display any inclination to ameliorate the situation.[72] Luke's rationale for allowing the Muslim demonstration was one of counter-balance to the Jewish demonstration and he said that the Muslims possessed legal documents of ownership whereas the Jews claimed historic rights. Indeed, in his confidential dispatch to Lord Passfield, he proffered his view that such was the tension that there was a growing feeling amongst the Jews 'that to die in the defence of the Western Wall was a martyrdom of which to be proud'.[73] He also suggested that the Jews believed that 'the Wall is Jewish property and the Muslims have no rights in the area about it'.

THE AFTERMATH OF THE DEMONSTRATION

When an incensed *Ha'aretz* had an opportunity to comment on the wave of Muslim anger, it castigated the British for being ineffectual and the Zionist leadership for being inactive. In an article entitled 'He who Sows the Wind shall Reap the Whirlwind', *Ha'aretz* reserved its venom for the Revisionists and *Doar Hayom*.

> The poison of propaganda was dripping from its columns daily until it poisoned the atmosphere and brought about the Thursday (Jewish) demonstration....and this served as a pretext to the wild demonstration of the Arabs.[74]

Anxious telegrams continued to fly from Jerusalem to the Zionist Executive at the Zurich Congress.

> Population again very excited and false alarms caused local panics in various quarters but no further incidents course of day. Arabs also excited and afraid

Jews. Desirable insist with home Government need of serious measures assuring public security. We are issuing appeal to public keep calm, refrain from demonstrations, and observe discipline, but feel embarrassed by militant attitude. *Doar Hayom* and also part of youth influenced by Revisionist agitation. Can you speak to Revisionist leaders?[75]

Ha'aretz called for national discipline 'at this hour of danger'.[76] But the die was cast. On the same day, the Mufti and his associates called upon Muslims to come to Jerusalem. This led to a general outbreak of violence in the Jerusalem area and to the subsequent killings of 59 Jews in Hebron on 24 August and 20 in Safed on 29 August. In all 133 Jews were killed in the 1929 disturbances and over 120 Arabs perished – mainly at the hands of the British. Indeed, Klausner's own home was plundered and scholarly manuscripts destroyed. Many Arabs had left their fields and their places of employment in the belief that they had to defend Islam against the Jews. They had been led to believe that the British had given the Wall to the Jews and armed them; that the British were permitting the slaughter of innocent Muslims; that a bomb had killed hundreds of Muslims on the Haram.

In his testimony in camera to the Shaw Commission, Major Alan Saunders, the head of the Palestine Police, said that after the two demonstrations, he believed that the Arabs were only interested in driving out the Jews.

> The whole Arab population wanted to make it clear to the world that they were not going to tolerate the Jews, the old or new ones. If a man was a Jew, it was good enough for him to be killed and stamped out.[77]

The Commission of Inquiry under Sir Walter Shaw sat at the end of 1929 and defined the Jewish demonstration 'as having been more than any other single incident an immediate cause of the outbreak'.[78] The actions of Professor Klausner's Committee, *Doar Hayom* and the demonstration of the Jewish youths was emphasized since it also provided a diversion from considering the inadequacy of the British response to Arab violence. In an in camera testimony to the Shaw Commission, Luke acknowledged that if he had taken a different view following the Yom Kippur incident in 1928 and supported Jewish historical claims for access to the Wall over Muslim legal ones, he could not have enforced this approach, given the negligible forces at his disposal. A brigade would have been required, he stated, rather than one or two divisions.[79] Many questioned Luke's wisdom in allowing both the Jewish and Muslim demonstrations to take place. Indeed, Weizmann wrote to Lord Passfield requesting that Luke be relieved of his duties.[80]

Both Luke and Sir John Shuckburgh, the Assistant Undersecretary of State for the Colonial Office were unsympathetic to Zionist claims and indeed tired of

Jewish exhortations. An irritated Luke told the Shaw Commission in camera that he found 'the Jews with whom the Government have to deal officially quite incapable of seeing more than just their own demands'.[81]

Sir John Shuckburgh similarly wished to divert attention away from the lack of British preparedness in Palestine and deflect any possible Zionist political comeback after the disturbances. In a memorandum to Sir Samuel Wilson at the end of September 1929, he commented:

> A discussion between myself and Dr Weizmann would serve no useful purpose. If a mere informal discussion is meant, it would be quite superfluous; I have given Dr Weizmann an immense amount of my time for the last eight years and have heard his views, and he mine, ad nauseam. If more formal discussions are intended, they could not be carried far. I should have no authority to agree to anything except a referendum. Moreover, if it got out (and it would be sure to get out: the Jews can keep nothing to themselves) that the Jews and the Colonial Office were co-operating in a revision of policy in Palestine, we should have a howl from the Arabs and the anti-Semites that might have awkward repercussions in Palestine itself.[82]

There was also an editing and detailed alteration of the reports of the officers in charge of the two population centres where a majority of Jews had been killed. This had resulted in a deletion of police criticism of Arab attitudes as well as the names of those who had been involved in violence. Comments which referred to 'Jewish vulnerability and non-aggression' were removed as was mention of the British failure to provide adequate police to protect the civilian population. A major failure for the absence of so many police and government officials was that they were on holiday. This was Luke's responsibility – and this too seems to have been airbrushed from the official report.[83]

Although Shuckburgh had been informed about the special preparations for Tisha B'Av in early August,[84] the condemnation of the Revisionist-inspired campaign, protests and demonstrations became a method of heading off both Zionist criticism and claims. Only a few days after the killings in Hebron and Safed – and before the Shaw Commission of Inquiry had even met – Shuckburgh had concluded that the Jewish demonstration of 15 August, 'apparently of an aggressive and provocative nature, was one of the immediate causes of the disturbances'.[85] He also believed that *Doar Hayom* had played 'a mischievous and provocative part'.[86]

Sir John Chancellor, the High Commissioner, hurried back to Palestine following the violence. He, too, was keen to deflect blame and to dissipate Zionist protests over the killings. In a private letter to his son, he remarked:

> There is evidence to show that the Jews, realizing the need for arousing interest in the national home among the Jews of the world and the need for a rallying cry to stimulate subscriptions, deliberately seized upon the Wailing Wall incident of a year ago, and worked it for all it was worth, and converted a religious question into a political one.[87]

The Jewish demonstration became the subject of much discussion. Although Siegfried Hoofien had been told by one of the leaders of Betar that it was not a Betar-sponsored demonstration,[88] the campaign in its entirety was clearly imbued with a Revisionist-Mizrachi ethos. The 'Betar' demonstration became a vehicle of attack by the opponents of the Revisionists. But there were also admirers of Jabotinsky such as Jacobus Kann who condemned both the youth for staging the demonstration and the British too for allowing the demonstration to go ahead.

The Shaw Commission Report's findings evolved into broader criticism of Zionist policy through the Hope-Simpson Report and the 1930 White Paper. The wisdom of allowing the Zionists to proceed with their plans became the focus of debate rather than the disturbances. The Revisionists themselves published a response to the Shaw Commission, but the demonstration and campaign was played down and merited only a couple of paragraphs.[89]

Instead the Revisionists selectively quoted the report to illustrate that the protest by contrast with the Muslim one was 'orderly and quiet'. The report and its authors were criticized for playing down the Mufti's 'incitement to disorder' and the belief of the Arabs that 'the Government was with them'. They also condemned the lack of British protection for the Jewish community. It further argued that the need for separate Jewish police units and the legalization of Jewish self-defence had been ignored.

The Zionist Executive also compared the conduct of the participants in both the Jewish and Muslim demonstrations. It clearly did not endorse the Jewish demonstration and pointed to the miscommunication between Luke, Major Saunders and the leaders of the demonstration as well. The Labour Party member of the Shaw Commission, Harry Snell, believed that the Palestine Administration should never have negotiated with the young people and should have been prepared to arrest '300 headstrong youths' if they deviated from Luke's orders.[90]

THE WIDENING SCHISM

REVERSING THE BALFOUR DECLARATION

Jabotinsky's first reaction to the Jewish demonstration on Tisha B'Av was one of great delight that the campaign for the Wall appeared to 'an initiative of the Revisionists and Betar'. In a letter to Meir Grossman, he explained that this could set the precedent for future activities. 'We must raise a hue and cry, the like of which has never been heard before.'[1] Initially, he did not appear to question the staging of the demonstration publicly or privately. It seemed to be less than important. Indeed, Jabotinsky had taken little notice of the demonstration until it became apparent that Luke and other British officials were intent on foisting the blame for the outbreak of violence on the organizers of the demonstration – and, in particular, the waving of the Zionist flag in front of the Wall. In a letter to Max Seligman,[2] he mentioned that he had met one of the young participants who stated that two British officials had been photographing the demonstrators with their 'Kodaks'. Jabotinsky further asked Seligman to ensure that this should be raised at the hearings of the Shaw Commission.

> It may be useful to investigate how much fact there is under this story. Not so much for the purpose of justifying the flag waving (much as I hate all kind of painted smartutim (dishcloths), blue or white or red), I do think that on August 15 even that was a psychological necessity; and if I believed for a moment that that was the "cause" of the outbreak, I should heartily congratulate the promoter, because it is the main thing in all strategy to force the enemy to attack before he is ready. A year later would have been infinitely worse. Not for justification, but for attack. It is most light-headedly provocative for 'high officials' to expose themselves filming an infuriated crowd: nothing can be better calculated to incite a crowd to excesses.[3]

Jabotinsky thus did not question the wisdom of staging the demonstration and the linkage to the Hebron and Safed killings. There were no words of remorse that the tragic outcome could have been avoided. There was no public reprimand for the nationalist youth. Instead, Jabotinsky exhibited a profound degree of fatalism. Violence, he surmised, was to be expected under the circumstances. It followed the logic of his well-known article 'The Iron Wall', published in *Rassvet* in 1923, which postulated that it was 'utterly impossible to obtain the voluntary consent of the Palestine Arabs' in building a country with a Jewish majority. As a general rule, Jabotinsky believed that this had always been the case in history.

> The native population, civilized or uncivilized, have always stubbornly resisted the colonists, irrespective of whether they were civilized or savages. And it made no difference whatever whether the colonists behaved decently or not. The companions of Cortes and Pizarro or (as some will remind us) our own ancestors under Joshua Bin Nun behaved like brigands; but the Pilgrim Fathers, the first real pioneers of North America, were people of the highest morality who did not want to do harm to anyone, least of all to the Red Indians; and they honestly believed that there was room enough in the prairies both for the Paleface and the Redskin. Yet the native population fought with the same ferocity against the good colonists as against the bad.[4]

For Jabotinsky, therefore, the killings were part and parcel of a self-fulfilling prophecy. This would be the shape of things to come until the Palestinian Arabs realized that they could not make 'a breach in the Iron Wall...and the leadership will pass to the moderate groups who will approach us with a proposal that we should both agree to mutual concessions.'[5] The logic of this position was that the focus of Zionist attention after Hebron should not be on the Palestinian Arabs, but on the weakening support of the British for the Zionist position and their inefficiency in protecting the Jews. Indeed, Jabotinsky praised the demonstration as a necessity and a noble act[6] which he wished Betar had organized.

Yet not all viewed the situation in such apocalyptic, predestined, predetermined terms – and certainly not the Zionist Left in an age of messianic socialism. They still believed in a rapprochement with Palestinian nationalism. They saw differences between the Zionist colonization of the present and the European colonialism of the past. Thus Shmaryahu Levin and the Zionist leadership in general blamed Betar for the procession.

Weizmann, himself, saw the demonstration as symbolic of the rise of a new type of Zionism. It was 'the spark which has kindled the flame and for which they (the Revisionists) will be one day called to account before the bar of history'.[8] Weizmann viewed the Revisionists as irresponsible at best, criminal at worst and their actions in wrecking terms. In a private letter to the New York lawyer, Morris Rothenberg, Weizmann expressed his frustrations and confided his fears:

> And still they and their supporters are blowing the big trumpet; they are the big noise on the Jewish street – Hitlerism all over in its worst possible form. I am not joining issue so much with the Revisionists. At least they are open and frank, although very dangerous. But all the others who are hidden Revisionists are infinitely much worse. There must be a thorough cleansing of the soul of the movement if we are to survive. The financial difficulties are merely a symptom of an internal serious disease which goes by many names: demagogy, intellectual falsehood, political expediency, chauvinism and injustice to others – Arabs for instance – of the worst character, and last but not least, a complete disregard of realities, a complete misunderstanding of the fact that we live in a distracted world, and that our problem is a function of the general situation, and that we Jews cannot afford to use the same weapons as the others to get drunk on the same phraseology as the others – k'col ha'amim (like all other nations). I hide my head in shame when I read our press and sometimes ask myself: are we worthy of the task which has fallen on us? [9]

Weizmann's outburst against 'these fire eaters'– albeit within the context of a private letter to a supporter – encapsulated the differences in strategy and temperament. It starkly delineated the paths open to the evolution of the Zionist movement in an age of emerging ultra-nationalism. Despite the violence and the Mufti's policies, it also symbolized his hope for a rational accommodation with the Palestinian Arabs. It implicitly signified an increasing recognition of a growing band of critics with his policies – a process which would come to fruition at the 17th Zionist Congress in 1931 and end in Weizmann's resignation.

The demonstration, the killings and the unrest had been utilized by Sir John Chancellor, the High Commissioner in Palestine and Sir John Shuckburgh, the long-term head of the Middle East desk at the Colonial Office to accelerate British backtracking on both the Balfour Declaration and indeed the Churchill White Paper. Thus the Shaw Commission led to the Hope-Simpson Report which in turn formed the basis for the Passfield White Paper. In developing the view of Chancellor in Palestine and Shuckburgh at the Colonial Office, Shaw exonerated both the administration and the police, but crucially went beyond his brief to examine the disturbances of 1929 to proclaim that a national home for the Jews was inconsistent with the Mandate. In January 1930, the High Commissioner for Palestine, Sir John Chancellor, clarified the two possibilities for future British policy to Lord Passfield:

> to withdraw from the Jews the specially privileged position (as compared with the Arab inhabitants of the country) which has been given to them under the Mandate but which is not justified by the terms of the Balfour Declaration and to grant the people of Palestine a measure of self-government;

or to continue the present policy unchanged and to enforce the provisions of the Mandate by maintaining in Palestine military forces of sufficient strength to keep order and to protect the Jews from attack by the Arabs in Palestine supported by their sympathizers in the adjacent territories.

I reject the second alternative because it is altogether repugnant to modern sentiment and because it would provide no permanent solution of the present difficulties in Palestine and no palliative apart from repression by force of arms for a situation which has become dangerous and if allowed to continue will become a menace to the Empire in its relations not only to the territories adjacent to Palestine but also to the whole Muslim world.[10]

The MacDonald government then began to look to its imperial interests and consider what its obligations were to the Palestinian Arabs and to investigate the possibility of curtailing Jewish immigration. Field Marshal Smuts, who was originally favoured to look into the issues raised by Shaw, was then passed over for his pro-Zionist views and Sir John Hope-Simpson, a member of the Indian Civil Service, appointed in his stead. He was asked to investigate the questions of land settlement, immigration and development. His report in October 1930 recommended a discouraging of the piecemeal purchase of land and condemned the refusal to employ Arab labour. It suggested that there was only room for another 100,000 immigrants and only half of these should be Jews – therefore a maximum of 20,000 Jewish families should be allowed in. It criticized the government for abdicating its responsibilities for labour certificates to the Jewish Agency and the Histadrut. The Passfield White Paper which emerged simultaneously out of the Hope-Simpson Report confirmed the about-turn of British policy. In a letter to his wife, Lord Passfield pointed out that 'it is really the work of the office, in consultation with Sir John Campbell (economic advisor to the Colonial Office 1930-1942), Sir John Chancellor and Sir John Hope-Simpson.'[11]

This campaign of Chancellor and Shuckburgh who had never looked on the Zionist experiment with any favour was probably initially an attempt to transfer immediate responsibility for the disturbances away from themselves and to secure a deeper explanation, emanating from the Balfour Declaration and Zionist ideology in general. Their strategy was initially successful because of the election of a Labour government under Ramsay MacDonald in the summer of 1929. MacDonald had travelled to Palestine in 1922 and had written a pamphlet on his return 'A Socialist in Palestine' in which he had commented that 'Palestine was placed at the Jews' disposal so they should settle it and govern it.'[12] MacDonald appointed as his Colonial Secretary Lord Passfield, the former Sidney Webb who together with his wife Beatrice were lifelong campaigners for democratic socialism and respected Fabian theoreticians. Passfield had no strong feelings initially about Zionism. His wife, Beatrice Webb, however, felt that it was 'hypocritical nonsense' and viewed it in neo-colonialist terms in comparing the Jews in Palestine with white settlers in Kenya.[13] One of the leading intellectuals of her time, she was convinced that the Jewish immigrants were 'Slavs or Mongols and not Semites and the vast majority are not followers of Moses and the prophets, but of Karl Marx and the Soviet Republic'.[14] She believed that the Balfour Declaration – 'a fatuous promise' – was at the root of all the difficulties.[15]

Following the Jewish and Muslim demonstrations and only days before the killings in Hebron and Safed, Lord Passfield agreed to the disarming of Jewish special constables in Palestine and explained his rationale in a letter to Weizmann. The decision to disarm, he explained, was 'taken as an unassailable principle and was in the best interests of the Jews as a whole since it removed an important irritant of the whole Arab population, both in Palestine and Transjordan'.[16] Weizmann, he pointed out, did not appreciate the greater danger of a general uprising by the Arabs and therefore they had to be placated. Passfield accepted the broad approach of both Shaw and Hope-Simpson in finding that nobody could be held to account for the disturbances of 1929. Significantly, Passfield ignored Snell's minority report as well as a suggestion from Hope-Simpson in a private letter that funding to the Arab Trust that looked after the Wall and its environs should be diverted to Palestinian Arab education. Hope-Simpson further suggested that the Mufti be removed from his post.[17]

Over the next few months, Passfield's relations with Weizmann progressively deteriorated. The White Paper brought with it protest from the Jews as well as condemnation from the Conservative and Liberal opposition. MacDonald, who was cultivating the US Administration to alleviate the effects of unemployment and the deepening recession, was aghast that the Palestine issue should have been raised at the same time since American Zionists began to campaign vociferously against the White Paper. MacDonald expediently decided to place Palestine affairs in the hands of a specially appointed cabinet committee and to marginalize Passfield. The final volte-face occurred when MacDonald wrote to Weizmann in February 1931 repudiating the White Paper.

Weizmann like Jabotinsky had often complained of the judeophobia of some of the British officials both in Palestine and in Whitehall. Colonel Richard Meinhertzhagen, who was a military advisor to the Middle Eastern Department of the Colonial Office between 1921 and 1924, felt that the Colonial Office was 'definitely hebraphobe' with Shuckburgh as 'its worst offender'.[18] The Jewish Agency's lawyers at the Shaw Commission sittings concluded that Sir Walter Shaw, a retired Chief Justice of the Turkish Straits settlements, was 'a reactionary and anti-Semitic type'.[19] The psychological difficulty in dealing with

Jewish nationalists who were not frightened to campaign for their views was also prevalent on the Left. Passfield complained to his wife about the 'Jewish hurricane' following protests against the White Paper. He felt that the Jews had no grounds for complaint – after all, the British were placing no limitations on 'continued colonization'.[20] Part of the problem was that he had difficulty in accommodating the Jewish question within socialist theory. Zionism did not fit into the classic British colonial enterprises that Passfield was encountering in India and Kenya. His wife was more certain in her views. She wrote that 'all the officials at home and in Palestine' had related to Passfield that they found Jews 'intolerable as negotiators and colleagues'.[21]

Beatrice Webb asked, 'Why is it that everyone who has dealings with Jewry ends by being prejudiced against the Jew?'[22] Lord Passfield was clearly out of his depth and fatigued by dealing with the complexities and sensitivities of the Palestine conflict. Weizmann viewed him in terms of his desire to support 'poor Arabs' against 'wealthy Jews'.[23] Yet such stereotyping was not merely Jewish paranoia or zealotry in promoting the Zionist case. An early biography of the Webbs in 1932 described the Jews as 'powerfully represented as they are in governing circles at home and abroad, they had, and used, all kinds of pressures and had and used all kinds of access'.[24] The image of the Jew as campaigning Zionist was thus difficult for the standard bearers of progressive humanity to come to terms with. Zionism fitted no ideological conformist theory and it became easier to fall back on less savoury images.

EXPULSION FROM PALESTINE

Jabotinsky above all personified the noisy Zionist gadfly who continued to bite the imperial elephant. The aftermath of the 1929 disturbances and the Colonial Office's pointed retreat from the Balfour Declaration provided a golden opportunity to bar him from living and campaigning in Palestine.

The logic of British tactics demanded criticism of the Jewish demonstration leading to attacks on Jabotinsky and the Revisionist movement, concluding with a marginalization of Weizmann and a rolling-back of the Zionist initiative. Jabotinsky had left Palestine on 19 July 1929 – almost a month before the demonstration which the Mandate police described as 'the result of undue activity of extremist propaganda by the Revisionists and Brit Trumpeldor'.[25] With Jabotinsky out of the country for a long period and the Shaw Commission sittings in progress, the British had to wait until the end of the year. On 23 December, Jabotinsky gave a speech to a crowd of thousands in Tel Aviv – the text of which was published in *Doar Hayom* the following day.

His speech was a response to the post-Hebron situation and the direction that the Shaw Commission sittings were taking. He commenced with an attack on liberal Zionist advocates of a rapprochement with the Palestinian Arabs. Elucidating his usual fatalistic approach, he said that all attempts would come to nothing:

> A social rapprochement is impossible and is but a dream like all other dreams; for in no country has the attempt to associate in social life two circles which are two worlds, two epochs and which have no common spiritual interests, succeeded. This does not mean to say that we are 'better' than they or vice-versa, but it is impossible.[26]

He referred to the tradition of the lamed-vavniks – the 36 righteous men, living in every generation who are privileged to see the Divine Presence. Where were the corresponding lamed-vavniks from the Arab side? He compared the idea of Jewish cantons – alongside Arab ones – as comparable to a new Pale of Settlement. He said that the learning of Arabic was secondary before the Hebrew language had become entrenched. Social rapprochement, he argued, would actually lead to assimilation, followed by anti-Semitism – as had been the case in the European past. He attacked the idea of a legislative body where 'the British and the Arabs' would together form a majority. He reminded his audience:

> For there are no paltry and casual remedies for Zionism, no roundabout way and no magic wand – there is only the way of a struggle for Zionism in its full scope. For a Zionism, of which many hate any mention. The expression of which is about a Jewish majority, a Jewish state, a Jewish Defence and a Jewish Legion – all this has become anathema. And if you are tired by these things, I am even more tired of this, but the doctor must always come with his remedy.[27]

He recalled the situation in 1917 when Weizmann and Sacher spoke openly about a Jewish state. Lloyd-George, Balfour and Smuts understood the Balfour Declaration, it was argued, as meaning a state – and not 'the creation of a new ghetto'. Cecil's comment – 'Armenia for the Armenians, Arabia for the Arabs and Palestine for the Jews' – summed up Zionist thinking at the time. Yet his demands of Britain were based on a humanitarian understanding for the Jewish problem down the centuries. He castigated the Zionist Executive for their docile approach and particularly before the Shaw Commission sittings where he compared the discussions to a 'society to combat anti-Semitism' of the past. 'The Jew was obliged to justify his existence by proving that he was of use to others, that he had no intention to govern, but only requested the right to breathe.' In conclusion, he said that an Arab rebellion would neither triumph over the Jews nor over the British. But the Jews were angry:

> Scores of thousands of Jews in the country and abroad are filled with fury. There is not a vestige of confidence in the present administration left in them. They are

only waiting for a strong call to rally round a movement of protest and we shall
not allow that national asset, the fury of the masses, to be wasted needlessly.[28]

Jabotinsky said nothing new, nothing that he had not commented upon
previously in other speeches and writings. Yet the British were nervous in the
aftermath of Hebron and Safed that passionate rhetoric would incite violence.
Following his digestion of the 26 page translation of Jabotinsky's speech,
Drummond Shiels, the Under-Secretary for State for the Colonial Office, wrote
that 'Jabo's speech is eloquent and logical, but certainly dangerous in its
tendency so far as law and order are concerned…Mr Jabotinsky's activities must
therefore be curbed.'[29] Clearly the Foreign Office had briefed the MPs with less
than accurate information. But in the House of Commons, primed questions
were addressed to Shiels which suggested that Jabotinsky had been deported
from Palestine in 1920 after serving a prison sentence and blacklisted. Yet he
had returned in 1922 and 1926 before settling on October 1928. Furthermore
his conviction had been quashed by the High Commissioner in 1920 and the
Army Council in 1921. It had also been claimed in Parliament that his speech
had been 'seditious'. Jabotinsky subsequently wrote to Shiels that he would take
any person to court who considered his speech to be seditious.[30]

Norman Bentwich, the Attorney-General in Palestine, was asked to read
Jabotinsky's speech and give his view. He concluded that there was 'not
sufficient on which to charge him with seditious publication under Section 9 of
the Criminal Law (Seditious Offences) Ordinance, 1929. His speech is a
declaration of a radical policy, but it does not come within any of the four
heads of sedition which are laid down in Section 9.'[31] Furthermore Bentwich
concluded that the speech could not be deemed to be 'an incitement to violence
and hatred'. Bentwich, however, was a Jew with liberal Zionist sympathies who
believed in reconciliation with the Palestinian Arabs and was actually opposed
to Jabotinsky's approach. A few weeks later Lord Passfield and Sir John
Chancellor decided that Bentwich's presence in the Palestine Administration
had become an embarrassing obstacle after a decade in position. 'It would not
be in the interests of Palestine for him to return to Palestine as Attorney-
General after his leave in September.' [32]

The other area of contention was Jabotinsky's comments about the
impossibility of reaching a rapprochement with the Palestinian Arabs.
Chancellor reported to Shuckburgh that the speech had caused 'considerable
excitement' amongst the Arabs.[33] He formally explained his views on excluding
Jabotinsky from Palestine because of his political activities. In selectively
utilizing Bentwich's evaluation of the speech, he commented:

I daresay Jabotinsky does not deliberately intend to foment trouble in the country; but he cannot avoid the temptation to indulge in public speaking; he is, I am informed, eloquent and his eloquence carries him away so that his speeches are frequently violent and inflammatory...there can be little doubt Jabotinsky's presence in Palestine would add to the tension. Bentwich shared my opinion that he should not be admitted to Palestine at present.' [34]

For good measure, Chancellor also suspended *Doar Hayom* – as well as two Arab papers – for publishing inflammatory articles. The British continued to survey Jabotinsky's pronouncements.

Jabotinsky's expulsion from Palestine meant that he was distant from the development of Revisionist opposition to the mandate. This left the field open to more radical forces to step in to fill the vacuum. *Doar Hayom* reverted to a more moderate position under its former editor and eventually severed its ties to the Revisionist movement. The Revisionist members of staff went on strike – they were bereft of both a daily vehicle for their views and a guiding leader.

On the other hand, Jabotinsky's treatment was viewed by Zionists as part and parcel of the British offensive to curtail the movement in general. It was a short step from identifying him as the central vocal opposition to Passfield's approach to the delegitimization of Zionism.

In addition, there was a widespread Jewish anger that the British had done little to protect the Jews of Palestine. Indeed, a *Jewish Chronicle* editorial on the Shaw Commission report commented that it was reminiscent of the Russian Government's report of the Kishinev pogrom.[35] The rise in identification with Revisionism was in parallel with disillusionment with Weizmann's inability to change British policy. At the annual Zionist conference of Congress Poland, the elections produced a majority for the Revisionists and the Al Hamishmar group of Radicals. The number of Revisionists elected increased from 8 to 100.[36]

The first Revisionist Conference in England in May 1930 spoke of their 'marching to victory'.[37] The 4th World Conference of the Revisionist movement in Prague in August 1930 was therefore one of anticipation. In a preparatory message to all its members, the movement suggested that it alone had remained unshaken by the reverses of 1929 and after. 'It has become strengthened and reinforced through continual confirmation of its predictions and the justification of its political direction.'[38] It had embarked on an 'inner Zionist offensive'[39] which it hoped would maximize its growing support amongst non-Revisionists and project the movement as the wave of the future. It publicized details of a registered membership of more than 30,000 in 29 countries, but particularly in Eastern Europe.[40] Yet it also revealed a virtual reluctance to take control. On the eve of the conference, the London Executive commented that:

> It must free itself from that dangerous psychological condition that sometimes leads an organization to regard itself as having arrived at the peak of its ideological and organization development. It must be remembered that the inner strength of Revisionism lay always in the fact that it was never content with present situations, seeking always for newer and more positive forms for the building-up of Zionism.[41]

The desire for opposition and catalytic activities seemed to predominate over a thirst for governance. The world conference opened in the Great Hall of the Produktenbourse in Prague with over 200 delegates in attendance. A focal point was the ongoing assault on Weizmann and the Zionist Executive whether it was the 'pusillanimous performance' before the Shaw Commission, the new mixed Jewish Agency of Zionists and non-Zionists, their inability to support openly the idea of a Jewish state or simply a Jewish majority on both sides of the Jordan. Yet the demands to some extent concealed the struggle between those who wished to secede from the Zionist Organization and those who wished to oust Weizmann. The discussions in the Political Commission led to an all-night sitting.

Selig Brodetsky, representing the Zionist Executive, warned that if the Revisionists opted for outright opposition, they would cause fragmentation in a united Zionist front against the Passfield policies. Both Grossman and Lichtheim postulated a Revisionist takeover of the Zionist Executive, but they also moved in Jabotinsky's direction of greater independence. Grossman argued that the Revisionists could no longer permit the Zionist Executive to be the only body to interpret the aims of Zionism. The Revisionists should feel free to engage in all forms of political activity. Lichtheim suggested that there should now be a new constitutional arrangement whereby the Revisionists should establish their own union like the religious Zionists of the Mizrachi. The Prague gathering abrogated the decisions of their last conference to effectively tow the line – they now decided to exercise the right to make direct demands to both the British Government and to the League of Nations. Jabotinsky felt very little sympathy for the beleaguered Zionist Executive. He recalled a long catalogue of insults and distortions which he felt that he had suffered in a letter to Grossman just before the Prague Conference.[42]

The decisions of the conference reaffirmed 'the joint interests of the British Empire and Zionism', but warned both the British and the Zionist Executive that the Revisionists would develop its own direction. It significantly reiterated its view that it was 'an integral part of the Zionist Organization', but that with its accelerating growth, 'it could not be doomed to a state of opposition with opportunity to exert its influence on the practical execution of Zionist work.' It concluded that unless there was a change in leadership and policy, the Revisionists would have to reconsider their membership of the Zionist Organization.[43] It also warned the British of unspecified dire consequences if 'the present crisis does not result in a transformation, more or less conforming with our demands, of a situation that has grown intolerable, it will not be possible to restore the Jewish people's shaken confidence in the Mandatory Power.' [44]

A NEW PSYCHOLOGICAL RACE

The Distraction of Youth

The 17th Zionist Congress proved to be a watershed in the development of the Revisionist movement, but its outcome was also a statement on Jabotinsky's brand of leadership. When it became clear that Sokolov would emerge as a neutered caretaker leader in place of Weizmann, several Revisionist delegates argued that two or three members could be elected to the Executive and their views would be highly influential. Jabotinsky would not hear any such suggestion, He would only enter the Executive as President with a Revisionist majority – otherwise no meaningful change was possible. Benjamin Akzin later recalled that:

> The most Jabo was prepared to accept was that a few Revisionists other than himself should join the Executive. This, we, of the internal opposition, would not agree to, because we thought that without Jabo on the team, the others would be unable to influence the Executive sufficiently. He then made another proposal: he would introduce a resolution formally defining the establishment of a Jewish State as the aim of Zionism; if the resolution was carried, he would agree to join the Executive... All the others agreed to that and I was about the only one to object:

'At last a majority in Congress is ready to part with Weizmann, but it is not yet ready to pass a resolution of this kind. The important thing is to have an Executive that would work for the establishment of a Jewish State – and to forgo this chance by insisting on a formal resolution.' Jabo's views prevailed, of course, the proposed resolution failed to be adopted and our chance to become the dynamic factor in the actual Zionist leadership was thrown away. Jabo's gesture in Congress in tearing up his delegate's card added to the drama; the grave error, in my view, was committed before.[1]

The implosion at the Congress had not brought satisfaction to the Revisionists. Despite the growing sense of victory which had been engendered amongst their followers and sympathizers, Jabotinsky had neither been elected President nor had a Revisionist Executive been formed. The Revisionists found themselves as impotent as they had been before the Congress despite the increased support for their position. The lessons which Jabotinsky drew from the Basle debacle were entirely different from those of his colleagues on the Revisionist Executive.

The Congress also bore witness to the embryonic alliance between Weizmann's faction of General Zionists and Ben-Gurion's Labour movement. Jabotinsky had not only opposed Weizmann's 'soft' approach, but he had also formulated 'an ideological contrast between Revisionism and Socialism'. Whereas some Revisionists wanted a degree of neutrality on social issues, Jabotinsky opened up a second front which undoubtedly reduced the chances of success.[2] Indeed there were members of Betar who envisaged themselves as part of the broad pioneering movement and ideological opponents of Labour Zionism.[3]

1931 was certainly not a good year for Jabotinsky – he was under attack both externally and internally. But the multiplicity of attacks was, in part, self-inflicted. If there was now hostility from both Weizmann's supporters and the Labour movement, he had, in addition, two foci of opposition within his own movement. Firstly, he had become concerned by the radicalization of the Revisionists in Palestine. His enforced absence left a vacuum into which Achimeir, Greenberg and Yeivin willingly stepped. There was a clear difference of approach. Thus, on the eve of the publication of the Passfield White Paper, Jabotinsky persisted in clinging to his tenet of truth – that everything depended on England. He attempted to prove rationally that 'a national home' could only mean a Jewish state according to the original interpretation of both the Balfour Declaration and the Mandate. Balfour's letter to Lord Rothschild, he argued, was a declaration of 'sympathy with Jewish Zionist aspirations'. Jabotinsky logically asked - 'And what were Jewish-Zionist aspirations at the time?' – if not a state? [4]

In contrast, Abba Achimeir favoured direct action. He was arrested for participating in a protest outside the Tel Aviv hotel of Drummond Shiels, the visiting Under-Secretary at the Colonial Office. Yet, in contrast to most of his long-time colleagues on the Revisionist Executive, Jabotinsky had been a strong advocate of permitting the Revisionists in Palestine to exercise their right to independent action. Meir Grossman was opposed to both independent actions as well as to radical methods. Moreover, Grossman was a strong supporter of remaining within the Zionist Organization despite his frustration at the Zionist Congress.

Despite Jabotinsky's seemingly erratic style of leadership – where he was not unhappy to see real power in the Zionist movement placed almost deliberately beyond reach – it also seemed less important to many of his followers. His tremendous charisma, his passion for his mission and his lack of personal opportunism kept many within his orbit of influence. Pragmatic politics for Jabotinsky seemed to suggest betrayal. It was better to remain pure in aim than tarnished through compromise. The 17th Zionist Congress brought such divergent aspects of Jabotinsky's character into conflict. He had to choose between the drudgery of the establishment and the theatre of the free but powerless. The former meant a directed gradualism, the latter an uncontrolled spontaneity. Although he would have liked a half-way house where he could combine a rational diplomacy with the drama of the Zionist experiment, in an age of ideology and polarizing positions, this became increasingly unlikely – and Jabotinsky had to choose. This meant that in the first half of the 1930s, he adopted – at least publicly – a seemingly more radical position as the adversary of what he termed 'small-time Zionism'. He promoted an opposition to the Zionist status quo through his mesmerizing rhetoric, yet this promotion and the pressure of events, both in Europe and Palestine, effectively boxed him in in such a fashion that he was unable to guide his followers to pursue a rationalized political direction. Above all, Jabotinsky's band of adoring youth could not see the world through the eyes of a seasoned veteran in his fifties.

Jabotinsky's ambivalence about formally participating in the official work of the Zionist Organization was complemented by a growing quasi-educational work amongst the young. In January 1929, Jabotinsky travelled to the first international gathering of Betar in Warsaw. But it was more than a Jewish meeting, it was also an emotional drama, defined by dreams of the future – a sense of anticipation symbolized in the visit of Jabotinsky. Several hundred uniformed members of the Betar youth group marched to the tomb of the unknown soldier, led by a band. There was a memorial service for Trumpeldor at the Central Synagogue on Tlomatska Street and a torch-lit procession through the Jewish quarter.

Jabotinsky was enthusiastically welcomed in Poland. The editorial in *Haynt* which often carried his articles commented that 'Betar aspires to develop in Jewish youth a sense of discipline and courageous endurance, to develop a strong willpower and a readiness for self-sacrifice in order to obtain the historic ideal. Youth like this – in the absence of ideas and beauty in our small world today – is the best guarantee that we shall not stand with our arms folded halfway along the road, but shall reach our goal.'[5] Jabotinsky spoke to a large audience of young people in Warsaw's Kaminsky theatre, but it was at a parallel meeting of some twenty commanders of Betar from different European countries that the restructuring of the movement began to take shape. Betar had been founded in Riga. The Warsaw meeting marked a transfer of power and influence from Latvia to Poland. It also marked the first clash between the Latvian model of Betar – a uniformed, demonstrative, if not militant, youth group designed to break the mould in Zionism and the alternative military image of the Palestinian Jews – an incipient national liberation movement. The former still embellished the framework of a youth group, the latter, in Jabotinsky's eyes, was the embryonic model for a reborn Jewish Legion which would protect the Jews in Palestine. It was not, as many of the Palestinian branch viewed it, a revolutionary national movement committed to the armed struggle against the British.

Jabotinsky viewed Betar in Palestine and in the Diaspora differently. In a letter in November 1928 to Menachem Arber,[6] the head of Betar in Tel Aviv, Jabotinsky argued that military training was to be promoted and that a school for madrichim (youth guides) should be established. He qualified this by suggesting, 'such a praiseworthy sense of physical might should not be misused in outbreaks of violence where other means would suffice.'[7] He particularly pointed out that the use of force should only be defensive – and not offensive – and certainly not be utilized in Jewish public life. As if to complement this, he suggested that a circular should be sent out to all brigade commanders in Palestine, stressing politeness, orderly dress and courtesy to all, especially women. Yet when he wrote to Betar in Latvia on its fifth anniversary three days later, Jabotinsky utilized religious imagery and language. 'I do not know how to pronounce the Ineffable Name of your (Betar's) holiness.'[8]

Jabotinsky was elected Rosh Betar – the head of Betar - and the commands in each country would thereby defer to him as supreme commander. Significantly Betar would be an autonomous institution with close ties to the Revisionist movement – the common denominator being Jabotinsky at the helm. Thus it was possible to be a member of 'the Jabotinsky movement', but not be a member of the Revisionist movement. Each Betar member was expected to undergo three levels of training and then emigrate to Palestine. Each darga (level) corresponded to age and a minimum of nine members of the same darga could form a zror – a military unit. In turn, four to seven zrorot would then form a gdud – a brigade. Examinations based on a comprehensive syllabus of Zionist history and culture had to be taken to move from one darga to the next. Jabotinsky's own library of writings were accumulated, distributed and discussed. For example, his 1911 article 'Instead of Excessive Apology' urged its readers to stand firm, not to give an inch in any discussion and tell the detractors of the Jews to 'go to hell'.[9]

The new uniform for members of Betar sported epaulettes and insignia of rank. The uniform of a member in 1929 was a brown shirt – 'the colour of the soil of Israel' – with a straight collar. For ranks two and three, members of Betar would wear a black tie. For the top rank, this would be replaced by a brown kerchief with a toggle ring – like the uniform of the scouts. The number of silver strips on the left arm and silver stars of David on the left breast denoted the seniority of the member. The top rank would also have to study the tenets of Revisionist Zionism, sport and defence.

> The members would greet each other by touching the brim of the cap with the right hand and exclaiming 'Tel Chai' (the site of Trumpeldor's death). This replaced the older 'Shomer' tradition of saying 'hazak ve'amets' (be strong and of good courage).
> Betar had to create a symbol for Jewish youth, and this was the call 'Tel Chai'. Whenever Jabotinsky was asked something, he replied, 'Tel Chai', just as we respond 'Shalom' to 'Shalom'.[10]

The Betar constitution exhorted members 'to be honest' and to be responsible for 'their words and deeds'. It forbade members to drink alcohol or to visit night clubs. Smoking was only permitted to darga gimel, the over-eighteens. Despite Jabotinsky's highly-developed secularism, members were forbidden to desecrate the Sabbath and to blaspheme publicly.[11] Aharon Propes, the founder of Betar in Riga, became the full time chief commander in Poland on the basis of a shoe-string budget. Publicly the adulation of Jabotinsky was encouraged. Several decades later, the official chronicler of Betar could write:

> The movement chose the warrior for the Hebrew state, the fighter for the glory of Israel, the perfect Zionist, the man of Hebrew culture and language alive in the Diaspora, the founder of the Jewish Legion, the defender of Jerusalem and the prisoner of Acre, the man who stood at the gate of the people – against external enemies and internal traitors, the man who awakened others, encouraged them, demanded from them and obliged them to act. This was a whole-hearted choice made by the entire movement, even if some of its leaders did not see the position of Head of Betar in the same way.[12]

Jabotinsky self-evidently saw himself as a man with a mission – an educator and transformer of Jewish youth, the creator of the new Jew. Yet this all came at a price. As early as 1926, he complained in a letter to his wife that he was being turned into a myth, akin to a wunder-rebbe.[13] In his article 'Fascist Zionism' in 1925, he ironically attacked the adulation of Weizmann, yet he too became 'a hero of the people', the object of the cult of personality. Indeed he expressed his profound dislike of this in a letter to Miriam Lange in August 1927.[14] This did not dissipate, however, but reached new heights of idolization.

Several weeks before the 17th Zionist Congress, Jabotinsky once more attempted to create a strong youth movement. This was, in part, his reaction to the perceived irrelevance of the Zionist Organization and his desire to convince his colleagues of this fact. The development of Betar offered a second opportunity to build an organization in his image. In April 1931, Betar staged its first formal conference in Danzig. Sixteen European countries with the exception of England attended and represented a membership of 22,000 in 21 countries. Significantly over 60 per cent of the membership resided in Poland. It was decided that children would become eligible for membership at 12 and after eight years of training and education would be expected to emigrate to Palestine. At 20 they could join the Revisionist movement, if they wished. Jabotinsky gave the opening address on 'The Task of Youth in the Zionist Movement' and he reiterated several themes which he would continue to repeat throughout the 1930s. Jabotinsky told his young audience that Jews were faced with the moral collapse of a generation that had originally been fired by heroism, but those brave intentions had dissolved in a series of compromises. The 'old Zionists' were once more covered in 'the grime of the ghetto'. They had started off as 'slaves who mutiny and leave Egypt (but) prove in the end to belong to Goshen'.[15] This, Jabotinsky explained, was due to the fact that Herzl's contemporaries were not up to his standard – and with his early death, matters had degenerated. Therefore a new generation – a Herzlian generation – must be prepared for tomorrow's struggles. He told them that:

> We must bring up the youth of Israel under the spell of three principles:
> Zionism means a Jewish state; and Jordan is the name of the river that runs in the middle of that Jewish state;
> No classes in Zionism whether capitalist or factory hand, farmer, lawyer, policeman, or chimney-sweep. In Zionism and in Palestine, you are but a puppet dangling from a wire and playing a prescribed part, and the hand that pulls the wire is called the state-in-building;
> Lawyer or farmer or chimney-sweep: learn above all, how to resist violence.
> If this education is successful, I believe that it will give us a Herzlian generation.[16]

Betar was based on the Czechoslovak youth group and gymnastic society, Sokol, which idolized the founder of the state, Tomas Masaryk. He was admired too by the Jews for defending the Jewish shoemaker, Leopold Hilsner, against a blood libel in Czechoslovakia that he had murdered a young girl. Moreover, Masaryk had declared his sympathies for Zionism and the national regeneration of the Jews as early as 1899.[17] But perhaps the most important reference point for Jabotinsky was the establishment of the Czechoslovak Legion in Russia during World War I and the successful emergence of the new state. This all followed a certain pattern. Sokol had actually been established in 1861 shortly after the triumph of the Risorgimento in Italy by Joseph Scheiner, a director of the Bank of Bohemia, in the hope that it would evolve into a national militia. Sokol, in turn, was based on the Turnverein – the gymnastic societies created by Friedrich Ludwig Jahn after the invasion of the German states by Napoleon. Jahn was an ardent nationalist who was also sympathetic to Polish and Italian nationalism, but he clearly did not believe in the emergence of a German state on the multi-national Hapsburg model. He believed in a mono-national state. 'Hybrid animals are incapable of reproducing themselves: bastard peoples, similarly, lack the life force of proper nations.'[18] Jahn disregarded the French concept of citizenship, but believed instead in 'the volk of deeds' which meant excluding all outsiders including Jews. 'Its outward community of state will maintain itself through the force of internal links, it will not lose its way in escapism in the manner of gypsies and Jews.'[19] Jahn opened the first gymnasium in 1811 amidst a mix of patriotism and fervent nationalism, but then commanded a volunteer corps in the final struggle against Napoleon. The gymnasia soon became centres for political gatherings and were subsequently closed down in 1818, Jahn was arrested in 1819 and sentenced to five years' imprisonment.[20]

For Jabotinsky who dreamed of building a new Jewish Legion from Betar, the Czechoslovak Sokol was the palatable paradigm – and the overtones of German nationalism safely glossed over. Above all, it was in clear contrast to the policies of Weizmann which were effectively 'a grotesque and distorted Ahad Ha'am's'. The latter, he argued, had definitely espoused the idea of a Jewish majority in Palestine.[21] He was extremely scathing about Martin Buber who at that time favoured a bi-national state of Arabs and Jews:

> To them (Jewish youth) is babbled the doctrine of Martin Buber, a typical provincial in outlook, a third rate would-be thinker, with nine parts twisted phrases to one part ideas – and these – neither his own nor of value. This youth is taught to regard Zionism as a dream and that it is desirable for it to remain a dream, never to become a reality.[22]

Zionism had been so watered down, he argued, that it needed a motivating injection of other ideologies such as socialism. In polemically attacking his other central opponent, the Labour Zionists, Jabotinsky argued that one could not have two ideals just as you could not have two gods:

> An ideal is jealous and exclusive; otherwise it is not an ideal. Grafting a bit of some other 'ism' upon the sapling of Zionism can only have the same result as grafting an orange twig onto a lemon trunk: the lemon disappears and the tree will bear oranges.[23]

Sometimes zealous members of Betar took this to unexpected lengths such as the criticism of jazz in the United States movement. Such music appreciation was deemed 'a disgrace to our Zionist ideal' – and what was wrong with Palestinian dances? [24]

Jabotinsky described this ideological monism in the context of the Biblical prohibition (Sha'atnez) in Leviticus of mixing different kinds such as wool and linen.[25] Other familiar images were projected. 'Within the Temple where the altar of Zion stands, there is no room for other altars.'[26] This, he surmised, did not denigrate the nobility or holiness of the excluded idea, but it did focus on the one – and only – ideal, that of building the Jewish state.

Fascism and Communism

In reality, on an ideological and socio-economic level, Jabotinsky opposed socialism. In this, he followed Herzl who even at the first Zionist Congress went out of his way to disclaim that the movement was social democratic, but represented the entire nation.[27] He viewed the class struggle advocated by the Histadrut as diversionary and counter-productive to the ideal of state-building. In Jabotinsky's eyes, there were no classes, no proletarians, and no well-to-do – only pioneers. Jabotinsky argued that conditions in Palestine were different from Britain and France:

> The worker, if he is a Zionist, cannot afford the luxury of running a factory because the scope of colonization is narrowed. The manufacturer, too, if he is a Zionist, must not tolerate impossible working conditions in his enterprise which then would lose its colonizatory significance. In other words, in Palestine, higher and mightier than class interests, the common interest of rebuilding the Jewish state reigns supreme. Consequently, there should be no talk of class war, a system, the harmful tendency of which is manifested when one side threatens the other by means of strikes and lockouts. In Palestine, such conflicts must always be settled in one manner only: through obligatory national arbitration.[28]

A 'herem' (proscribing), Jabotinsky stated, would be pronounced on the 'two national crimes – strikes and lockouts'.[29] Jabotinsky railed against the Histadrut's commanding monopoly of workers' interests. The Histadrut demanded that all workers should be members of the Histadrut. If a manufacturer employed non-Histadrut labour – they were often members of Betar – a strike would be declared. Jabotinsky went further and advised the members of Betar to break the strike.

> Such a strike must not merely be disrupted, it must be made impossible; whether one is cursed with the cry of 'scab' or not. An unjust and state disintegrating strike must be mercilessly broken as well as any other attempt to damage the reconstruction of the Jewish State. Finally, it is the right and duty of Betar itself to decide as to the justice or injustice of a conflict, help the former and break up the latter.[30]

Thus, in the strike at Frumin's Biscuit factory in 1932, there was violence when non-Histadrut labour was employed. Jabotinsky urged his followers to confront the Histadrut in articles such as 'Yes, Break it'[31] and 'The Rule of the Fist in the Yishuv'[32] Betar publications spoke, in turn, of the 'Left terror', 'the red tainted rulers of Palestine'[33] and suggested, 'the red propaganda of the teachers among the children in our schools must be stopped.'[34] 'Haneder' (The Vow) – the poetic oath which Jabotinsky wrote for Betar – proclaimed that no 'redness' would be added to the blue and white of the Zionist flag. The language of the European right was well and truly employed.

Betar workers were organized in the Irgun HaTsohar u Betar (the Organization of Revisionist and Brit Trumpeldor Workers). Following the Revisionists' Conference in Vienna at the autumn of 1932, a decision was taken to establish a second 'national Histadrut' whose members would not be governed by the class struggle. Moreover, Jabotinsky criticized the 'soft-hearted' Jewish bourgeoisie who financially supported the Zionist enterprise without condemning the Histadrut's practices and the Left in general. Such a weak-kneed approach, Jabotinsky argued, would undermine liberty in Palestine and compromise the freedom to build a Jewish land.[35] Jabotinsky's solution to the problem of strikes and lockouts was to replace the class struggle with a Supreme Institute of National Arbitration. This judicial body would be 'entrusted with the task of fixing in every single instance the limit up to which the wages of the workers and the employees can be increased without disturbing the opportunity of making normal profits.'[36] The class struggle, Jabotinsky pointed out, would weaken the Zionists in Palestine both economically and politically and allow their opponents to exploit such a division. The National Arbitration plan had first been mooted at the Revisionist World Conference at the end of 1928. The Histadrut and the Labour movement angrily accused Jabotinsky of imitating the doctrine of economic corporativism of European authoritarian states.

Jabotinsky projected a growing antipathy for the USSR. In his eyes, Soviet Communism had uprooted the idyllic Odessa of his youth and besmirched Russian culture through its mindless indolence. From a political point of view, Jabotinsky argued that the international Communist movement and Zionism were in conflict in key areas. Marxism-Leninism had always opposed Zionism and since 1924 had actively suppressed the Zionist movement in the USSR through arrests, imprisonment and exile. Moreover, the Soviet Union promoted the Arab national cause in the hope of creating a unitary Arab state as a bulwark against British imperialism. He also argued that espousing Communism would mean alienating the Jewish middle class – and 90 per cent of the funding for construction was provided by the Jewish bourgeoisie. 'Zionism cannot live in Communist air…for our Zionist lungs, Communism is a suffocating gas.'[37] He advised those of his followers who saw beauty in the universalism of

Communism to choose – there could be no diversionary distractions in the construction of the Jewish state.

There was a parallel approach towards Italian Fascism. The distinction was that few Jews were attracted to Fascism – although some Italian Jews had been among the founders of Mussolini's movement. For example, a former chairman of Pro Israele, Giovanni Colonna di Cesarò, had been an early Fascist, but generally it attracted semi-assimilated Italian Jews with no interest in Zionism. Jabotinsky understood Fascism as an attack on individualism, rationalism and the legacy of the French revolution. Although an admirer of D'Annunzio,[38] Jabotinsky, in the 1920s, had been scathing in condemning Italian Fascists:

> There is today a country where 'programmes' have been replaced by the word of one man. Whatever he says is the programme. Popular vote is scorned. That country is Italy; the system is called Fascism; to give their prophet a title, they had to coin a new term – 'Duce' – which is a translation of that most absurd of all English words – 'leader' – buffaloes follow a leader. Civilized men have no 'leaders'.[39]

Indeed, Italian Fascism was not anti-Semitic even if Mussolini blew hot and cold towards the Jews per se.[40] Although Mussolini had ousted the Jewish socialist, Claudio Treves, as editor of *Avanti* in 1912, several Jews were members of the Fasci di combattimento and participated in the march on Rome. Jabotinsky's main supporter in Italy, Leone Carpi, had attacked Mussolini in an article after the latter invoked the idea of a 'complici ebrei' – a Jewish conspiracy in the aftermath of the October Revolution connecting the capitalist Rothschild and the Communist Bela Kun.[41] In 1922, Mussolini denounced Zionism for being a tool of British imperialism which compromised the loyalty of Italian Jews. Jabotinsky, himself, criticized Mussolini in a long letter to him for his suggestion that Italy should become a supporter of pan-Arabism and that it would ultimately benefit the country.[42] Later in the 1930s, Jabotinsky was less condemnatory of Italy. In 1935, he argued – from the point of view of the Jewish situation in Italy – that although there was a total absence of freedom of speech and civic rights per se, 'the Italian brand of Fascist ideology is, at least, an ideology of racial equality'. In 1936, he told an audience in Prague that Italy regarded the equality of Jewish rights as 'something sacred' and that it had 'honestly fulfilled all its obligations' to the Mandate.[43] The reason for this apparent volte-face was the possibility that Italy might replace Britain as the dominant power in the Middle East. Jabotinsky finally concluded that it would actually be in the Zionist interest for a British-Italian rapprochement to take place. Rivalry in the Mediterranean area between the two powers would mean Italy utilizing pan-Arabism as a stick with which to beat its British rival. Therefore, co-operation between Britain and Italy would benefit Zionism. The British believed, however, that the Revisionists were wholeheartedly sympathetic to the Italians and noted that only *Hayarden*, from all the Zionist press in Palestine, reported the invasion of Abyssinia from a pro-Italian perspective. *The Times* reported that the Italian government was the only one which sent official greetings to a Revisionist Conference in Vienna.[44] When official sanctions were threatened against Italy following the Abyssinian adventure, a leading Jewish Fascist, Corrado Tedeschi, was despatched to Palestine to garner support amongst right-wing Zionists. Indeed, following a meeting with Itamar ben-Avi, the editor of *Doar Hayom*, a pro-Italian article appeared in the paper.[45] Although Tedeschi met with different representatives of the Jews in Palestine, he subsequently reported that Italy's best friends in Palestine were the Revisionists.[46] In addition, Betar possessed a Marine school in Civitavecchia during the 1930s and Jabotinsky presumably did not wish to prejudice its operations. Therefore in addressing Betar's sea cadets in Italy in 1934, Jabotinsky instructed its members not to become involved in domestic politics:

> Do not intervene in any party discussions concerning Italy. Do not express any opinions about Italian politics. Do not criticize the present regime in Italy or the former regime. If you are asked about your political and social beliefs answer, 'I am a Zionist. My greatest desire is the Jewish state, and in our country I oppose class warfare. This is the whole of my creed.' [47]

In the fraught age of mesmerizing ideologies, Jabotinsky proclaimed his pride in and adherence to nineteenth century liberalism. He instinctively attempted to distance himself from the extremes of Left and Right. Yet the 1930s was not the decade to preach liberalism to increasingly radicalized and discriminated youth.

In one sense, any public mention of the virtues of liberalism was to implicitly condemn those of his followers – especially in Palestine – who had an 'understanding' for authoritarian regimes such as Mussolini's and derided parliamentarianism. In an article entitled 'Grandpa Liberalism' in 1932, he predicted that liberalism would ultimately triumph.[48] In a private letter to the editor of the British liberal daily *News Chronicle* in December 1938, Jabotinsky predicted a come-back for liberalism to triumph over the 'barrack-room religions' of Fascism and Communism. He wrote:

> I understand some Jewish opponents of my brand of Zionism pretend to suspect me of being pro-Fascist. I am just the opposite: an instinctive hater of all kinds of polisei-staat, utterly sceptical of the value of discipline and power and punishment.[49]

As Europe approached a new World War, Jabotinsky's sentiments about a faded liberalism were uttered in private rather than in public. They were uttered at a time when the Maximalists in his movement were in the ascendancy. The spirit of the times had changed. Liberalism had decidedly been rejected.

THE COLOURING OF BETAR

Ironically, Jabotinsky's model for Betar was not the Italian Fascist Ballila but the Czech Sokol of Masaryk.[50] Yet his forging of Betar projected other images. What Jabotinsky saw as inspirational, others saw as totalitarian. Jabotinsky defined the self-sacrificing Zionist pioneer:

> It is a piece of iron ready to be transformed into any part of the great machine which is building the Jewish state. You want a wheel? Take me. A cog, a plug, a screw, a nail? Here I am. A stonebreaker, a doctor, a teacher, a soldier for cannon-fodder? I am ready. I have no face, no features, no whims, and no name even: I am just an embodied abstraction of the word 'service'.[51]

Without expounding it, Jabotinsky saw himself as a second Herzl whom he described as a 'true aristocrat' – someone who had 'nothing to do with idiotic and ludicrous titles'.[52] Jabotinsky argued that the Jews had to discipline themselves and operate as a collective if they wished to succeed:

> What we Jews need, above all, is to learn moving as one, stepping with one step, striking with one stroke. I know the value of individualism – it is a great asset too. But the highest rung of civilization belongs to those who, though conscious and proud of their individuality, possess the power, at the moment of need, to conquer their own will, to fall in with the alignment of a nation, to act in their millions as though they were one single man or one single machine. A multitude incapable of acting together, though each of its members be a genius, is called a mob: only the lore of unison makes of them a nation. This is what Herzl wanted to teach us when he created the Congress: a Big Parade. Let our boys and girls learn it on small parades. A day may come when much will depend on the question whether the Jewish people are able, at a sign given from one centre, to respond all the world over, with one voice – like a man, 'like a machine'.[53]

'Discipline,' Jabotinsky argued, 'is the subordination of a mass to a leader.'[54] That leader, in turn, would submit to another along the chain of command. The imagery – and the reality – of brown-shirted Jewish youth, seemingly robotically operating as a machine, conjured up images of the authoritarian etatist regimes of interwar Europe in the minds of their liberal and leftist opponents. In the age of Mussolini, Salazar, Franco – and of course, Hitler – Jabotinsky had created a controversial persona for Betar – albeit unintentionally. Jabotinsky countered that it was a reactionary idea to ban uniforms from civil life – and that dress was a matter of ceremony – and gave the example of the Englishman's penchant to dine alone in a dinner jacket. Yet the perception remained in the Jewish psyche that Betar was simply another branch of

European Fascism. Thus a young leader of Betar in South Africa could write in 1934: 'We cannot be Zionists and socialists at the same time. In that Betar monism – one leader, one aim, one ideal – lies the great difference between us and other youth bodies.'[55] Herzl was portrayed in Revisionist circles as a radical. Joseph Klausner wrote in a Betar publication that:

Herzl's extremism belongs to that type which is positive and creative; the extremism which builds a nation and creates a state. Such extremism is always successful. It always creates even when it seems as if it were destroying; it creates even when it criticizes. It is not the extremists who are dangerous but the opportunists. Those who yield and compromise are dangerous because they weaken the creative forces and the power of resistance to the evil, and the strength of revolt against the existing and outworn. Nothing really great emerged from opportunism.[56]

Yet Jabotinsky also brought certainty to marginalized and directionless youth. The religiosity of the cause attracted many who required clarity and unambiguity in their lives:

There are no 'brands' of Zionism, but one real Zionism. The Zionism that knows not of discrepancies, the one that is logical, faithful to the whole aim of a virile, revolutionary movement. It does not suffer from contradictory qualms and does not seek a raison d'être.[57]

In an era of persecution where the Jews haplessly awaited their fate, Jabotinsky gave both hope and a vision of the future. Betar, he proclaimed, would be 'a new psychological race of Jewry'.[58] The opening stanza of the Hymn of Betar proclaimed:

Betar
From a heap of decay and dust
With blood and sweat
Will arise a generation
Proud and generous and strong

Betar were told that whatever their background, each one was a descendant of the Kings of Israel –

Crowned with the diadem of David
In light or in darkness never forget your crown

To remind his young audience of what had been, Jabotinsky would retrieve the past of old, frightened Jews by quoting Bialik's epic poem of the Kishinev pogrom – of Jews hiding in the cellar, silently watching killing and mutilation through cracks in the wall. The Betar oath was formulated and defined the parameters of Jabotinsky's new psychological race:

> I shall devote my life to the revival of the Jewish State with a Jewish majority on both sides of the Jordan;
> To this ideal of state building, I shall subordinate my own interests, as well as the calls of my house and class;
> The Hebrew language will be my language and the language of my offspring, both in Eretz Israel (Land of Israel) and in the Galut (Diaspora);
> I shall prepare and train myself for the defence of my people and the re-establishment of my motherland;
> I shall carefully endeavour to fulfil the principles of 'hadar' (majesty) in thought, word and deed, for I am conscious of the noble heritage of my people;
> I shall rise and answer the Betar mobilization – be it for the Legion or for labour, to go up to Zion, or for service in the Galut, be it near or far, I shall rise and go;
> I shall harken to the laws of Betar and obey the commands of its leaders as a man listens to his conscience; for the law of Betar reflects my own personal wishes and its leaders are my representatives.

A central defining feature of Betar's philosophy was that of self-defence. After all, as early as 1904, following the death of Herzl, Jabotinsky had spoken of 'we, the soldiers of his regiment'.[59] Clause 4 of the oath of Betar was to pledge to prepare and train 'for the defence of my people'. Jabotinsky defined 'the backbone of Betarism' as the great and stern business of training for defence'.[60] This was crucial to the national renaissance of the Jews. The ability to defend themselves conferred a sense of self-dignity – hadar. After Danzig, Jabotinsky reflected:

> To what do these youngsters who have so many names for their strivings aspire? They want a Jewish state; they want to be soldiers in a Jewish generation; they also want to drill, they want to behave with pride. I watched them for a week and was in quest of the riddle and finally thought that I found it in a Hebrew dictionary. It was the term that covered all they wanted, it was 'hadar betari'.[61]

History had maimed the Jews. The injury could only be healed through hadar, but it meant behaving with noblesse oblige:

> The new Jews must consist of noblemen who choose to chop wood, to hew stones and to carry water. The knave and the proverbial hick should be inconceivable among these new Jews. The street cleaner among them must not only possess a noble soul, but also the external finished manners of an exclusive caste – a soft, concise way of talking and knightly courtesy extended alike to the weak and powerful, to the friend and enemy.[62]

It meant sensitivity towards self-hygiene. A member of Betar should not eat noisily and quickly or stick out his elbows at dinner. He should walk quietly and not run upstairs at night. In the street, he should give up the right of way to a

lady, to a child, to every man. In Poland, such encouragement took on the
colouring of the Polish nobility. Herzl had promoted similar virtues amongst
his followers – all of which were derived from the Prussian nationalist
influences that he had absorbed in his university days. Girls were shown the
examples of Shulamit, Catherine the Great of Russia and Elizabeth I of
England rather than the 'empty headed flappers' of the 1920s.[63]

The new Jewish state would be a model of European civilization. Members of
Betar were educated to be the shapers of Israel. As Herzl had remarked, the
homeland would be a new Venice, not a Boer republic.
But above all, such educational sculpting meant military preparedness and the
ability to defend embattled Jews. In his closing speech to the Danzig
conference, Jabotinsky called for the militarization of Betar. Addressing Jewish
parents in 1939, Jabotinsky commented:

> Ever since I took up my first pen I have followed one vocation. I have spoilt your
> children; taught them to break discipline (and sometimes even windows), tried to
> persuade them that the true translation of 'komatz-alef-o' is not 'learn to read'
> but 'learn to shoot'. I have always done this and I have a suspicion that so far it
> has not done the children much harm.[64]

Girls were not exempt – they should not only be taught military training such
as 'shooting, marching and signalling' but also how to organize supplies and
sanitation.[65] But Jabotinsky's mention of 'komatz-alef-o' conjured up the
imagery of an old rabbi teaching children the alef-bet – the Hebrew alphabet.
In a seminal article entitled 'Afn Pripitshek' (By the Hearthside), Jabotinsky
utilized the familiarity of this image to tell his followers that the equivalent
learning curve was to learn military skills and above all – 'learn to shoot':

> For this generation now growing before our eyes and on whose shoulders will fall
> the responsibility for the greatest turning point in our history, the alef-bet is very
> plain and simple: Young men, learn to shoot!
> The force of historical reality teaches us a very simple lesson. We should all be
> educated people and learn to plough the land and to build houses and all be able
> to speak Hebrew and know our whole national literature from the Songs of
> Devorah until Avigdor Hameiri and Shlonsky but if we do not know how to
> shoot, then there is no hope.[66]

While Jabotinsky utilized the imagery of frightened Jews in a cellar to contrast
the old with the new, it was the massacre of Jews in Hebron in August 1929
which both shocked and galvanized young Jews. Many members of Betar such
as Yitzhak Shamir only joined the movement in the aftermath of the Hebron
massacre and Jabotinsky's encouragement ensured recruits who would be
willing 'to defend Jewish lives, honour and property'.[67] Shamir – whose parents
were originally Bundists – was also radicalized through reading Jabotinsky's

articles in *Haynt* and *Moment* and attending his speeches in Bialystok and Warsaw, but, above all, he was particularly impressed by the sentiments expressed in the article 'Afn Pripitshek'.[68]

In Jabotinsky's eyes, the situation had worsened and the British were unable – and perhaps unwilling – to protect the Jews. The nucleus of a Jewish army could be established from a cadre of motivated youth. The military training would further inspire the disillusioned and the apathetic and induce a sense of national self-esteem. With the lack of progress at the Zionist Congress and his irritated frustration with its deliberations, Jabotinsky envisaged Betar as the builders of the Iron Wall which would protect the Jews.

In an article entitled 'The Meaning of Preparedness', Jabotinsky predicted in 1932 that 'restlessness and ferment' in the Middle East had 'almost always ended in a brawl. We must be realistic'.[69] A new war, he argued, must find the Jews prepared. This had not been the case in World War I when hardly ten thousand had volunteered for the Jewish Legion. If a hundred thousand had served, Jabotinsky pointed out, it would have made a great difference to the evolution of Zionism – not least at the Peace Conference. Any future opportunity must be seized.

> Dante has called it Fortuna. He tells us she passes by rapidly and inscrutably. Her hair is long, and by her hair we must seize her. One moment too late and we can no longer grasp her.[70]

Everyone was expected to play their part in the operation of the national machine. Jabotinsky threatened that those Betarim who had neglected their military training would no longer be tolerated. 'We must not allow any halfway measures about it.'[71]

The radicals in the Revisionist Party who were already beginning to influence the members of Betar enthusiastically followed Jabotinsky's line – and interpreted it differently. Yeivin, for example, believed that the carnage in World War I had buried the last vestiges of liberalism and justice. Only armed legions could guarantee the future. Pilsudski and Masaryk understood this, but, according to Jabotinsky, Weizmann did not. 'Thus they received the Balfour Declaration not as an act that demands physical reinforcement on the part of the Jews, but as a confirmation of their puerile faith that "the justness of the Zionist ideal will naturally triumph".'[72]

Training centres were established for members of Betar. Naval training was provided in Civitavecchia (1934) and in Riga (1935). Air force training was provided in Paris (1934), Lydda (1938), Johannesburg (1939) and New York

(1941). The symbolism of the first flight of a Betar glider at Rechovot in April 1937 was understood very well by Jabotinsky. But it was the maritime dimension of Zionism that was heavily promoted. The great increase in trade, immigrants and tourists since the end of World War I stressed the necessity to develop a Jewish fleet. Imports into Palestine more than quadrupled between 1920 and 1935. In 1934, only one school, the Zevulun Association, existed in Palestine with a support group in Poland. The Revisionists' Tel Chai fund subsidized a Betar squad for the training of seamen at the Consorzio della Scuale Professionali per la Maestranza Marittima of Civitavecchia in Italy at a cost of £5000 in the mid-1930s.[73] Other funding through the Jewish League for Navigation came from the Kirschners and Rothschilds of Paris.[74] Instruction in Italian and Hebrew accompanied a detailed course on navigation and was followed by advanced courses in ship-building, fishing and mechanics. Twenty-four cadets trained on the *Sara I* and visited numerous Mediterranean ports. During the second year, 50 trainees came from as far apart as Lithuania, Tripoli and Rhodesia. In Riga, Latvian Jews trained on the *Theodor Herzl*.[75] The very idea of Jews as sailors and airmen, fishermen and aircraft mechanics assisted in the creation of the image of the new Jew. Home-made uniforms and self-appointed officers raised the vision of what could be. Significantly, in all the ports that *Sara I* visited, large numbers of Jews came out to greet them in their astonishment. In the Diaspora, a 'kibbush ha'yam' (conquest of the sea) programme became part of the Betar agenda.[76]

MODELS FOR THE RADICALS

ITALY AND THE RISORGIMENTO

In his address to the world conference of Betar in Danzig in 1931, Jabotinsky spoke effusively about the new Jew – a creature who would be democratically self-abnegating, noble and patrician. Someone who would exude a knightly courtesy to the weak and powerful, to friend and foe alike. This 'remoulding of our habits'[1] – so as to repair 'the mutilations of history' – was defined by a programme of military training. Betar would emerge as the kernel of a new Jewish Legion. A resolution passed at the Danzig conference stated that:

> The aim of Betar is to organize and to educate the Jewish youth to be a vanguard for the Jewish people in their creation of a state. Every member of Betar is ready, at any moment, to be mobilized for the up building of a Jewish state and for its defence, if it so be requested by the leadership.[2]

Such military training was defined within the context of defensive and not offensive tactics. Military discipline was also viewed as a psychological bulwark against other attractive contemporary ideologies. Jabotinsky warned in several articles that it was all too easy for Jewish youth to become attached to the ideologies of the day:

> When a procession with fine banners parades on that avenue, they cannot restrain themselves; they must shove their heads out of the window, stretch forth their hands and yell 'Me too!' Although what 'too' means is not important – it may signify Marx, Lenin, Gandhi, perhaps tomorrow Mussolini.[3]

The prime model – to which all aspirations were directed - was the Jewish Legion. Jabotinsky had written unambiguously about the necessity for an Iron Wall to protect the Jewish people in Palestine. Yet the Legion had been disbanded by the British – and the responsibility for this act, according to the Revisionists, was attributable to the vacillating attitude of the 'old Zionists'. Yehoshua Heschel Yeivin had written on Jabotinsky's fiftieth birthday in 1930, 'All the Jews had laughed at Mr Jabotinsky's idea of building a living wall out of Jewish youths armed with swords, but Zionism will only succeed with Legions and fail without it.'[4] The Jewish Legion thus possessed enormous symbolic value – and not least in the eyes of the Jews themselves. Supporters of the idea of the Legion such as Jabotinsky, Weizmann, Ben-Gurion and Yitzhak Ben-Zvi all noted that the national revival of nations as the Poles, Czechs. Armenians, Ukrainians – and indeed the Arabs – had gone hand-in-hand with the formation of their own military forces. Political ends and the use of military force could not be divorced from one another. Ben-Zvi had even argued that the Jewish Legion was merely the complementary obverse of the Zionist Congress.[5]

But such military formations had to have their models. Three were dominant for Betar in the 1930s. The first, projected fulsomely by Jabotinsky, was the example of Garibaldi and the Italian Risorgimento which was supremely representative of his admiration for nineteenth century national liberalism. This was also manifested in the struggle of the Poles against Tsarist domination and their internationalist slogan 'for your liberty and ours'. In addition, there was another Polish model – the exclusionist narrow nationalism of Pilsudski's new Poland in the inter-war years. Finally, the struggle most pertinent to their own – both in terms of time and in terms of opponent – the Irish demand for independence from the British. Italy, Poland and Ireland were all Catholic nations with a strong national-religious identity.

Jabotinsky strongly promoted Garibaldi as an icon and in its train, the romanticism of Italian nationalism. This, he implied, derived from his sojourn as a student in Rome at the turn of the century. In the 1930s, he recalled, often in the most idealistic terms, the liberalism of fin-de-siècle Italy – perhaps almost as a mechanism to distance himself from the tainting influence of Mussolini's regime. Herzl's conversation with the King of Italy was often remembered as a benchmark of tolerance and the successful integration of Jews into Italian society.[6] During his 'evacuation' campaign to exit the distressed areas of Eastern Europe in the late 1930s, Jabotinsky continually praised pre-1914 Italy for its negotiations with the United States, Argentina and Brazil to secure facilities for its emigrants to those countries. In his autobiography, Italy famously became his 'spiritual homeland' and he recalled that the legend of Garibaldi was all-pervasive at that time in Italy.[7] His views on 'the nation, state and society' were said to have emerged during his time in Italy. In his biography, he writes about the legend of Garibaldi and the writings of Mazzini,[8] but he also admits that the coalescence of the idea of a Jewish state and the

Risorgimento only took place somewhat subconsciously – 'perhaps I didn't realize it.'[9] Moreover, recent research has noted that nowhere in his numerous articles for the Odessa press in his student days in Rome between 1898 and 1901 does he embrace Italian nationalism – or any of its great figures. In fact, his early writings suggest someone of 'radically individualistic, anti-nationalistic, quasi-nihilistic and aestheticistic' views who denounced the monarchy and attempts at empire building.[10] Indeed, in 1933 Gabriele D'Annunzio was described as 'closer to his heart than Tolstoy and Turgenev',[11] yet Jabotinsky had attacked the writer in 1901 for moving to a nationalist position and abandoning progressive causes.[12] Significantly, on his return to Russia, Jabotinsky secured the post of chief cultural critic of *Odesskie novosti* rather than that of a political journalist. Back in Odessa, he corresponded with his friend Arrigo Rizzini and others in Italy, but no mention was made of Italian nationalism in any pre-1914 letters. An article written in 1912 utilizes a statue of Garibaldi to defend the national struggle of the Italians.[13] It was only the possibility of Italy's reversing its early declaration of neutrality during World War I and entering the war on the side of the Allies – with all the implications for British policy in the Middle East and the revived hope of establishing a Jewish Legion – that propelled Jabotinsky to write about Italy. Garibaldi and Cavour were thus raised in correspondence a couple of days after Italy declared war on Austro-Hungary, but specifically in the context of Zionist policies.[14] It is clear that by the 1930s, early Italian nationalism was being promoted for the benefit of Betar and the Revisionists. Labriola and Ferri were recalled in the autobiography (1932-3) and Benedetto Croce in 'The Revolt of the Old Men'[15] (1937). Even his teacher, Maffeo Pantaleoni, was mentioned positively in the article, 'Crisis of the Proletariat'[16] (1932), despite the fact that he had attacked Mussolini for being susceptible to the blandishments of Italian Jews.[17] Hence the Hymn of Betar concluded with a veritable echo of Garibaldi and his followers – 'to die or conquer the mountain'. This was not only intended to encourage his followers, but also to counteract the accusations of his Labour opponents that the Revisionists were no better than Jewish Fascists. For example, his recollections of his early life in Odessa were written at the height of the Revisionist-Labour strife in Palestine.

Jabotinsky in his student days in Rome never seemingly warmed to Filippo Marinetti and Futurism.[18] But Marinetti condemned anti-Semitism in May 1933[19] and Jabotinsky's romanticist and cosmopolitan outlook could well have owed something to Futurism. As Marinetti commented in a speech in November 1919:

> Futurism carries within it a moral foundation more cosmopolitan than nationalist, despite its nationalist appeal, its calls to the Italian race, its wilful amorality, and remains difficult to categorize within strict and coherent racist

parameters of the classical type.[20]

There were several conflicting emotions in Jabotinsky's attitude towards inter-war Italy. He retained a great affection for the Italy of his youth and his teachers, but he ridiculed Mussolini and his ideology. He was also irritated that some Italian Revisionists were sympathetic to the Fascist regime as were the Maximalists and Activists in Palestine. Yet he explored contacts with Mussolini's Italy as a means of placing pressure on Britain prior to the passing of anti-Jewish legislation in November 1938. By 1939, Jabotinsky was arguing that Italy's relations with the Arabs far outweighed its concern with the Jewish question. There was, he believed, 'a gigantic, irreconcilable, "fiendish" conflict' between Italy and Arab nationalism.[21] He suggested that within a generation or two, the British and the French would leave Egypt and Tunisia as still part of the Arab world. The Italians, he believed, wished to colonize Tripoli and Tunis to relieve over-population in Italy itself. The Italians and the Arabs would eventually fight each other – and this would give the Jews 'political elbow room'.

Moreover, the attempt of Jabotinsky to counteract the accusations of 'Fascist' and jibes such as 'Vladimir Hitler' were hindered by the desire to maintain and expand the Maritime School at Civitavecchia. An internal note in the Italian Foreign Ministry detailed a meeting with Jabotinsky at the end of 1935. It commented:

> (Jabotinsky) confirmed the favourable attitude toward Italy and Fascism on the part of Zionist Revisionism since its position towards General Zionism, which is now under the control of the democracies, is the same as the position and function Fascism has toward liberal and socialist democracies.[22]

Given that Jabotinsky was attempting to secure more assistance from the Italians who in turn were attempting to exploit any anti-British stance, this probably does not reflect his innermost views. A bigger question mark hangs over the radical Revisionists in Palestine who were far more sympathetic to the Italians. In October 1934, Wolfgang Von Weisl sent a telegram to the Italian Ministry of Foreign Affairs requesting them to admit:

> as assistants in Fascist institutes of any kind, for the entire period necessary, four young Zionists the Revisionist Party would send to the kingdom at its own expense, with the intention of having them understand the spirit – and learn in detail – the mechanisms of Fascist organizations.[23]

Von Weisl further pointed out that if successful, the four would become instructors of the Revisionist masses. All this pointed to the widening ideological chasm between Jabotinsky and his radical adherents in Palestine.

POLAND AND PILSUDSKI

Jabotinsky also took a considerable interest in Poland – and in the parallels between Poles and Jews. Poland fought to overcome the effect of three partitions. Indeed, Poland did not exist as a sovereign state between 1795 and 1918. During that period, four major insurrections were crushed by the Russians. Both Prussia and Russia conspired to suppress Polish culture, language and faith. This, in turn, catalysed the development of a creed of self-sacrifice within a burning romantic nationalism. Priests and poets combined to create a messianic vision of a Poland that had been liquidated but would rise again. The last partitions of Poland had taken place during the French Revolution and Kosciuszko's revolt at the beginning of 1794 was inspired by the Jacobins. The belief of the Poles in France was absolute and intense and two legions served Napoleon in Italy, Germany and Spain. Moreover, the Grand Duchy of Warsaw existed for eight years and more than 100,000 Poles participated in Napoleon's invasion of Russia in 1812. Napoleon, the liberator-emperor, evolved into an icon for Polish romantic nationalists. Indeed, throughout the nineteenth century, he was transformed into a Polish beacon of hope amidst all the suffering. A woodcut on the centenary of Napoleon's death in 1921 shows the leader of the new Poland, Jósef Pilsudski, awarding the Virtuti Militari Cross to Napoleon. The song of the Polish Legion which became the National Anthem in 1926 commenced with the survivalist sentiment, 'Poland has not perished yet.'[24] Jews travelled along a similar pathway – both because they were affected by the same historical currents and that they comprised a sizeable national minority in Poland. Jews had fought in the Polish revolts of 1794, 1830 and 1863 and were even encouraged by the principal poet of the Polish struggle, Adam Mickiewicz, to establish their own Legion in order to liberate Palestine.[25] Yet the Jews ultimately were outside the Polish national revolt – excluded as non-Poles.

Like the Jews, the Poles felt betrayed by the promises of the West, but were sustained by a purposeful religion. A Polish Diaspora had been created – and with the crushing of each revolt, was reinforced and supplemented through a new exodus of the intelligentsia. Generations later, the Diaspora still expressed a deep solidarity with the homeland even though most had never lived there. Poles wanted a restoration of national sovereignty, but few expatriate Poles had any idea where the borders should be situated. Some Poles even adopted the idea of a permanently dispersed people, Polonia. All these currents resonated in the Jewish psyche.

Modern Poland emerged in 1918 out of the collapse of the great empires that had originally devoured it. An independent Poland under Jósef Pilsudski had truly arisen from the ashes and although the national movement was, at best, indifferent to Jews, it was indirectly highly influential in shaping the Revisionist movement and Betar. Pilsudski's objective was not simply to restore Poland to the European community of nations, but to reverse the tides of history and to create a federation of Poland, Lithuania, Byelorussia and the Ukraine. Poland would become a great power once more.

Pilsudski reasoned that Russia would only be brought to her knees by her imperial neighbours, Germany or Austro-Hungary. The logic of 'the enemy of my enemy is my friend' was first employed by Pilsudski during the Russo-Japanese war of 1904. Japanese intelligence trained Polish Socialist Party (PPS) militants in bomb making in order to cause as much difficulty for the Russians on their western border and also funded Pilsudski. Following a split in the ranks of the PPS, Pilsudski remained with the nationalist faction and was left in control of the military wing. Killings, harassment and armed robberies were an integral part of the armed struggle.

With the drift towards world war, Pilsudski embarked on developing a military force and secured the backing of the Austrians. The Japanese had previously refused Pilsudski's request to support a Polish Legion, composed of American expatriates and prisoners of war, but the Austrians were not so squeamish. Thus, within a couple of days of the outbreak of World War I, Pilsudski had mobilized three companies of Polish riflemen and invaded Russian territory. Both sides on the Eastern front attempted to utilize Polish discontent to embarrass their enemy. It was not long before both Germany and Austro-Hungary promised to establish a new kingdom of Poland. In response, the Tsarist regime too hinted at Polish independence whilst Kerensky's Provisional Government promised a free Polish state after the February revolution.

In the 1930s, both Jabotinsky and Betar attempted to draw lessons from Pilsudski's political and military odyssey. The focal point of any analysis was the use of force. Jabotinsky saw as paramount the development of an army which Pilsudski had used to great political effect. The Polish brigades of 1914, as Jabotinsky noted, were symbols of Polish nationalism. Indeed, in his autobiography, Pilsudski commented that he 'wanted Poland which had forgotten the sword so entirely since 1863 to see it flashing in the air in the hands of her own soldiers'.[26] The Jews were similarly promised help to advance the Zionist cause by both Britain and Germany – of which the Balfour Declaration and the Jewish Legion were the most self-evident examples. Both Jabotinsky and Pilsudski appreciated grand gestures, military marches and the psychological importance of a smart uniform – often as a substitute for real political support. Pilsudski and Jabotinsky were both indifferent to religion unless it could be used to further the cause. Pilsudski had actually converted from Catholicism to Protestantism to marry – and then back again for political reasons. Both looked to an embellished, sometimes mythical, past which could be utilized in the political struggle. Jabotinsky also realized that there were fundamental differences – the most central was that a majority of Poles were living in Poland. Their dispersion had been recent and limited. While Poland had been seen by the Russians as the repository to keep out unwanted Jews, Jabotinsky understood it as the focus of concerted Revisionist Zionist activity amongst the Jewish masses.

Betar and the Revisionist radicals in Palestine viewed the figure of Pilsudski differently from Jabotinsky. In contrast to Jabotinsky, they selected instead his period of armed struggle – the PPS as a national liberation movement – as their model rather than the Legion. Pilsudski's alliances with Russia's wartime enemies impressed. He was the leader of his men – the 'Kommendant' who was adored by all. As he wrote on the eve of the Bezdany train robbery in September 1908:

> I fight and die only because I cannot live in the shithouse that is our life. It is an insult – do you hear? It insults me as a dignified, unenslaved human being. Let others play at growing flowers or at socialism, or at Polishness or at whatever. I cannot! This is not sentimentality, not procrastination, not a route to social evolution or anything else. It is ordinary human dignity. I wish to win….neither despair, nor self-sacrifice, guide, but the will to win and to prepare for victory.[27]

Even as leader of Poland after his coup, he favoured non-party blocs and entertained the possibility of pre-emptive military strikes – against Hitler and Germany in particular. He also suffered from depression. Pilsudski was a distant man of few words and not averse to using coarse language on public occasions. He had no real policy for national minorities and did not truly understand the economic difficulties that his country was plunging into, yet he remained deeply admired by his men. Moreover, his Legionnaires coalesced into a political grouping so as to establish a political base for him. This took place at the same time as Mussolini's march on Rome – and many Legionnaires looked with favour on the rise of Italian Fascism. The assassination of the Polish president, a general strike and the collapse of the economy paved the way for Pilsudski's coup d'état in 1926. Civil rights were often held in abeyance and a dictatorship prevailed for the best part of a decade. But the regime did not rule through the application of naked terror and the suppression of representative bodies, although Pilsudski undoubtedly retained the power to make the final decision. All these events moulded the world outlook of the inter-war generation of Polish Jews – and especially the young members of Betar. It was Pilsudski the conspirator and advocate of the armed struggle that was dominant, not Pilsudski the legionnaire and politician.

Jews in an independent Poland were, however, in a parlous position. Poles consisted of less than 70 per cent of the population – the rest were Ukrainians, Byelorussians, Germans, Russians, Lithuanians – and Jews. Yitzhak Gruenbaum's admonitions to secure the rights of autonomy for national minorities in the Polish constitution were rejected. His suggestions for autonomy in the Minorities Treaty were not acceptable to the international community. The Jews in Poland manifested all the attributes of an ethnic group meriting autonomous instruments of governance – newspapers and publishing houses in Hebrew, Yiddish and Polish, large numbers of Jewish schools, numerous and varied social and welfare organizations. Jabotinsky viewed the situation of the Jews as something endemic to the Jewish condition in Eastern Europe, a core product of the mixing of peoples and the continual redrawing of borders in Eastern Europe. He argued that governments could in reality do little to change this – that the organic hostility to a scattered minority was inherent in the situation.[28] Jabotinsky believed that most of the blame originated with Polish governments before Pilsudski's regime had attained power – his coup d'état had merely exacerbated the hardship inflicted on the Jews. Poland had thus become 'the most tragic of all the ghettos'.[29] Jabotinsky therefore wrote an appreciation of Pilsudski, but in the sense that Poland characterized the definition of an anti-Semite as one who dislikes the Jews more than he should:

> Pilsudski was neither a friend of the Jews nor their enemy: he was politely indifferent – 'politely' at all events in public. One cannot help suspecting (although he never said so) that he would not have thought it regrettable had Poland had only 1 per cent of Jews instead of 10 per cent; and as there were never enough jobs to go round, one may imagine (though he never mentioned it) that he wanted them to go to the Poles and not to the Jews. But pogroms and ghetto laws and such things were to him like a boil on the tip of the beloved's nose: Pilsudski would not have them in his Poland.[30]

Such sentiments decisively divided Polish Jewish opinion. Jabotinsky argued passionately that the Jews were ultimately unable to change their objective situation and that emigration was the only way out. The impoverishment of Polish Jewry and the broad discrimination against Jews in Poland had worsened dramatically in the 1930s.[31] In 1934, 25 per cent of the Jews living in major urban areas needed subsistence relief. Even donations for Palestine had decreased; the Palestine Foundation Fund (Keren Hayesod) was only able to collect 797,947 zloty in Congress Poland in 1933, compared to 1,194,463 zloty in 1930. For those Jews who believed that they could change Polish society for the better, Jabotinsky's comments were heretical and defeatist.

Pilsudski and the PPS had accepted a multi-national solution – perhaps within the much hoped-for parameters of a federated Greater Poland. Pilsudski's rival, Roman Dmowski, and the Endecja, on the other hand, believed in a Catholic mono-national state where Jews and other national minorities would occupy inferior positions – a Poland for the Poles. An ideology based on a belief that it was better demographically to secure a smaller Poland, but one where national minorities would either leave or accept polonization. While there was great bitterness between the two national camps, the increasingly difficult situation of their large Jewish minority did not preoccupy either movement.

In early November 1933, fighting between the supporters of Pilsudski and the Endecja forced the closure of Warsaw University. Two weeks later on the anniversary of the killing of Stanislaw Waclawski, an Endecja student, in the anti-Semitic riots in Vilna in 1931, supporters of Dmowski at the School of Commerce distributed leaflets urging Polish students not to sit next to Jewish ones. In response. Pilsudski's supporters did just the opposite and sought out Jewish students.[32] For Pilsudski, the Endecja was nothing more than 'a spit soiled gnome'.[33] Caught in between these two less than friendly power centres, the Jews broadly supported Pilsudski – both before and after the coup. His containment of Dmowski and the extreme Right proved to be the dominant factor in Jewish attitudes towards him.

Yet Polish nationalism was exclusivist; Jews were prevented from integrating. No de facto recognition was given in reality to national minorities. Many Jews found themselves in an undefined limbo outside the ghetto, but had found no place for themselves within normative society. While Polish Jews such as Yitzhak Shamir went to a Polish school and learned about the Polish national struggle and its great writers such as Mickiewicz and Sienkiewicz, he discovered that Jews had to inhabit a different world from the Poles. With growing discrimination and a deteriorating economic situation, Polish nationalism ironically served as a model for the aspiring Betar movement even though they were barred from entering its portals. Poland, on the one hand, personified the 'tragic ghetto', on the other it was seen by both Polish nationalists and Revisionist Zionists as a great power. Jabotinsky had certainly clarified his past ambivalence about Polish nationalism in the debate with Dmowski and his followers.[34] His sentiments changed from suspicion to appreciation. Pilsudski, for Jabotinsky, had been the great guide and educator of his people. He had overcome the tendency for schism and self-abasement and put Polish Romanticism to good use. On his death in 1935, Jabotinsky compared him with Trumpeldor, in a public eulogy in Cracow.[35] Yet most segments of the Polish Zionist movement had recoiled from overtly embracing Pilsudski and the promotion of military ritual. While he was certainly preferred to Dmowski, they also believed that Polish nationalism had taken a turn into a sectarian dead-end street. Revisionism, however, moved in the diametrically opposite direction from most Polish Zionists. Jabotinsky rationally explained Polish dislike of Jews as 'the anti-Semitism of things', caused essentially by the economic situation as opposed to 'the anti-Semitism of men', as typified by Nazi Germany,[36] and launched his evacuation plan to meet the situation. Polish nationalism was emulated and admired. The members of Betar – whether consciously or not – were fashioned by Pilsudski's Poland.[37] The fallacy was that Pilsudski's Poland was not a strong military power, Betar was not the Polish Legion and the liberation of Palestine was different from and more complex than the liberation of Poland. Its opponents claimed therefore that Revisionism had created a fantasy world, fuelled by a false messianism, to shield it from the numbing reality of powerlessness. In the words of one writer, 'Revisionism, it was held, created a fictitious militaristic world, a Zionist version of the imaginary world of Polish militarism' and this reflected the sad reality of oppressed Polish Jewry.[38] As the situation worsened in Poland and Pilsudski's successors were unable to hold back the forces of the Endecja, the raison d'être for military training to defend the Jewish homeland went beyond Jabotinsky's intention of mere education and character formation. In a period of general radicalization in Europe, members of Betar began to ask – to what purpose could military training be best applied? But for Jabotinsky, it was a question of defining and exalting the new Jew:

> Ritual demonstrates man's superiority over beast. What is the difference between a civilized man and a wild man? Ceremony. Everything in the world is ritual. A court trial – ceremony. How else is a case conducted in court? The judge opens the session and gives the floor to the prosecutor; then to the counsel for defence.... It may be that the most important of all the new ideas which Betar has given to the Jewish ghetto is the idea of ceremony. The special uniform seemed strange to the Jewish public fifteen years ago. And so did all our other habits – standing upright, walking straight, and so on.[39]

Yet the young were also fashioned by the times they lived in and the environment they inhabited. Betar grew up in the aftermath of World War I when nationalism was an all-embracing creed, guided by strong – and often authoritarian – leaders. A time when the coup d'état, as Pilsudski had demonstrated, was as valid a pathway to power as the democratic election. Although Jabotinsky taught that individual will and determination could overcome all, the collective attitude of his disciples was a far cry from that of their cosmopolitan liberal outlook of the Russian-born mentor.

The incendiary poetry of Uri Zvi Greenberg provided a potent vehicle to transmit Polish messianism to the Revisionists and Betar. Greenberg epitomized the Jew in transition. His forebears were Talmudic scholars and he was born into a Hasidic family in Eastern Galicia, but his experiences in World War I via Yiddish expressionism established him as a major Hebrew poet in the Palestine of the 1920s. Greenberg combined the religiosity of his past with the nationalism of the present to create fiery poetry with a messianic sense of expectation. In his poem 'Radiance' which was published in 1926, he writes as someone charged with messianic anticipation:

> Bright shining in the body
> I am so much of Jerusalem
> My glowing ribs chant Messiah:
> Come; gather the shed blood to the arteries!
> Yehuda! Shomron!! Galil!
> My hills! My valleys!
> My deserts and my seas!
> En Harod, Tel Yosef, the two seething Deganias![40]

Greenberg was always somewhat ambivalent about his status as a man of the Left. The events of Yom Kippur 1928 and the killings of 1929 confirmed his move away from Labour Zionism and the implicit hope of Arab-Jewish coexistence. Following the Hebron massacre, Greenberg formally joined the Revisionists. His poetry was the poetry of suffering which advocated redemption in the future. Greenberg's poetry informed and fired the Betar generation. It cross-referenced the great poets of nineteenth century Poland such as Mickiewicz, Slowacki and Krasinski with the situation of the Jews of Palestine in the 1930s. Moreover, the members of Polish Betar had grown up with the poets of the Polish struggle and could recite long extracts without hesitation.[41]

IRELAND AND THE IRA

The Irish 'troubles' also attracted the attention of Betar and the Revisionists. The Easter Uprising in 1916, the successful struggle for independence and the violence between Irishmen provided a model worth studying. The example of Ireland even attracted mainstream Zionists.[42] Yet throughout his life, Jabotinsky virtually ignored the fight of the Irish republicans because he clearly believed that the path of armed struggle on the Irish model would not succeed in Palestine. Jabotinsky rarely mentioned the Irish question at the beginning of World War I. In a letter in May 1915, he argued that the British had only moved towards Home Rule for the Irish for the same opportunist reason that the Russians issued a manifesto for the Poles.[43] In time of war, nation states cultivated their potential fifth columns.

A year later, Jabotinsky was insisting to his newspaper, *Russkie vedomosti* that he should remain in Europe for the duration of the war and that he was collecting material for a series of articles on Canada, Australia, Holland, British imperialism – and Ireland.[44] Jabotinsky was clearly moved by the stirring proclamation of Padraig Pearse:

> In every generation the Irish people have asserted their right to national freedom and sovereignty: six times during the past three hundred years they have asserted it in arms in the face of the world. We hereby proclaim the Irish Republic as a sovereign independent state and we pledge our lives and the lives of our comrades-in-arms to the cause of freedom, of its welfare and of its exaltation among the nations.

Although this should have been welcomed without reservation, Jabotinsky was totally dismissive about the Easter Uprising.[45] In 1916, he was, of course, cultivating the British in the hope of establishing the Jewish Legion – and even a fleeting sympathy with Irish nationalism would have been counter-productive. In an article in mid-May 1916, in *Russkie vedomosti*, he commented, 'The worst thing is not that these people (the rebels) perished, but that they perished for an unjust cause and the country which loved many of them was obliged in both conscience and honour to reject them and abandon them to their destruction.'[46] Jabotinsky further commented that although Ireland's past was terrible, a revolution could not be undertaken simply to avenge the past.

In further articles, he repeated his criticism and argued that life was actually becoming better under British rule and Irish demands could have been attained through non-violent means. He suggested that a Home Rule compromise was the best solution with autonomous status for the six Protestant provinces of Ulster. Jabotinsky's belief in England and diplomacy continued throughout the period – even when he was advocating in the 1930s that young people should 'learn how to shoot'. Moreover, he warned his followers that the Irish model had also been shown to contain the seeds of civil war:

> There are cases – for example, in America eighty years ago, in South Africa forty years ago and in Ireland twenty years ago – where the way to unity passed through violent internal struggles. Let us hope that we Jews will be spared the physical horror of such fights.[47]

The Irish national movement was subsequently only mentioned to illustrate specific points of policy rather than the veracity of the armed struggle. Thus Ireland was invoked when discussing economic interests[48] or the legitimacy of political disunity on genuinely divisive national issues such as Home Rule.[49] It was only in 1938 that Jabotinsky acknowledged Irish Republicanism when he met De Valera – but as the head of the Irish state rather than as an IRA revolutionary. The Irish had opposed the proposed partition of Palestine because of their own experience. De Valera had addressed the Assembly of the League of Nations on the Peel Commission and strongly opposed its recommendations. Ireland had also just introduced a new constitution: this and support for Jabotinsky was De Valera's way of demonstrating Irish independence.[50] Significantly Jabotinsky did not refer to his support for the precursor to partition in Ireland in 1916 in the context of his opposition to partition in Palestine in 1937. Jabotinsky saw De Valera as an interlocutor with Britain,[51] but in his discussion drew parallels between the Irish and the Jews – including the revival of Gaelic and Hebrew.[52] Robert Briscoe, the only Jewish member of the Dail Eireann and a long time supporter of De Valera pointed out that there was a similarity between Betar and Republican organizations. In Ireland, 'boys graduated to the Republican Army....having had a thorough education in Irish nationalism and having been prepared in mind and spirit for the necessity of the work they were to do.'[53] The Revisionists depicted De Valera as an Irish Woodrow Wilson, but like Pilsudski, its radical wing looked to a totally different period of the Irish revolutionary's history. Unlike Jabotinsky they did not view the connection with Ireland in terms of a step in the diplomatic struggle with England. For example, in his notes for his Dublin speech, Jabotinsky took up another theme from the Peel Commission which distanced him from the radical wing of the Revisionists. This was the proposal of transferring the Palestinian Arabs from the proposed Jewish state. Jabotinsky commented:

> It must be hateful for any Jew to think that the re-birth of a Jewish State should ever be linked with such an odious suggestion as the removal of non-Jewish citizens.[54]

Despite Jabotinsky's reticence about the Irish struggle, many young people began to turn their attention to it after the disturbances of 1929 and the Hebron killings. Understanding and learning from Irish Republicanism became an integral part of devising a more militant stand.[55]

In October 1930, Abba Achimeir published an article in *Doar Hayom* entitled 'Sinn Fein'.[56] In contrast to Jabotinsky's frequent liberal comments about 'the conscience of the world', he stated that:

> One of the greatest sins of Zionism is its faith in the kindness of nations. Zionism has forgotten Sinn Fein's principle, the principle of 'If I am not for myself, who will be for me?': the principle that the nationalist Irish have placed first and foremost in their movement.

His fellow radical, Yosef Katznelson, surveyed the Irish 'in slavery and in liberation' in the autumn of 1934.[57] Avraham Stern even translated part of P. S. O'Hegarty's book *The Victory of Sinn Fein: How it won it and how it used it* into Hebrew.[58] O'Hegarty argued that prior to 1916, the employment of force was 'a last reserve' and that its actual use was understood as being suicidal. It was a means of 'arousing the nation's soul rather than as a policy'. He also reminded his readers that although Sinn Fein won the 1918 election, they were not allowed into the Versailles conference:

The insurrection of 1916 was a forlorn hope and a deliberate blood sacrifice. The men who planned it and led it did not expect to win. They knew they could not win. They knew that the people were against them and that the people would hate them for it. But they counted upon being executed afterwards and they knew that would save Ireland's soul. The European war had shown Ireland to be less Irish and more Anglicized than ever she had been in her history, had shown Ireland to be more than three fourths assimilated to England; and they offered up their lives as a sacrifice to recall the nation to heroic deeds, to remind the people that they were a nation and not a dependency. Never did any body of men go forth on a more desperate enterprise, with purer hearts or more unfaltering courage. They played for the soul of Ireland and they knew it was a sheer gamble.[59]

This 'philosophy of blood sacrifice' struck a chord amongst the leadership of Betar and the radical Revisionists in Palestine. The experience of the Irish struggle was an exemplar for Avraham Stern and Lehi in their attacks on the British in the 1940s. It also influenced Menachem Begin, as a prime figure in Betar in the late 1930s and certainly his leadership of the Irgun in the 1940s. One essential ingredient which was noted by this younger generation was the importance of attacking Britain when the country was at war. Both Stern and Begin proclaimed their revolts against British rule in Palestine when the British were still fighting the Nazis – albeit at different stages of the conflict. Avraham Stern noted that Ireland refused to join Britain in the struggle against Hitler in World War II.[60] Israel Scheib (Eldad), later one of the triumvirate of Lehi, when still in Kovno in 1940, pointed to the fact that the Irish understood the necessity of attacking Britain when she was distracted by war. Although there were no contacts between Lehi and the IRA, another member of the triumvirate, Yitzhak Shamir, studied Irish Republican literature during his time in the underground and adopted the name of 'Michael' as his nom de guerre after Michael Collins.[61] As head of operations for Lehi, Shamir based himself on Collins amongst others. As O'Hegarty remarked:

But right through it Mick Collins was its eyes and its ears, its push and its determination, its support, its cornerstone. Everybody looked to him; everybody depended upon him. He represented to the people and to the British the embodied spirit of militant Irish nationalism and he was that. It was not for nothing that the British got him on the brain and they offered reward after reward for him.[62]

Indeed, Lehi later compared itself to the participants in the Easter Uprising.[63] Although Pilsudski was seen as a model, the figure of Sir Roger Casement was also promoted in Revisionist publications. He, of course, wished to divert the Irish during World War I towards fighting the British instead and travelled to Germany to achieve that expressed goal. Some Revisionists understood that just as Casement wanted to move the Irish problem onto the European stage, it was similarly important to transform the Jewish problem into an international problem. Moreover, in contrast to Jabotinsky's view, it was emphasized that fighting on England's side in time of war did not guarantee eternal gratitude afterwards. Casement, his doomed quest in Germany, his execution and the Easter Uprising brought the Irish question to the attention of both the Irish people and world opinion.[64] For Avraham Stern and his successors in Lehi, the Irish version of 'the enemy of my enemy is my friend' was particularly pertinent and was cemented by contacts first with the Italians, then the Germans, and latterly the Soviets.

ON TWO FRONTS

Jabotinsky's Problems

Jabotinsky's irritation with the radical Revisionists in Palestine was the least of his concerns in the aftermath of the 17th Zionist Congress. Despite his assertion that the tactics at the Congress had been 'consistent, resolute and wise',[1] the Revisionists had neither taken power nor left the Zionist Organization. This lack of resolution of their position intensified the dissension within the Revisionist Executive despite a statement by Grossman to the contrary. Jabotinsky was still advocating a total withdrawal from the Zionist Organization and the establishment of a new independent body. Moreover, he was strongly supported by an alliance of the Palestinian Revisionists, Betar and occasional long-time adherents such as Vladimir Tiomkin, but generally his old colleagues showed their allegiance to Grossman and the principle of remaining within the mainstream Zionist fold. An acrimonious meeting of the Revisionist Executive in Calais at the end of September 1931 concluded with a compromise. Those who wished to pay the shekel and remain members of the Zionist Organization could do so and those who did not want to remain members through non-payment were also very welcome under the Revisionist umbrella.[2] Paragraph 8 of the Revisionist Constitution was amended to state that:

> The membership of the Union of Zionist Revisionists will in the future not be restricted to shekel payers. Revisionists who acquire the shekel exercise the functions arising out of their membership of the Zionist Organization under the direction of the shekel paying members of the Executive Committee of the Union.'[3]

All who wished to remain members of the Zionist Organization were still subject to the discipline of the Revisionist movement. Jabotinsky's compromise for the sake of unity of neither being totally within nor totally outside weakened his position amongst the radicals and the younger generation. It was not a clear black and white position, but he argued that it was a step in the right direction.[4] On the other hand, the radicals in Palestine were antagonizing the moderates by their actions. Thus, a number of moderate Revisionists signed a letter to *Doar Hayom* stating that they did not recognize the authority of 'the extremist Zionist Revisionist Executive' in Palestine.[5]

But the main attack on the thinking behind the Calais compromise came from the Labour Zionist movement. Like the radical Revisionists, figures such as Arlosoroff argued that being halfway in was not an option. On the eve of the conference of the Polish Revisionists, the Zionist Executive condemned the Calais resolutions and argued that membership of the Zionist Organization involved compliance with its rules and decisions. There could be no negotiations with the British government or the League of Nations without the approval of and in consultation with the Zionist Organization. It further stated:

> Revisionist associations, arbitrarily established without the Zionist federations, are unauthorized within the meaning of the Constitution of the Zionist Organization (Article 3) and are not entitled to describe themselves as Zionist or to claim the rights of Zionist federations or groups of separate unions.[6]

On 27 December 1931, the Polish Revisionist Conference opened in the Einstein Hall of the Jewish Students' residence in Warsaw. The deliberations went on for four days and attracted 250 delegates from over 100 locations. Grossman opened the proceedings and claimed that Britain had moved from a position of co-operation in 1917 through Samuel's policy of 'neutrality and holding the balance' to 'active assault' as epitomized by the Passfield White Paper. Britain had to choose between a Jewish or an Arab majority in Palestine:

> Under present conditions, Britain's presence in Palestine is rather obstructing our development and we must draw the logical inferences from the situation. The position has changed radically. The Mandatory is hostile. It is a state of affairs that requires new methods adapted to the struggle. Until today we have been only parliamentary combatants...further proclamations, protests and resolutions in which many have no faith and which are of little effect, can only succeed in making Zionism appear ludicrous before the world.[7]

Jabotinsky's speech on the following day similarly alluded to the development of new directions in pointing out that over a hundred young people had been arrested in protests against the census. England, he argued, was in 'psychological and economic decline. The impulse to empire had died away or fallen into slumber'. Therefore England could not be relied upon to introduce 'a comprehensive colonization regime'. Jabotinsky maintained that an attitude of mind – 'kremola' as it was known in Tsarist Russia – had developed in

Palestine. This was a sense of permanent and active disaffection of the population towards the regime.

> If conditions remain as they are, there will come into being, in Zionism, a new form of movement which will take all things into account. The effect of this situation will, no doubt, be that it will become as uncomfortable for England to rule Palestine as it is for the Jews of Palestine to be ruled by her. All this is liable to cost our people a great deal of further suffering; but I am afraid we shall not be the only ones to suffer. The whole world may have to pay for England's action in Palestine. That action threatens to drive the Jewish masses, and especially our youth, along a very dangerous road. The youth of a people faced with such a plight as ours cannot live without some kind of faith: faith either in a great reconstruction or in a great destruction.[8]

Such dire warnings about a slide towards an uncontrollable radicalism – and implicitly towards violence – did not change the situation. Jabotinsky had no option but to continue in his attempts to persuade the British. In a letter to *The Times*,[9] Jabotinsky reiterated and clarified his approach. In two final paragraphs which were not published, he drew attention to the development of 'anti-English feeling' amongst the world's fifteen million Jews.

> In this term, 'anti-English feeling', I imply no hint of futile threat: no Jew dreams of trying 'reprisals', nor would it save us if we tried. But the feeling itself is a fact; it grows and spreads and deepens day by day, and it can no longer be stemmed.[10]

Even so, Jabotinsky had to take note of the general lack of faith in the British. *Haynt* published an article by Jabotinsky entitled 'Disobedience'[11] This article advocated an attitude of hostility and disobedience towards government measures which hindered the establishment of a Jewish National Home. It adopted a fatalistic approach in arguing that nothing positive could be expected of the government in the future. Jabotinsky predicted that the situation would deteriorate because of the British government's determination to placate Arab sensitivities following the failure of the Round Table Conference on India to bridge the divide between Muslims and Hindus.[12]

Clearly Jabotinsky had come to the conclusion that a more radical approach of protest and civil disobedience – but not armed struggle – should be pursued in parallel with diplomatic initiatives. This would mollify feelings of frustration and steal the thunder from the radicals. Only a year previously in a speech at the State Opera House in Kovno, he had spoken of 'the honesty and morality of the British nation and reliance on its promises and undertakings'.[13] The observation of British diplomats who reported to Arthur Henderson, the Foreign Secretary, was that 'the lecturer does not seem to have adopted any violently hostile attitude to His Majesty's Government'.[14] Even more to the point, Jabotinsky's speech was made in the context of the publication of the

Passfield White Paper.

TEACHING THE YOUTH

Jabotinsky was keenly aware of the growing restlessness within his own movement following the killings in Hebron and in a broader sense within the Zionist movement. He understood the importance of channelling such frustrations into productive directions. He thus privately complained about the 'passivity' of the Revisionists and expressed an understanding of the radicals in Palestine.[15] Moreover, Jabotinsky believed that figures such as Abba Achimeir could serve as a great example to the youth and his activities could serve to catalyse another area of meaningful opposition to British policies, defusing any attacks on Jabotinsky's own diplomatic initiatives. Jabotinsky debated with his friends that such 'excitable elements' were useful. Indeed, the very future of Revisionism, he envisaged, would be tied to such elements rather than to the passive establishment. While he commented that they undoubtedly showed all the shortcomings of inexperienced youth, this ultimately could be corrected. Jabotinsky clearly saw Achimeir in May 1931 as a motivated leader of nationalist youth – and that he would grow into a responsible role as he matured politically.[16] Thus Jabotinsky famously referred to Achimeir as 'our teacher and guide' amidst a torrent of other accolades.[17]

Achimeir was in a position to influence youth since he was employed as an instructor for the madrichim (youth leaders) for nationalist youth. His close colleague, Yeivin, recalled Achimeir's approach towards his followers:

> True, it was a very small group, but it was well-suited to the aims of protesting that were impressed on it. And it was this group that he educated and shaped to his ideology with great assiduousness, hard work and tenacity. A small back room, bursting with books, in the house of the artist and legal figure Mordechai Avniel in Nachlat Tsadok in Jerusalem, served Achimeir as the schoolhouse for the dissemination of the teachings of national resistance among the young people of Israel. With good reason, one of his students, from among his student-disciples, said of him, 'You gave me more than my own father gave. My father only gave me my body; whereas you gave me spirit.'[18]

All this tended to be without the formal approval of Betar in Palestine whose leadership came to resent the polarizing Achimeir for influencing their members in his role as a teacher.

The idea of a military training school had originally evolved from the Revisionist desire to maintain Betar as a renascent Jewish Legion. The Asefat Ha'nivcharim – the elected assembly of Palestinian Jews – had formally rejected the idea of military training. One of its Revisionist delegates, Menachem Arber, who had served in the Legion disagreed with the approach of the Assembly. In April 1927, he formally became the head of the 'sports section' of Betar in Palestine. The person responsible for bringing Achimeir into the school for training Betar madrichim was Yirmiyahu Halperin, shortly after he had become its director. Halperin had been involved in the Haganah in 1920 and subsequently served the Betar movement in many capacities. During the same year, he and Moshe Rosenberg became active in the development of Betar's military training programmes. He resigned as commander of Brigade 41 in April 1928 because of the lack of ideological direction and motivation in Betar. He complained to Jabotinsky that there was no spirit of self-sacrifice and no independence of character amongst its members. The legacy of the Legion lay moribund.

Halperin and Rosenberg decided to organize a school for the Betar madrichim. Yet this was not as clear-cut and self-evident a process. Halperin took advantage of two flaws in the evolving identity of Betar. Was it a pioneering movement similar to those in other Zionist parties? Or was it an embryonic military organization? The Latvian headquarters perceived Betar as the former while the Palestinian, Polish and Czechoslovak branches placed emphasis on the latter – as did Jabotinsky himself.[19] In addition, the relationship between Betar and the Revisionists was unclear. Betar, although nominally independent, identified – and was identified – with the Revisionists. It seemingly deferred to the Revisionists in all things political. However, the pressure of the situation in Palestine effectively enforced a blurring of these lines of division. Halperin, in particular, wanted a more independent status for his school – and this led to disagreement with Arber. This situation was exacerbated by growing political differences between the Labour movement and the Revisionists in Palestine. Jabotinsky encouraged Halperin to pursue his goals, but not to fragment Betar in Palestine.[20] The Halperin group which considered forming a separate organization did not want to accept the authority of the Betar leadership in Riga. Jabotinsky promised Halperin that if he and his friends remained within Betar in the capacity of individual members, they could develop their plans for a school for madrichim. But he denied them 'constitutional autonomy' for the school and demanded a veto over who taught there.[21] Halperin deferred to Jabotinsky and together with his friends accepted the conditions and joined the movement.[22] Yet in any case, the school seemed to go its own independent way. It became, in effect, both radically politicized and organized itself as a separate entity. A dispute with Menachem Arber led to Jabotinsky demanding that the military command structure of Betar should be respected and its principles taught at the school.

> Under no circumstances is it permissible for Betar members to settle accounts – regarding an insult, an injustice or anything else – in front of a crowd, even if

they are members of Betar.[23]

The matter was referred to a Betar court of honour. In a letter to the teachers at the school, Jabotinsky recognized that there was considerable hostility to the school in some Betar circles. He further stated that 'a sectarian spirit' was prevalent in the school. 'Students and madrichim tend to see themselves as an aristocracy and even demonstrate this trait outside....I will not hesitate to take steps to stop the manifestation of this attitude.'[24] At a disciplinary hearing in May 1929, Halperin was demoted for a period of two months. Jabotinsky thereafter attempted to iron out differences between Betar in Palestine and the Halperin group which was running the school and employing its teachers.[25]

Achimeir taught the cadets at the school when they had become very disillusioned with the direction of the movement. He liked them because 'they don't sabotage me as do Betar'. Even so he described Halperin as one whose 'head is full of porridge from an ideological point of view'.[26] In a letter to Achimeir, Halperin told him that 'although we are opponents in our opinions...we are friends in practice'.[27] Achimeir was asked to set examination questions and, after his move to Jerusalem,[28] was asked to travel to Tel Aviv once a week to teach the students. But both Jabotinsky and Halperin agreed on the need to provide the Betar movement with more drive and a greater momentum. They both understood this within the context of educating the new national Jew and not in terms of deviating extensively from the Revisionist line. Yet the school was following an increasingly radical line. Military training was seen not as preparation for a new Jewish army, but as the means of establishing the military wing of a national liberation movement. In this interpretation, there was a distinct difference of opinion between Betar in Palestine and the school. Under the guidance of Halperin and later Achimeir, the 24 cadets took the lead in organizing demonstrative activities outside Betar. This included taking the initiative in the Tisha B'Av procession to the Western Wall in August 1929. The school's cadets in adhering to a policy of direct action formed the nucleus for the Maximalist tendency in the Revisionist movement. Achimeir was able to disseminate his very different approach through Helperin's direction of the Betar school. Jabotinsky saw this development in a purely educational framework. He hoped that if the school adapted to the general discipline of the Betar youth group, it would emerge as the movement's central educational institution.[29] Instead, the complementary approaches of Halperin and Achimeir contributed to both the evolution of the Irgun and to the emergence of Maximalism in the Revisionist movement and support for that tendency within Betar.

The personalities and characters of the two contributed to the formation of the two schools which differed in their very essence: the first a military one (the

Irgun) unreservedly accepting Jabotinsky's authority as the organization's commander, and the second, the revolutionary school (the Maximalists) which paused to consider Jabotinsky's orders and totally disassociated itself from the Revisionist leadership.[30]

ACHIMEIR AND REVOLUTIONARY ZIONISM

Achimeir set great store on the promise of nationalist youth. He conveyed to them an image of their future and their destiny. He suggested that only their acts at this juncture, 'perhaps the most decisive moment in the history of our people since the destruction of the Temple', would make a difference.[31] In an article in 1928, Achimeir spelled the weltanschauung of Betar.

> What is the aim of Betar? The aim is clear. To create the 'national guard' of the state that is gradually being built. If the realization of the Zionist idea has been delayed in recent years, this is because of the lack of such a guard. A state is built by political means. Diaspora politics is the politics of *shtadlanut* (intercession) which at most aspires to rights, received as a gift. Creative politics does not receive, it takes. One gives when one wants to give, but one takes when one has sufficient strength to take. We must develop the 'will to rule' in the youth, to use Nietzsche's expression.[32]

A 'national guard' – presumably on the French Revolutionary model – was a far cry from Jabotinsky's desire for gdudim (brigades) and a renascent Jewish Legion. Nationalist youth should be untainted by Diaspora mores.[33] Achimeir preached the importance of preparedness. He gave the example of the enthusiasm for sport amongst the youth of Czechoslovakia, Finland and Germany. This, he suggested, was a euphemism for military training – and Betar should be no different. In an article titled 'Betar and the Revolution in Zionism', his colleague, Yeivin, commented that:

> Betar means a new Bar-Kochba Zionism. It signifies that we shall not cease to fight for our ideal, although the world insists on remaining evil and stained with blood, for we reinforce the power of the Jewish nation. We believe that the day will come and that the strength of a small nation may prove superior to that of a powerful one. The rise of Czechoslovakia, Lithuania and Yugoslavia furnish proof'.[34]

Achimeir saw the spirit of self-sacrificing defiant Jewish youth in the classics of Hebrew literature. He claimed that 'Hebrew culture is shot through with the ideals of Betar to an extent undreamed of by the Zionist world'. The best of the maskilim, with Y. L. Gordon at their head, all preached Betarism. So did Tchernikovsky, Schneur, Berdichevsky and Yaakov Cohen. 'Does not Bialik,' he asked, 'in his 'City of Slaughter', appeal to the very same spirit that we want to instil in youth?'

Many of our writers envisioned Betarism without knowing what they foresaw. The German-Zionist writer Max Brod, for instance, in his book *Reubeni, Prince of the Jews*, places pure Betar ideas in the mouth of his hero. Nobody could suspect Brod of affection for Betarism, any more than one could suspect Balaam of love for the Israelites ... but his book should be in every library, in every club, in every Betar platoon's reading room.[35]

Joseph Klausner similarly located Maximalism in the recent Zionism past. Herzl's genius, he suggested, was to combine the two essential elements of Maximalism – 'bold statesmanship and the romance of the messianic idea'.[36]

Achimeir truly believed that 'whoever has the youth – has the state'[37] and directed all his intellectual and organizational energies towards influencing that youth. For him, Jewish honour took precedence over the expansion of Jewish settlement.[38] But he struck a considerably different path from Jabotinsky. A fundamental difference was the role of England. For Achimeir and his friend Yosef Katznelson, England was the central obstacle. Achimeir considered the Arabs to be merely an instrument in British hands.

The killings of 1929 were undoubtedly a turning point for both Jabotinsky and Achimeir. Both praised the march of nationalist Jewish youth to the Wall on Tisha B'Av, but as the dust settled, Jabotinsky still had faith in England. To calm the situation, he tried to place the massacres in Hebron and Safed in context. In a speech in Paris only days after the news broke, Jabotinsky said:

> Don't exaggerate! What has happened to us in Eretz Israel (the Land of Israel) is a terrible humiliation for us, and a shame on the British nation—but it is not a holocaust. The Arabs don't have the strength to wreak a holocaust in Eretz Israel. Don't overstate the brigand's power: he may be a strong brigand, but he's not an Attila.[39]

For Achimeir, the events of 1929 simply deepened his antipathy towards England and fortified his belief in revolutionary Zionism. He believed that English fair play in Palestine was merely a metaphor for nativization and eroding the Jews' just demands. Unlike Jabotinsky, he did not believe in 'the kindness of nations'.[40] Moreover, the 'vegetarianism' of the leaders of the Yishuv restrained the youth and simply assisted the British in their aims.[41] Achimeir took the long view and predicted that the British Empire would be a temporary phenomenon. Contemporary events had to be set within the context of Jewish history. Growing Italian influence in the Mediterranean was perceptible and Italian Fascism for Achimeir now looked even more seductive.

Achimeir had joined the Revisionists in 1927, but he was clearly no Revisionist.

Achimeir's political Maximalism and revolutionary Zionism was an implant from the Left. Like Uri Zvi Greenberg and several others, Achimeir and his friends were originally members of Achdut Ha'avodah and Hapoel Hatzair who had grown disillusioned with the Labour movement. This followed a pattern of many European political thinkers such as Georges Sorel who moved from the dissident left towards a radical nationalism. Later with the spur of the 1929 killings, they had crossed the line to Revisionism with the fervour of the newly converted. Lenin was admired as an example of what single-mindedness, ruthless expediency and revolutionary determination could achieve. For Achimeir, the Bolsheviks were motivated more by Russian nationalism than the international class struggle. Indeed, he spoke about preparing and training for 'our own 1917'.[42] Other times he spoke about facilitating an 'October Revolution' in Zionism. It therefore became easy to identify with such former socialists as Pilsudski and Mussolini who had similarly moved away from their left wing ideological moorings. Achimeir was highly influenced by the writings of Osvald Spengler and especially the publication of 'The Decline of the West' in the aftermath of World War I. His own doctoral thesis 'Bemerkungen zu Spengler's Auffassung Russlands' utilized Spengler's theory of the growth and decay of cultures to focus on Russia. Achimeir's interest in Spengler was his reaction to the advent of Communism – not least in the short-lived Soviet republic in Munich in April 1919 – and to thereby scientifically utilize 'the morphology of history' to predict the future. Spengler wrote:

> I foresee that the old Prussian element with its incalculable treasures of discipline, organizing power and energy will take the lead, and that the respectable part of the working population will be at its disposal against anarchism in which the Spartacus group has a remarkable relationship with the left liberalism of the Jewish newspapers, pot-house pamphlets, jobbers and doctrinaires.[43]

Thomas Mann called Spengler 'a defeatist of humanity', but his writings clearly influenced the National Socialists. Indeed, Spengler supported Hitler's Munich putsch in November 1923.

Achimeir's membership of Hapoel Hatzair lasted a few short years, but even at the onset of this period, it was clear that his views were in transition. By the mid-1920s, he had begun to perceive that the ideology of democracy and the method of democratic rule were often in opposition to each other and he cited the examples of Poland, Mexico and Turkey.[44] Past examples of the co-existence of democracy and dictatorship were illustrated by the examples of Napoleon and Julius Caesar. In an article written in August 1926, Achimeir commented that:

> Democratic rule, the creation of liberalism, has been conquered throughout the

world by conservatism. Those who espouse democratic ideology and who aspire to social change cannot reconcile themselves to this situation and are increasingly turning to dictatorship in one form or another. The recognition that parliamentarianism is detrimental to the realization of modern ideas and aspirations also encourages the creation of a new ideology of democracy. [45]

Thus Mussolini was seen by Achimeir as the heir to the ideology of Mazzini, Garibaldi and Cavour. He even claimed that Mussolini's Fascism was a resurrected form of Bonapartism.[46] Mussolini, moreover, had not enacted anti-Semitic policies even though he was cool towards Zionism. Both Weizmann and Sokolov had met him during the 1920s. Achimeir, in particular, looked to the work of Robert Michels, a German sociologist and socialist who had followed Mussolini into Fascism and became a well-known Fascist theoretician at the University of Perugia. Achimeir read Michels' 'Socialism and Fascism in Italy as Political Currents' and was clearly impressed by it.[47] Michels' area of expertise was oligarchy in organizations and elite theory which argued that the domination of the body politic by focused minorities was an inevitability. It was this which provided the theoretical underpinning of Italian Fascism. It was this that struck a chord with Achimeir. Thus only a few days after Jabotinsky's arrival in Palestine at the end of 1928, Achimeir was already penning articles such as 'On the Arrival of Our Duce'.[48] The advent of an authoritarian regime in Yugoslavia in 1929 persuaded Achimeir that 'Red dictatorship' was not inspiring imitations in the rest of the world and that attempts to transplant the Soviet experiment to countries such as China and Germany had been abject failures. The very idea of 'world revolution' was now bankrupt. The Communist model, he suggested, had been superseded by one of national dictatorship. He gave the examples of Italy, Hungary, Spain, Poland, Lithuania, Turkey, Persia and Egypt – all this and without a murmur of dissent.

> The national dictatorship is striking root, without claiming any victims. It is absurd to speak of Italian Fascism as a murderous regime. Capital punishment is no more common there than in 'democratic countries', such as France. Italian dictatorship has inspired imitations in many countries, thus providing the best proof for this type of dictatorship's superiority.[49]

Achimeir suggested that the parliamentary system suited secure countries with strong capitalist economies such as the USA, France and England. There were other countries such as Estonia and Latvia who were simply satisfied with their lot. Finally there were those unstable countries where parliamentarianism was being eroded by national dictatorship. Significantly, Achimeir looked to the parliamentary democracy of Germany in 1929 and ominously predicted:

> But even there, it is not a strong regime. It still relies upon the republic. And the more the supporters of dictatorship in Germany free themselves from the monarchy there, the greater danger there is to parliamentarianism, and the more

likely that it will have to make way for another regime which is not an imitation of the French system.[50]

Moreover, he argued that 'pure nationalism' made a distinction between individual and group morality.

Laws and commandments that bind the individual do not apply to the group. What is forbidden to the individual is permitted to the group. The distinction between individual and group is not merely one of quantity. The group is an organism, with its own special laws, which differ from those of the individual. The 'absolute command' of the individual, for instance, forbids him to kill someone for the sake of his own interests. Raskolnikov, the hero of *Crime and Punishment*, killed someone for his own private reasons, and was therefore punished. But Napoleon, who executed hundreds of thousands of people, suffered no pangs of conscience, since he did what he did for general reasons.[51]

Achimeir further pointed out that 'the sons of political Judaism' made a distinction between the morality that obtains between man and man – and between man and society. Applied to Betar, this cemented the symbiotic relationship between noblesse oblige and 'the use of the bow'.[52] Assassination of public figures could therefore be justified for national reasons. Thus Achimeir expressed an understanding for the assassination of the French President, Paul Doumer, by a deranged Russian émigré Dr Paul Gorgulov in May 1932.[53] Achimeir had also read the memoirs of Vera Figner, a member of the Narodnaya Volya who was implicated in the assassination of Alexander II in 1881. He marvelled at her idealism and at her fortitude in enduring two decades in the Schusselburg fortress.[54]

His unpublished work, *Megilat Hasikarikin* (The Scroll of the Sicarii) which developed such ideas and was publicized when he was on trial for the murder of Arlosoroff in 1934, had in fact been written several years previously. Moreover it was dedicated to two women – to the Girondin Charlotte Corday who murdered Marat in his bath and to the Russian social revolutionary Fannie 'Dora' Kaplan who attempted to kill Lenin in 1918.

THE RISE OF BRIT HABIRYONIM

Achimeir, Greenberg and Yeivin were of a generation which had been conditioned by the permissible exercise of arbitrary violence, experienced in a world war. Achimeir had lost a brother and Greenberg witnessed the fake execution of his family. Achimeir's Maximalist views had emerged in the aftermath of his experiences in Russia and pointedly he left Hapoel Hatzair before the disturbances of 1928 and 1929 in Palestine.[55] His disillusionment with Labour Zionism was a reaction to his bearing personal witness to the war and to the new Bolshevik regime during his years in Russia and Byelorussia after 1914. Like Jabotinsky, his many writings indicated a continuing involvement in Russian culture and politics, commenting on such figures as the novelist and poet Dmitri Merezhkovsky[56] and the chairman of the Constituent Assembly in 1917, Viktor Chernov.[57] On the tenth anniversary of the October Revolution in 1927, he wrote a series of articles[58] in *Ha'aretz* in which he reacted with the full vehemence characterized by many Russian émigrés, at Soviet authoritarian rule. Achimeir considered Lenin and Trotsky to be false messiahs who seduced Jewish youth in great numbers by their dreams of an assimilationist utopia. Jabotinsky shared this view which became accentuated as the western democracies proved unable to grapple with the growth of authoritarian regimes in the 1930s.[59] In particular, Achimeir witnessed the split in Gdud Ha'avodah – originally called the Yosef Trumpeldor Labour Battalion – which had been founded in 1920. It attracted young people aged 18-22 mainly from those who had emigrated early on from Russia before the negative manifestations of Bolshevism were truly felt. In 1926, the economic situation in Palestine worsened and this induced several splits in the left wing of Gdud Ha'avodah. The group of Menachem Elkind, 'communalist' rather than 'Communist', returned to the Crimea between the end of 1927 and the beginning of 1929 where they established a commune called 'Vojo Nova' (Esperanto for the 'New Way'). For Achimeir, this was both rank betrayal and a dangerous precedent. He therefore endeavoured to create a polar alternative to attract revolutionary youth. Brit HaBiryonim, which Achimeir founded in October 1931, created 'revolutionary space'.

The choice of the name was in itself instructive about Achimeir's world outlook. The 'biryoni' of antiquity were said to have been a specific type of robber-zealot in a Jerusalem besieged by the Romans.[60] The Babylonian Talmud comments:

> The biryoni were then in the city. The rabbis said to them: 'Let us go out and make peace with them (the Romans).' They would not let them, but on the contrary said: 'Let us go out and fight them.' The Rabbis said: 'You will not succeed.' They then rose up and burned the stores of wheat and barley so that a famine ensued.[61]

Abba Achimeir's nom de plume in publications such as *Hazit Ha'am* and *Doar Hayom* was often Abba Sikra. The Babylonian Talmud refers to Abba Sikra as the head of the biryoni. Significantly Joseph Klausner, whose academic expertise was in this area, regarded the biryoni as the forerunners of both the French revolutionary sans-culottes and the Bolsheviks. Achimeir clearly understood the Brit HaBiryonim in this light. He commented to his friend Yeivin:

> I am certain that if the Brit HaBiryonim had existed during the split in the Labour battalion, Elkind's people would not have returned to Russia and become lost to the Zionist cause, but would have found their rightful place within the structures of the Zionist Revolutionary Movement.[62]

Yet Lenin showed what was possible by a dedicated minority. A small dedicated group of zealots could be more effective than the combined forces of any Jewish Legion. Moreover, the success of Communism indicated the need for a strong driven leader. Yet the Left, from whence he had come, came in for scathing criticism. Socialist Zionism was, in reality, monastic Zionism. Political parties who followed Zionist ideologues, Borochov and Syrkin, were 'nothing but a modern monastery to the socialist religion'.[63] Yet Achimeir, for all his fiery writings, did not advocate Brit HaBiryonim as a vehicle for causing violence – at least not in 1931 – the various protests staged by the group elicited no bloodshed. He did, however, advocate individual terror in his writings and was sanguine about the justice of assassination of public figures in certain circumstances. The determined protests of Brit HaBiryonim, based on Halperin's school, did, however, act as a precursor for those who would utilize violence in the context of the armed struggle. There were three main protests in the winter of 1931-1932. These protests were against the visit of Drummond Shiels, Under-Secretary of State for the Colonies, the conducting of a population census and the appointment of Norman Bentwich, suspected of Brit Shalom sympathies, to a chair at the Hebrew University.

Like Jabotinsky, Achimeir suggested military training as a means of rejecting the lack of zeal in the mainstream Zionist movement. Brit HaBiryonim was seen as a new start and decidedly different from Betar.[64] It also looked to Bar-Kochba and the Jewish revolt against the Romans in the year 132 for its military inspiration. Indeed, 1932, the anniversary of the revolt, provided a platform for both Achimeir and Yeivin to compare the current situation of the Jews to those of their ancestors. Yeivin introduced one article with a fragment of Uri Zvi Greenberg's poetic allusions to the Sicarii – the zealots who fought the Romans – which had been written as a reaction to the killings of 1929. He contrasted the Torah of a normal people, epitomized by the self-sacrificing leadership of Bar-Kochba, with the Torah of the rabbis which preached withdrawal and the conversion of the Jews into 'a kingdom of priests'. Yeivin accused the rabbis of rewriting the history of the Jews so as to minimize Bar-Kochba and his followers:

> The bodies of the heroes of Israel were trampled and destroyed by the external victor but the souls of the heroes of Israel, and the very mention of their heroism, were trampled underfoot by the spiritual dictators from within. If not for Josephus and the Christians who preserved his book, we would not have

known the name of Bar Giora. [65]

Accusing the rabbis of censoring Jewish history, he singled out the zealots who fought the Romans who were no longer regarded as heroes, but instead as criminals and ruffians (Biryonim). For Yeivin, the Josephuses – the Jewish turncoats – of 1932 were the purveyors of 'the Torah of mercy, the socialists and the non-socialists who are today in control' of the Zionist movement.

For Achimeir and Yeivin, the Bar-Kochba anniversary was an occasion to advocate the development of military prowess. Following the disruption of Norman Bentwich's inaugural lecture on peace, Achimeir commented, 'It is not a cathedral to international peace in the name of Bentwich that we need, but a military academy in the name of Ze'ev Jabotinsky.'[66]

The leaflet handed out by the demonstrators stated that the creation of a chair of peace studies was 'the work of Satan'. It was 'an anti-Zionist measure, a stab in the back of Zionism'. It pointed out that most universities – even those without the security problems of Palestine – did not have peace chairs, but military academies. Jerusalem was not – as Bentwich viewed it – 'a city of peace', but a volcano ready to erupt. It asserted that 'the peace-keepers' in Jewish history always symbolized national betrayal, assimilation and the blurring of reality. It concluded that 'we can defend the honour of Israel…not by filling our bellies with lectures on peace…but rather by learning the doctrine of Jabotinsky.' [67]

Achimeir and his followers regarded Jabotinsky as 'the Jewish Pilsudski'. For Achimeir, Jabotinsky was a Jewish hero who followed in the footsteps of Herzl – just as Mussolini was an ideological descendant of Mazzini and Garibaldi. Their objective, therefore, was to save him from the clutches of Grossman and his colleagues. In a letter to the youth of Betar from the central prison in Jerusalem, following his arrest after the Bentwich demonstration at the Hebrew University, Achimeir was highly specific about Jabotinsky's role in the unfolding of this stage of the Zionist dream:

Zionist youth has not been dedicated to sacrifice, and this is why there have been so few creators of revolutionary Zionism. This is why the voice of Trumpeldor, of Aharon and Sarah Aharonson, and – may he be spared for life – of Jabotinsky have been voices crying in the wilderness. Few followed them. The tremendous opportunities that opened up in front of Zionism – the war and the destruction of Russian Jewry – these opportunities ended in despair. One part of the youth (a minority) went to the monastery of A. D. Gordon, and another part (the majority) to the Cheka of Dzerzhinsky and the Red Army of Trotsky.
If Zionism were an illusion, it would not have been able to rise again after these failures. But the fact that Jabotinsky founded a mighty Zionist youth movement

after the war is an encouraging sign for our ideal. A miracle has happened. On one hand, international socialism has gone bankrupt, on the other, there is a leader of political Zionism.[68]

Jabotinsky, however, declined the honour. It was their very lack of political perception that distanced Jabotinsky from the Maximalists. As one scholar has succinctly remarked, 'Revisionist political monism was undergirded by an ontological monism, which embraced the passions while rejecting the Cartesian divide between mind and body.'[69] From the very formation of Brit HaBiryonim, Jabotinsky's tactics were to contain this new outburst of radicalism and to direct it along rationalist lines. He utilized the language and style of radicalism, praised its exponents, supported their freedom to act, but also asked pointed questions and expressed qualifications.

Achimeir was already regarded by Jabotinsky as 'too much a Fascist'[70] in late 1928. Indeed, he had commenced his work for *Doar Hayom* with his column entitled 'From the Notebook of a Fascist'. Achimeir expressed admiration for Mussolini and espoused a Zionist interpretation of integral nationalism. Moreover, he had clear views how Revisionism should evolve. Within a couple of weeks of Jabotinsky's arrival in Palestine, Achimeir had written to him addressing him as 'the Leader':

> This was not because I wanted to please or flatter you, but it was simply an expression of my feelings. I long for someone superior to stand above me and show me the way…
> Sir, why do you consult with us so much? Command us more. We have to obey your orders. You have to stay in touch for the sake of information, but don't ever leave a problem for someone else to have the last word. You should separate your personal inclinations from the inclinations of your position.[71]

THE FALL AND RISE OF THE
MAXIMALISTS

MAXIMALISTS AND ACTIVISTS

The Revisionists in Palestine were severely divided. At least three factions could be discerned. The Maximalists – intellectuals such as Achimeir, Yeivin, Greenberg and their tactician, Katznelson – were supported by a group of activist youth who were mainly Betar cadets from Halperin's school. Their belief in direct action distinguished them from Revisionists who still believed in the efficacy of political and diplomatic intervention. Yet the ability of the moderates to confront the Maximalists and activists was constrained not only by the radicalizing impetus of the general situation, but they were also divided by the issue of whether to remain within the Zionist Organization. The Weinshall brothers wanted to leave whereas the chairman of the Revisionist central committee, Israel Rosov, wished to remain.[1] In the aftermath of the Hebron killings in 1929 and the Shaw Commission Report in 1930, many young people were attracted to the radicalism of Achimeir and the energetic propagation of the Maximalist position. This was in distinct contrast to the staid politics of the Revisionists. The release of the Passfield White Paper in October 1930 – and its negative consequences for the Zionist experiment – impelled the Maximalists to call for an extraordinary party conference. Despite appeals to the World Executive, the Revisionist leadership in Palestine eventually accepted the need for such a conference. Confronted by an 'Activist-Revisionist' list, the old guard were roundly defeated and replaced by a new Maximalist leadership. Achimeir, Katznelson and Von Weisl rejected both instructions and pleas from the World Executive for a compromise solution – especially as Rosov had retained the loyalty of the large Tel Aviv branch.[2]

Achimeir stipulated that two tasks now confronted the movement – the conquest of youth and the dissemination of Revisionist doctrine:

> The idea of Revisionism is a much broader idea than just opposition to the political system operated here by the government. It is a different concept from 'Weizmann out! Hurrah for Jabotinsky!' Revisionism is a revolution within our people whose political sense has been dimmed.[3]

It was therefore not by chance that *Haynt* published one of Jabotinsky's most famous articles 'Afn Pripitshek' on 16 October 1931 which exhorted young people to 'learn to shoot'. Jabotinsky, of course, placed it in the educational context of defensive military training and the evolution of the new Jew. It was remembered long after the original reasons for its composition were forgotten. But from Jabotinsky's perspective, its very success was counter-productive since it encouraged Brit HaBiryonim and its activist supporters in Betar to consider the virtue of armed struggle through the vehicle of a national liberation movement. Throughout 1932, Jabotinsky attempted in several articles to apply 'corrections' to the growing exuberance of the Palestinian Maximalists and their adherents in Betar in the Diaspora, while simultaneously protecting their freedom of action in neutralizing the criticisms of Grossman and the Revisionist Executive.[4] Thus while the Revisionist Executive expressed 'its appreciation to those in Palestine who, at considerable personal sacrifice, have so valiantly fought against the Palestine Census',[5] the containment of 'adventurism' within limits was the subject of two articles by Jabotinsky where he argued that such behaviour had to be applied selectively. His journalism assisted in pointing the way – 'when to press the accelerator, when to use the brake'.[6] Thus, in his article 'On Adventurism' which appeared in *Haynt* at the end of February 1932.

Jabotinsky pointed out that he supported an effective selective adventurism not an unpredictable sans-culottism. In particular, he did not accept the Jacobins' identification of the sans-culottes with the intrinsic will of the nation. Jabotinsky was well aware of the excesses of the Jacobins and the self-destructive forces unleashed in the French revolution. As someone who defended the bourgeoisie in Palestine and publicly embraced liberalism, he did not warm to that phase of the Revolution. There was no meeting of minds with Hébert who proclaimed, 'To your pikes, good sans-culottes, sharpen them up to exterminate aristocrats.'[7]

Jabotinsky attempted to bridge differences in the hope of keeping an increasingly fractious party together. He even warned the London secretariat not be so dogmatic and to allow the Palestine branch to produce their own documentation 'as they were very touchy'.[8] There was no overt criticism of Italian Fascism since it was favoured by the Maximalists. Yet both Jabotinsky and Weizmann explored the possibility of utilizing Mussolini for the good of the cause. Thus although Achimeir fervently embraced Italy ideologically,

Jabotinsky saw courting Mussolini's regime as a means of putting pressure on Britain. In a letter to the Executive Committee in London, he wrote, 'Why is Mussolini an exception? Nobody suggests that we should offer him the Mandate; but if we tell him that we are dissatisfied it would only be natural.'[9] Italy, of course, had its own reasons for meeting Zionists. In fact, when Weizmann was received by Mussolini in 1934, an article in *I Poplo D'Italia* not only came out in favour of a Jewish State, it discussed the possibility of granting Palestinian citizenship to Jewish national minorities in the Diaspora while allowing those who considered themselves assimilated or acculturated to remain citizens of their countries.[10] These were views that even Weizmann did not dare to expound. Mussolini's only interest was to further Italian interests in the Mediterranean and he was willing to play up to Zionist disillusionment with Britain to further that goal.

Jabotinsky still believed that he could pursue his goal of training Betar to become the kernel of a future Legion rather than the Maximalists' model of the nucleus of those conducting the armed struggle. In the same letter, he proposed following up on the possibility of establishing a school of instructors in Italy.[11] Jabotinsky was extremely keen on promoting Italy amongst the youth of Betar,[12] but he emphasized culture and literature rather than politics and history. Indeed, he even believed that the proliferation of the Italian language would be beneficial for 'the harmonization of Hebrew pronunciation'.[13] He believed that his love of Italy could be transmitted to Betar – and that it somehow could be separated from Mussolini's Fascism. Jabotinsky had written critically to Mussolini in 1922 – months before the march on Rome – and little had changed in his approach.[14] Yet the Revisionists in Italy who faced the daily reality of Fascism glossed over any such distinctions. They often spoke in adulatory fashion about the regime. For example, on the 14th anniversary of the Balfour Declaration, the chairman of the Italian Revisionists addressed Mussolini as someone who was 'driven by a higher sense of justice and humanity'.[15]

Jabotinsky's individualism had long been a bulwark against any personal belief in the cult of the personality. In 1926 he had ridiculed Mussolini's Fascism when he wrote 'Buffaloes follow a leader. Civilized men have no "leaders".'[16] The nineteenth century liberalism that partly defined Jabotinsky still resided in an appeal to the world to recognize the justice of the Zionist case. For example, he still retained the notion that the partition of Palestine and the creation of Transjordan could be reversed by a benevolent world.[17] Jabotinsky claimed that Transjordan had little meaning for the Arabs of Palestine – the central Islamic sites were located in Jerusalem and Hebron and the intelligentsia, the bourgeoisie and the industrialists all resided on the West Bank.[18] He also pressed for a powerful international petition that would capture the world's imagination. Significantly Jabotinsky wanted to avoid any hint of radicalism, cautiously suggesting that even phrases such as 'transforming the country into a Jewish National home' should be omitted.[19]

Achimeir, on the other hand, interpreted Jabotinsky's manoeuvres as his genuine beliefs or else did not notice his repeated qualifications. He wished to supplant conventional Revisionism with its Maximalist version and believed that Jabotinsky would go along with him. Thus, the petition was deemed to be a time-wasting exercise by activist youth. Achimeir held up the example of similar international petitions to the Disarmament Conference in February 1932 – the signatures of eight million women had not made the slightest bit of difference.

At the end of April 1932, the Revisionists in Palestine held their conference. A letter from Jabotinsky was read out where he distinguished between 'the two ways of recognizing truth: propaganda and action'. The former, as exemplified by the petition, served the Diaspora well, but 'the Herzl movement' in Palestine ought to find another way. He advised the conference that this required 'the ability to examine the situation soberly and rationally and to be prepared to make great sacrifices'.[20] Jabotinsky's qualified recognition of the special case of Palestine and his advice regarding the direction in which to proceed was ignored by the Maximalist leadership.

Achimeir's speech instead was a critique of the liberal tendencies within the Zionist movement. The focus of his delivery was the newly established Hebrew University which he heavily associated with the Brit Shalom movement. The University Chancellor, Judah Magnes, a follower of Ahad Ha'am, a leader of Brit Shalom, was an advocate of a bi-national state. The lesson which Magnes drew from the disturbances of 1929 was that there had to be new ways of examining the Jewish-Arab division. For example, he argued at the beginning of the academic year 1929-1930 that Zionists should not do anything that could not be justified before the conscience of the world. Most Zionist parties criticized the approach of Brit Shalom and especially any consideration of limiting immigration, but even Ben-Gurion occasionally entered into discussion with Magnes' circle. The Revisionists, on the other hand, viewed Brit Shalom as beyond the pale. The demonstration against Bentwich in February 1932 by Achimeir and Brit HaBiryonim was, in essence, a demonstration against Magnes and Brit Shalom. Achimeir described Magnes in his speech as a fellow traveller with Communism – someone who 'sees and cavorts with Lenin'. As Magnes had called in the police to prevent the disruption of Bentwich's lecture, Achimeir likened him to a Tsarist minister who relied on bayonets to impose his will. Most teachers at the University were second-rate, Achimeir insisted, and you had to be a disciple of Claude Montefiore, the theologian of Liberal

Judaism and determined opponent of Zionism or a blind follower of Stalin to gain employment at the institution. The only students who received bursaries, he claimed, were those affiliated to Mapai and Mizrachi. Revisionist students, although far brighter, he claimed, were being excluded. Achimeir's harangue against the university authorities reached its apogee with the observation that even the site of the university depicted vacillation and acquiescence. After all, Mount Scopus was the place where Titus's legions encamped prior to their assault on Jerusalem and where the British had their military cemetery. In concluding his speech, Achimeir cited Jabotinsky's opposition to the original conception of the university as an elitist research institution rather than as a mass vehicle for higher education. Although Jabotinsky's views had actually modified, the very mention of his name was designed to stamp Achimeir's views with the seal of approval. Yet Achimeir was continually interrupted by members of the audience who opposed his views and were irritated by his rhetoric. For him, the university personified all the demons that he had set himself against. It is also significant that the intellectual Achimeir was critical of the liberal intellectualism of Brit Shalom and its 'educated' leading figures.[21]

Jabotinsky shared some of Achimeir's views on pacifism and bi-nationalism and had written several articles on the need to remain militarily vigilant especially after the opening of the international Disarmament Conference in Geneva at the beginning of 1932.[22] But Achimeir utilized the opportunity not simply to embrace 'the Revisionism of the prison', but also to denounce liberalism per se.

> Zionism's calamity was that it was raised and educated on the knees of liberalism, and its methods were those of liberalism, of speech. We want methods of action. Liberalism is good for other peoples who live in peace on their land...but for enslaved and oppressed peoples like us, there is another law of liberation. Our ideal and example is Aharon and Sarah Aharonson. The youth are going to a place where sacrifices will be demanded – to prison and to the gallows...we have lost two generations of the Jewish people to Zionism. We do not want to lose the third generation, and therefore we want the methods of Zionism to be those of a liberation movement which follows revolutionary paths. Zionism will be realized not by gentlemen but by sans-culottes, the 'barefooted' who are ready for any sacrifice.[23]

Several new journals were established to express the new activism. *Ha'am*, a daily which listed Jabotinsky as its editor-in-chief, had Yeivin as its responsible editor. This lasted only a few months during 1931 but attracted writers such as Achimeir, Uri Zvi Greenberg, Avigdor Hameiri, Yonatan Ratosh and Ben-Zion Netanyahu as contributors. At the beginning of 1932, *Hazit Ha'am* was launched as a weekly organ of the Revisionist movement and Betar in Palestine. It soon became the stronghold of the Maximalists. Significantly Jabotinsky was not listed as its editor-in-chief this time, yet his articles appeared in most issues.

He supported *Hazit Ha'am* over *Doar Hayom* which was no longer part of the Revisionist movement.[24] His style became overtly populist in an attempt to maintain a foothold in the Maximalist camp. In an early edition, he warned that its contributors should utilize moderate language and a non-antagonistic style. 'Criticism that appears in a velvet glove has double benefit.' Moreover, Jabotinsky argued that the British administration had lost its moral justification to rule the Land of Israel – and that the confrontation was first and foremost with them:

> Don't allow the Jewish public to settle for a confrontation against the Sanbalatim (Jewish governors of Samaria during the Persian Empire). There is a danger that they will be satisfied with that since it is easier to attack Bentwich and Mr Magnes than an external opponent.[25]

This, of course, was an open criticism of Achimeir and the demonstration. *Hazit Ha'am* also followed a clear anti-Communist line – especially in the midst of the bitter confrontation with the Labour movement. Thus Von Weisl could predict that the world was on the eve of a new war in 1932, but between Britain and Russia. Jewish youth – and especially Betar – should therefore be trained and mobilized to fight alongside Britain, 'but only on receipt of secure and clear pledges, not cloudy empty promises'.[26] Jabotinsky too followed this approach towards Britain – in such articles as 'According to the Marxist Worldview'.[27]

Jabotinsky's attention at this time was given to a plan for an international petition to the British Parliament to be signed by Diaspora Jews. Achimeir, bound by his distaste for diplomacy and England, suggested that breaking the windows of 'a well-known embassy in Warsaw' would be far more valuable than a petition.[28] He further declared that the Maximalists would oppose the petition. He and his followers directed their efforts towards making an impact at the 5th World Revisionist Conference in Vienna at the end of August 1932. The Maximalists even published their own manifesto in which they called for 'the raising of the prestige of the leader to the status of dictator'.[29]

The electoral breakthrough of Hitler in July 1932 convinced Jabotinsky that it was important that his movement should not be contaminated by acts and accusations of extremism. He once again promoted the virtues of nineteenth century liberalism and castigated the mindless masses 'hysterically saluting in a chloroformed state, a castor-oiled salute in a deranged nightshirt dress'.[30] In another article 'More on Adventurism',[31] he was less ambiguous in his choice of language:

> Adventurism? There are moments when it might bring benefits. An underground? Yes, too. But Betar is not and cannot be part either of adventurism or of an underground; yet not anti-adventurism and not anti-underground. Betar,

as I conceived it, is a school with three 'levels' where youth will learn to control their fists, their batons and all other means of defence; to be able to stand to attention and to march well; to work; to foster beauty of form and ceremony; to scorn all forms of negligence – call it whatever you wish, hooliganism or ghetto mentality; to respect women and the elderly; and prayer – no matter what religion, democracy and many other things which may seem obsolete, but which are everlasting. This is the type of school that Betar has to be. Yes, a school like that, for if not, better that Betar not exist at all.[32]

Yet he persisted in praising adventurists in other parts of the article – 'those square-jawed men, resourceful, undaunted by hardships and failure'.[33] A few days later, he was much more candid in a letter to Yeivin who had written to him urging him to change his line. In an angry formal letter which damned both Yeivin and Achimeir with faint praise for their 'generous spirit of self-sacrifice', he said that he had been expecting such a letter and prepared its content long ago. Jabotinsky wrote that 99 per cent of Yeivin's opinions had nothing in common with the principles that Zionism was founded upon:

Your sanctity is mistaken, in my eyes; it destroys the building which I have laboured so long to erect, and in its place creates a shrine which I do not desire. I will not go with you. Nor do you have the moral right to go with me and to be considered as members of the party in which I participate, from the moment when you came to believe that all its basic principles 'had perished' . . . your attempts to make your views prevail in the Revisionist movement and Betar instead of the former views are nothing but attempts to drive me out. If these views had triumphed, I would have left the party. The Revisionists comprise a movement founded on nineteenth century democracy, on the rebuilding of the land, on the conquest of positions, on governmental and patrician education. Its revolutionary nature, which justifies *kremola* when it is necessary and appropriate, is also imbued with this ideology, and will remain so. If not – then I will not remain in it.[34]

Yet he concluded with a vigorous defence of their right to take independent action, if the Revisionist movement did not want to participate, as long as it was not under an official party banner – and he would defend this principle within the governing councils of the movement.

I shall not say, nor agree that others should say, that there is no room within our ranks for those of our members who do more than the official measure and outside the official camp – as long as they act in the name of the same outlook. However, I will not move an inch as regards the principles of this outlook.[35]

For Jabotinsky, Betar in Palestine and elsewhere was an organization that aspired to reach 'a legal goal by legal means'. Yet Betar in the summer of 1932 was torn between Jabotinsky's blueprint for youth based on 'moral and cultural education on the one hand, and military preparation (for defence) on the other' and the militancy of the Achimeir school of radicalism.[36] Although Jabotinsky extolled the virtue of youth and their single-minded mission to rebuild the Jewish state, he was ambivalent about the multitudes which looked to him as their overarching leader and guide. In an article in an American student magazine, entitled 'If I were young in 1932', Jabotinsky advised his youthful readership, 'Every generation is a separate country with a different climate; what we know about ours may not be worth knowing in yours.'[37] Yet in a revealing letter to Ben-Gurion in 1935, Jabotinsky bemoaned the fact that the inter-war generation demanded clear and simplistic solutions to problems – a generation which neither knew nor recognized the soul-searching that preceded the arrival of 'conclusions in the quest for truth'.

> There seems to be a new characteristic among our present-day youth, Jewish and Gentile alike, who refrain from delving into matters and seek a simple 'yes' or 'no', primordial and brutal. Of these two threads they seek the thicker and shiny one; and that love which in the past moved you to measure again and again those proportions in the blend, they look upon compromise as weakness or even worse. With what then will you fight this brutality, with which blend? Will you attempt to teach them your convictions? I have grave doubts as to whether this generation is capable of understanding it. This generation is very 'monistic'. Perhaps this is no compliment, but it is definitely a fact.[38]

THE VIENNA CONFERENCE

Achimeir laid out the approach of the Maximalists in an article entitled 'Basle or Zimmerwald'[39] a month before the opening of the 5th World Revisionist Conference in Vienna. He argued that the 'Basle' type of conference was all right for Herzl's time because such conferences were effectively public demonstrations, a declaration of purpose. What was required now, he argued, was a 'Zimmerwald' conference where true Zionists would proclaim their fidelity to the cause and rebuild the movement as Lenin did in September 1915. Achimeir recalled that only a few dozen socialists had gathered in the Swiss village of Zimmerwald to declare their continued loyalty to international socialism and to condemn those who had been seduced by the rival nationalisms of the trenches. Lenin argued for a transformation of the world war into a revolutionary assault on the bourgeoisie. Achimeir pointed out that two years later the Bolsheviks took power due to the indecision and spinelessness of the moderate socialists:

> The Bolsheviks won because they were prepared. They put their efforts not into the smoke-filled rooms of the official committees, but into the small and serious congresses in Swiss villages such as Zimmerwald and Kiental.[40]

Achimeir repeated his claim that the collection of signatures by 'an army of youth' was a waste of time and commented that 'a single deed by a brave young man, a deed that for the usual reasons the writer of these columns does not find it possible to write about— such a deed would raise far greater interest in the Land of Israel'.[41] Clearly the nature of the deed was left to the reader's imagination.

In the prelude to the World Revisionist Conference in 1932, Jabotinsky not only had to confront the Palestinian radicals, but also his opponents on the Revisionist Executive who despite the Calais compromise voiced their disaffection. These two fronts within Revisionism were matched by the uncompromising assaults of Ben-Gurion and the Labour movement as well as the Zionist Executive's unwillingness to accommodate the Calais compromise in accepting second place on the question of discipline.

In August 1932, the 5th World Revisionist Conference opened in the Renz Circle House in Vienna with a two hour speech by Jabotinsky on 'The Position of Zionism and the Task of Revisionism'. The Maximalists had prepared themselves well. Not only had their advocates kept up the ideological momentum through articles in *Hazit Ha'am*, but they had even issued a manifesto in the paper a few weeks before the formal opening of the conference. The manifesto opened with the statement that there would be an ideological split in Vienna and that they represented the majority of Revisionists in Palestine. The Maximalists stated that their objective was to extract Revisionism from its liberal entrapment:

> Should we continue along the path of the ringing phrase, should we carry on the Revisionist tradition of criticism for the sake of criticism, the internal idleness – or should we renew Zionism, refresh the Movement with spirit and thunder, replace the endeavours of opposition with revolutionary deeds – action in place of talk! [42]

The Maximalists stated several demands. The first was the elevation of Jabotinsky to the status of dictator. It implicitly attacked Grossman and his supporters by demanding that the Revisionist headquarters should be moved from London to Paris where Jabotinsky lived. It also argued that the Revisionists should have their own independent unaffiliated organization which would reflect the Maximalist view and that it should be 'a tool for liberation, as it is with all other peoples who have fought or are fighting for their freedom'. The manifesto placed considerable emphasis on the role of youth – from combating discrimination in allocating funds for pioneers to fighting anti-Semitism. It concluded, 'Long live the Leader! Long live the Kingdom of Israel!' The use of 'malchut israel' – the kingdom of Israel – was significant since it represented an almost messianic strain of some Maximalists in telescoping the present with the Jewish past. All this had come in the wake of the increasing electoral success of the Nazis throughout 1932 and their emergence as the largest party in the Reichstag elections of 31 July. Indeed, Yeivin, probably one of the authors of the manifesto, referred to the NSDAP two days previously as a vehicle for national liberation – in the same category as the revolutionary organizations of the Italians, Poles and Czechs.[43]

Jabotinsky thus faced the impossible task of bridging the gap between Maximalists with pro-Fascist tendencies with their reliance on direct action and revolutionary ardour and his colleagues on the Revisionist Executive who wished to remain within the Zionist Organization and pursue diplomatic initiatives with Britain. In an article written on the eve of the conference, Jabotinsky had argued optimistically that 'internal differences of opinion' might not break up the movement, but it would certainly impede its growth.[44] On arrival in Vienna, Jabotinsky met the representatives of all three factions, the Maximalists, the activist youth and the older Revisionists who were mainly close to Grossman. In his opening speech, he strongly condemned the British and called upon all Jews to unite behind the idea of a mass petition which would shame the British government into changing their policies. Achimeir and the Maximalists had already rejected the petition as a futile exercise in gesture politics. Yet Jabotinsky attempted to integrate the Maximalists as a legitimate part of the movement by suggesting that they would play an important role in the future since the political differences between the administration and the Revisionists in Palestine would become deeper and broader.[45] He warned of the dangers of disunity in the movement, but was exceedingly careful not to offend any of the contending factions.[46] He suggested that some believed that the most important item on the agenda was the creation of a self-defence force, others that political pressure was central, still others believed that the problems in Palestine would only be solved 'as result of a major cataclysm similar to the events of 1914-1918'. Jabotinsky warned that there was nothing wrong in having a central concern, but when all other concerns were regarded as unnecessary or harmful, the effect was factionalism and fragmentation.

In his speech, Achimeir stated that two things characterized the twentieth century – youth and dictatorship. The time had now arrived to change the nineteenth century ideal of a leader. Democracy had now reached the limits of bankruptcy. Achimeir, himself, had long despaired of parliamentarianism and 'the intrigues of professional politicians'. He had approved of inviting the military to take over a country[47] – as in the case of Yugoslavia in 1929 – and even quoted from the book of Isaiah to substantiate this view. 'Come, be thou our ruler and let this ruin be under thy hand.'[48] Achimeir had refused to go the previous Zionist Congress in 1931 but now challenged Jabotinsky with his revolutionary view of the future – not to become a second Arthur Ruppin, but to assume the role of dictator. Nineteenth century liberalism had run its course. He juxtaposed the petition with the prospect of armed struggle:

> This is the cause of our tragedy. Zionism has always been coloured by the ghetto mentality with grandiose declarations, but the road to the kingdom of Israel does not pass through a bridge of paper, but through a bridge of steel.[49]

Achimeir was also critical of his erstwhile allies, the activist youth. He said that Betar had become fossilized and had begun to resemble their elders in the Revisionists. 'The difference between them is not great, it is a chronological difference.'[50] He was very clear as to what he expected from the activist youth:

> What Von Weisl offers is merely duplication (of the old order); I bring a new social form that is free of principles and of party; a fighting covenant. The Jesuits saved the Catholics; I bring you neo-Revisionism.[51]

Yosef Katznelson reiterated the Maximalist plea that the Revisionists were becoming too much like the mainstream Zionists and that the economy should be based on private enterprise.[52] Uri Zvi Greenberg accused the Revisionists of being on the verge of adopting 'the Weizmann ambience' and of being dangerously out of touch with the situation in Palestine.[53] He reminded his audience that people like himself had left the Left because of the regression of Zionism, but now Revisionism itself was becoming fossilized. Leone Carpi, the chairman of the Italian Revisionists and a member of Mussolini's Party[54] gave the Fascist salute as he rose to speak – and was in turn saluted by the Palestinian Maximalists.[55] This was also the first time that Jabotinsky had been openly criticized for his policies and ideological approach. Ben-Horin accused him of sacrificing the very idea of Revisionism in an attempt to prevent schism and called upon him to return to his 'original' views – 'Back to Jabotinsky.'[56] The Maximalists genuinely revered and publicly supported Jabotinsky against his opponents on the Revisionist Executive, but they were also quite willing to criticize him 'outside the committee rooms'.[57]

Jabotinsky's response to this was a four hour speech in Yiddish in which he condemned 'the dream of dictatorship among the younger generation which has reached epidemic proportions'. He said that he viewed Hitlerism with profound contempt and hoped that there would be no new world catastrophe, but he emphasized that he was 'an opponent of egoistic, aggressive nationalism or militarism'.[58] In criticizing the cult of the personality, he launched into an explanation of his understanding of the term 'leader'. Jabotinsky repeated his view that 'cattle have a leader while people have a chairman'[59] and told his audience that the idea of an all-knowing, divinely inspired leader in history was often a mechanism to assist people in deferring responsibility for thinking for themselves.[60] It was neither a question of status nor a desire for hero worship, but one of ideas that influenced people. In reacting to the demand for adventurism and imitating the need for dictators, Zionists, he argued, were pandering to the dictates of assimilation.[61] For Jabotinsky, a true party leader was the main thinker of his movement. People of ideas such as the Russian philosopher Nikolai Mikhailovsky impressed him as individuals who personified leadership. He professed his faith in the ideological heritage of the century of Garibaldi, Lincoln, Gladstone and Hugo:

> The ideological fashion of today is that man is naturally dishonest and foolish, and therefore should not be given the right to rule himself; freedom leads to destruction, equality to falsehood, so society needs leaders, orders, and truncheons. I do not want this type of faith. It is better not to be alive at all than to live under such a regime. I would rather disappear and die than to agree to a worldview that sees my son and the son of my neighbour as being of different value, or my son and the cobbler's son as unequal. I stand with all my strength by the democratic nature of our movement.[62]

He concluded by telling his audience that if this was the sort of society they wished to create with him as its dictator, he did not wish to breathe its air – 'and you cannot, in any circumstances whatsoever, impose this post upon me'.[63] In his evaluation of the conference afterwards, he played down the drama of the clash of views and wrote that that there was no room for real Fascists in the Revisionist movement. Publicly, he suggested that Achimeir and the Maximalists were playacting and were not serious in their beliefs:

> Such men, even in the Maximalist and activist factions, number no more than two or three, and even with these two or three – pardon my frankness – it is mere phraseology, not a worldview. Even Mr Achimeir gives me the impression of a man who will show flexibility for the sake of educational goals . . . to this end he has borrowed some currently fashionable (and quite unnecessary) phrases, in which this daring idea clothes itself in several foreign cities.[64]

Jabotinsky expressed his confidence that 'they will be amused by this and then drop it'. Clearly a mixture of ridicule and a charge of lack of seriousness was an effective tool against his opponents. This was clear when the resolution on endorsing the Calais agreement was passed by 82 votes to 24. Yet he pointed out that while the conference did not launch 'a new era', it did create 'a future full of possibilities'. However, a decision was taken to establish a political bureau of the Executive Committee in Palestine – half of whose members would consist of the Palestinian central committee. This was done to ensure coordination and political harmony between the Revisionists and its Palestinian branch while preserving the level of autonomy for the latter.[65] However, it was the revelation of Nazism and the reality of anti-Semitism that really led to the abandonment of the idea of a dictatorship and the overt rhetorical flourishes used by the Fascists. But Maximalism as an ideology continued because

Jabotinsky had permitted a pluralistic approach to emerge within the Revisionist movement which was authenticated by the autonomy of the Palestinian branch. The Maximalists had absorbed the Hapoel Hatzair notion that national redemption would arise 'in blood and fire'. Jabotinsky asked, 'why not water as well?' in reference to methods other than through direct action. 'No one should say that whereas I can work with water, you are not allowed to work with fire.'[66] The understanding of 'fire' was open to interpretation. Clearly Jabotinsky in 1932 interpreted it in one fashion and Achimeir in another.

SAVED BY THE BRITISH

Jabotinsky was not only fortunate that his opponents on the Revisionist Executive were unappealing figures, but also that there had been no overt manifestations of violence since 1929 or any dramatic displays of British determination to retreat from the Balfour Declaration. Jabotinsky was therefore able to put off the day of reckoning with the Maximalists – not simply through his charismatic style of leadership, but through two unexpected events: the appointment of Hitler as German Chancellor in January 1933 and the arrest of Achimeir by the British in July on suspicion of involvement in the assassination of Arlosoroff.

There had been murmurings of 'understanding' from the Maximalists when Hitler attained power. They viewed the wave of idealism that swept through German youth with a certain sense of vindication. Germany, they reasoned, now had a direction and a determined leadership. It was a return to the era of Bismarck and Prussian values. The pernicious influence of the Marxists had been halted. Nazi anti-Semitism was deemed to be unreal and thereby assumed a secondary importance in the eyes of the Maximalists. Achimeir's blindness led him to assert that German racism was no different from that of whites in South Africa or in the American south. 'Those who accuse Hitlerism of anti-Semitism should know that Hitler learned it from progressive Americans, with the constitution of Franklin and Jefferson.' Just as Italy and now Germany had reclaimed their national heritage from their past so should the Jews. After all, he wrote, 'It is the (political) heroes who are the creators of history — it is not history that creates heroes!'[67] The Maximalists downplayed the centrality of anti-Semitism in Nazi ideology and suggested that both movements espoused a common anti-Marxism. On the appointment of Hitler as German Chancellor, the Maximalists reacted to the universal condemnation of Nazism. They asked why there was no similar condemnation of Stalinism and the Comintern, which had assumed demonic proportions in their eyes. Their vehemence against Communism blinded them to the evils of Nazism. There was therefore little difference between Hitler and Thaelmann, his Communist rival. Moreover, the rise of Nazism laid down lessons for the Jews. It was an eye-opener for the assimilated and – in Achimeir's words – 'it is forbidden to tread proudly on a people's soul.'[68]

> The socialists and various types of democrats think that Hitler's movement is all shell, while we think that it has both shell and kernel. The anti-Semitic shell must be discarded, but not its anti-Marxist kernel.[69]

Following Hitler's appointment as Chancellor, the Nazi assault on the Jews from below began straight away. Anyone who stood in the path of the Nazi revolution was swept away. The ascendancy of the Nazis removed any constraints on violence – and humiliation and degradation of the Jews became the norm in February and March 1933. The threat of an unofficial Jewish boycott against German goods induced Hitler to declare an internal boycott against Jewish businessmen and Jewish-owned department stores as well as the dismissal and isolation of German Jews – doctors, schoolchildren and civil servants. It was this intensification and legitimization of anti-Semitism in April 1933 which was the turning point for the Maximalists in Palestine who now began to see the national revolution in Germany in a different light.

However, in the intervening months before April 1933, Jabotinsky had to contend with two divergent views on the meaning of Hitler's ascendancy to power. In the week after Hitler's appointment, he warned that he had heard all the explanations – that Hitler would not last long as Chancellor or that he was not intelligent and would make mistakes or that extremists become moderates once confronted with the realities of power – and found them unconvincing. He wrote that he had read *Mein Kampf* and that while this was 'talentless, naïve and pedestrian' gutter literature, he recognised that Hitler knew how to argue a point and how to relate it to everyday life. Moreover, Hitler, he suggested, could always depend on his more astute colleagues, Goebbels and Strasser. The likes of Hindenberg, Von Papen and Hugenberg would be unable to stem the tide of rising anti-Semitism and protect the Jews. Responding to the argument of the Maximalists, Jabotinsky wrote that Hitler had 'an excellent mentor' in Mussolini and:

> If we too easily differentiate between hatred of the House of Israel and the rest of the Hitler's ideology, if we try to sell ourselves the idea that the Nazis will mechanically carry out their programme – and forget about us – then we are being excessively optimistic. It is very possible that both Hitler and his aides, even those who aren't stupid, don't have the necessary talent to carry out their grandiose plan, in all its massive ramifications. But the problem is enormous. It is for the first time ever that the main question of our very existence in the Diaspora has been put before us in such a prominent way.[50]

There had been an internal debate within Betar in Palestine whether to devote all its energies to the kind of militancy proposed by Brit HaBiryonim.[71] But now the head of Betar in Palestine began to advocate that the youth movement should base itself on purely Jewish models – Bar-Kochba rather than Hitler or Mussolini.[72] With the enactment of the Nazi boycott of the Jews, Jabotinsky vociferously denounced Hitler in a broadcast on Radio Warsaw. Betar and the Revisionist Union in Germany were formally disbanded to prevent conflict with the Nazi authorities.[73] In this matter of 'Jews against Germany', he urged Revisionists and Betar to adopt the role of whistleblowers in the Jewish community – 'to remind shopkeepers and consumers, to flush out traitors…and to fight them until they get used to it'. The Jews, he suggested, had an interest in preventing a belligerent Germany from rearming and remaining 'weak and helpless'. Moreover, Jews should not allow others to lead the condemnation of Hitler's Germany. The Revisionists should take the lead in being overt and not covert in their campaign. 'The Jewish voice …will truly be the sound of the human conscience' and would serve to give the stamp of approval to an international campaign 'to restrain Germany'.[74] Jabotinsky supported the boycott movement, but opposed the controversial Transfer Agreement whereby Jewish immigrants to Palestine would buy German goods and redeem them in the local currency. This proved to be another bone of contention between the Labour movement's Mapai and the Revisionists. Moreover, Mapai's gradualism meant that Jabotinsky's call for mass evacuation was a non-starter.[75]

All this was ironically taking place at the same time as the Revisionist movement was falling apart at the Katowice conference – in the aftermath of failed attempts to bridge the differences with Grossman. Achimeir and the Maximalists saw Jabotinsky's taking control as proof of strong leadership and probably the first step on the road to dictatorship – despite Jabotinsky's categorical condemnation of such a role. Jabotinsky's vehemence reached its zenith in a letter to the editors of *Hazit Ha'am* where he angrily complained that such articles about Hitler and the Nazi movement was 'a stab in the back for me personally and for all of us'. He ridiculed those who found elements of 'a national liberation' movement in Nazism and demanded the complete disappearance of 'all this dirty hysteria' from the pages of *Hazit Ha'am*.

> If even one more line is published in *Hazit Ha'am* that could be interpreted as an attempt by small-minded Jews to find favour before such a crude tyrant who happened by chance to be elected, I will insist on removing the newspaper from the party and will cut off all personal contact with those who are causing my work to flounder for the sake of such cheap mass sarcasm.[76]

Brit HaBiryonim had already seen the light. They proceeded to remove the Nazi flag from the German consulate in Jerusalem – leaving the German imperial flag in place – and daubed slogans on its gates.[77]

On 16 June 1933, the rising star of the Labour movement Chaim Arlosoroff, the head of the political department of the Jewish Agency, was assassinated by unknown assailants as he strolled along the Tel Aviv coastline with his wife. Betar in Palestine participated in his funeral cortège. Five weeks later, fifteen Revisionists and members of Betar were arrested. Achimeir, Yeivin and Katznelson were amongst those charged. The Revisionist archives, Achimeir's own writings and even the letter written by Yeivin wherein Jabotinsky contemplated expelling them from the Revisionist Party were confiscated by the police. The arrests and indictments were an attempt to attach the murder of Arlosoroff to Brit HaBiryonim – and to blur the two cases. The indictment against Achimeir eventually collapsed and he and some of his co-defendants were acquitted.

Attention was intensely focused on the death sentence passed on one of the defendants, Avraham Stavsky, a recent immigrant from the US and a member of the Egroff (fist) group,[78] for the killing of Arlosoroff. Jabotinsky and the Revisionists embarked on a campaign to overturn the verdict on appeal. This led to a request for the appearance of the editors of *Doar Hayom*, *Hayarden* and *Ion Meyuchad* in the High Court for publishing bitter condemnations of the sentence. Indeed Jabotinsky's article 'At the Crossroads' in *Hayarden* was deemed to be the most offensive.[79] On the diplomatic front, Jabotinsky warned in a letter to the Colonial Secretary that the death sentence on Stavsky would be a disaster which threatened 'to poison Anglo-Jewish relations beyond repair'.[80] Significantly, this deep-seated belief in Britain permeated Jabotinsky's responses through his campaign to save his ideological opponents in the Revisionist movement even when Stavsky was formally acquitted.[81]

While his release was greeted with jubilation, it also overshadowed the separate trial of Achimeir and members of Brit HaBiryonim who had remained in prison. Although Jabotinsky publicly promoted the hope for another acquittal, there was not the same passionate and energetic commitment as in the Stavsky affair.

Achimeir and his co-defendants were tried on four counts: conspiring to effect acts in furtherance of seditious intention; advocating and encouraging unlawful acts; being a member of an unlawful and seditious association; and being in possession of seditious literature. At the end of a long trial, the judge found Achimeir guilty on three counts and sentenced him to 21 months' imprisonment. He was cleared of instigating unlawful acts. In his summing-up, the judge attempted to unravel the nature of Brit HaBiryonim. Utilizing interpretations from the classic dictionary of modern Hebrew by Eliezer Ben-Yehuda – the father of the Hebrew language – the judge interpreted the Biryonim of the 1930s as 'terrorists' and distinct from the ancient forebears of the same name. Achimeir's defence commented that he had always been interested in terrorism as a historian and intended to write a history of the Russian revolution. While the defence argued that Brit HaBiryonim was nothing more than a faction within the Revisionist movement, the judge clearly believed that it was something more. He referred to the founding of an 'Organization of Revolutionary Zionists' which was considerably different from Revisionism. In particular, he mentioned the material confiscated – 12 documents written by Achimeir, another nine addressed to him and 20 found in his possession. Achimeir's 'Scroll of the Sicarii' which was written shortly after an attempt to assassinate Mussolini in the 1920s was considered to be a moral licence to kill for political reasons. The judge termed it 'a glorification of political murder'. Achimeir's diary which was 'illuminating as showing his intentions and thoughts' included a comment that 'acts are needed to drag the Jabotinsky movement out of the mud.' Other tracts included phrases such as 'with blood Judea will arise'; 'Zionist Revolutionary Order'; 'Long live the Jewish Revolution and the Jewish Dictatorship.' A student testified that he had heard Achimeir speak in Haifa in the summer of 1933 where he expressed the view that there was no one within the Jewish student body who had the tenacity of the German students who had killed Rosa Luxembourg, Karl Liebknecht and Walter Rathenau.[82] Another witness at the meeting, however, said she heard nothing of the kind. Achimeir, in response, asked the witness to produce a stenogram of the speech.[83] A letter written by one of the defendants, Chaim Dviri, did suggest that there was a distinction between Brit HaBiryonim and the Revisionist movement. Brit HaBiryonim did not 'care for' Parliament and its manners. In order 'to fight pitilessly in any way against British imperialism', it was necessary for the movement to train people for revolutionary action and that youth should be prepared to sacrifice themselves on the scaffold and on the guillotine.

The ideas of Achimeir and the activities of Brit HaBiryonim were considered to be seditious by the British. Indeed, the trial judge concluded that 'a dangerous conspiracy has been unearthed'. Significantly he also stated that the Jabotinsky-Yeivin correspondence on the ideology of Revisionist Zionism was unimportant – the effect of this was to separate Brit HaBiryonim from the Palestine Revisionists. Labour, the Revisionists and the British all had something to gain from the suppression of Brit HaBiryonim.

Throughout all this, Jabotinsky nominally supported Achimeir and his co-defendants. He significantly did not refer to the ideology and future plans of Brit HaBiryonim, but only to their past demonstrations. Here too, when the sentence on Achimeir was reduced on appeal by a couple of months, he did not suggest acquittal as in the case of Stavsky, but that the demonstration against Bentwich at the Hebrew University only merited a sentence of hard labour.[84] This was a double-edged approach. On the one hand, it allowed Jabotinsky to marginalize Achimeir and to displace the Maximalists by taking the lead in the Revisionist campaign to help them. On the other, Jabotinsky appeared as the standard bearer for the nationalist camp. The Labour movement which had convinced itself that the Revisionists were responsible for the murder was aghast at the overturning of the verdict. There was now a deep-seated belief in the Labour Zionist movement that the Revisionists were nothing less than Palestine's version of European Fascism. Ben-Gurion had already published a book on relations with the Revisionists in which he accused Jabotinsky of following in the footsteps of Hitler.

When Stavsky visited the synagogue immediately on his release and was called up to the weekly reading of the Torah portion, this was a signal for the overturning of benches and for the throwing of stones from the ladies' gallery.[85] All this fortified Jabotinsky's status as the defender of patriotic nationalist youth against the unforgiving onslaught of the socialists. He could thus unofficially order the smashing of windows in British embassies and consulates in order to protest the reduction in the number of immigration certificates.[86] The control of militancy was now in his hands rather than Achimeir's. In essence, Jabotinsky's broad strategy to extinguish Brit HaBiryonim worked since Achimeir never recovered his status as an ideologue after his release. However, he had performed his historic role as a catalyst and Jabotinsky's public support for him enhanced the drift towards Maximalism within the Revisionist movement and within Betar especially.

Despite their defeat at the Vienna Conference, the Maximalists still believed that the Revisionists would leave the Zionist Organization and continued to place their faith in Jabotinsky. On a visit to Palestine in January 1933 Grossman was told a political bureau would never be established there – even though it was in accordance with the conference resolutions – until Jabotinsky had taken all the political work out of the hands of the London office. In a heated debate with Grossman, the Palestinian Revisionists advocated that the leading positions in the movement should be held only by those who recognized the primacy of Revisionist discipline – as opposed to that of the Zionist Organization – and this would be under the jurisdiction of Jabotinsky. Faced with such uncompromising opposition, Grossman took the first steps towards fortifying his own faction in the Revisionist movement by attempting to establish a rival newspaper to *Hazit Ha'am*. The weekly *Hamatarah* under Grossman's editorship lasted only five months.

Jabotinsky believed that the Vienna Conference had resolved the question of the primacy of discipline – and that the primacy of Revisionist discipline had prevailed. It later transpired that his colleagues on the Revisionist Executive did not share his interpretation.[87] The Zionist Organization had recognized the existence of a Separate Union of Revisionists and, indeed, conditions relating to the Calais agreement. They presumed that the separate union which had subscribed to the Zionist Organization would thereby be under its broad discipline. The resolutions at Vienna cast doubt on all this. All approaches to the Separate Union met with ambiguous responses[88] and the Zionist Organization suspended the Separate Union in January 1933. During the next few months, the disagreement over the question of discipline and by extension membership of the Zionist Organization grew worse. Jabotinsky wished to amend the resolutions adopted at Calais and Vienna to ensure Revisionist discipline. Grossman was happy to remain in a sea of ambivalence and argued that Revisionist campaigns were not hampered by the discipline of the Zionist Organization.

The Revisionists in Palestine demanded strong leadership that would 'save the young people from the claws of Marxism and other bankrupt ideas',[89] and addressed an open letter to the world movement.[90] It protested against the implied threats that to leave the Zionist Congress would meet discrimination and exclusion from public bodies in Palestine. It called for 'the realization of mass Jewish immigration' and commented that Jewish youth were becoming increasingly embittered by the state of affairs. The heated discussions at a meeting of the party council at Katowice in March 1933 led nowhere and both sides refused to submit a resolution. The meeting ended in confusion, yet the day afterwards, Jabotinsky announced that he had suspended the central institutions of the movement and was personally taking control. This statement known as the Lodz Manifesto announced that he was also establishing a provisional secretariat to replace the Revisionist Executive and a provisional commissariat for the Separate Union. Grossman and his colleagues cried 'putsch' while the headlines from the Polish press announced that 'the Jews have a Dictator'. Jabotinsky explained his actions in *Moment* while Grossman attacked him for authoritarianism and inconsistency in *Haynt*. Grossman complained that Jabotinsky changed 'his coats in the same fashion that an oriental dancer changes her veils'.[91] In mid-April all Revisionists over the age of 18 were asked by Jabotinsky to vote in a plebiscite. The Executive called upon them not to take part.[92] They were requested to effectively endorse Jabotinsky's actions in taking personal control until the next world conference. 93.2 per cent approved, but only 6.2 per cent did not. Grossman produced figures to show that a majority of Revisionists had not bothered to vote. Moreover, Jabotinsky's opponents argued that there was nothing in the Revisionist Constitution which allowed him to assume control. The situation was also confusing because Jabotinsky played two roles. One was as the advocate of a specific point of view, the other as the neutral, objective President of the movement. The Maximalists, however, now saw Jabotinsky as 'the energized and assertive leader that he had been in his best years'. They even contemplated that Jabotinsky would head a Betar list – rather than a Revisionist one - in the elections to the next Zionist Congress.[93]

Achimeir viewed Jabotinsky's attempt to take control as a vindication of Maximalism. It was 'separation' rather than 'unification' which pointed to his understanding of the future. It was only those national regimes associated with separatism and strong leaders – Kemal Attaturk, Mussolini, Pilsudski, De Valera and Hitler – which were successful. In a concession to Jewish sensibilities, Achimeir added, 'whatever we may feel, it is clear that in each case the Maximalists won.' He was fearful that the developments at Katowice would only lead to a display of Maximalist rhetoric and that coalition building would continue with other Zionist parties. Instead he advocated a Third Zionist movement. The first had been established by Pinsker and Lillienblum in Katowice in 1884, the second by Herzl and Nordau in Basle in 1897; it was now time to break with the past and to establish a new movement.[94]

Yet Jabotinsky went ahead and attended the 18th Zionist Congress in the summer of 1933. The split in the Revisionist movement was essentially formalized when 46 delegates represented the official Revisionists while seven represented the Separate Union of Grossman and the former Executive. Grossman's group seceded to become the Jewish State Party which remained affiliated to the Zionist Congress. Jabotinsky's supporters left shortly afterwards. Concurring with Achimeir's approach, Jabotinsky formed a new movement to rival the old. In Hitler's first year of power, accompanied by the doctrine of official anti-Semitism, the Zionist movement split. Separation was deemed more important than unity. The Revisionists subsequently emerged as the central force in Jabotinsky's New Zionist Organization which remained outside the mainstream Zionist Organization. Both Poland and Palestine fervently supported Jabotinsky, but the split meant that he lost the support not only of the moderates, but also the many intellectuals in the movement. The adherents of Maximalism especially in Betar suddenly attained an increasingly important role.

RAZIEL, STERN AND BEGIN

The Aftermath of Vienna

At the Vienna Conference, Achimeir admitted that the Maximalists had been placed in 'splendid isolation' both by the other delegates and especially by those from Palestine.[1] Yet by its end, he also believed that, he had made a great impact on the youth. The leader of the Activists, Von Weisl, commented in his speech:

> Achimeir is more radical than me, but because I know that he has a brilliant mind, I do not consider him to be a madman. He has a definite manner about him and I am filled with a sense of brotherhood towards him. We will ensure that this will penetrate into the ranks of the Revisionist movement.[2]

Thus despite Jabotinsky's stand and the crushing defeat of Achimeir and his supporters on the resolution on the Calais agreement, Maximalism had not been extinguished, but instead became increasingly influential and dominant within Betar. The full comprehension of Hitler's attitude towards the Jews may eventually have diminished any pro-Fascist inclinations, but it did not alter the general political approach of the Maximalists. Following the Vienna conference, the contacts made by Achimeir began to bear fruit and their attempts to spread their ideas were well received. The representatives of Maximalism in Poland sent a memorandum to the Katowice conference in which they bemoaned the failure of the Revisionist movement to inhibit the atrophication of Zionist youth. It listed several past goals of the Revisionists such as unrestricted immigration and active resistance to the British administration in Palestine – and asked why these goals had not been achieved. They suggested instead that the Revisionist movement should be reconstructed on a hierarchical basis, firm discipline and total obedience to 'the higher echelons of the movement':

> The movement must be united. Discipline must be introduced and it must be brought under the unconditional dictate of the Leader. Our movement was born

as a result of the act of the genius of our era of national revival. The Leader must be the sole influential element in our movement who must guide the movement and lead it along the route of recovery from its childhood illnesses – the fear of independence and the feelings of inferiority.[3]

The Polish Maximalists advocated 'a closing of the English chapter'. If the British continued to rule the Land of Israel, they would view them as 'a government of occupation'. Moreover, the British would be opposed by 'large scale political action' – and for this reason, it was important to allow the Revisionists in Palestine 'wide-reaching autonomy and far-reaching political independence'. The fifteen signatories from all over Poland included the local Betar commander in Brest-Litovsk, Menachem Begin.

In 1932, Aharon Propes, the effective founder and organizer of Betar, appointed Begin to one of Betar's nine regional commands, the Polsia area of Eastern Poland, shortly after he had arrived in Warsaw to study law. Begin was also given the Betar's organization portfolio. In addition, he was involved with two new publications which appeared at the same time. *Madrich Betar: A Platform for Ideological and Educational Issues* appeared in Warsaw in September 1932. The solicited articles came not only from the leadership of Betar in Poland and beyond, but also from the Maximalist intellectuals such as Achimeir and Greenberg. Achimeir, in particular, was idolized by Polish Betar, and in the first issue, he warned that:

> we have not exploited the 'chance' given to us by the crisis of 1914-1918 because of the intellectual dominance of the socialists in the Jewish street and the 'wimpishness' of a Zionism which wants to please everybody . . . a military movement, the Betar movement, will prevail among Jewish youth. And we must prepare Betar for the world crisis – a crisis, for if we are worthy, will see the birth pangs of the Jewish state emerge out of the sufferings of war. [4]

In contradistinction to Jabotinsky, who was head of Betar, Achimeir told his young readers that 'education for the purpose of defence is not appropriate' and instead compared 'our army' with that of Cromwell from the English revolution. Betar leaders such as Benno Lubotsky suggested that the world did not listen to the Jews because they manifested 'physical weaknesses' and their 'ethical fervour' was deemed irrelevant and mocked. Waiting for the messiah and the end of days solved nothing, only 'an iron wall of a sophisticated defence army' would help the Jews.[5] *Madrich Betar* was distributed throughout all the central branches of the movement in Poland and in turn spawned local versions.

Similarly *Hamedina* appeared in Riga in February 1933 and was transferred to Warsaw a year later. Appearing in Hebrew, Yiddish and Polish, its high standard attracted the Maximalists. In the second issue Achimeir was quoted as saying that it was now the time for youth to 'cleanse its soul of idolatry and to create battalions for the war against anti-Semitism.' They had to learn from Garibaldi, Pilsudski, Gandhi 'and especially De Valera' so that 'a revolutionary Zionism must be created'.[6] Lubotsky described the paradoxical situation which Betar inhabited and fortified only by the dream of the future:

> Betar is a magic circle: a movement that aspires to create a state which does not yet exist (and whose entire raison d'être is this aspiration), and trying to construct itself on organizational foundations that will only exist in this state.[7]

Jabotinsky found himself in a complicated and sometimes desperate situation in the summer of 1933. By seizing control of the Revisionist movement and initiating a plebiscite, he catalysed the exodus of Meir Grossman and his followers. Although he opposed their wish to remain within the Zionist Organization, he also needed their support as a counter-balance to the Maximalists and Activists. With them gone, he effectively strengthened the militant tendency within the Revisionists and moved the movement towards the authoritarian Right and away from his brand of nineteenth century liberal conservatism. It meant the exit of old colleagues of Herzl such as Max Bodenheimer who felt that Jabotinsky had fallen 'under the spell of Von Weisl and Achimeir'.[8]

The Maximalist *Hazit Ha'am* was overjoyed at the turn of events and greeted the schism at Katowice with the banner headline: 'Jabotinsky's Way: Zionism takes on a struggle against the Bosses, the Marxists and the Scroungers.' But importantly it suggested that the true Revisionists now were the youth who really understood their leader and 'followed his path without doubt'.[9] It left the movement with a hard core of Maximalist intellectuals and activist youth, a rapidly radicalizing Betar and an adulatory mass following who paid more attention to the spirit of Jabotinsky's pronouncements than their substance.

With the split, Aharon Propes, the head of Betar in Poland was appointed by Jabotinsky to the temporary Executive. The vast majority of Betar's members remained with Jabotinsky and very few left to join Grossman's new youth movement, Brit HaCana'im. Jabotinsky met the Council of Regional Commands of Betar in Warsaw at the end of March 1933. Menachem Begin spoke about the new training schemes that had been initiated to help Betar immigrants prepare for Palestine such as the agricultural school in Vilna and the foundry in Suwalki. There were military training squads, courses in self-defence and a series of meetings to celebrate the 15th anniversary of the establishment of the Jewish Legion.[10] While he welcomed the Betar Commanders' support, he also warned them to use tact in their polemics against his long-time former colleagues. Unlike the Maximalists, Jabotinsky still felt that there was a place for

Grossman and his allies once the contentious issues had been resolved by a vote. He related his vision of the future to the Betar commanders. Echoing Achimeir's prophecy, he stated that:

> This is the third attempt to forge the Zionist movement. Pinsker made the first attempt, Herzl the second, and we are currently engaged in the third. The Revisionist movement will develop and grow. It will first become a majority within Zionism, and then will become Zionism itself. Betar will be the moral and spiritual lawgiver for all Jewish youth.[11]

The Maximalists and many in Betar including Menachem Begin saw through Jabotinsky's repackaging of the movement's image and simply did not agree. They argued for revolutionary Zionism, not evolutionary Zionism. Begin had already begun to express his views on the militarism and patriotism in the Betar journal, *Hamedina*.[12] Yet Jabotinsky's pronouncements in 1934 suggested a more engaged situation with Betar. For example, 'The Idea of Betar' – an explanation of the movement's raison d'être, its guidelines and effective constitution was written and disseminated by Jabotinsky. He may well have wished to counter the influence of the Maximalists upon the youth, but such emphasis on youth, militancy and self-sacrifice seemed only to augment it. Even a question mark which he placed over the Western democracies and their policies illustrated this trend. Jabotinsky presented the persona of a wise, but aged rebbe – he was then in his mid-fifties – urging his pupils to understand the principles of Herzlian Zionism and to grasp the standard as it metaphorically fell from his tired hands. Both teacher and students enthusiastically played their parts. Yet the spread of Maximalism and its pervasive influence within Betar ensured that there were continuous departures from the original script.

In an article entitled 'A Legend in His Lifetime', Begin bemoaned the fact that Achimeir had been imprisoned and was impotent to influence events. He praised Achimeir as 'a brilliant journalist' whose articles came from within the genre of 'spiritual literature that incites the blood'. But Begin also saw Achimeir as a poor speaker and a poor organizer, although he pointed out, the ideas that he conveyed went far beyond the lecture hall. Begin wrote about the impact that the legend, the personal example and accomplishments of Achimeir had made upon Jewish youth:

> This legend... has recently struck even deeper chords in the hearts of Jewish youth. Why? Because Achimeir epitomized a new way for the struggle for freedom: a way which – no matter how difficult it becomes – contains a halo of honour; a way which as cruel as it is – has in it something that invites enthusiasm: the way of being willing to go to prison. And he epitomizes this way, body and soul.[13]

Begin significantly wrote this article in August 1935 on the eve of the founding conference of the New Zionist Organization. It was an implicit criticism of the transformation of Revisionism into the NZO rather than an evolution into a body embracing direct action – and ultimately the armed struggle. Others such as Uri Zvi Greenberg attempted to link Maximalism to Jewish tradition. At a Betar conference in Warsaw in 1934, Greenberg claimed that Moses had been a Maximalist as had been the rabbis who excommunicated Spinoza.[14] The Labour Zionists were now 'sanbalatim' – the equivalent of local stooges of a foreign empire.

Maximalism therefore found its time and place because events – the rise of Nazism, the Arab Revolt of 1936, increasing Polish anti-Semitism and Jewish degradation, the inability of the British to live up to Zionist aspirations, the powerlessness of the mainstream Zionist Organization – all conspired to overwhelm normative Jewish responses. Jabotinsky and Begin inhabited different worlds. The former – the cosmopolitan man of letters who had never shaken off the attraction of assimilationism. The latter – the youth from the provincial shtetl who was not allowed to forget his Jewishness.

Jabotinsky increasingly mentioned his age and looked back nostalgically to a pre-1914 world of liberal values and intellectual endeavour. Begin embraced a future of self-sacrifice and national liberation, framed by Darwinian definitions. Israel Eldad, later a leader of Lehi and highly critical of Begin's approach, offered an incisive observation of the two men in the late 1930s. Begin was depicted as a Roman pupil attempting to travel the same path as his Greek teacher but unable to attain his mentor's lofty heights both intellectually and in the manner he exhibited graciousness and dignity:

> Jabotinsky often closed his eyes to see more clearly and remained tight-lipped to think more deeply. His pupil, not so. The teacher exuded an inner beauty compared to his charge. But the reality of the situation overwhelmed both of them – and it was here where they were forced to act.[15]

At the second world conference of Betar in Cracow in January 1935, Jabotinsky spoke about 'the pain and suffering' which the members of the movement had endured at the hands of the Left and repeated his views set out in 'The Idea of Betar'. He mourned the passing of Bialik and Baron Rothschild as well as complimenting Chief Rabbi Kook for his support.[16] Above all, Jabotinsky was effusive in his praise of Betar:

> I love the Tsohar (Revisionists); I love the Brit Ha'chayal and the young Brit Yeshurun, but above all I love Betar. The Tsohar is the branches of the tree; Betar is the root from which we all receive their nourishment until the final victory is achieved. This is my firm belief. [17]

In contrast to Jabotinsky, Menachem Begin spoke during the second session and criticized the lack of meaningful contact between the leadership and the youth. Moreover, he called for the politicization of the youth of Betar.[18] In the 6th World Revisionist Conference which followed the Betar gathering, he criticized the accord struck between Jabotinsky and Ben-Gurion in London which was designed to put an end to the bitter rift between the Revisionists and the Labour Zionists. Both movements in the end decisively rejected their leaders' attempts to make peace. Begin was vociferous in his attacks on the possibility of reconciliation and even condemned the imprisoned Achimeir's call for a truce as 'a serious breach of movement discipline'.[19] The extreme antagonism between Left and Right helped to define the Betar generation and their opponents both in Palestine and in the Diaspora. For example, in 1933, when hundreds of members of Betar in Palestine came to honour Trumpeldor on the anniversary of his death, they were met by local left wing demonstrators at his graveside.[20] Begin reminded Jabotinsky that the Labour Zionist press had referred to him as 'Vladimir Hitler'[21] and the Revisionists were continually branded as 'Jewish Fascists' by Ben-Gurion and the Mapai leadership – and such slurs were keenly felt.[22]

But Begin's determined approach was rewarded by his appointment as head of the propaganda department of Betar in September 1935. At the beginning of 1936, in addition to all his other duties, Begin was asked to become head of Betar in Czechoslovakia and to revive its fortunes. Jabotinsky and Propes dismissed Begin's radicalism as the prerogative of youth and such 'adventurism' – as in the case of Achimeir – was to be encouraged within rational parameters. Thus, Begin had assisted Jabotinsky in his Polish campaign to save Stavsky from the hangman. Jabotinsky embraced this spirit of commitment and penned both the Betar anthem 'To Die or Conquer the Mountain' and 'The Idea of Betar' in 1934.[23] But such encouragement also allowed Betar to absorb the central features of Maximalism – to which Jabotinsky was so adamantly opposed. Jabotinsky was always keen to prevent youth from becoming enthusiastic about rival ideologies. The bitterness between Betar and the Labour movement in Palestine ensured a distancing from Communism. But Jabotinsky also condemned Betar in Germany for its flirtation with the Nazi representatives during the pre-boycott period:

> Hitlerism remains schweinerei in spite of the enthusiasm of millions which impresses our youth so much in a manner similar to that which Communist enthusiasm impresses other Jews. It is a very cheap and common type of assimilation.[24]

Yet the hostility between the Revisionists and Betar and the Labour movement often took a physical form – even in Nazi Germany. Although the Revisionists and Betar had formally been disbanded, an article in Goebbels' *Der Angriff* – headlined 'Jewish secret meeting, grave fighting between co-racials' – commented that, 'it is time to proceed rigorously against these people who have apparently forgotten how to live in a National Socialist state, enjoying here hospitality as a guest people.' The pretext of the fighting led to a raid on the Zionist headquarters in the Meinekestrasse and searches of the homes of leading Zionists were conducted. The chairmen of all nineteen branches of the Zionist movement were called in to the Gestapo.[25]

THE GENESIS OF THE IRGUN

In parallel with the growing radicalization of Betar, another group of dissidents began to coalesce in Palestine. The 1929 killings catalysed a split in the Haganah. The reasons were anchored both in the powerlessness of the Jews and in the indecision of the British. The members of Haganah Bet (B) – 'the National Haganah' – complained about the docility and acquiescence of its mother body. A disaffected group in Jerusalem formed HaSukhba which began to publish a new periodical, *Hametsuda,* in 1932.[26] HaSukhba comprised many young men in their early twenties such as Avraham Stern and David Raziel who would later emerge as leaders of the Irgun Zvai Leumi and Lehi. The members of HaSukhba initially were non-aligned nationalists who warmed to the actions of the Maximalists rather than to their ideas. They focused on military training and armed struggle – and were thereby naturally drawn towards and influenced by figures such as Achimeir, Yeivin and Greenberg. *Hametsuda* served as a means of disseminating the views of the Maximalist thinkers within both wings of the Haganah, but also more widely within the Revisionist movement and Betar.

In the first issue, Yeivin wrote the main ideological article in which he described the sanctity of their mission. In a second article he criticized 'The Pacifism of Jewish Youth in Germany'. Chaim Shalom Halevi and Peretz Carmeli examined national liberation movements in Bulgaria and Czechoslovakia. Future issues looked at the Western Wall disturbances or commemorated the outbreak of the Bar-Kochba revolt eighteen hundred years previously. Articles were attributed to the surname initial or pseudonyms were used – 'Infantist' (Raziel) and 'The Recluse' (Klausner).[27] Avraham Stern was an admirer of the Polish romantic poet, Juliusz Slowacki[28] who wrote about the suffering of the Poles in the long years of struggle for national independence. As a young classics student at the Hebrew University in Jerusalem, he had been involved in the Bentwich demonstration. *Hametsuda* published his own poetry including the well-known 'Chayalim Almonim' (Unknown Soldiers).[29] Stern's poems spoke of self-sacrifice and martyrdom, of blood and fire. He wrote:

Yes
I am both a soldier and a poet
Today I write with a pen, tomorrow I will write with a sword
Today I write in ink, tomorrow I will write in blood
Today on paper, tomorrow on the torso of a man
Heaven gave us the book and the sword
Fate has decreed it
Soldier and poet[30]

This was written in June 1934 in Florence where he had gone to study and where he was increasingly impressed by Mussolini's new Italy. Stern's poem gives an understanding of how he viewed himself. It began with a quotation from the first Book of Samuel whereby King Saul searched for a young man 'who is skilful in playing (the harp) and a heroic man of valour and a man of war'.[31] This, of course, referred to the future King David – the shepherd boy who would become ruler of Saul's domain. It was also accompanied by a fragment of a poem by the Greek mercenary and poet, Archilochus: 'I am a follower of my lord Enyalius (the God of war), and I understand the lovely gift of the Muses.' Archilochus was eventually killed in battle, but significantly he was the first European writer to give vent to his personal experiences as the central theme of his poetry. His famous comment, 'the fox knows many things, but the hedgehog knows one big thing' could well have been adapted to Stern's understanding of Zionism and its goals. All this – Biblical romanticism, Greek mythology and Italian Fascism – propelled Stern towards the armed struggle of the Jews of Palestine.

David Raziel who worked with Stern in the early days of the Irgun came from a rabbinical background and indeed enrolled at Mercaz Ha'Rav Kook, the seminary of Chief Rabbi Kook.[32] He, too, was affected by the killings in 1929 and the lack of response by both the Zionist leadership and the British. He had intended to enrol at the yeshiva (seminary) in Hebron where the massacre had taken place, but had chosen Jerusalem instead. He became a member of the student group 'El Al' which had been established by Joseph Klausner.[33] Like Stern, he was involved in the Bentwich demonstration. He, too, had been expelled, apologized and reinstated. Unlike Stern, he was closer to the Revisionists and studied military history and theoreticians such as Clausewitz and Mazzini. In 1933, he became the Irgun commander in charge of the Old City of Jerusalem. Raziel educated himself about military strategy and techniques and wrote 'the Theory of Training' and 'Parade Ground and Field Drill' for dissemination within the Irgun. Together with Stern, he wrote a military manual *Haekdach* (The Pistol). When Raziel gave a copy to his future wife, he inscribed it with familiar quotations from traditional Jewish sources such as 'to learn and teach, to heed and to do' from the daily 'Shema' prayer as well as Ben Bag Bag's famous dictum from the Ethics of the Fathers: 'Turn it and turn it over again, for everything is in it, and contemplate it.' The Irgun oath was taken over a flag, a gun and a Bible. Raziel used a Biblical quote, symbolizing the bond between the Jewish Naomi and her Moabite daughter-in-law, Ruth, as the oath of allegiance. 'Where you die, I will die and there will I be buried; God will do this for me and even more so, only death will part us.' While this certainly epitomized a geographical return to Zion, Jewish tradition also viewed this Biblical episode as an echo of Ruth's act of conversion to Judaism. All these selective quotes clearly omitted the name of God.[34] Thus, for Raziel, the oath not only symbolized self-sacrifice, brotherhood and solidarity between the members of the Irgun, but also an act of conversion to a new understanding of Jewishness in the Land of Israel.

While the Irgun began to attract members of Betar, as well as university and yeshiva students, Jabotinsky kept his distance from the organization despite its Board of non-socialist party representatives. Although approached on several occasions to involve him and to take a seat on the Board, Jabotinsky was ambivalent and refused to give his moral backing to the Irgun. He reacted negatively to operations that had not been sanctioned, but more importantly he did not believe that a Jewish Legion could be created out of the framework of an underground.[35] The events of the mid-1930s conspired to deny Jabotinsky room to manoeuvre and to think through a rational policy. The outbreak of the Arab Revolt in 1936 closed the gap between words and deeds. Jabotinsky was no longer able to maintain the distinction between encouraging youth to be militant and defiant and their increasing desire to take up arms and retaliate. While Achimeir had been marginalized through his imprisonment and the Brit HaBiryonim neutralized, his message of direct action was far more potent amongst the youth than any tarring by his flirtation with Fascism. Even though the onset of the Spanish civil war catalysed a new outburst of 'understanding' for European Fascism from Achimeir and the Maximalists,[36] it was the prospect of casting off the passivity of doing nothing that transformed the Irgun into a home for Maximalist Revisionists and members of Betar. Indeed the professional and educated offspring of the Palestinian Arab notables organizing themselves into parties and the forces of rising Arab nationalism were ready to confront both the British rulers and the Zionists. With the advent of Nazism, Jewish immigration increased dramatically and the Jewish population of Palestine doubled between 1931 and 1936.

The Arab Revolt brought with it attacks on Jewish civilians as well as on the British military. Yet the official policy of the Yishuv was one of 'havlagah' – self-restraint on moral and ethical grounds. Much of this policy was rooted in the fusion of Jewish and socialist traditions that condemned the shedding of blood. Self-restraint against violent provocations served to elevate the self-image of the Zionist pioneer to a new moral plain. Many Revisionists argued that such a policy would not bring political dividends from the British and blurred the reality in Palestine. Reaction and retaliation was the only rational choice.

Jabotinsky had written to the Colonial Secretary to protest the low level of British policing despite the 1929 disturbances – an issue to which the Inspector-General of Police in Palestine had drawn attention publicly. Jabotinsky argued that in other British colonies, settlers were encouraged to form military units such as the Planters' Rifles in Ceylon, the Burghers' Force in West Africa and the Kenya Defence Force.[37] As the Jewish casualties began to rise, many in both the Haganah and in the Irgun began to question the veracity of such a policy. Throughout 1936 Jabotinsky resisted calls to embrace havlaga in the hope of securing British agreement to establish an armed Jewish force in Palestine. In addition, British influence in the Mediterranean seemed be waning with a resurgent Rome taking its place. Mussolini's Italy – Fascist but not yet anti-Jewish – was still an attraction for nationalist youth. For them, Britain was a failure – Jabotinsky's God who had repeatedly let them down – a great power which seemed to be perpetually reneging on its promise to the Jews in the Balfour Declaration. The killings of 1920, 1921 and 1929 were being repeated once more in 1936 and the Jews were left unprotected. The urge to retaliate grew stronger with each passing month and privately Jabotinsky professed that he did not have an answer 'as long as the earth's surface is still wriggling'.[38] He stipulated that perhaps Italy or 'a condominium of less anti-Semitic states' or the League of Nations were remote possibilities in replacing Britain as a colonization regime. He also considered the improbability of a unilateral withdrawal of British forces leaving behind the Mandate under Jewish auspices with an armed Jewish force to empower it.[39] Jabotinsky went some way to becoming a fellow-traveller with the Italian option of other Revisionists - even 'understanding' the invasion of Abyssinia. He regarded Italy's re-alignment with Nazi Germany as mere window dressing and didn't take seriously the subsequent introduction of anti-Jewish legislation.[40] Perhaps this was part and parcel of his attachment to the liberal Italy of his youth. In the end, his ties with Britain proved stronger. He was too embedded in the political process and in diplomatic engagement with Britain to contemplate changing course. While he called for the resignation of Sir Arthur Wauchope, the British High Commissioner in Palestine, he also told the Peel Commission that despite everything he still believed in Great Britain. At a dinner at the Trocadero restaurant in London in February 1937 to commemorate the 20th anniversary of the founding of the Jewish Legion, Jabotinsky toasted the brotherhood of Britain and Israel, but he had great difficulty in convincing hundreds of thousands of Jews in the distressed areas that Britain really intended to carry out her promises.[41] In an address to the 8th Conference of the Polish Revisionists in October 1937, he placed the relationship with Britain within a familial framework:

> We may have a number of grievances against England but the English
> government is and will be the government of a well-disposed mother. We must
> have patience. We shall finally achieve our aim of a Palestine on both sides of the
> Jordan. This will be achieved with the aid of the England who always puts
> obstacles in our way and always helps us.[42]

In the Diaspora, he could advocate long-term solutions such as the Evacuation
Plan[43] where one and a half million would emigrate to Palestine over a ten year
period. 75,000 would leave Poland alone each year. The economic
discrimination in the 'distressed regions' of Central and Eastern Europe
threatened an estimated six million Jews. Over several generations, they would
gradually descend the socio-economic ladder to occupy the lowest rung and
would be shunned by all other peoples.[44] Such campaigns which demanded
evangelizing the idea of departure to Jewish communities and the co-operation
of less than friendly governments – the Poles were happy to assist in the
departure of their Jewish population – demanded commitment and
involvement on the part of the Revisionists and Betar. These were Diaspora-
centred struggles.

In Palestine, however, the situation was significantly different because the
problems were often immediate rather than long term, practical rather than
theoretical. Jabotinsky was therefore unable to stop the radicalization of his
movement in Palestine because the process was related to the deteriorating
situation. Moreover, his enforced absence from Palestine meant that he could
not exert any influence over those who symbolically looked to him. Both the
evacuation plan for Poland as well as the idea of a Jewish armed force for
Palestine was doomed to failure because they required the co-operation of the
British – and that was not forthcoming. Indeed just the opposite – Britain,
along with Italy, was moving closer towards the Arab nationalist position. In
the absence of a new Jewish Legion, young Jewish nationalists in Palestine
joined the Irgun and preached retaliation.

There were also converging issues such as the Partition debate which united
nationalists in both Palestine and Poland. Thus over a thousand Revisionists
gathered in Muranowski Square and marched through the Nalewski quarter of
Warsaw in July 1937.[45] On Tisha B'Av – August 1937 – there were
demonstrations against partition in both Poland and Palestine.[46] Menachem
Begin was involved in these protests as well as later ones in support of the
Irgun.

During the second half of 1936, Jabotinsky came under great pressure to accommodate the views of his followers. In July 1936, he had openly written about his reservations in opposing havlagah while there was still a possibility that the British might consent to the formation of a Jewish Legion.[47] But by December 1936, he had met the Commander of the Irgun Avraham Tehomi in Paris, and concluded an agreement with him. The appointment of the Commander of the Irgun now became the responsibility of the President of the New Zionist Organization and it would be organized in the spirit of his instructions. In concluding this agreement, Jabotinsky no doubt felt that the overwhelmingly Revisionist Irgun could now be directed along rationalist lines and would counter the Maximalist influence within. It would pose an alternative to the Old Zionist Organization's hegemony and induce harmony within a restless Revisionist family. Yet Jabotinsky was unable to foresee the tremendous distance between the militant youth who joined the Irgun and the Revisionist diplomats who scurried through the parliamentary corridors of one unsympathetic European regime after another. There was a profound difference between 'the Jabotinsky movement' and 'the Revisionist movement'.

Even within the Irgun, there were those who were clear-cut about rejecting havlaga and those who kept their options open as events unfolded. As early as March 1937, Irgun radicals, with no instructions from the leadership, threw a bomb into an Arab coffee house outside Tel Aviv. The reservations within the Irgun about opposing havlagah came mainly from the non-Revisionists – the Religious Zionists and General Zionists. There had been negotiations with the Haganah since the summer of 1936 and by the spring of 1937, Tehomi felt that he could advocate a merger publicly. While many endorsed this approach, Jabotinsky vehemently opposed it as he believed that it would compromise his stand against partition which many of his Mapai opponents supported. Tehomi and the non-Revisionists defected and returned to the Haganah.

The new Irgun was therefore homogeneously Revisionist and deeply imbued with the spirit of the Maximalists. They argued that Jabotinsky had chosen this course – against all predictions – because he 'anticipated the contingency of breaking havlagah and having recourse to retaliation' as well a future 'open military confrontation with the British'.[48] Jabotinsky's words and actions in the last couple of years of his life do not bear witness to this approach, but instead to an ambivalence on the question of retaliation and a moral distancing from taking a clear-cut stand. Jabotinsky performed a balancing act between his different constituencies. With Betar and the Irgun in Palestine, he said that if the British attempted to impose partition, he would authorize an uprising against them: 'so that we can fight together, go together to prison and, if need be, die together.'[49] Jabotinsky, of course, qualified this by commenting that he thought that the British would never implement the scheme. To the head of the Haganah, Eliahu Golomb, a year later, Jabotinsky implied that in the worst case scenario, he would have to adjust to the fait accompli of partition and live with it.[50] Jabotinsky's desire was clearly to outmanoeuvre the radicals and modify their wilder schemes in the hope that somehow the situation in both Europe and Palestine would stabilize and thereby offer the possibility of new constructive policies.

In addition to Tehomi, there were another two Commanders of the Irgun in 1937. The changes reflected not only the inner turmoil of the Irgun, but also Jabotinsky's difficulties in resolving the question of retaliation and armed struggle in his own mind. In July 1937, he met the Irgun Commander, Robert Bitker, Moshe Rosenberg his eventual successor and Avraham Stern in Alexandria. Despite an abundance of qualms about such a course, Jabotinsky agreed to preparations for military retaliation in the future. As Commander of the Irgun, he would give the signal for action in the form of a telegram signed 'Mendelson'.[51] Jabotinsky partially resolved his moral reservations by requesting that he did not wish to be informed about every last detail. In this fashion, he distanced the Revisionists from controversial military action, but also bequeathed to the young commanders a degree of autonomy that was dangerously elastic. This provided the raison d'être for the comment that he was unsure whether his orders would be obeyed as well.[52]

Bitker's reputation was tarnished through involvement with a bank robbery staged by former members of Brit HaBiryonim in September 1937 and the unexplained death of an Irgun member whose body was found in the River Yarkon. His successor, Moshe Rosenberg, was one of the graduates of Yirmiyahu Halperin's School for Betar Madrichim at the end of the 1920s. The Revisionists condemned the robbery and stated that such actions could not be reconciled with Revisionist ideology. It commented that 'such methods have nothing to do with havlagah' and warned that there was no place in the movement for such methods.[53] The bank robbers were members of the Sadan group – Maximalists who opposed havlagah and had been expelled from the movement in Palestine.[54] Many members of Sadan joined the Irgun, but were viewed as inept and a danger to the group.[55] Rosenberg took over at a time when the Arab Revolt was degenerating into internecine Arab violence and nihilist attacks on Jews. The Irgun responded in kind, but there was concerted pressure from within the organization to do more. Independent action by Maximalist members of Betar was only averted when the Jerusalem Commander of the Irgun, David Raziel, agreed to a coordinated assault on centres of Palestinian Arab militancy. This took place on 'Black Sunday' 14 November 1937. Jabotinsky appears not to have known in advance of these actions which included firing on buses and the bombing of coffee shops. His later approach was to regard the military exploits of the Arab bands as 'child's play' and to downplay their importance: 'Arab resistance is a purely moral effect, not the physical force which appears.'[56] Amongst the Jewish public in Palestine, there was a deep sense of disbelief that Jews could have been behind the attacks.[57] However, Jabotinsky reacted to condemnations of the attacks by focusing instead on the arrests of Revisionists and Betar which had been carried out by the British authorities in the aftermath of Black Sunday. In particular, the Jewish Agency made no comment about the arrests in its stringent criticism of the attacks.[58] In a speech in East London, Jabotinsky stated that:

> No party was responsible for the reprisals. It was the spontaneous result of dissatisfaction and despair consequent on the failure or unwillingness of the Government to do its duty as a government…could they wonder that here and there were found people who regarded themselves as called upon to assume the task which should have fallen to the Government. Let there be an end to hypocrisy and let those who inveighed against the reprisals come forward and say what Jewish youth were to do in such circumstances.[59]

Significantly, none of the dozens of the arrested were actually members of the Irgun[60] – this was a clear demonstration of where the British felt that the real responsibility for the attacks lay. Yet Jabotinsky avoided all public discussion and pronouncement on the Irgun and its actions. Jabotinsky obviously felt that his adeptness as a political figure would allow him to exist in this twilight world between legality and illegality. Although publicly a fellow traveller with the Irgun, expressing 'understanding' at the right time and the right place, when he was actually confronted with the brutality of such actions, Jabotinsky privately reacted with anger and condemnation.

Yet even before Black Sunday, the Irgun had been organizing cells within Betar in Poland. In November 1937, Avraham Stern arrived in Poland to accentuate this development. His intention was to formalize the ideological break between the Revisionists and the Irgun. Unlike Raziel and the other Commanders of the Irgun, Stern was neither an admirer of Jabotinsky nor a member of his movement. The battleground, however, was Betar. Stern envisaged the Irgun as a conduit for Betar to secure training and arms in order to carry out the armed struggle which would secure a Jewish state. Two newspapers – the daily *Di Tat* in Yiddish and the Polish language weekly *Jerozolima Wyzwolona* – were founded in Poland in 1938 to convey the Irgun worldview rather than the Revisionist approach. Without Jabotinsky's knowledge, military training courses under the aegis of the Polish government were established in several cities. The emergence of military Zionism – the progeny of the Maximalists – was a direct threat to traditional Revisionism. Raziel and Begin shared to a large degree Stern's emphasis on the centrality of the use of armed force. All relegated the Revisionist movement to history, but whereas Raziel and Begin preached nominal loyalty to Jabotinsky, Stern privately referred to Jabotinsky as

'Hindenberg' – old, feeble, senile, yesterday's man. 'The days of parades have passed. In place of all this military exhibitionism – no more than children's games – there is the sound of automatic weapons and bombs.'[61]

Such bravado struck a chord with Polish Jewish youth who had come to see the activities of their elders as high theatre. The disdain that their Labour opponents reserved for the Revisionists now began to be adopted by the members of Betar:

> The Revisionists arrived by truck and train for the manoeuvres. The recruits – of assorted ages and sizes – gathered in the Plonsk market place to march before the commander-in-chief. Striplings left their homework; elderly Jews doffed their long frock-coats, closed their shops and entrained for Plonsk to parade before the reviewing-stand in brown uniforms, glittering with gold braid and medals. Of gold braid, epaulettes, clanking spurs and honourable decorations, there was an abundance – perhaps to conceal the absence of swords and pistols. The Polish government permits the legionnaires to dress up in fancy uniforms, but, unfortunately, it forbids the use of arms. However, the weapon-less warriors drilled, marched and presented arms with earnestness worthy of the 'generals' who led them.[62]

Armaments had been smuggled in by the Irgun from Finland, Poland and Czechoslovakia since 1935. But it was only in late 1937 that they were used in an active fashion. The Irgun regarded Black Sunday as a day of liberation from old thinking. Raziel believed that the best form of defence was attack. He wrote:

> The goal of every war is to break the will of the enemy and to impose the will of the victor. Yet this goal cannot always be achieved without first breaking the strength of the enemy. A struggle between opposing powers and the subjugation of one of them is a necessary means of achieving the goal of every war in the world.[63]

In his tract, 'Active Defence' which was distributed to the leadership of the Irgun after Black Sunday, Raziel blamed the situation on the Zionist Left. He accused them of lacking 'the will and mental readiness for war' and blamed their passivity not only for the deterioration of the situation in Palestine, but also for allowing the ascendancy of Nazism in Germany and Austria. Even 'the severing of Transjordan' was caused by a policy of docility and 'passive resistance'. Raziel argued that the Jews had to rely on their own force of arms to combat Arab attacks. 'The stories of world sympathy are stories only for fools or children.'

Uriel Halperin (Yonatan Ratosh) was another graduate of Yirmiyahu Halperin's School for Betar Madrichim.[64] He was close to Abba Achimeir and Brit

HaBiryonim in the early 1930s. He was on the editorial board of *Hayarden* and a member of Haganah Bet. With the formal alignment with Jabotinsky and the Revisionists, he worked with Raziel and Stern to develop a different approach within the nationalist framework. Like Achimeir, he admired Mussolini and saw Italy's growing influence in the Mediterranean as a positive development. After the invasion of Abyssinia, Italy was viewed as the spearhead of a benign imperialism. Like Stern, Halperin wished to throw off the British orientation of Jabotinsky and the Revisionists – a Jewish state in Palestine as a European bridgehead, perhaps aligned with Italy rather than Britain was proposed. Like Stern, he was not captivated by Jabotinsky's personal magnetism. In 1937, Halperin published a series of articles in *Hayarden* which outlined his views. These were collected and published as *Our Eyes are Turned towards Self-Government: The Liberation Movement's Future Front* at the end of 1937. In addition to the broad line of Maximalist Zionism, Halperin epitomized the colonialist – rather than the colonizatory – element in the nationalist camp. The Jews were depicted as an advanced superior society – and this alone permitted them to take power and establish a state. There was no need therefore to press ahead with Jabotinsky's cry for a Jewish majority in Palestine. Halperin's views coincided with a deepening of Jewish resentment at the violence of the Arab Revolt. During the same period, Uri Zvi Greenberg published *The Book of Indictment and Faith* – a series of fiery poems which became a paean to the cause of Zionist nationalism. One section was an apocalyptic cycle of poems written during the summer of 1936 under the influence of the Arab revolt.[65] Arabs were demonized amidst prophecies that Judea would not rise once more without blood letting and self-sacrifice.[66] Like Halperin, the poems projected an orientalist approach to the Arabs and to the conflict.

THE CONFRONTATION

Prague and After

At the end of January 1938, Jabotinsky opened the first world conference of the New Zionist Organization in the Luzerne Hall in Prague. His opening speech was a broad overview of the diplomatic initiatives and policy stands of the NZO. He spoke about the partition plan, evacuation, and the reform of the Jewish Agency and called on Britain to participate in an international conference with other 'friendly powers'. The vexed subject of havlagah was submerged deep within the speech. Jabotinsky protested at the arrest of Revisionists and members of Betar and sent a message of solidarity to those imprisoned. Black Sunday was once more 'a spontaneous outbreak of the outraged feelings of the nation's soul and must never be attributed to one party alone'.[1] In an implied reference to the Haganah's threat to take action against the Irgun, he raised the spectre of internecine conflict within the Jewish community in Palestine and cited past examples of the United States, South Africa and Ireland. While all this kept the NZO in the clear, the Betar supporters of the Irgun were unhappy.

The British closely followed the proceedings in Prague and noted in particular the call for the garrison in Palestine to be manned by Jewish regiments. Another resolution suggested that at the end of a ten year period, a representative assembly of the citizens of Palestine should be called, the Mandate cancelled and an independent Jewish state established. The new state would then negotiate with the British Empire as to its future relations with Britain. All this was conveyed by the British Legation in Prague to Anthony Eden, the Foreign Secretary.[2]

Following Black Sunday, the British closed down *Hayarden*. The central committee of the Revisionists in Palestine thereafter published it under different guises. A few weeks before the conference, it appeared as 'For the Sake of the Homeland' and within its pages, Menachem Begin and other members of the Initiative Group published the manifesto of the 'Activist-Revisionist Front'.[3] The tract was an unequivocal attack on Jabotinsky – without naming him – and his policies. It commenced:

> When it was founded and during the first years of its existence, Revisionism was understood by the Jewish masses, especially by the youth, as a revolutionary fighting movement, aiming at national liberation by means of uncompromising military action, both against the external enemy and against the internal traitors and unbelievers. However, in recent years Revisionism has restricted itself to the method of secret diplomacy, which we have mocked so much, in the direction of a completely pro-British orientation. The postulate of mass pressure on the external political factors has been completely forgotten. Within the Jewish people, the party executive has pursued an unceasing policy of seeking peace, thus ignoring the historic chances for a victorious crusade against liquidatory Zionism.

The manifesto bemoaned Jabotinsky's negotiations with Ben-Gurion in an attempt to put an end to the conflict between Revisionism and the Labour Zionists. It condemned the NZO's call for a round table with the mainstream Zionists. It was absolutist in calling for 'waging the battle until final victory'. The signatories complained that 'our fighting units in the Land of Israel, who adopted the way of active opposition in their war against the mandatory government' were effectively abandoned by the leadership of the party. They suggested that the Revisionist movement needed to be reconstructed on more radical lines:

> The Revisionist movement must be completely rebuilt, from the foundations upwards. It will cease to be a mass movement and become a closed pioneering group of faithful members, ready for self-sacrifice. Therefore the focus will be transferred from the branch to the individual member. Entrance into the movement will be made more difficult, and everyone who enlists will have to pass through several levels of status until he becomes a member of the Union of Zionist Revisionists with full rights.

Jabotinsky was not disavowed, but selectively endorsed. His inspiration rather than his policies was embraced by these – 'the spiritual sons of the iron typewriter of Jabotinsky'. It concluded:

> We do not despair, for we consider Jabotinsky's teaching to be the true and sacred Torah, by means of which the people will rise to rebirth in our great, free, and independent state.

Since Black Sunday Jabotinsky had begun to argue that a dispersed people such as the Jews did not have the luxury of a military uprising at their disposal.[4] Towards the end of the Prague conference, he devoted a separate speech for the assembled commanders and members of Betar where he discussed the meaning of the term 'revolutionary' with his critics and supporters.[5] He attempted to draw his youthful charges into the reality of securing a state within ten years – and how this might best be achieved. Diplomacy, he argued, could not be abandoned, and held up Masaryk as the supreme realist.[6] Yet there were voices of dissent. Uriel Halperin was allowed to present his published views to the political committee in Prague despite Jabotinsky's disapproval. According to Halperin, the state would come into existence without a Jewish majority. Its government would be elected through the vote of all Jews in the Diaspora who intended to emigrate and the current residents of the Land of Israel. While the old Revisionists – and even members of the Irgun – rejected it for its utopianism, Halperin's views struck a chord with the youth of Betar and certainly with Menachem Begin.[7] One of the delegates from Palestine, Shimshon Yunitchman, who had been one of the Maximalist signatories to the statement on the eve of the Katowice conference in 1933, criticized Jabotinsky for underestimating Arab strength. He also spoke about readiness and preparation and about an era of turning 'silver into iron'. Menachem Begin was less elliptical; he told the conference:

> The Land of Israel is not being built by money and now not even by diplomacy. The world's conscience is asleep and will not awaken through acts of diplomacy. An act of despair is required – the despair of heroism – this is our historic mission.[8]

He defined the different tasks of members of Betar in the Diaspora and in the Land of Israel. 'Our function in the Diaspora is to educate this generation. Our function in the Land of Israel is to fight.'[9] Military training should not be defined in defensive terms, but in preparation for a revolutionary role. Moreover, he did not view the Arab Revolt as merely a passing phase, but felt it would continue for an undeterminable period.

Avraham Stern was also present at the conference in Prague. There were private discussions between Betar and the Irgun which resulted in a temporary agreement.[10] It testified to the friction between the two organizations and the rivalry between Begin and Stern. It drew attention to the duplication of authority which meant that Betar members were uncertain and confused. More importantly, this related to the distribution of weapons. The agreement, however, clearly acknowledged that many members of Betar preferred the Irgun's vision of the future to that spelled out by Jabotinsky and the Revisionists.

Aharon Propes, the head of Betar in Poland and a Jabotinsky loyalist, wrote in *Hamedina* that the conference of Betar commanders had 'exceeded all expectations'.[11] Yet he acknowledged that the movement in general had lost direction and the ability to produce clear answers. He also referred darkly to 'enemies from outside and from within'. In contrast, Menachem Begin in a speech in Bielitz-Biala said that the movement in Palestine felt let down by its supporters in Poland and asked rhetorical questions on the way forward. He also called for a strengthening of the relationship between Betar in Poland and the movement in Palestine.[12]

The Arab Revolt had created a split between the British civil administration in Palestine and the military. The former believed that Arab national aspirations could somehow be accommodated, the latter simply wished to use its own force to crush the revolt. The killing of Lewis Andrews, the District Commissioner for Galilee in the autumn of 1937, and the resurgent Arab assaults, persuaded the British to introduce emergency laws to deal with the situation. These came into force a few days before Black Sunday. The failure of the initiative of the Arabs kings to quell the violence and open the path for a political solution effectively tipped the balance in favour of the view of the British military. In early October 1937, the Colonial Secretary, William Ormsby-Gore, outlined the rationale for the removal of the High Commissioner, Sir Arthur Wauchope, in a memorandum to the British Cabinet. This came in the wake of the Peel Commission Report which commented that 'the elementary duty of providing public security has not been discharged'. Wauchope's policy of 'extreme conciliation' became the instrument for his downfall. Ormsby-Gore believed that the High Commissioner had lost the confidence of both Jews and Arabs, and 'forfeited the confidence of British officials in Palestine':[13]

> The moment is not one for half measures. We have got to make it clear, to both the Jews and the Arabs, and indeed in all quarters, not only that we are finally determined to repress sedition and to maintain order, but also that our very real imperial interests in Palestine, with all the strategic importance that arises from its geographical position, are going to be permanently safeguarded against all comers.[14]

Ormsby-Gore went on to remark that 'the civil administration in Palestine may have to hand over full powers to the GOC'. The early retirement of the High Commissioner Sir Arthur Wauchope was subsequently and abruptly announced. On 1 April 1938 Colonel Robert Hadden Haining, who had been a strong advocate of military action, was appointed General Officer Commanding Palestine and Transjordan. A few weeks later, Shlomo Ben-Yosef, a member of Betar and recent illegal immigrant, and two others attempted to attack an Arab bus in northern Palestine. Their action was designed to be a freelance attempt at avenging the killing of Jewish civilians in a van along the same stretch of road a few weeks previously. Their attempt was hopelessly incompetent – their bullets missed the bus and their grenades refused to explode. On being apprehended by police, the young men adamantly proclaimed their guilt. A few months earlier, another member of Betar, Yechezkiel Altman, had had his death sentence commuted after he had shot dead an Arab boy. Given the determination of the British now to crack down on violence, Ben-Yosef was sentenced to death and hanged at the end of June 1938, despite the best efforts of Jabotinsky to save him. For Jabotinsky, the convergence of unexpected events destabilized the uneasy equilibrium that had existed since the Prague conference. In a plea to Malcolm MacDonald, the Colonial Secretary, to save Ben-Yosef's life, Jabotinsky wrote:

> The whole atmosphere is madness. The Jewish people would never get reconciled to a situation which first drives them to the verge of madness and then hangs them. This kind of martyrdom would only serve to release thousands of similar urges, ill-mastered even now; would only set a match to trails long laid.[15]

At the same time, Jabotinsky finally did send a message to Raziel before Ben-Yosef's execution. 'If final, invest heavily, Mendelson.' It was final and the Irgun did invest heavily – 76 Arabs, 44 Jews and 12 members of the security forces were killed in three weeks in July 1938. Jabotinsky was shocked since he did not expect such devastation. In particular, he was outraged by the killings in a marketplace in Haifa where no warning had been given. Jabotinsky's private protests surprised and indeed were even ridiculed by the Irgun leadership. On the eve of the Irgun offensive, Jabotinsky had addressed a mass meeting in London to mourn Ben-Yosef.:

> I declare to the British: Be careful. Jews are beginning to think whether Ben-Yosef's way is the best. Be careful! This has happened before in history. A martyr became a prophet and graves became shrines. Be careful! Ben Yosef's example may prove too much for suffering Jewish youth. Is Jewish youth dust or is it iron? The hangmen of Ben Yosef think it is dust. We shall see![16]

The Irgun had taken Jabotinsky at his word. Events were spiralling out of control – to the extent that Jabotinsky had been warned by the Haganah that they would act militarily against the Irgun. In reality, Jabotinsky had reached the limit of his influence: mesmerizing rhetoric and dramatic declamations for justice were not enough, the youth wanted more. Jabotinsky's dualism of approach had been punctured by the Irgun's determination to turn words into deeds. The death of Ben-Yosef had not only produced a martyr for the cause, but also induced a dramatic radicalization within Betar. They were captivated by Raziel's words in commemorating Ben-Yosef:

> And the keen eyes of victory see also what they must. They see courage, the spirit

that can overcome the flesh. They see the advantage of the dead lion over the living dog. They see cursed reality being transfigured by immense power to a unifying ideal. They see the hopes of the past and the dreams of the future materializing – for there is no mountain that cannot be conquered by the power of sacrifice.[17]

On the thirtieth day – the 'shloshim' – after the hanging, Menachem Begin wrote an article in *Hamedina* in which he constructed an imaginary conversation between Ben-Yosef and his friends on the eve of attack. Begin used Ben-Yosef to comment that since 1929, there had been a wave of apathy and indifference. There were no protests from the Jews, just a desire to obtain peace at any price. Begin further blamed the Arab Revolt for destroying the economy and stopping immigration. He ridiculed the idea that the Land of Israel could be built through 'peaceful work' when blood was being spilled. He then used Ben-Yosef to state:

> I don't understand diplomacy. In the Land of Israel, there are two peoples who struggle – the Arabs and the English – while the Jews merely defend their settlements. The Land will not belong to a third people who simply observe what is taking place simply by defending positions. We have to actively enter into the struggle and to give our lives – otherwise the people and the Land will be lost.[18]

In contrast to Propes[19], Begin utilized the hanging of Ben-Yosef to promote his vision of the future. Unlike Stern, he recognized the importance of staying within the fold. Thus he criticized the unauthorized actions of Ben-Yosef and his friends as 'foolish and immature'. In Begin's eyes, the central lesson from the tragedy of Ben-Yosef was that he willingly offered his life for an ideal.

Jabotinsky was traumatized by his failure to save Ben-Yosef and the events that followed. Yet he devised two strategies in an attempt to regain control of his movement. He approved the Irgun's desire for a merger with the Haganah in August 1938. The Irgun wanted to gain access to superior training for their members, the Haganah wanted to limit the counter-productive military actions of Raziel and his subordinates. Jabotinsky also wished to limit the Irgun's infiltration of Betar, yet he had no instruments at his disposal to do this except grandiose gestures and brilliant speeches. In a letter to a Betar leader, he commented that 'it is an iron rule that only the Revisionist movement bears responsibility for any actions of policy – major, medium, minor – by vote or by acclamation or by any other way – and Betar only carries it out.'[20] Moreover, his diplomatic standing with the British had been severely jeopardized. A classified CID report for the new High Commissioner in August 1938 characterized Revisionist policy 'as similar to Fascism, and in fact the majority have always been pro-Italian'. Jabotinsky was seen as instructing the Irgun to obtain arms and plan 'retaliatory outrages'.[21]

THE THIRD WORLD CONFERENCE OF BETAR

The Third World Conference of Betar opened in the Teatr Nowosci in Warsaw in September 1938. It provided the stage for the public clash between Jabotinsky and Begin. It was the confrontation between the two visions of the future for Betar, the diplomacy of the Revisionists or the armed struggle of the Irgun. In the end, it proved to be the turning point for the Zionist Right – a defeat for Jabotinsky and the older generation and a victory for the Maximalists and military Zionism.

The conference was held just months after the execution of Shlomo Ben-Yosef and a wave of new attacks by the Irgun after a period of silence. It was also taking place against the unfurling of the Munich crisis. Hitler's speech in Nuremberg warned the Czechs of 'lying propaganda' and 'intolerable persecution' of the Sudeten Germans. As if to warn the world as well as the Zionists, Hitler commented:

> The poor Arabs of Palestine may be unarmed and without help, but the Sudeten Germans are neither without arms nor without help…..No new Palestine shall arise. Unlike the Arabs of Palestine, the Germans of Czechoslovakia are not defenceless or deserted.[22]

The ideas of the Maximalists had profoundly influenced nationalist Jewish youth - given the situation in which they found themselves. Having failed to make any political headway in Prague, Uriel Halperin now presented his ideas in formal proposals to the Betar Conference[23] and publicized them in the press beforehand.[24] He stressed the importance of transforming Betar into an independent revolutionary force. Much had changed since the Prague conference and this time he found a far more receptive audience. Revisionism was perceived as docile and unreactive. Moreover, in the Poland of the 1930s, the policy of havlagah did not reflect their conception of Zionism and indeed confused many. There was 'a feeling of relief' by many Polish Revisionists on first hearing about the reprisals of the Irgun and an end to 'paralysing inaction'.[25] In Poland, they accepted the discrimination and degradation, but Palestine was not supposed to be a second Poland. This was not their image of the new Jewish state. This had led to great turmoil within Polish Betar and to members dropping out. The head of Betar in Poland, Aharon Propes, could do little to stop it, but more importantly was opposed to any change in ideology.[26]

Menachem Begin, who had espoused Maximalism at its inception, was fortified in his beliefs in viewing the gradual dissolution of Czechoslovakia and its abandonment by Britain. After his tenure as head of Betar in Czechoslovakia, he had closely followed the development of the crisis. But the problem for

Begin was not the existence of an adulatory youth for the exploits of the Irgun, but the fact that they were deserting Betar for the Irgun. This undermined his own power base. Stern's forays into his territory by training members of Betar in Poland were more a political threat to him personally than an ideological one. Begin's speech at the conference was thus not only an attempt to confront Jabotinsky, but also one to undermine Stern by openly stealing his policies. He therefore had to steer a line which would profess loyalty to Jabotinsky while attacking the roots of his Zionism.

Begin's speech began with the supposition that Betar should be addressing the question 'How?' rather than the question 'What?'[27] He said that the reason why this had never been raised before was due to the lack of definition of the relationship between the Revisionists and Betar. While he acknowledged the inspiration of the Revisionist movement, he commented, 'but there have been changes in the world.'

Begin then began to elucidate such changes. Firstly, the conscience of the world was no longer responding. Refugees from Germany and Austria were being turned back. Secondly, the League of Nations had outlived its usefulness. England was a fair-weather friend who had advocated partition where the Jews would receive only 5 per cent of the Land of Israel. Begin noted the determination of the Arabs to fight – 'and they fight bitterly' – even though they had received 95 per cent of the Land.

> We have to appreciate the Arab war as a national war. We should regard it with respect even though it is barbarous. In the eyes of the non-Jews, the Jewish home is a chimera, while the Arabs have a genuine home. England, which quelled several rebellions in the empire, cannot quell it here. It is impossible to give equal weight to the agony of the Jews on one hand and the Arab war on the other hand. We have to draw the conclusion and say: there is no hope in a moral war by means of the methods we have been using.

Begin further argued that Zionism would not be realized if this situation continued. Arab nationalism would undoubtedly continue their armed struggle. It was possible to compel 'a mighty empire at the expense of another people if force is threatened'. To applause, he declared, 'we have had enough of renunciation; we want to fight – to die or to win.'

He said that Betar stood at the beginning of a new era, the era of military Zionism. This would later be 'fused' with political Zionism. In a reference to Jabotinsky's often quoted example, Begin pointed out that Italy would not have been liberated solely through the efforts of the diplomat Cavour – the military campaign of Garibaldi was just as important. Begin then implicitly attacked the official Revisionist stand on partition if it had been implemented:

We shall win with our moral strength. If the partition plan had been implemented, would we have been silent, would we have been contented with speeches? I am sure that even with the proportions of today we would have raised a living wall against partition, and even if we had fallen – we would have fought.

He came next to the central point of his speech – a striking amendment to the Betar oath which Jabotinsky had formulated in 1934. He suggested a change in the wording and meaning of clause four: 'I will train to fight in the defence of my people, and I will only use my strength for defence.' Instead Begin proposed, 'I will train to fight in the defence of my people and to conquer the homeland.' This change displaced the interpretation of the clause from a primarily defensive understanding to one which entertained the idea of offensive action. 'Conquest' could only mean the use of armed struggle against the British and the Palestinian Arabs. Begin maintained that Betar had reached a stage of military maturity where this had become possible – and it was all due to the teachings of Jabotinsky:

We have always aspired to strength. That strength has been created. There are millions who have nothing to lose. Our mission is to make use of their latent strength, so that outsiders do not exploit it. We must follow in the footsteps of the one who taught us.

His speech was greeted by tumultuous applause. Jabotinsky, however, was considerably irritated. He had interrupted Begin several times during his speech and made points demonstrating a distinction between the situation in Garibaldi's Italy and present-day Palestine. He also asked Begin pertinent questions such as the comparative strength of Arab and Jewish military forces in Palestine or how he would ensure the passage of the soldiers of Betar into Palestine without the help of an outside power. Jabotinsky realized that he could no longer resort to the argument of qualified adventurism which he had propagated in 1932 and resolved to confront his Maximalist critics in Betar and in the Irgun.

Permit me to say some harsh words; as your teacher, I have to do this. There is a special relationship to a teacher. Forgive me if I speak somewhat harshly. There are all sorts of noises, such as squeaking, and my attitude and the attitude of others to squeaking can be very different. I can bear the squeaking of a machine, or of a cart, and so on. And this is obvious. But I cannot bear the squeaking of a door, because it has no use, it is unnecessary. Both this speech and the applause it received are like the squeaking of a door, with no sense and no benefit. There is no place in Betar for this kind of nonsense. Sometimes this squeaking can even be attractive, but we should beware of it. The things said here by Mr Begin is squeaking of this sort, and all such squeaking should be cruelly rejected. The face of reality is terrible.

It is true that we need Garibaldi's spirit, and this has a place in Betar, but if we want to go over to this method – this is the squeaking of a door. What Garibaldi did is a matter of arithmetic. He placed his trust in the spirit of the Italians, but it was simply speculation on his part. It never occurred to Garibaldi that someone would just come along and succeed because the overwhelming majority lived in Italy. In nationalist Ireland too, the attitude of the Catholic Irish inhabitants was the same. We began Zionism in disgrace – and the disgrace lies in the fact that we are not in the Land of Israel. And even if we become heroes, against whom shall we rise up? The question of getting into Land of Israel comes before outbursts of heroism. We have come to the Land of Israel by the power of non-Jewish humanity's conscience, and thanks to this, some of us have the audacity to say such things today. And our situation in relation to Arab strength in the land? In the Yishuv there are all sorts of Jews. But the hearts of all the Arab youth are inclined to the gangs, and they are many. And we should pay special attention to the strategic situation in the land: the Arabs hold the hills. Apart from this, they can get help from across the Jordan or from the other neighbouring states, but as for us – only from the distant Diaspora. They bring weapons from the neighbouring states, but as for us – the distance between the Land of Israel and the lands of the Jewish dispersions are as far apart as heaven and earth. When the Arabs need help, they simply cross the Jordan or Taggart's barbed-wire fence. That is easier than bringing Jews on foot from Poland to the Land of Israel. No strategist in the world would say that in this situation we could do something like Garibaldi and De Valera. It is nonsense. Our situation is very different from that of the Italians or the Irish, and if you think that there is no other way than for Mr Begin to offer you weapons – you are committing suicide. If there is no longer conscience in the world – there is the Vistula River and there is Communism...

What has been said about the Jewish refugees, that no free states will take them in — it is because of this very fact, that the doors have been shut in the face of the Jewish refugee, that we have built our hope on conscience, ever since Herzl's days. There are limits to conscience. If they ask me to collect funds for an orphanage, I will do it. But if they want me to support the orphanage for the rest of my life, I won't do it. What forces me to build an orphanage – except for my conscience? I see both the gold and the thorns in reality. The question is: is there a move in the world to become involved in and to discuss the building of an orphanage or not? I think that there is.

Why did England issue the Balfour Declaration? If I am wrong, I suggest that we disband Betar, but if I am not wrong — accept the consequences boldly: we need an outsider to help us to hold the doors of Land of Israel open until a sufficient number of people and tools can get in. When there is a Jewish majority, then we'll thank the door-keeper and do the rest ourselves. But as long as the arithmetically (critical mass) isn't there, we need the outsider. If an outsider can't be found, then we must put off the realization of Zionism. Perhaps the current door-keeper is not suitable; perhaps we should look for another one; perhaps we'll find one.

Perhaps we should speculate further – I learned from Herzl. Perhaps we should take advantage of English political developments and exploit them. My speculation is: As long as there are more and more orphans in front of people's houses, their inner compulsion to find a way out and to build an orphanage will grow. Roosevelt wanted to call an international conference to solve the refugee question. The first attempt did not succeed. We must demand a second attempt. Outbursts of heroism in the Land of Israel certainly help. But how do they help? They help to arouse the conscience – the decisive factor. This is also necessary for education.

Peel buried the partition plan himself. Obviously, heroism is important in order to educate and to prove a point. Its aim is to educate the non-Jews, with an education based on the hope or the illusion of conscience. To say that conscience no longer exists—this is despair. It is not even worth publishing an article about this. We will sweep this idea away. Obviously each of us is allowed to express his opinion, but there is a limit to this. Conscience rules the world. I respect it. It is forbidden to mock it and ridicule it. I understand the pain, but to sink into despair because of it is dangerous. It is a useless and unnecessary squeaking of the door.

Jabotinsky's assault on military Zionism and Begin's advocacy of it made an impression, but it did not change the minds of the Betar leadership who voted for the change in clause four. The conference also prevented Betar members from joining the Irgun without the sanction of its leadership which was moving strongly in the direction of Menachem Begin. The days of Aharon Propes, the head of Betar in Poland, who had supported Jabotinsky's approach, were numbered.

DIFFERENT VERSIONS

There have been different versions of the Jabotinsky-Begin altercation. The Revisionist press deliberately did not mention it. Future generations of Betar were handed down a surrealistic appraisal of what had transpired. For example, in South Africa in 1952, it was related:

A prophet is speaking. He castigates and teaches, and when from his lips the words are …'Whither Jewish youth?' then you feel that before you stands a father with a big heart, a heart that bleeds because of the fate of his children and at the same time does not fail to show the true way. [28]

The published version of the proceedings of the conference in Bucharest in 1940 differs in a slight, yet significant manner from the handwritten protocol.[29] The edited version presented a much more rationalized, hard-nosed and sympathetic version of Begin's speech. For example, there was an excising of his mention of the Revisionist movement in the introduction. The official version suggests that in the past, the members of Betar were naïve and 'innocent believers' – and thus Begin was characterized as the realistic leader who was now forced to speak out. There was an accentuated anti-British line throughout. Hence the addition of the comment, 'our "partner" sends the flower of our people's sons to the gallows and to prison.' This reflected not only the execution of Ben-Yosef, but subsequent British moves to suppress the Irgun. The nationalist nature of 'the Arab war' was downplayed and the passivity of the Old Zionists and the acquiescence of the Revisionists in facilitating partition emphasized. Question marks were raised about the veracity of applying moral pressure. The logic of all this was the rationale of embracing military Zionism. In the official version, Begin presents it as the third period of Zionism. It is framed as an historical development – a natural and logical superseding of Revisionism.

> Honoured assembly, we have the impression that we are about to enter the third period of Zionism. The national movement of Israel began with 'practical Zionism', then came 'political Zionism' and now we are standing on the threshold of 'military Zionism' which will eventually emerge from political Zionism.

This was not only a displacement of Revisionist Zionism, but also a displacement of Jabotinsky. The phrase 'we must follow in the footsteps of the one who taught us' –with which Begin concluded his speech – was omitted in the official version. Even so, Jabotinsky's riposte to Begin was faithful to the handwritten protocol and certainly more authentic than the treatment of Begin's speech. Yet Jabotinsky's attempt to pose as the realist was downplayed. Thus phrases such as 'the face of reality is terrible' and 'I see both the gold and the thorns in reality' were omitted. Similarly the need for an outside power to assist the Zionists as long as the Jews were a minority in Palestine was excised. Finally, Jabotinsky's acerbic and ultimately derisory comment that it was not even worth writing an article about Begin's suggestion that 'conscience no longer exists' was cut out.

Many years later, Begin reconstructed his own unpublished account of his speech at the fateful Betar conference in Warsaw.[30] Clearly he felt the need to vindicate his position and to set the record straight. His latter-day version was a selective and simplistic recollection of his speech. As a post-Holocaust tract, it emphasized the plight of 'the Jewish masses' who were barred from entering the gates of Zion. New information was inserted. Thus the Evian conference was included. Moreover, Begin repeated the phrase 'the agony of the Jews' several times throughout his version and utilized it to necessitate the urgency of military Zionism 'to break the siege around us'. The League of Nations – used to settling disputes such as that between Paraguay and Bolivia – did not have the will to help a small people against a larger one.

> Military Zionism means – and I think that this should be stated explicitly – a war of liberation against those who hold the land of our fathers, and who have clearly

decided, against their promise and undertaking, to steal it from the Jewish people. We must conquer our land; this is the way. We shall not reach the goal by any other path.

Begin once more develops the historical vein and rationalizes the surpassing of practical and political Zionism. No good emerged from the Weizmann interregnum – 'the period of spiritual recidivism'. The British 'with the help of their Jews' emptied the Balfour Declaration of any meaningful content. Jabotinsky and the Revisionists are reinstated once more in the introduction and there is a mention of Begin's presence at the Prague conference at the beginning of 1938. The conclusion, however, deals with Begin's attempt to explain his amendment of clause four of the Betar oath. 'I will train to fight in the defence of my people, and I will only use my strength for defence.' This meant, according to Begin's interpretation, 'I will strengthen myself.' Begin postulated that Jabotinsky's intention in formulating this clause referred only to internal matters, presumably the cause of self-defence, but 'we cannot undertake to abide by this in external affairs.' In Begin's understanding, this did not cover 'the conquest of the historic homeland', and hence the need to amend the clause. As Prime Minister of Israel in 1980, Begin denied that he was ever in any serious dispute with Jabotinsky, but that indeed there had been an altercation with him at the Betar conference in Warsaw. He said that Jabotinsky had not really understood him and believed that he had suggested that there was no place for political Zionism. In private conversation later, Jabotinsky, according to Begin, understood his error.[31]

The Warsaw conference in September 1938 heralded the end for Revisionism and after his death two years later, the selective recasting of the historic Jabotinsky by Begin and his followers. There was always a tension between Jabotinsky, the man of ideas and Jabotinsky, the man of political action. The Bolsheviks cut off his contact with Russia. The British prevented him from living in Palestine. As the political options diminished, his homeland increasingly became one of intellectual discourse. By 1938, the situation had worsened to such an extent that his radical followers argued that it called for a new approach – that armed struggle should be integrated into the realm of political action – and Jabotinsky, the believer in England and diplomacy, would not oblige. For Israel Eldad, who like Begin had spoken in the debate in Warsaw, it was a clash of generations and a fundamental difference in the vision of the future. It was also a fundamentally different understanding of the meaning of Zionism. The altercation revealed the very different societies from which Jabotinsky and Begin had emerged - and the events that had forged them. Unlike Begin, Eldad did not pursue a politician's agenda and tried to explain the underlying factors which galvanized the confrontation:

On the morrow we, the anguished, triumphed over him, the angel (Jabotinsky). We, whose youth had not flowed to the beat of Pushkin and Lermontov, whose hearts did not bleed as his heart had bled for the cruelties of the Russian Revolution. We, who had no leisure between the First and Second World Wars to enjoy the melodies of Italy and its skies, who did not care whether the Fascist regime was good or not, and did not understand, with our dry political analysis, why he refused to meet Mussolini; we, who were not from the generation of those who fought for the freedom of the citizen, for liberalism and parliamentary democracy, who did not grasp the secret of his sympathy for the democratic British regime and the freedom of the individual and respect for the individual in Britain itself. This was the psychological background to the argument and the struggle that went on at the conference that day.

POSTSCRIPT

THE LAST GASPS

The clash with Begin – and indirectly with Raziel, Stern and the Irgun – was seemingly relegated to being a matter of lesser significance by Jabotinsky. Perhaps the Munich crisis and the deteriorating situation in both Eastern Europe and Palestine overshadowed the significance of Begin's challenge. Perhaps it was a matter of self-denial on Jabotinsky's part who now often recalled easier times in the past. Yet between the end of the Betar conference in September 1938 and his death in the United States in August 1940, Jabotinsky's authority underwent a process of systematic erosion by an alliance of Betar and the Irgun – by a new generation of young men and women who had taken him at his word and 'learned to shoot'. Effectively, this last period of Jabotinsky's life saw a transfer of Betar's loyalty from the Revisionists to the Irgun. The Irgun's sense of self-reliance impressed the young. Jabotinsky told them to believe in the efficacy of politics, but they saw the reality of 1939 differently. In March 1939, an Irgun radio broadcast proclaimed:

> Do not believe in the conscience of the world and in the graces of strangers. Only an independent Jewish force, fighting with Jewish arms under the orders of Jewish officers, can conquer our homeland for our people.[1]

This was a long way from Jabotinsky's idealization of inter-dependent national revolutionary movements of the first half of the nineteenth century and his personal pride as a national liberal. His pronouncements during these last two years bear witness to the verbal tightrope that he had decided to walk in order to keep the various components of his movement together. In employing political and rhetorical devices which often reflected style rather than substance, he attempted to maintain his status as an ideological glue and unifying figure. Apart from Avraham Stern, all still deferred to him even if they profoundly disagreed with his views. Even so, his influence was waning and his authority was weakening.

In a letter which was written just a few days after the Warsaw conference, he positively contrasted the spirit of Betar with the 'all round defeatism' of the Revisionists.[2] At this time Jabotinsky believed that he had cemented a draft agreement between the Irgun and the Haganah regarding self-restraint and retaliation. Indeed, this may also have accounted for his response to Begin during the conference. Any reprisals would be decided by a committee of four – two from each organization – and the Irgun would be represented by autonomous units in all local self-defence bodies in Palestine.[3] But Jabotinsky's optimism was abruptly dissipated when Ben-Gurion torpedoed any possible reconciliation. Ben-Gurion was unequivocal in his opposition:

> These biryonim now want two things: to enter the legal forces of defence in order to make themselves kosher for the Jewish public after the negative reaction on the kidnapping of (Zecharia) Kykoin – the Bartholomew declaration of Jabo. I do not see why we have to help them in the second thing, but I am absolutely opposed to the first one.
> As long as the Revisionist Party with Jabo at its head does not accept in political affairs the discipline of the Zionist Organization, there is no basis for negotiations with the biryonim on defence problems.[4]

The collapse of the initiative was catastrophic for Jabotinsky and allowed Stern to further develop the Irgun's military training programmes in Poland with the assistance of the Polish government and to bypass Jabotinsky, Propes and the Revisionist movement. Under Stern's guidance, the Irgun began to develop its own organizational framework and to propagate a clear-cut ideology of military Zionism. It also allowed Irgun publications to proliferate and to spread their ideas. At a press conference of the editors of Irgun publications in Poland in the office of *Jerozolima Wyzwolona*, Jabotinsky was referred to as 'an ex-activist' who now espoused complacent policies.[5] He complained privately that the editors had made unauthorized comments in the name of the Irgun which covered 'essential fields of policy not only military, but also (even mainly) political'. This, he argued, would lead to disorder and anarchy.[6] Jabotinsky was clearly annoyed at the intrigues and the whispering campaign to undermine him and privately conveyed his intention to crush them 'like Grossman' if it continued.[7]

In an attempt to resolve the situation, at the beginning of February 1939 in Paris, Jabotinsky brought together representatives of Betar, the Revisionists and the Irgun including Raziel who had come from Palestine. The discussion was heated and the disagreements bitter, but Jabotinsky accepted a division of labour. Betar would operate in the Diaspora while the Irgun would achieve dominance in Palestine. Betar would essentially be militarized and serve as a stepping stone for service in the Irgun. Jabotinsky conceded responsibility and supervision of Betar in Palestine to Raziel as commander of the Irgun – as long as the violence of the Arab Revolt continued. Jabotinsky's strategy in this and other situations was to sympathize with the supporters of military Zionism and make concessions at the expense of the Revisionists and diplomatic endeavour, but to ensure in the final analysis that the Maximalists remained subservient to his authority and his ultimate control of the organization. However, the tactic of integrating the Irgun into the Revisionist web of organizations only worked through the acceptance of the figure of Jabotinsky. Raziel, with reservations, concurred, but Stern – who wished to develop the Irgun as an independent body – adamantly opposed both Jabotinsky and Revisionism. Stern perceived Jabotinsky as a relic of times past, an aged and absent leader leading the yes-men from another epoch. He did not believe in Britain and its promises; instead he looked for other national allies, first Italy and later Nazi Germany. He did not believe in a renewed Jewish Legion working in conjunction with the British, but in an army of national liberation which would fight and vanquish them. Indeed, Stern believed that in co-operating with the Polish military, he could create an army of 40,000 European Jews who would rise up against the British in 1940.[8] Jabotinsky seemingly played along with such pretensions even to the point of offering to participate in an 'invasion' of Palestine in October 1940. Initially he felt that he could win over Stern as he had done Raziel, but such planning – real and imaginary - came to a shuddering halt with the invasion of Poland and the rapid collapse of its forces before the Nazi onslaught.

An important outcome of the Paris meeting was the effective ousting of Propes from his post as head of Betar in Poland. In 1939, Propes was already 35, ten years older than Begin. He had always opposed the transformation of Betar into a conduit for the Irgun and the Maximalists. After fifteen years service as 'the first member of Betar', he was sent to the United States to establish the organization on a new footing. Menachem Begin who was the advocate of the Irgun and Maximalist Zionism within Betar was appointed in his stead. Begin occupied this position because he was amenable to both Betar and the Irgun. He opposed both Stern's radicalism and the Revisionists' conservatism. He was not a member of the Irgun, but could cement a symbiosis between the two groups. At a meeting of Betar commanders at the end of March 1939 where the handover formally took place, Begin formally paid tribute to 'our teacher' Propes, but also said that the only way forward was the path of conquest, not cultural preparations. He also believed that youth rather than children should become members of Betar. He put forward a new slogan to attract young people to Betar: 'Kumt tsu undz un tsuzamen veln mir derobern undzer foterland' (Come to us. Together we will conquer the fatherland).[9] Immediately after his appointment, Begin began to work with the Irgun representative in Warsaw who had ignored Propes. The language of Betar publications in Poland began to change as he employed the revolutionary rhetoric of national liberation to fire nationalist youth. Mordechai Katz who represented Betar at the Paris meeting subsequently wrote:

> We must create the bayonets – and many of them. We must prepare ourselves for a decisive struggle on a scale and with methods different from those that even we 'militarists' imagined. And therefore the formula from now on must not be 'defence training' but 'military training'.[10]

Menachem Begin began to propagate the new approach through publications such as *Hamedina*. He castigated the Zionist Left for placing class solidarity above national solidarity because a strike had been called on May Day. Jewish socialists, he pointed out, were prepared to give up Jerusalem, but not their general strike. 'Diaspora socialism is as degenerate as the Diaspora itself.'[11] In contrast to Jabotinsky, he vehemently attacked British policy. He told Britain that there could be no third way – either open up the doors of the Land of Israel or the Jews would break them down. 'What Britain is doing is undermining her moral standing…and can lead it to behave like the Nazis in Berlin.'[12] In introducing this new acerbic style, Begin was not shy in criticizing the Jewish intelligentsia.

All this was a far cry from Jabotinsky's world, but he, too, emphasized the absence of wholeness, beauty and heroism in Jewish life. 'Not the passive heroism of suffering which we could teach all the other peoples, but the heroism of attack.'[13] In a much quoted article 'Amen' in *Moment*,[14] Jabotinsky raised the moral dilemma of retaliation where innocent bystanders were killed. He described the moral choices – the situation was not between good and bad, but between bad and worse since the British would disarm and arrest any group of Jews who pursued the actual perpetrators of Arab violence. Jabotinsky recalled the British raid on Karlsruhe during the First World War as a retaliatory response to Zeppelin raids on London. Jabotinsky also qualified the British response in suggesting that this was a special case. The effect of the article was one of painting the landscape of choices. For example, Jabotinsky asked whether 'from both the moral and the national point of view, may an honest Jew assist in catching refugees or in helping those who help the hunters?' From the standpoint of Jewish national interests, Jabotinsky pointed out that the only question that should be asked was which choice was worse. It was articulate in describing the dilemmas, but it did not advocate any clear-cut solutions. It was also suggested that *Moment*'s editor, Uri Zvi Greenberg had 'substantially rewritten' the piece.[15] Whether this was the case or not, it was the closest that Jabotinsky had come to embracing the Irgun line. Begin, on the other hand, did not suffer the pangs of conscience. He did not pander to diplomacy as a vehicle and did not keep faith in Britain. In a demonstration outside the British

Embassy in Poland in April 1939, he was arrested and imprisoned for three weeks before securing a release through the intervention of the US Ambassador in Warsaw.

The White Paper of 1939 which indicated a strong movement towards the Palestinian Arab position was seen by Weizmann and the mainstream Zionists as a deep betrayal of Jewish trust in British promises and as a self-evident vehicle to safeguard British interests in the event of an outbreak of war. 75,000 Jews would be admitted to Palestine over the following five years and thereafter Jewish immigration would be in the gift of the Palestinian Arabs. For the Irgun, it was a defining watershed which initiated a new campaign – this time, not only against Palestinian Arabs, but also against the British. However, what initially concerned Jabotinsky was action against Arab civilians. In a telegram from 'Mendelson' to the Irgun,[16] he quoted from a report in *The Times*[17] which suggested that four Arab women had been shot 'with premeditation'. He advised the Irgun either to deny it or to punish the assailants. He said that it was better not to shoot at all than to endanger the lives of women.

The Irgun issued a long statement which delineated its approach to the White Paper. It proclaimed that no nation in history had ever succeeded in winning its independence without resorting to military force. The British, the statement claimed, 'instigated, favoured and allowed to continue' episodes of Arab violence in order to backtrack on the Balfour Declaration and ultimately nullify the promises made to the Jews. It warned that 'a Jewish ghetto in Palestine will be established only over our dead bodies.' The IRA and other national movements were hailed as examples of what was possible. Weizmann was depicted as a British stooge and the Zionist Organization was condemned for its bequest of 'pacifism at any price'. The Round Table conference of early 1939, the Irgun argued, had brought them to this impasse and the only way forward was to 'reconquer the Land of Israel'.[18] Yet they also perceived the virtue in the existence of a military force as a chess piece in any future diplomatic contest. In the event of world war only an armed force of 100,000 would assure the defence of Palestine and thereby place them in a strong bargaining position to induce Britain to agree to the creation of a Jewish state. Moreover, Jabotinsky's less than wholehearted support for the Irgun's approach created further criticism of the aging leader. An Irgun delegation consequently decided to attend the Zionist Congress in Geneva without Jabotinsky's authorization and this was clearly against Revisionist policy.

A week before the invasion of Poland, the Irgun killed three British CID members whom they accused of torturing an Irgun commander. The day before the Germans crossed the border with Poland, the British arrested and imprisoned the entire high command of the Irgun.

As history records, Jabotinsky immediately took the opportunity to throw his personal support and that of the Revisionist movement behind the Chamberlain government. David Raziel in a communiqué from prison resolved to do the same and declared a ceasefire – much to the surprise of Stern and the rest of the Irgun high command. This was the first step in a series of political and personal disputes between Raziel and Stern who had been formerly close colleagues. It ended in a split with Stern leading his own group out of the Irgun. This was known pejoratively by the British as 'the Stern Gang' – later as Lehi - which still saw the British as the central enemy. Stern devoutly believed that 'the enemy of my enemy is my friend' so he approached Nazi Germany. With German armies at the gates of Palestine, he offered co-operation and an alliance with a new totalitarian Hebrew republic. He hoped that with German assistance, he could now bring 40,000 Jews from occupied Europe to Palestine to overthrow British rule. Both the Germans and fellow Maximalists such as Achimeir did not take Stern seriously. An increasingly isolated Avraham Stern forged ahead with his fatalistic political and military campaign until he met his death at the hands of the British CID in early 1942. Raziel, too, died young, ironically serving the British in Iraq.

There was a deepening animosity, however, between the Irgun and Lehi amidst conspiratorial accusations of betrayal of the other side to the British. Indeed, following the wave of arrests in November 1940, the Stern Group threatened to kill both Raziel and Altman.[19] The Raziel-Stern debate was reflected by members of Betar and the Irgun in Poland who had fled eastwards towards the Soviet zone of control. Begin's position was once more a halfway compromise: he believed that Britain's weakness – even when fighting Nazism – had to be exploited, but the enemy of my enemy was not 'always automatically' my friend.[20] He maintained that the European war was not 'our war'.

Jabotinsky died suddenly of heart failure while inspecting a Betar camp in New York in 1940. Yet his last book, *The Jewish War Front*, written at the beginning of 1940, testified to his profound belief that Britain should be supported in the struggle against Nazism.[21] As he pointed out in his letter to Chamberlain, 'Great Britain's resolve to cut out the cancer choking God's earth carries a message that transcends political disagreements.'[22] Moreover, Jabotinsky began a campaign to resurrect the Jewish Legion, an army of 200,000.[23] On this occasion, Weizmann agreed.[24] In a short period of time, therefore, death had claimed Jabotinsky, Raziel and Stern. Begin was eventually arrested by the NKVD – the Soviet secret police – in Lithuania and sentenced to eight years in the Gulag. With the breakdown of the Molotov-Ribbentrop pact and Hitler's invasion of the USSR, Begin found himself a member of the newly formed Polish Army of General Anders which eventually made its way to the Middle East. Despite the fact that he had never been engaged in military combat either in Poland or in Palestine, in December 1943, Begin became the sixth commander of the Irgun Zvai Leumi in Palestine. Two months later, he proclaimed 'The Revolt' against British rule.

THE RISE OF THE HEBREW REPUBLIC

The war concluded as a victory for the Allies, but a defeat for the Jews. The murder of six million in the Shoah concentrated minds as to the future. The legacy of Jabotinsky had evolved into those who actively participated in the armed struggle and those who did not. The Revisionists of Aryeh Altman remained Jabotinsky loyalists. The Irgun under Begin interpreted Jabotinsky selectively. Lehi, first under Stern, then Yellin-Mor, Eldad and Shamir, were advocates of a post-Jabotinsky ideology.

The official Revisionists reversed the decisions of Katowice in 1933 and reunited with Grossman's breakaway faction, the Jewish State party, and once more became part of the Zionist Organization. In early 1948, Meir Grossman became the leader of the Revisionist movement. Begin had attempted to draw Lehi back into the Irgun in the autumn of 1944, but it had rejected all his overtures. A prime point of disagreement was the recognition of the authority of Jabotinsky. Moreover, Begin tried to adopt Jabotinsky's tactic of posing as a fair and neutral arbiter between the warring factions.[25]

Although the Irgun had formally broken with the Revisionists at the end of 1943, Begin resisted considerable pressure for his organization to rejoin the Revisionist family. Propes, who had been replaced by Begin, spoke of him as 'the brilliant commander of the Irgun Zvai Leumi'.[26] In spite of all this, Begin defended the independence of the Irgun as a separate entity and proceeded to turn it into a political party, the Herut movement. Which group, therefore, – the official Revisionists or Herut – represented the legacy of Jabotinsky? Begin understood that his standing as the commander of the Irgun in the emotional aftermath of the establishment of the state of Israel commended him to a section of the Israeli electorate. His defiant rhetoric and flair for the public relations of polarization embellished his position. For Begin, all nationalists, regardless of the path taken, became the children of Jabotinsky 'our father and teacher'.[27] Moreover, he began to develop a public perception of himself as Jabotinsky's sole heir and only interpreter of his political teachings. In his broadcast on Irgun radio on the eve of the declaration of Israel's independence, Begin invoked Masaryk, Lafayette, Jefferson and Thomas Paine, followed by Herzl, Nordau, Trumpeldor, 'and the father of modern Jewish heroism, Ze'ev Jabotinsky'.

The Revisionists meanwhile ploughed a political path in remaining in the

Provisional Governing Council. The sinking of the arms ship, *Altalena*, in June 1948 provided them with the opportunity to unite all nationalists in a torrent of outrage against Ben-Gurion. Grossman and Altman believed that Begin's conduct in the *Altalena* affair had weakened his position and that this would facilitate Herut's merger with the Revisionists. Yet even his well-known and emotional broadcast, following the sinking of the *Altalena*, suggested a blurring of differences with the Revisionists and an implicit suggestion that the Irgun was the true heir of Jabotinsky's legacy.

> Do they really think that by liquidating me they would have achieved something? Who and what am I?
> They could have learned from past history. When Jabotinsky died in exile in 1940 they rejoiced; his party would disintegrate. But it did not. It arose step by step. We raised the banner of freedom and came as far as capturing Jaffa and liberating Tel Aviv.[28]

Begin resisted any enticement to capitulate, but continued to negotiate with the Revisionists. Publicly he began to portray Herut as the central voice of opposition to Ben-Gurion and his conduct of the war. He warned that the 'statelet' of Israel could become a ghetto unless the East Bank – Abdullah's Transjordan – was conquered. 'Either we advance eastwards, or, sooner or later, we shall be pushed into the sea.'[29] Israel, moreover, had not taken advantage of the ceasefires of 1948 to press home its military superiority. For all intents and purposes, Begin appeared to be campaigning for the elections. Indeed, Herut had already opened an office in Tel Aviv.

At a public meeting in August 1948 in Jerusalem, Begin challenged Ben-Gurion to arrest him. Seated under a large poster of Jabotinsky and the slogan 'Moledet v'Herut' (Homeland and Freedom) he promised to erect the Third Temple in Jerusalem.

The Revisionist World Council met in Israel to discuss the situation of two parties and to find a solution to the problem. The Revisionists, for their part, were concerned whether Herut would be a truly democratic party or one based instead on a military structure. They also asked how Herut would separate itself from the Irgun. For example, they demanded that Herut drop its symbol of a rifle. Begin and Herut were once more opposed to any membership of the Zionist Organization. One plan which was mooted was the dissolution of the Revisionists in Israel and their replacement by Herut. The former would now be active only in the Diaspora while the latter would be the parliamentary representative in Israel. The Revisionist leadership which was now represented on the Zionist Executive vehemently opposed the suggestion. These disagreements were brought to a head during the conference of the Israeli Revisionists at the end of August 1948. A resolution was brought to unite the

Revisionists with Herut. A vote to postpone the resolution was rejected by 61 to 32. When the vote was finally taken, 61 voted in favour – and the remainder walked out.

Begin's attempt to reconstruct memory and to selectively mould Jabotinsky's views reached an apogee on the eve of the first Herut conference in October 1948. He had already spoken of him in quasi-religious terms – 'to learn a portion of his Torah' – in an article which commemorated the eighth anniversary of his death.[30] Begin further wrote a similar article on Jabotinsky for the Jewish New Year which was translated and distributed throughout the Revisionist Diaspora. Jabotinsky was lauded not only as the teacher of Betar, but of all Zionists:

> In the period of the eclipse of Israel's light, when its aim, conceived by the vision of our fathers and interpreted by Herzl, became obscured, when the captains cast the compass to the sea's bottom and wandered lost, in the period when deception was twisted by men of folly and malice into high sounding political wisdom, Jabotinsky arose.

Begin castigated Weizmann and Ben-Gurion for not believing in the possibility of a Jewish state. For them, 'a noble Jewish state was a stupid dream, a reactionary and detrimental desire.' Even though Jabotinsky had believed in 1939 that war would not break out and did not predict the enormity of the Shoah, Begin hinted that the policies of his opponents were instrumental in the destruction of European Jewry:

> The 'reality' mouthed by those of little vision turned to ashes. Of that, nothing was left, nothing save the rivers of blood that streamed from our nation. Still clinging to its erupting volcano, still trusting in its deceitful and faithless leaders.

Moreover, Jabotinsky, Begin argued, had shown the path to political fulfilment through his advocacy of force rather than diplomacy:

> Through statesmanship and construction, but principally through the strategy of warfare. I say this because statesmanship is nothing more than hollow persuasiveness unless it can be upheld in battle. Even construction, and be it of the most noble proportions, becomes null and void unless the war of freedom transforms it into statesmanlike construction.

Such a statement defined Begin and his transition to Herut in 1948 rather than Jabotinsky and his eve of war dilemma and ambivalence on the Irgun's actions. Yet it was utilized to retroactively define Jabotinsky. Begin reminded his readership of Jabotinsky's article 'Afn Pripitshek' where he advocated that young people should learn the art of self-defence and 'learn to shoot'. Begin interpreted this as 'he taught us how to shoot' and thereby transformed

Jabotinsky into 'the father of the Revolt'. Defence against Arab violence became synonymous with conquest of the homeland. Begin further suggested that there had been nothing like the Revolt of the Irgun since the days of the ancient Maccabees:

> Our generation learned the methods of warfare from Ze'ev Jabotinsky. He was a rebel and a revolutionary, a despiser of conventions and a stern enemy of defeat. He called for revolt and actuality soon proved that there could be no life without revolt, no freedom without war and no future without striving.

Begin concluded by cementing his relationship – and that of the Irgun – to Jabotinsky:

> Your sons – the sons of your dreams and doctrines – have done what you have taught. They have arisen and revolted. They were persecuted and martyred, but they fought.

All this was well received by the emerging nationalist camp in Israel, but less so by Jabotinsky's colleagues and co-workers and by the intellectuals in the Revisionist movement. At the first Herut conference at the end of October 1948, Begin declared that he was ready to form a government if Herut won the forthcoming elections. He spoke about 'the mutilation of our country' due to the partition of 1947 and condemned Ben-Gurion and his supporters for a failure to prepare a sufficiently large military force at the right time. He said that there would be no negotiations with Arab countries and criticized the United Nations. All this was predictable. What was not was the support given by the Jabotinsky family to Begin. Jabotinsky's widow greeted him on a visit to New York. Jabotinsky's son was a candidate on the Herut electoral list while Jabotinsky's sister, Tamar, accompanied Begin when he triumphantly entered the Ohel Shem hall at the start of the first Herut conference.[31]

The first Israeli elections saw Herut trounce the official Revisionists. Begin collected 14 seats while the Revisionists were unable to secure the election of even one candidate. Begin had drawn up the Herut list of candidates himself.[32] The official Revisionists were thereafter absorbed by Herut. Grossman, Altman and other long-time Revisionists were confined to the political wilderness. Both Jabotinsky's family and colleagues – those who were initially loyal to Begin and those who joined Herut after the rout of the Revisionists – were eventually marginalized in terms of political power. In Begin's eyes, they belonged to a nostalgic past, but not to the hard reality of the political present. Even so, the Revisionist intelligentsia as well as Jabotinsky's son began to depart from Herut because of Begin's centralized rule. There were many who unhesitatingly had obeyed Jabotinsky – even when they disagreed with him – but now vehemently argued with Begin.

At the first Herut conference, Begin was surrounded by portraits of Jabotinsky, Raziel and Stern. In turn, he paid tribute to them. Differences were not mentioned. Fate had bequeathed them early deaths and in so doing removed any potential rival. Achimeir, Propes and even Uri Zvi Greenberg retreated to cultural and intellectual pursuits. Begin had outmanoeuvred Altman's Revisionists, Grossman's State Party, Stern's Lehi and Hillel Kook's Hebrew Committee of National Liberation.

Raziel and Stern were now presented as the David and Jonathan of the nationalist cause. Begin in the 1960s recalled 'the proximity of hearts' between himself and Avraham Stern some thirty years previously.[33] Jabotinsky's name was enthusiastically proclaimed on public occasions, but it was a selective and often fictional Jabotinsky that was honoured and exalted. Herut became a highly centralized party defined by loyalty to Begin – and often to his interpretation of the past. Indeed he implied that Jabotinsky had chosen him as his successor.[34] Yet Begin fulfilled a role in terms of the party apparatus more akin to Grossman's function in the Revisionists.

But Begin lived in different times. By shrewd coalition building with anti-Labour parties and by a covert reversal of some of Jabotinsky's policies such as belonging to the Histadrut[35] or membership of the World Zionist Organization, Herut became Gahal in 1965 which in turn was transformed into the Likud in 1973. Begin attained neither Jabotinsky's intellectual stature nor an admiration from friend and foe alike, but it was a rare combination of political astuteness, a fair share of luck, a steely stubbornness and the implosion of his political opponents which secured his election as Prime Minister of Israel at the ninth attempt at the age of 64 in 1977. But Begin's imagery of Jabotinsky also triumphed. It provoked adulation amongst the heirs of the Irgun in Herut and profound disdain amongst Begin's enemies on the Left. The real Jabotinsky disappeared into the mists of time. Shortly after his election, Begin delayed a first meeting with President Carter to commemorate the anniversary of Jabotinsky's death. He was announced firstly as Commander of the Irgun Zvai Leumi and only then as Prime Minister of Israel. There was no speech. Begin solemnly stood alone before Jabotinsky's grave on Mount Herzl in Jerusalem to silently inform him that his disciples now constituted the government of Israel.

REFERENCES

INTRODUCTION

1.Vladimir Jabotinsky, 'Points from V. Jabotinsky's address', Dublin, 12 January 1938, Jabotinsky Archives.

2. *Jewish Herald* 7 January 1938.

3. Vladimir Jabotinsky, 'A Talk with Zangwill' *Jewish Herald* 4 August 1939.

4. Derek J. Penslar, 'The Foundations of the Twentieth Century: Herzlian Zionism', in *Israel Studies* vol.6 no.2, Summer 2001.

5. Walter Laqueur, *History of Zionism* (London 2003) pp.381-382.

6. Eran Kaplan, *The Jewish Radical Right: Revisionist Zionism and its Ideological Legacy* (Wisconsin 2005) p.156.

7. Vladimir Jabotinsky, 'Italy', *Hayarden* 21 August 1936.

8. Raphaella Bilski Ben-Hur, *Every Individual a King: The Social and Political Thought of Ze'ev Vladimir Jabotinsky* (Washington 1993) pp.13-14.

9. Vladimir Jabotinsky, Letter to Shlomo Gepstein, 10 December 1928 *Igrot 1928-1929* (Jerusalem 2002).

10. Vladimir Jabotinsky, Letter to Avraham Weinshall, 29 December 1930 *Igrot 1930-1931* (Jerusalem 2004) pp.154-156.

11. Roger Griffin, *The Nature of Fascism* (London 1991) p.26.

12. Sasson Sofer, *Begin: An Anatomy of Leadership* (Oxford 1988) p.27.

13. Ben Zion Netanyahu, 'Jabotinsky and His Generation' *Zionews* September 1942.

14. Benjamin Akzin, *Mi-Riga L'Yerushalayim* (Jerusalem, 1989), p.176.

15. Ibid. p.157.

PROLOGUE

1. Vladimir Jabotinsky, 'Why I Resigned', *Jewish Chronicle* 2 February 1923.

2. Vladimir Jabotinsky, *Jewish Chronicle* 9 February 1923.

3. *The New Palestine* 25 November 1921.

4. Saul J. Cohen, *Jewish Chronicle* 9 February 1922.

1. THE PARTING OF THE WAYS

1. Memorandum presented to the King-Crane Commission by the General Syrian Congress in *The Israel-Arab Reader: a Documentary History of the Middle East Conflict*, ed. Walter Laqueur and Barry Rubin (London 1984) p.33.

2. Chaim Weizmann, Letter to Lord Curzon, 2 April 1920; GB165-0252, Herbert Samuel Archives, Oxford.

3. See Dvorah Barzilay-Yegar, *Bayit Leumi La'am Hayehudi: Hamusag Bekhashiva – 1923* (Jerusalem 2004).

4. Chaim Weizmann, 'Our Relations with the Authorities', Report to the Zionist Executive 7 November 1919, Herbert Samuel Archives, Oxford.

5. Seder Nashim, Ketubbot 111a, *Babylonian Talmud*.

6. Herbert Samuel, Note of conversation with Sir Edward Grey, 9 November 1914, Herbert Samuel Archive, Oxford.

7. Ibid.

8. Ibid.

9. Vladimir Jabotinsky, *The Story of the Jewish Legion*, translated by Shmuel Katz (New York 1945) p.30.

10. Ibid.

11. Chaim Weizmann, Letter to C. P. Scott, 12 November 1914, *Letters and Papers of Chaim Weizmann* Series A Letters, vol.7 August 1914-November 1917.

12. Chaim Weizmann, Letter to Lord Curzon, 2 February 1920, Herbert Samuel Archive, Oxford.

13. Herbert Samuel, Note of conversation with Sir Edward Grey, 9 November 1914, Herbert Samuel Archive, Oxford.

14. Chaim Weizmann, Letter to Ahad Ha'am, 14 December 1914 *Letters and Papers of Chaim Weizmann;* Series A Letters, vol.7 August 1914-November 1917.

15. Herbert Samuel, 'The Future of Palestine: For the Use of the Cabinet', January 1915, Herbert Samuel Archive, Oxford.

16. *Jewish Chronicle* 6 November 1919.

17. Herbert Samuel, Letter to Lucy Franklin, 3 May 1920. See Evyatar Friesel, 'Herbert Samuel's Reassessment of Zionism in 1921', *Studies in Zionism* vol.5 no.2 Autumn 1984, p.217.

18. H. St. J. B. Philby, 'Memorandum on Transjordan and other Near East Problems', 26 June 1926; Herbert Samuel Archive, Oxford..

19. Herbert Samuel, *Memoirs* (London 1945) p.151.

20. *The Rise of Israel*, vol.12 ed. Isaiah Friedman (New York 1987).

21. *The Times* 2 September 1920.

22. Joseph B. Schechtman, *The Jabotinsky Story: Rebel and Statesman 1880-1923* (New York 1956) p.416.

23. Herbert Samuel, *Creative Man* (London 1949) p.123.

24. Herbert Samuel, *Liberalism: An Attempt to State the Principles of Contemporary Liberalism in England* (London 1902) p.396.

25. Norman Bentwich, *England in Palestine* (London 1932) p.53.

26. Gideon Biger, 'Where was Palestine? Pre-World War I Perceptions', *Area XIII* no. 2 (1981) pp.133-160.

27. *Encyclopaedia Britannica*, 11th edition, 1910-1911 pp.600-601.

28. Norman Bentwich, 'The Future of Palestine', *Zionism and the Jewish Future,* ed. Harry Sacher (London 1916) p.208.

29. Book of Judges 20.

30. Gideon Biger, *An Empire in the Holy Land: Historical Geography of the British Administration in Palestine 1917-1929* (Jerusalem 1994) pp.47-63.

31. Sir George Adam Smith, *The Historical Geography of the Holy Land, especially in relation to the History of Israel and the Early Church* (London 1891).

32. In a letter to Lord Curzon, 12 July 1920, Samuel comments, 'Adam Smith's atlas is inaccurate in many points. Before a formal argument is made, no doubt the latest maps will be consulted.' Herbert Samuel Archive, Oxford.

33. A. M. Hyamson, *Palestine under the Mandate* (London 1950) pp.1-12.

34. *The Times* 26 January 1870.

35. Blanche Dugdale, *Arthur James Balfour: First Earl of Balfour* vol.1 (London 1936) p.433.

36. *Jewish Herald* 5 May 1939.

37. Herbert Samuel, 'Palestine', March 1915, Herbert Samuel Archive, Oxford.

38. Joseph Klausner, *Menachem Ussishkin* (London 1944) pp.61-62.

39. Cypher telegram from the Foreign Office to Sir George Buchanan, Petrograd, 11 March 1916.

40. Cypher telegram from Sir George Buchanan, Petrograd, to the Foreign Office, 14 March 1916.

41. Memorandum PRO/FO 371/E 14954944, 29 November 1919.

42. J. Ramsay MacDonald, *A Socialist in Palestine* (London 1922).

43. Bernard A. Rosenblatt, 'Zionism and the British Labour Party', *The New Palestine* 6 October 1922.

44. Chaim Weizmann, Letter to Winston Churchill, 1 March 1921, *Letters and Papers of Chaim Weizmann*; Series A Letters; vol. 10 July 1920-December 1921 (Jerusalem 1977).

45. Ibid.

46. Vladimir Jabotinsky, 'What the Revisionist-Zionists Want' in *The Jew in the Modern World: A Documentary History* ed. Paul R. Mendes-Flohr and Jehuda Reinharz (London 1995) pp.594-596.

47. Vladimir Jabotinsky, Memoranda 4 November, 12 December, 29 December 1922, in CZA S25-2073.

48. Vladimir Jabotinsky, *Jewish Herald* 29 April 1938.

49. Vladimir Jabotinsky, *Jewish Herald* 30 September 1938.

50. Vladimir Jabotinsky, 'What the Revisionist-Zionists Want' in *The Jew in the Modern World: A Documentary History* ed. Paul R. Mendes-Flohr and Jehuda Reinharz (London

1995) pp.594-596.

51. Vladimir Jabotinsky, *Jewish Herald* 29 April 1938.

52. Mopsim: Mifleget Poalim Sotsialistim Ha'Ivrim.

53. Sondra Miller Rubenstein, *The Communist Movement in Palestine and Israel 1919-1984* (Boulder 1985) p.60.

54. *The Times* 14 May 1921.

55. Herbert Samuel, Speech on the King's Birthday, 3 June 1921 CZA Z4/6055.

56. For an overview of the question of emigration during this early period, see A. M. Hyamson, *Palestine Under the Mandate* (London 1950) pp.51-69.

57. Chaim Weizmann, Letter to Winston Churchill, November 1921, *Letters and Papers of Chaim Weizmann;* Series A Letters; vol.10 July 1920-December 1921 (Jerusalem 1977) p.344.

58. Helen Bentwich, *Tidings from Zion: Letters from Jerusalem 1919-1931,* ed. Jennifer Glynn (London 2000) p.68.

59. Vladimir Jabotinsky, Letter to Chava and Tamar Jabotinsky, 10 June 1921, *Igrot 1918-1922* (Tel Aviv 1997) pp.230-231.

60. Vladimir Jabotinsky Letter to Joanna Jabotinsky, 16 June 1921, *Igrot 1918-1922* (Tel Aviv 1997) p.235.

61. Vladimir Jabotinsky, Letter to Joanna Jabotinsky, 21 June 1921 *Igrot 1918-1922* (Tel Aviv 1997) p.236.

62. Shmuel Katz, *Lone Wolf: A Biography of Vladimir Ze'ev Jabotinsky*, vol.1 (New York 1996) p.735.

63. Herbert Samuel, Letter to Chaim Weizmann 10 August 1921, in Evyatar Friesel, 'Herbert Samuel's Reassessment of Zionism in 1921', *Studies in Zionism* vol.5 no.2 Autumn 1984 p.224.

64. Herbert Samuel, *Memoirs* (London 1945) p.168.

65. Palestine: Disturbances in May 1921: Report of the Commission of Inquiry with correspondence relating thereto. Command 1540. (London 1921).

66. Herbert Samuel, Letter to Winston Churchill, 26 August 1921, PRO CO 733/396.

67. M. Mossek, *Palestine Immigration Policy under Sir Herbert Samuel* (London 1978) p.43.

68. Vladimir Jabotinsky, Letter to the Zionist Executive, 24 November 1921 *Igrot 1918 -1922* (Tel Aviv 1997) pp.260-265.

69. Yehoshua Freundlich and Gedalia Yogev, eds., *Minutes of the Zionist General Council* vol.1 February 1919-January 1920 (Tel Aviv 1975).

70. Vladimir Jabotinsky, *The Story of the Jewish Legion* (London 1945) p.71.

71. This was a sensitive subject for the British Colonial Office. MacMahon wrote to Sir John Shuckburgh on 12 March 1922 to make clear that he had intended to exclude Palestine from Arab area. 'Damascus', in fact, meant the vilayet of Damascus. In a letter to Sir Herbert Samuel, Shuckburgh commented, 'You doubtless saw Mr Churchill's reply to Ormsby-Gore's question in Parliament on the 11th July. The wording of that reply was drawn up with the most meticulous care and represents, I think, the best that can be said on the subject.'

72. Vladimir Jabotinsky, 'Why I Resigned', *Jewish Chronicle* 2 February 1923.

73. *Daily Express* 22 October 1922.

74. Helen Bentwich, *Tidings from Zion: Letters from Jerusalem 1919-1931*, ed. Jennifer Glynn (London 2000) p.77.

75. *The New Palestine* 17 March 1922.

76. Ibid.

77. Vladimir Jabotinsky, *New York Evening Post* 22 April 1922.

2. THE ROAD TO RESIGNATION

1. Vera Weizmann, *The Impossible Takes Longer* (New York 1967) p.104.

2. Chaim Weizmann, Letter to Vera Weizmann, 21 March 1920, *The Letters and Papers of Chaim Weizmann*; Series A Letters; vol.9 October 1918-July 1920 (Jerusalem 1977) p.324.

3. Vladimir Jabotinsky, 'Zionist Administration in Palestine', *Jewish Chronicle* 14 April 1922.

4. Vladimir Jabotinsky, Interview in the *Jewish Chronicle* 20 May 1921.

5. Ibid.

6. Ibid.

7. Vladimir Jabotinsky, Memorandum to the Zionist Executive, 5 November 1922.

8. Louis Lipsky, 'Max Nordau', *The New Palestine* 26 January 1923.

9. Max Nordau, *Zionism: Causes of Failure and Conditions of Success*, New Zionist Organization, London 1943); *Max Nordau to His People* (New York 1944), introduction by Ben-Zion Netanyahu p.57.

10. Max Nordau, 'Colonization insecure without Political Zionism', *Jewish Herald* 14 January 1938.

11. Max Nordau, 'Yesterday, Today and Tomorrow', *Le Peuple Juif* 1920.

12. Max Nordau, 'To American Jewry', *Zionews* 2 January 1943.

13. Chaim Weizmann, 'Zionism and the Jewish Problem', *Zionism and the Jewish Future* ed. Harry Sacher (London 1916) pp.7-8.

14. Max Nordau, *Zionism: Its History and Victims* (English Zionist Federation 1905) p.18.

15. *Jewish Herald* 27 May 1938.

16. Max Nordau, 'La Guerre et L'Organization Sioniste', *Le Peuple Juif* 19 November 1920.

17. *Jewish Herald* 27 May 1938.

18. Max Nordau, 'Thus Spoke Nordau', *Hadar* February 1940.

19. Vladimir Jabotinsky, *The Story of the Jewish Legion* (New York 1945) p.31.

20. Ibid., p.31. Nordau regarded France as his 'true homeland'.

21. Vladimir Jabotinsky, Letter to Israel Rosov, 5 November 1914 *Igrot 1914-1918* (Jerusalem 1995) pp.6-7.

22. Although Nordau's views were attacked by Jabotinsky in 1919, his supporters were happy to publish them in 1943 *Zionews* 2 January 1943.

23. Vladimir Jabotinsky, 'Aliya Hadashot', *Ha'aretz* 14 November 1919.

24. Ibid.

25. *L'Echo Sioniste* 23 December 1921.

26. 'Weakness in the Zionist Organization' 19 January 1922 in Jehuda Reinharz, *Chaim Weizmann: The Making of a Statesman* (Oxford 1993) p.369.

27. *The New Palestine* 19 January 1923.

28. Chaim Weizmann, *Zionist Review* September 1920.

29. Vladimir Jabotinsky, Letter to Chaim Weizmann, 7 October 1920 *Igrot 1918–1922* (Jerusalem 1997) pp.149-150.

30. Chaim Weizmann, Letter to Nachum Sokolov, 27 November 1920, *Letters and Papers of Chaim Weizmann*; Series A Letters; vol.10 July 1920-December 1921 (Jerusalem 1977).

31. Chaim Weizmann, Diary 2 January 1921 *Letters and Papers of Chaim Weizmann*; Series A Letters; vol.10 July 1920-December 1921 (Jerusalem 1977).

32. Chaim Weizmann, Letter to Vladimir Jabotinsky, 20 March 1921 *Letters and Papers of Chaim Weizmann*; Series A Letters; vol.10 July 1920-December 1921 (Jerusalem 1977).

33. *Jewish Chronicle* 3 June 1921.

34. Chaim Weizmann, Telegram to the Zionist Executive CZA Z4Å059.

35. *Jewish Chronicle* 1, 8 September 1922.

36. Chaim Weizmann, Letter to Vera Weizmann, 29 August 1922 *Letters and Papers of Chaim Weizmann*; Series A Letters; vol.11 January 1922-July 1923 (Jerusalem 1977).

37. Joseph Schechtman, *The Jabotinsky Story: Rebel and Statesman 1880-1923* (New York 1956) p.424.

38. Vladimir Jabotinsky, Introduction to *Chaim Nachman Bialik: Poems from the Hebrew* ed. L. V. Snowman (London 1924).

39. Chaim Weizmann, *Trial and Error* (London 1949) p.37.

40. 'Vladimir Jabotinsky's address to the inaugural meeting of the South African branch of the New Zionist Organization', 26 June 1937 *Eleventh Hour* vol.1 no. 16, 2 July 1937.

41. *Jewish Chronicle* 2 February 1923.

42. See Saul S. Friedman, *Pogromchik: The Assassination of Simon Petliura* (New York, 1976).

43. *Jewish Chronicle* 30 December 1921.

44. Joseph B. Schechtman, *The Jabotinsky Story: Rebel and Statesman: The Early Years 1880-1923* (New York 1956) pp.412-414.

45. Colin Shindler, 'Jabotinsky and Ukrainian Nationalism: A Reinterpretation', *East European Jewish Affairs* vol.31 no.2 London 2001.

46. Vladimir Jabotinsky, 'K voprosu o natsionalizme (otvet g. Izgoevu)' (On Nationalism: A Reply to Mr Izgoev), *Obrazovanie* (St Petersburg), no.10 October 1904, pp.87-98.

47. Vladimir Jabotinsky, 'A Letter on Autonomy', *Ketavim Tsionim Rishonim*, Ketavim 8 ed. E. Jabotinsky (Jerusalem 1949) pp.59-74; *Evreiskaya zhizn* no.6 June 1904.

48. Vladimir Jabotinsky, 'The Lessons of Shevchenko's Anniversary', *Odesskie novosti* 27 February 1911 in *Al Sifrut Ve-Omanut*, Ketavim 6, ed. Eri Jabotinsky (Jerusalem 1958) pp.133-141.

49. Vladimir Jabotinsky, Letter to Yona Machover, 9 March 1922 *Igrot 1918-1923* (Tel

Aviv 1997) p.297.

50. Vladimir Jabotinsky, 'Vopros o Petliure', *Rassvet* 8 March 1925; Nachum Levin, 'Jabotinsky and the Petliura Agreement', *Jewish Standard* 16 August 1940.

51. In a letter to Richard Lichtheim, 6 January 1922, Jabotinsky refers to the opposition of Poale Zion to the accord with Slavinsky. This arose in a congress in Vilna 27-30 December 1921. In Vladimir Jabotinsky, *Igrot 1918-1923* (Jerusalem, 1997) p.273.

52. Chaim Weizmann, *Trial and Error* (New York 1949) p.82.

53. Ibid.

54. *Zionews* 28 July 1941.

55. Vladimir Jabotinsky, 'Shiva', *Evreiskaya zhizn* no.6 June 1904; *Hadar* November 1940.

56. Vladimir Jabotinsky, 'Leader', *Moment* 3 July 1934.

57. Chaim Weizmann, Letter to Nachum Sokolov, 18 February 1923 *Letters and Papers of Chaim Weizmann*, Series A Letters; vol.10 July 1920-December 1921 (Jerusalem 1977).

58. *The New Palestine* 9 February 1923.

59. Vladimir Jabotinsky, *Jewish Chronicle* 2 February 1923.

3. A STRANGE ODYSSEY

1. Vladimir Jabotinsky, Letter to Chava and Tamar Jabotinsky, 21 January 1923, *Igrot 1922-1925* (Jerusalem 1998) p.57.

2. For an appraisal of post-World War I Czechoslovakia and the Jews, see Howard M. Sachar, *Dreamland: Europeans and Jews in the Aftermath of the Great War* (New York 2002) pp.132-160.

3. Alain Dieckhoff, *The Invention of a Nation: Zionist Thought and the Making of Modern Israel* (London 2003) pp.198-199. Sokol was based on the model of Turnverein, the gymnastic societies created by Friedrich Ludwig Jahn following Napoleon's invasion of the German states.

4. Vladimir Jabotinsky, 'Ha-Hasmonai ha-Riga', *Reshimot*, Ketavim 16, ed. Eri Jabotinsky (Tel Aviv 1958) pp.189-198; *Rassvet* 28 February, 7 March 1926.

5. There had already been a Zionist presence in Riga such as the youth group Ha'Techiya. Benjamin Akzin, *Mi-Riga L'Yerushaliyim* (Jerusalem, 1989) p.154.

6. Vladimir Jabotinsky, 'Ha-Hasmonai ha-Riga', *Reshimot*, Ketavim 16, ed. Eri Jabotinsky (Tel Aviv 1958) pp.189-198; *Rassvet* 28 February, 7 March 1926.

7. Ibid.

8. Joseph Trumpeldor was Jabotinsky's close collaborator in the formation of the Jewish Legion. He was killed at Tel Chai in 1920 by attacking Arabs. Jabotinsky commemorated him as a one-armed hero in poetry and literary endeavours – and of course, through Brit Trumpeldor, Betar.

9. Aaron Z. Propes, 'Those Evenings and Nights', *Hadar* November 1940.

10. Vladimir Jabotinsky, Letter to Paul Diamant, 8 December 1923, *Igrot 1922-1925* (Jerusalem 1998) p.57.

11. Zalman Shazar, 'The Great Violin has been Shattered', *Davar* 5 July 1940.

12. Vladimir Jabotinsky, 'My Typewriter Speaks', *Moment* 18 November 1932.

13. Benjamin Akzin, *Mi-Riga L'Yerushalayim* (Jerusalem, 1989), p.157.

14. Vladimir Jabotinsky, 'The Other Max Nordau', *Moment* 3 February 1933; *Hadar* February-March-April 1941.

15. Ibid.

16. Vladimir Jabotinsky in his address to the first NZO conference in South Africa on 26 June 1937 *Eleventh Hour* 15 July 1937.

17. Ben-Zion Netanyahu, 'Jabotinsky and his Generation' *Zionews* 1 September 1942.

18. Gabriel Preil, 'Max Nordau on the 9th anniversary of his death', *Betar Monthly* February 1932.

19. Vladimir Jabotinsky, *Avtobiografia: Sippur Yamai*, Ketavim 1, ed. E. Jabotinsky (Jerusalem 1958) p.113.

20. *Eleventh Hour* 23 April 1937.

21. Max Nordau, 'Speech to the First Zionist Congress', *The New Palestine* 26 January 1923.

22. Theodor Herzl, 'The Menorah', *Die Welt* 31 December 1897.

23. Aviezer Ravitzky, *Messianism, Zionism and Jewish Religious Radicalism* (Chicago 1996) pp. 10-13.

24. Max Nordau, *Max Nordau to His People* introduction by Ben-Zion Netanyahu (New York 1944)

25. Max Nordau, Letter to Reuben Brainin, 16 June 1896, *The New Palestine* 26 January 1923.

26. Anna and Maxa Nordau, *Max Nordau* translated from French (New York 1943) p.127.

27. Max Nordau, 'The Psychological Roots of Religion' in *The Meaning of History* (London 1910) p.214.

28. Ibid. pp.212-213.

29. *Zionews* 28 July 1941.

30. A. Misheiler, 'The Man and the Symbol', *Jewish Herald* 9 August 1940.

31. Benjamin Akzin, 'Apostle of Freedom', *American Jewish Chronicle* vol.1 no.9 15 March 1940.

32. According to Michael Stanislawski, it is doubtful whether Jabotinsky actually met Herzl, see p.162.

33. Michael Stanislawski, *Zionism and the Fin de Siecle: Cosmopolitanism and Nationalism from Nordau to Jabotinsky* p.168, quoting Jabotinsky's article in *Odesskie novosti* 23 August 1903. Israel Zangwill similarly compared Herzl to 'the Assyrian kings whose sculptured heads adorn our museums'. Walter Laqueur, *History of Zionism* (London 1972) p.98.

34. Vladimir Jabotinsky, Letter to Maxim Gorky, 28 July 1903 *Igrot 1898-1914* (Jerusalem 1992) pp.13-14.

35. Vladimir Jabotinsky, 'On the Wrong Path', *Feuilletons* (St. Petersburg 1913) pp.253-254 in Israel Kleiner, *From Nationalism to Universalism: Vladimir Ze'ev Jabotinsky and the Ukrainian Question* (Toronto and Edmonton 2000) p.40; *Felyetonim*, Ketavim 13, ed. E. Jabotinsky (Tel Aviv 1953-1954) pp.161-173.

36. Vladimir Jabotinsky, *Avtobiografia: Sippur Yamei*, Ketavim 1, ed. E. Jabotinsky

(Jerusalem 1947) p.27.

37. Arthur Hertzberg, *The Zionist Idea* (Philadelphia 1997) p.227.

38. *Jewish Herald* 27 May 1938.

39. Vladimir Jabotinsky, 'Shiva', *Evreiskaya zhizn* no.6, June 1904; Hadar (5-8) November 1940.

40. Ibid.

41. Anna Isakova, 'Review of Yevgenia Ivanova's Chukovsky and Jabotinsky: A History of their Relationship in Texts and Commentary', (Jerusalem 2004) *Ha'aretz* 25 February 2005.

42. Vladimir Jabotinsky, 'Shiva', *Evreiskaya zhizn* no.6, June 1904; *Hadar* (5-8), November 1940.

43. Vladimir Jabotinsky, 'Dr Herzl', *Kadima*, 1905; *Ktavim Tsionim Rishonim*, Ketavim 8, ed. E. Jabotinsky (Jerusalem 1949) pp.77-105.

44. Vladimir Jabotinsky, 'Hesped', 1904; *Shirim*, Ketavim 2, ed. E. Jabotinsky (Jerusalem 1958) pp. resh-lamed-zayin-resh mem.

45. Theodor Herzl, *The Complete Diaries of Theodor Herzl* ed. Raphael Patai, vol.1 (London 1960) p.231.

46. Ibid. p.283.

47. Vladimir Jabotinsky, 'Chloroformed', *Jewish Herald* 30 June 1939.

48. Vered Levy-Barzilai, *Ha'aretz* 19 April 2001.

49. Mordechai Nurock, 'My Meetings with Dr Herzl', *Igeret Lagolah* no.31 July-August 1954.

50. Theodor Herzl, Entry 6 June 1895, in *The Complete Diaries of Theodor Herzl* vol.1 ed. Raphael Patai (New York 1960) p.34.

51. Jacques Kornberg, *Theodor Herzl: From Assimilation to Zionism* (Indiana 1993) p.53.

52. Ibid. p.122.

53. J. L. Talmon, *Israel Among the Nations* (London 1970) p.118.

54. Jacques Kornberg, *Theodor Herzl: From Assimilation to Zionism* (Indiana 1993) p.122.

55. Theodor Herzl, Entry 3 September 1898, *The Complete Diaries of Theodor Herzl* vol.2 ed. Raphael Patai (New York 1960) pp.655-656.

56. Theodor Herzl, Letter to Bertha von Suttner, 16 January 1899 *The Complete Diaries of Theodor Herzl* vol.2 ed. Raphael Patai (New York 1960) p.783.

57. Theodor Herzl, Entry 6 February 1899, *The Complete Diaries of Theodor Herzl* vol.2 ed. Raphael Patai (New York 1960) p.785.

58. Theodor Herzl, Letter to Baron Hirsch, 3 June 1895 *The Complete Diaries of Theodor Herzl* vol.1 ed. Raphael Patai (New York 1960) p.27.

59. Ibid. p.28.

60. Ibid. p.28.

61. Ibid. p.33.

62. Theodor Herzl, Letter to the Family Council, 10 June 1895 *The Complete Diaries of Theodor Herzl* vol.1 ed. Raphael Patai (New York 1960) p.65.

63. See David H. Weinberg, *Between Tradition and Modernity* (New York 1996).

64. Robert Weinberg, *The Revolution of 1905 in Odessa* (Bloomington 1992) pp.7-11.

65. Vladimir Jabotinsky, 'Isa Kremer's City', *Jewish Tribune* 14 May 1926.

66. Vladimir Jabotinsky, 'Odessa: City of Many Nations', *Jewish Standard* 12 September 1941.

67. Vladimir Jabotinsky, 'Isa Kremer's City', *Jewish Tribune* 14 May 1926.

68. Vladimir Jabotinsky, 'My Typewriter Speaks', *Moment* 18 November 1932.

69. Chaim Tchernowitz, 'His Origin and Destiny', *Zionews* 1 September 1942.

70. Vladimir Jabotinsky, *Avtobiografia: Sippur Yamai*, Ketavim 1, ed. E. Jabotinsky (Jerusalem 1947) p.41.

71. Joseph B. Schechtman, *The Jabotinsky Story: Fighter and Prophet 1923-1940* (New York 1961) pp.284-285.

72. Benjamin Akzin, *Mi-Riga L'Yerushalayim* (Jerusalem 1989) p.161.

73. Vladimir Jabotinsky, 'Chloroformed', *Jewish Herald* 30 June 1939.

74. Vladimir Jabotinsky, 'The Idea of Betar' (Tel Aviv 1934) *Ba-derech la-medina*, Ketavim 11, ed. Eri Jabotinsky (Jerusalem 1952-3) p.308.

75. Vladimir Jabotinsky, 'Afn Pripitshek', *Haynt* 16 October 1931; *Jewish Herald* 12 September 1947.

76. Vladimir Jabotinsky, *Evreiskaya zhizn* no.11 1905.

77. The British Chief Rabbi, Dr Hertz, even referred to Jabotinsky as an incarnation of Bar-Kochba at a memorial service at the Great Synagogue in London on 21 August 1940 *Jewish Herald* 27 September 1940.

78. Vladimir Jabotinsky, Introduction to *Chaim Nachman Bialik: Poems from the Hebrew* ed. by L.V. Snowman (London 1924).

79. Vladimir Jabotinsky, 'Address to Betar', Danzig 1931 *Hadar* November 1940.

80. Joseph Nedava, *Trotsky and the Jews* (Philadelphia 1972) pp.195-197.

81. Chaim Weizmann, *Trial and Error* (London 1949) p.63.

82. Vladimir Jabotinsky, 'On Jewish Education', *Kadima* 1905.

83. Vladimir Jabotinsky, 'A Letter on Autonomy', *Ktavim Tsionim Rishonim*, Ketavim 8, ed. E. Jabotinsky (Jerusalem 1949) pp. 59-74; *Evreiskaya zhizn* no.6 June 1904.

84. Amnon Rubinstein, *From Herzl to Rabin* (New York 2000) p.58.

85. Vladimir Jabotinsky, *The Story of the Jewish Legion* (New York 1945) p.32.

86. Vladimir Jabotinsky, 'The Iron Wall', *Rassvet* 4 November 1923; *Jewish Herald* 26 November 1937.

87. Ibid.

88. Karl Renner, *Der Kampf der österreichischen Nationalen um den Staat* (Vienna 1902).

89. Rudolf Herrmann von Herrnritt, *Die Nationalitaet als Rechtsbegriff* (Vienna 1899); *Nationalitaet und Recht* (Vienna 1899)

90. Karl Renner (Rudolf Springer), 'Gosudarstvo I Natsiia' (Odessa 1906) in Israel Kleiner, *From Nationalism to Universalism: Vladimir Ze'ev Jabotinsky and the Ukrainian Question* (Toronto and Edmonton 2000) p.16.

91. Mark Levene, 'The Limits of Tolerance: Nation-State Building and what it means for minority groups', *Patterns of Prejudice* vol.34 no.2 (London 2000) pp.24-27.

92. Vladimir Jabotinsky, 'An Exchange of Compliments', *Feuilletons* (St Petersburg 1913) in *Uma V'Chevra*, Ketavim 9, ed. E. Jabotinsky (Jerusalem 1949-1950) pp.145-158.

93. Vladimir Jabotinsky, 'Race', (1913) in *Uma V'Chevra*, Ketavim 9, ed. E. Jabotinsky (Jerusalem 1949-1950) pp.123-136.

94. For an exposition of Jabotinsky's views, see Oscar K. Rabinowicz, *Vladimir Jabotinsky's Conception of a Nation* (New York 1946) pp.32.

95. Vladimir Jabotinsky, 'A Lecture on Jewish History', *Haynt* 13 May 1932; in *Uma V'Chevra*, Ketavim 9, ed. E. Jabotinsky (Jerusalem 1949-1950) pp.159-170.

4. THE NATIONAL REVOLUTIONARY LEGACY

1. Vladimir Jabotinsky, 'The Ten Books', (1904) in *Al Sifrut Ve-Omanut*, Ketavim 6, ed. Eri Jabotinsky (Jerusalem 1958) pp.13-45 quoted in Joseph Heller, 'Ze'ev Jabotinsky and the Revisionist Revolt against Materialism: In Search of a World View', *Jewish History* vol.12 no.2 Fall 1998 p.62.

2. Vladimir Jabotinsky, 'The East', *Rassvet* 26 September 1926 in *Reshimot*, Ketavim 16, ed. Eri Jabotinsky (Tel Aviv 1958) pp.275-283.

3. Edward W. Said, *Orientalism: Western Concepts of the Orient* (London 1995) pp.154-155.

4. Vladimir Jabotinsky, 'The East', *Rassvet* 26 September 1926 in Reshimot, Ketavim 16, ed. Eri Jabotinsky (Tel Aviv 1958) p.280.

5. Ibid. pp.278-279.

6. Vladimir Jabotinsky, *The Zionist* 14 May 1926.

7. Vladimir Jabotinsky, 'Edmee' in *Pocket Edition of Several Stories – Mostly Reactionary* (Paris 1925).

8. Vladimir Jabotinsky, 'The East', *Rassvet* 26 September 1926 in Reshimot, Ketavim 16, ed. Eri Jabotinsky (Tel Aviv 1958) p.282.

9. Vladimir Jabotinsky, *Neumim 1927-1940*, Ketavim 5, ed. Eri Jabotinsky (Jerusalem 1958) pp.184-185. See also *The Political and Social Philosophy of Ze'ev Jabotinsky: Selected Writings* ed. Mordechai Sarig (London 1999) pp.56-57.

10. Ibid. p.57.

11. Simon Dubnov, 'Jewish History: An Essay in the Philosophy of History', in Simon Dubnov, *Nationalism and History* (New York 1970) p.263.

12. Vladimir Jabotinsky, 'Zionism and the Land of Israel' (1905) in *Ketavim Tsiyoniyum Rishonim*, Ketavim 8, ed. Eri Jabotinsky (Jerusalem 1949) p.118 quoted in Raphaella Bilski Ben-Hur, *Every Individual a King* (Washington 1993) pp.123-124.

13. Shlomo Avineri, *The Making of Modern Zionism* (London 1981) pp.14-22.

14. Simon Dubnov, 'Jewish History: An Essay in the Philosophy of History', in Simon Dubnov, *Nationalism and History* (New York 1970) p.259.

15. Moses Hess, *Rome and Jerusalem* (New York 1918) p.77.

16. Isaiah Berlin, 'The Life and Opinions of Moses Hess' in *Against the Current: Essays in the History of Ideas* ed. Henry Hardy London 1979) p.221.

17. For Hess's religious odyssey, see Shulamit Volkov, 'Moses Hess: Problems of Religion and Faith', *Studies in Zionism* vol.2 no.1 Spring 1981 pp.1-15.

18. Alain Dieckhoff, *The Invention of a Nation: Zionist Thought and the Making of Modern Israel* (London 2003) pp.200-207; Joseph Heller, 'Ze'ev Jabotinsky and the Revisionist

Revolt against Materialism: In Search of a World View', *Jewish History* vol.12 no.2 Fall 1998 (Jerusalem) p.52; Yaakov Shavit, 'The Use of Jewish Intellectuals in Eastern Europe in the Doctrine of Thomas Henry Buckle', *Zion* 49 (Tel Aviv 1984) pp.410-412.

19. Vladimir Jabotinsky, 'By Intellect?', *Moment* August 1934 in *Al Sifrut Ve-Omanut*, Ketavim 6, ed. Eri Jabotinsky (Jerusalem 1958) p.361.

20. Vladimir Jabotinsky, 'Jewish Rebelliousness' (1906) in *Felyetonim*, Ketavim 13, ed. Eri Jabotinsky (Jerusalem 1953) p.48.

21. David Footman, *The Primrose Path: A Life of Ferdinand Lassalle* (London 1946) p.119.

22. J. L. Talmon, *Israel Among the Nations* (London 1970) p.96.

23. Eduard Bernstein, *Ferdinand Lassalle as a Social Reformer* (London 1893) p.19.

24. Walter Laqueur, *History of Zionism* (London 1972) p.379; Joseph B. Schechtman, *The Jabotinsky Story: Fighter and Prophet 1923-1940* (New York 1961) p.477.

25. 'Diary of Ferdinand Lassalle 1 February 1840', in David Footman, *The Primrose Path: A Life of Ferdinand Lassalle* (London 1946) p.11.

26. 'Diary of Ferdinand Lassalle 21 May 1840', in George Morris Cohen Brandes, *Ferdinand Lassalle* (London 1911) pp.9-10.

27. Eduard Bernstein, *Ferdinand Lassalle as a Social Reformer* (London 1893) p.35.

28. Arno Schirokauer, *Ferdinand Lassalle: The Power of Illusion and the Illusion of Power* (London 1931) p.189.

29. Joseph Heller, 'Ze'ev Jabotinsky and the Revisionist Revolt against Materialism: In Search of a World View', *Jewish History* vol.12 no.2 Fall 1998 pp.52-54.

30. David Footman, *The Primrose Path: A Life of Ferdinand Lassalle* (London 1946) p.106.

31. Benedetto Croce, *History of Europe in the Nineteenth Century*, translated from the Italian by Henry Furst, (London 1934) p.18.

32. Max Nordau, *Fernbeben Zionistische Schriffen* (Berlin 1923) p.394. See Robert S. Wistrich, 'Max Nordau and the Dreyfus Affair', *Journal of Israeli History* vol.16 no.1 (1995).

33. Benedetto Croce, *History of Europe in the Nineteenth Century*, translated from the Italian by Henry Furst, (London 1934) p.21.

34. Raphael Mahler, *A History of Modern Jewry 1780–1815* (London 1971) p.32.

35. Ibid. p.44.

36. David Vital, *A People Apart: The Jews in Europe 1789-1939* (Oxford 1999) p.48.

37. Alexis de Tocqueville, *On the State of Society in France before the Revolution of 1789* (London 1888) pp.198-199.

38. Rousseau witnessed the disturbances in Geneva in 1737 and opposed the idea of bloody insurrection. See *Confessions* Book 5 Oevres Complèes (Paris 1995).

39. See Jean Starobinski, 'Rousseau and Revolution', *New York Review of Books* 25 April 2002.

40. Harry Sacher, 'A Century of Jewish History', *Zionism and the Jewish Future* ed. H. Sacher (London 1916) pp.34-35.

41. Vladimir Jabotinsky, 'The Ideology of Betar', (1934) *Ba-Derech la-Medina*, Ketavim 11, ed. Eri Jabotinsky (Jerusalem 1952) p. 309; 'This is Betar' (South Africa 1952).

42. Vladimir Jabotinsky, *The Story of the Jewish Legion* (New York 1945) pp.178-179.

43. Franz Kobler, *Napoleon and the Jews* (Jerusalem 1975) p.56.

44. Vladimir Jabotinsky, 'ABC of the Jewish Army', *American Jewish Chronicle* 20 June 1940.

45. Vladimir Jabotinsky, 'When the World was Young', *Haynt* 23 January 1931; *Jewish Herald* 25 July 1947.

46. Vladimir Jabotinsky, 'A Lecture on Jewish History' (Warsaw 1933) *Uma ve-Chevra*, Ketavim 9, ed. Eri Jabotinsky (Jerusalem 1949) p.168.

47. Adam Zamoyski, *Holy Madness: Romantics, Patriots and Revolutionaries 1776-1871* (London 1999) pp.80-82.

48. Ibid. pp.309-311.

49. William Wordsworth, 'The Prelude'.

50. Adam Zamoyski, *Holy Madness: Romantics, Patriots and Revolutionaries 1776-1871* (London 1999) p.280.

51. Ibid. p.328.

52. *Palestine Post* 5 August 1938.

53. Michael Graetz, *The Jews in Nineteenth Century France: From the French Revolution to the Alliance Israélite Universelle* (Stanford 1996) p.244.

54. Vladimir Jabotinsky, *Avtobiografiya: Sippur Yamai*, Ketavim 1, ed. Eri Jabotinsky (Jerusalem 1958) p.27.

55. Giuseppe Mazzini, 'Faith and the Future', (1835) in *Essays of Joseph Mazzini* ed. William Clarke (London) pp.24-25.

56. Benedetto Croce, *History of Europe in the Nineteenth Century*, translated from the Italian by Henry Furst, (London 1934) pp.116-117.

57. Giuseppe Mazzini, 'Faith and the Future', (1835) in *Essays of Joseph Mazzini* ed. William Clarke (London) p.54.

58. Benedetto Croce, *History of Europe in the Nineteenth Century*, translated from the Italian by Henry Furst, (London 1934) p.219.

59. George Meredith, 'For the Centenary of Garibaldi', *The Times* 1 July 1907.

60. Michael Stanislawski, *Zionism and the Fin de Siècle: Cosmopolitanism and Nationalism from Nordau to Jabotinsky* (London 2001) p.134.

61. Rakhel Pavovna Magolina, *I ee perepiska Korneei Ivanovichem Chukovskim* (Jerusalem 1978) p.20 in Israel Kleiner, *From Nationalism to Universalism: Vladimir Ze'ev Jabotinsky and the Ukrainian Question* (Toronto 2000) p.3.

62. S. Poliakoff-Litovtseff, *Zionews* 1 September 1942.

63. Vladimir Jabotinsky, 'The Obscurantist', (1912) *Uma ve-Chevra*, Ketavim 9, ed. Eri Jabotinsky (Jerusalem 1949) pp.101-110.

64. Vladimir Jabotinsky, Letter to Victor Jacobson, 25 May 1915, *Igrot 1914-1918* (Jerusalem 1995) p.40.

65. Vladimir Jabotinsky, 'My Odessa', *Zikhronot ben-dori*, Ketavim 15, ed. Eri Jabotinsky (Jerusalem 1958) p.27.

66. Joseph B. Schechtman, *The Jabotinsky Story: Rebel and Statesman 1880–1923* (New York 1956) p.18.

67. Vladimir Jabotinsky, 'On Zionism', *Odesskie novosti* 8 September 1902.

68. Vladimir Jabotinsky, 'On Nationalism' *Odesskie novosti* 30 January 1903.

69. Zeev Sternhall with Mario Sznajder and Maia Asheri, *The Birth of Fascist Ideology: From Cultural Rebellion to Political Revolution* (Princeton 1994) p.21.

70. Richard Bellamy, *Modern Italian Social Theory: Ideology and Politics from Pareto to the Present* (Cambridge 1987) pp.1-11.

71. Antonio Labriola, *Socialism and Philosophy* translated by Ernest Untermann (Chicago 1934) p.319.

72. Ibid. pp.90-91.

73. Ibid. p.67.

74. Antonio Labriola, Letter to G. Sorel 10 May 1897 ibid. p.41.

75. Ibid. p.60.

76. Antonio Labriola,' Concerning the Crisis in Marxism', *Revista Italiana Di Sociologia* vol.3 1899.

77. Vladimir Jabotinsky, *Avtobiografiya: Sippur Yamai*, Ketavim 1, ed. Eri Jabotinsky (Jerusalem 1958) p.31.

78. Herzl's entry in his diary, 23 January 1904 in *The Complete Diaries of Theodor Herzl* vol.4 ed. Raphael Patai (London 1960) p.1596.

79. Vladimir Jabotinsky, 'A Lecture on Jewish History' (Warsaw 1933), *Uma ve-Chevra*, Ketavim 9, ed. Eri Jabotinsky (Jerusalem 1949) p.161.

80. Vladimir Jabotinsky, *Odesskiy listok* 13 March 1899 in Michael Stanislawski, *Zionism and the Fin de Siècle: Cosmopolitanism and Nationalism from Nordau to Jabotinsky* (London 2001) pp.136-137.

81. Antonio Labriola, *Socialism and Philosophy* translated from the Italian by Ernest Untermann, (Chicago 1934) pp.156-157.

82. Vladimir Jabotinsky, *Avtobiografiya: Sippur Yamai*, Ketavim 1, ed. Eri Jabotinsky (Jerusalem 1958) p.27.

83. Vladimir Jabotinsky, 'La Rivolta Russa: L'attegglamento del publico in Russia', *Avanti* 10 April 1901; 'Cosa Sono e cosa vogliono gli studenti russi', *Avanti* 16 April 1901.

84. Vladimir Jabotinsky, *Avtobiografiya: Sippur Yamai*, Ketavim 1, ed. Eri Jabotinsky (Jerusalem 1958) p.40.

85. Vladimir Jabotinsky, '(M.G.A.) Mirabeau', *Rassvet* 15 March 1931.

86. Vladimir Jabotinsky, *Avtobiografiya: Sippur Yamai*, Ketavim 1, ed. Eri Jabotinsky (Jerusalem 1958) p.38.

87. Vladimir Jabotinsky, 'An Open Letter to M. M. Vinaver', *Ryetch* 4 January 1907 in Joseph B. Schechtman, *The Jabotinsky Story: Rebel and Statesman 1880-1923* (New York 1956) pp.118-119.

88. Vladimir Jabotinsky, 'Jewish Rebelliousness'(1906), in *Felyetonim*, Ketavim 13, ed. Eri Jabotinsky (Jerusalem 1953) pp.43-51; Joseph Nedava, 'Jabotinsky and the Bund', *Soviet Jewish Affairs* vol.3 no.1 1973.

89. Vladimir Jabotinsky, 'Sketches without a Title', *Evreiskaya misl* 12 October 1906, in Joseph B. Schechtman, *The Jabotinsky Story: Rebel and Statesman 1880-1923* (New York 1956) p.51.

90. Theodor Herzl, *Die Welt* 10 September 1897.

91. Theodor Herzl, *Die Welt* 18 June 1897.

92. Vladimir Jabotinsky, *Avtobiografiya: Sippur Yamai*, Ketavim 1, ed. Eri Jabotinsky (Jerusalem 1958) pp.28-29; *Jewish Herald* 10 November 1939.

93. Vladimir Jabotinsky, 'Crisis of the Proletariat', *Nasz Przeglad* 12 February 1936; *Reshimot*, Ketavim 16, ed. Eri Jabotinsky (Jerusalem 1958) pp.275-283.

94. Vladimir Jabotinsky, 'The Revolt of the Old Men' (1937), *Uma ve-Chevra*, Ketavim 9, ed. Eri Jabotinsky (Jerusalem 1949) p.231.

95. Richard Bellamy, *Modern Italian Social Theory: Ideology and Politics from Pareto to the Present* (Cambridge 1987) p.88. See Benedetto Croce, *Liberalismo La Critica*, NI (Rome 1925) pp.125-128.

96. Vladimir Jabotinsky, 'The Revolt of the Old Men' (1937), *Uma ve-Chevra*, Ketavim 9, ed. Eri Jabotinsky (Jerusalem 1949) pp.225-236.

5. The Challenge of the Revisionists

1. Vladimir Jabotinsky, *Rassvet* 20 January 1925.

2. Vladimir Jabotinsky, 'What the Revisionist-Zionists Want' in *The Jew in the Modern World: A Documentary History* ed. Paul R. Mendes-Flohr and Jehuda Reinharz (London 1995) p.596.

3. Report on the Palestine Disturbances of August 1929, Command Paper 3530, March 1930, pp.108-109.

4. *The Times* 6 September 1929.

5. *Jewish World* 30 April 1925.

6. *Jewish Chronicle* 5 June 1925.

7. Vladimir Jabotinsky, 'Mesimot Mediniyot shel Ha-Ve'ida', *Rassvet* 19 April 1925; Yosef Nedava, ed. *Ha-Revizionizm Ha-Tsioni B'Hitgubshuto* (Tel Aviv 1985) pp.70–71.

8. In a letter to Eliahu Ginzburg on 18 April 1925, Jabotinsky asks after 'our movement' in America. In a letter to the French politician Anatole de Monzie, probably on the same day, he refers to the 'party' of the Zionist-Revisionists, *Igrot 1922-1925* (Jerusalem 1998) pp.209-210.

9. Joseph B. Schechtman, *The Jabotinsky Story: Fighter and Prophet 1923-1940* (New York 1961) p.39; Vladimir Jabotinsky, Letter to Joseph Schechtman 4 June 1925, *Igrot 1922-1925* (Jerusalem 1998) pp.222-223.

10. Vladimir Jabotinsky, Letter to Chava and Tamar Jabotinsky, 30 December 1924 *Igrot 1922-1925* (Jerusalem 1998) pp.184-185.

11. Vladimir Jabotinsky, 'What the Revisionist-Zionists Want' in *The Jew in the Modern World: A Documentary History* ed. Paul R. Mendes-Flohr and Jehuda Reinharz (London 1995) pp.594-596.

12. Vladimir Jabotinsky, 'Initial Discussions on the Revisionist Programme', 19 February 1925 in *Neumim 1905-1926*, Ketavim 4, ed. Eri Jabotinsky (Jerusalem 1957-8) p.253.

13. Vladimir Jabotinsky, 'What the Revisionist-Zionists Want' in *The Jew in the Modern*

World: A Documentary History ed. Paul R. Mendes-Flohr and Jehuda Reinharz (London 1995) pp.594-596.

14. Vladimir Jabotinsky, 'Address to the first meeting of the Revisionists', April 1925 in *Neumim 1905–1928*, Ketavim 4, ed. Eri Jabotinsky (Jerusalem 1957-8) p.261.

15. Ibid.

16. Vladimir Jabotinsky, *Jewish Chronicle* 19 June 1925.

17. Ibid.

18. Vladimir Jabotinsky, 'The Aims of Zionism', *The Zionist* 14 May 1926.

19. Meir Grossman, *Jewish Chronicle* 22 May 1925.

20. Vladimir Jabotinsky, 'The Idea of Betar' (Tel Aviv 1934) in *Ba-Derech la-medina*, Ketavim 11, ed. Eri Jabotinsky (Jerusalem 1952-3) pp.307-336.

21. Vladimir Jabotinsky, 'What the Revisionist-Zionists Want' in *The Jew in the Modern World: A Documentary History* ed. Paul R. Mendes-Flohr and Jehuda Reinharz (London 1995) p.596.

22. Vladimir Jabotinsky, *Jewish Chronicle* 19 June 1925.

23. Vladimir Jabotinsky, 'Dangerous Propaganda', *The Zionist* 11 June 1926.

24. *Jewish Chronicle* 6 March 1925.

25. *Jewish Chronicle* 19 June 1925.

26. Chaim Weizmann, Letter to Stephen S. Wise, 9 May 1926 *Letters and Papers of Chaim Weizmann;* Series A vol.13 March 1926-July 1929.

27. *Jewish Chronicle* 28 August 1925.

28. Chaim Weizmann, Letter to Stephen S. Wise, 9 May 1926 *Letters and Papers of Chaim Weizmann;* Series A vol.13 March 1926-July 1929.

29. Chaim Weizmann, Letter to Stephen S. Wise, 9 April 1926 *Letters and Papers of Chaim Weizmann;* Series A vol.13 March 1926-July 1929.

30. Chaim Weizmann, Letter to Vera Weizmann, 28 October 1926 *Letters and Papers of Chaim Weizmann;* Series A vol.14 July 1926-October 1930.

31. Benjamin Akzin, *Mi-Riga L'Yerushalayim* (Jerusalem 1989) p.159.

32. *The Times* 30 August 1925.

33. *Jewish Chronicle* 4 September 1925.

34. Vladimir Jabotinsky, 'About Cassandra', *The Zionist* 17 September 1926.

35. *Jewish Chronicle* 7 January 1927.

36. Vladimir Jabotinsky, 'We the Bourgeoisie', *Rassvet* 17 April 1927.

37. *Jewish Chronicle* 21 August 1925.

38. Vladimir Jabotinsky, 'I Believe', *Doar Hayom* 2 December 1928.

39. Vladimir Jabotinsky, Letter to Meir Grossman, 28 November 1928, *Igrot 1928-1929* (Jerusalem 2002) p.178.

40. Vladimir Jabotinsky, Letter to Shlomo Gepstein, 10 December 1928, *Igrot 1928-1929* (Jerusalem 2002) p.178.

41. *Jewish Chronicle* 2 August 1929.

42. Ibid.

43. Vladimir Jabotinsky, 'The Iron Wall', *Jewish Herald* 26 November 1937; 'The Ethics of the Iron Wall', *Rassvet* 11 November 1923; *Jewish Standard* 5 September 1941.

44. Rabbi I. Z. Kantor, 'Jabotinsky and the Student Corporations', *Hamashkif* 20 August 1940.

45. Vladimir Jabotinsky, 'To the Jewish Youth of Wloclawek' in *Michtavim*, Ketavim 18, ed. Eri Jabotinsky (Jerusalem 1958) pp.362-363.

46. Vladimir Jabotinsky, 'Lessons of a Forgotten Case', *Doar Hayom* 28 January 1929.

47. *Jewish Chronicle* 28 September 1928.

48. The Western or Wailing Wall in Jerusalem, Command Paper 3229, HMSO 1928.

49. Simcha Kling, *Joseph Klausner* (New York 1970) pp.113-114.

50. Vladimir Jabotinsky, 'But by Spirit', *Moment* August 1934; *Al Sifrut Ve-Omanut*, Ketavim 6, ed. Eri Jabotinsky (Jerusalem 1958) p.367.

51. *Doar Hayom* 23 July 1929; 25 July 1929.

52. *Doar Hayom* 6 August 1929.

53. *Davar* 1 August 1929.

54. *Davar* 7 August 1929.

55. Ibid.

56. *Ha'aretz* 18 August 1929.

57. *Davar* 1 August 1929.

58. Exhibit no. 96 p.1091.

59. *Doar Hayom* 7 August 1929.

60. *Doar Hayom* 9 August 1929.

61. *The Palestine Weekly* 9 August 1929.

62. *Doar Hayom* 12 August 1929.

63. Although the intelligence summary of 15 August suggested 6,000, Exhibit 94b, *Doar Hayom* of 16 August increased this to 10,000. Palestine Commission on the Disturbances of August 1929, Colonial no.48, 1930

64. The intelligence report of 15 August refers to Ben-Avi and 'Ben-Aviv – the latter is of Jerusalem' and clearly was unfamiliar with the son of Eliezer ben-Yehuda. Palestine Commission on the Disturbances of August 1929, Colonial no.48, 1930

65. *Doar Hayom* 16 August 1929.

66. Report on the Palestine Disturbances of August 1929, Command Paper 3530, March 1930, p.53. *Doar Hayom* 18 August 1929.

67. *Doar Hayom* 18 August 1929.

68. *Doar Hayom* 16 August 1929.

69. Harry Luke, Letter to Lord Passfield, 22 August 1929, Commission of Enquiry on the Disturbances of August 1929. Evidence taken in camera. PRO CO 96791.

70. Palestine Commission on the Disturbances of August 1929, Colonial no.48, 1930. Testimony of Dr Wolfgang Von Weisl pp.233-234.

71. Testimony of H. C. Luke, Commission of Enquiry on the Disturbances of August 1929. Evidence taken in camera. PRO CO 96791.

72. Joseph Klausner, Letter to Pinchas Rutenberg, 19 August 1929 PRO CO 96791.

73. Harry Luke, Letter to Lord Passfield, 22 August 1929, Commission of Enquiry on the Disturbances of August 1929. Evidence taken in camera. PRO CO 96791.

74. *Ha'aretz* 18 August 1929.

75. Telegram from the Zionist Executive in Palestine 21 August 1929, Report on the Palestine Disturbances of August 1929, Command Paper 3530 pp.57-58.

76. *Ha'aretz* 22 August 1929.

77. Testimony of Major Alan Saunders, Commission of Enquiry on the Disturbances of August 1929. Evidence taken in camera. PRO CO 967/1.

78. Report on the Palestine Disturbances of August 1929, Command Paper 3530 p.155.

79. Testimony of H. C. Luke, Commission of Enquiry on the Disturbances of August 1929. Evidence taken in camera. PRO CO 967/1.

80. Chaim Weizmann, Letter to Lord Passfield, 29 August 1929, PRO CO 733/175/2.

81. Testimony of H. C. Luke, Commission of Enquiry on the Disturbances of August 1929. Evidence taken in camera. PRO CO 967/1.

82. Sir John Shuckburgh, Memorandum to Sir Samuel Wilson, 26 September 1929, PRO CO 733/175/2.

83. Donald H. Hedworth, The British Response to Religious and Ethnic Conflict in Mandatory Palestine MA thesis, Anglia Polytechnic University, Centre for Jewish Christian Relations, Cambridge 2004 pp.31-36.

84. F. H. Kisch, *Palestine Diary* (London 1938) p.249.

85. Sir John Shuckburgh, General memorandum on the disturbances, 3 September 1929 PRO CO 733/175/2.

86. Sir John Shuckburgh, Memorandum to Sir G. Grindle, 21 September 1929 PRO CO 733/175/2.

87. Sir John Chancellor, Letter to his son, Christopher, 30 September 1929, J.C. box 16/3 in Yehuda Taggar, *The Mufti and Jerusalem and Palestine Arab Politics 1930-1937* (London 1986) p.142.

88. Testimony of Siegfried Hoofien. Evidence heard by the Commission in open sittings; Palestine Commission on the Disturbances of August 1929: Colonial No. 48, (London 1930) vol.2 p.659.

89. Examination and critique of the Shaw Commission, Executive Committee of the World Union of Zionist Revisionists (Jerusalem 1930) p.6.

90. Report on the Palestine Disturbances of August 1929, Command Paper 3530, March 1930, p 174; *The New Palestine* 4 April 1930.

6. THE WIDENING SCHISM

1. Vladimir Jabotinsky, Letter to Meir Grossman, 26 August 1929, *Igrot 1928-1929* (Jerusalem 2002) pp.316-317.

2. Vladimir Jabotinsky, Letter to Max Seligman, 24 October 1929, Jabotinsky Archives.

3. Ibid.

4. Vladimir Jabotinsky, 'The Iron Wall', *Rassvet* 4 November 1923; *Jewish Herald* 26 November 1937.

5. Ibid.

6. Vladimir Jabotinsky, *Doar Hayom* 15 January 1930.

7. Vladimir Jabotinsky, *Doar Hayom* 7 January 1930.

8. Chaim Weizmann, Letter to Morris Rothenberg, 31 January 1931 *Letters and Papers of Chaim Weizmann;* Series A Letters vol.14 July 1929-October 1930.

9. Ibid.

10. Sir John Chancellor, Memorandum to Lord Passfield, 17 January 1930 PRO CO 7331853.

11. Sidney Webb, Letter to Beatrice Webb 10 September 1930 in *The Letters of Sidney and Beatrice Webb* ed. Norman Mackenzie vol.3 'Pilgrimage 1912-1947' (Cambridge 1978) p.330.

12. Ramsay MacDonald, *A Socialist in Palestine* London 1922.

13. Beatrice Webb, diary entry, 2 September 1929 in *The Letters of Sidney and Beatrice Webb* ed. Norman Mackenzie vol.3 'Pilgrimage 1912-1947' (Cambridge 1978) p.315.

14. Beatrice Webb, diary entry, 2 September 1929 in *The Letters of Sidney and Beatrice Webb* ed. Norman Mackenzie vol.3 'Pilgrimage 1912-1947' (Cambridge 1978) p.334.

15. Ibid.

16. Sidney Webb, Letter to Chaim Weizmann, 20 August 1929 in *The Letters of Sidney and Beatrice Webb* ed. Norman Mackenzie vol.3 'Pilgrimage 1912-1947' (Cambridge 1978) pp.315-318.

17. Sir John Hope-Simpson, Letter to Lord Passfield, 18 August 1930 PRO CO 7331832.

18. Richard Meinertzhagen, *Middle East Diary 1917-1956* (London 1959) p.99.

19. Chaim Weizmann, Letter to Felix Warburg, 16 January 1930 in *Letters and Papers of Chaim Weizmann;* Series A Letters vol. 14 July 1929-October 1930.

20. Sidney Webb, Letter to Beatrice Webb, 22 October 1930 in *The Letters of Sidney and Beatrice Webb* ed. Norman Mackenzie vol. 3 'Pilgrimage 1912-1947' (Cambridge 1978) p.334.

21. Beatrice Webb, diary entry, 30 October 1930 in *The Letters of Sidney and Beatrice Webb* ed. Norman Mackenzie vol. 3 'Pilgrimage 1912-1947' (Cambridge 1978) p.334.

22. Ibid.

23. Chaim Weizmann, Letter to Felix Warburg, 13 November 1929 in *Letters and Papers of Chaim Weizmann;* Series A Letters vol.14 July 1929-October 1930.

24. Mary Agnes Hamilton, *Sidney and Beatrice Webb: A Study in Contemporary Biography* (London 1932) p.232.

25. Police Weekly Appreciation Summary, 17 August 1929.

26. Vladimir Jabotinsky, PRO CO 7331863.

27. Ibid.

28. Ibid.

29. Memorandum of T. Drummond Shiels, Under-Secretary for State for the Colonial Office, 1 February 1930 PRO CO 7331863.

30. Vladimir Jabotinsky, Letter to Drummond Shiels, 11 February 1930, Jabotinsky Archives.

31. Norman Bentwich, Evaluation of Jabotinsky's speech, 31 May 1930 PRO CO 7331863.

32. Note of minutes of a meeting held in the Secretary of State's room at 3 p.m. on 18

July 1930. Passfield, Chancellor and others were in attendance. PRO CO 7331853.

33. Sir John Shuckburgh, Internal Memomorandum, 30 May 1930 PRO CO 7331863.

34. Sir John Chancellor, Letter to Sir John Shuckburgh, 11 June 1930 PRO CO 7331863.

35. *Jewish Chronicle* 4 April 1930

36. Ibid. 10 January 1930.

37. Ibid. 16 May 1930.

38. Circular letter no.17 World Union of Zionist-Revisionists, Executive Committee, London, 3 July 1930.

39. Circular letter no.1, 2nd series, World Union of Zionist-Revisionists, Executive Committee, London, July 1930.

40. *Jewish Chronicle* 25 July 1930.

41. Ibid.

42. Vladimir Jabotinsky, Letter to Meir Grossman, 1 July 1930 in a written report of a press conference of the World Union of Zionist-Revisionist Executive Committee 7 July 1930.

43. Revisionist press conference, London, 8 September 1930.

44. Circular letter 2/I, World Union of Zionist-Revisionists 19 September 1930.

7. A New Psychological Race

1. Benjamin Akzin, *Mi Riga L'Yerushalayim* (Jerusalem 1989) p.162.

2. Ibid.

3. See Binyamin Eliav, *Zikhronot min Hayamin* ed. Danny Rubinstein (Tel Aviv 1990).

4. Vladimir Jabotinsky, 'What England Promised', *Jewish Chronicle* 10 October 1930.

5. *Haynt* 1 January 1929.

6. Vladimir Jabotinsky, Letter to Menachem Arber, 2 November 1928, *Igrot 1928-1929* (Jerusalem 2002) pp.160-163.

7. Ibid.

8. Vladimir Jabotinsky, Letter to Betar, Riga, Latvia, 5 November 1928, *Igrot 1928-1929* (Jerusalem 2002) p.163.

9. Vladimir Jabotinsky, 'Instead of Excessive Apology', 1911 in *The Maccabian Online*, August 1997.

10. *Sefer Betar: Korot umekorot*, vol.1, 'From the People', ed. H. Ben-Yerucham, April 1964, Tel Aviv, p.175.

11. *Betar Monthly* 15 September 1931.

12. *Sefer Betar: Korot umekorot*, vol.1, 'From the People', ed. H. Ben-Yerucham, April 1964, Tel Aviv, p.177.

13. Vladimir Jabotinsky, Letter to Joanna (Anya) Jabotinsky, in *Shmuel Katz, Lone Wolf* vol.2 (New York 1996) pp.1018-1019.

14. Vladimir Jabotinsky, Letter to Miriam Lange, 27 August 1930, *Ha-Umma* vol.3-4 (61-62) September 1980 pp.332-337 in Yaakov Shavit, 'Fire and Water: Ze'ev Jabotinsky and the Revisionist Movement', *Studies in Zionism* no.2 Autumn 1981 p.224.

15. Vladimir Jabotinsky, 'The Jewish State: The Way to Achieve that Goal', *Betar Monthly* 15 October 1931.

16. Ibid.

17. Howard M. Sachar, *Dreamland: Europeans and Jews in the Aftermath of the Great War* (New York 2002) pp.146-148.

18. David Vital, *A People Apart: the Jews in Europe 1789-1939* (Oxford 1999) pp.248-249.

19. Friedrich Ludwig Jahn, *Deutsches Volkstum, Werke* (Berlin 1884) p.234 in Peter Pulzer, *Jews and the German State: The Political History of a Minority 1848-1933* (Oxford 1992) p.15.

20. Isaiah Berlin talks about 'the sinister nationalism of Gorres and Jahn, Arndt and Treitschke' in 'Herder and the Enlightenment' in Isaiah Berlin, *The Proper Study of Mankind* (London 1998) p.399. See Alfred P. Pundt, *Arndt and the National Awakening in Germany* (New York 1935).

21. Ahad Ha'am, 'Shalosh Madregot' in *Kol Kitvei Ahad Ha'am* (Jerusalem 1956) p.153. See also Steven J. Zipperstein, *Elusive Prophet: Ahad Ha'am and the Origins of Zionism* (London 1993) pp.155-158.

22. Vladimir Jabotinsky, 'Sha'atnez Lo Ya'ale Alekha', *Hadar* November 1940.

23. Vladimir Jabotinsky, 'The Jewish State: The Way to Achieve that Goal', *Betar Monthly* 15 October 1931.

24. *Betar Monthly* March 1932.

25. Leviticus 19:19; Deuteronomy 22:11.

26. Vladimir Jabotinsky, 'Sha'atnez Lo Ya'ale Alekha', *Hadar* November 1940.

27. Theodor Herzl, *Die Welt* 10 September 1897.

28. Vladimir Jabotinsky, 'The Idea of Betar', (Tel Aviv 1934) in *Ba-Derech la-medina*, Ketavim 11, ed. Eri Jabotinsky (Jerusalem 1952-3) p.315; 'This is Betar' (South Africa 1952).

29. Ibid. p.317.

30. Ibid. p.316.

31. Vladimir Jabotinsky, 'Yes, Break it', *Haynt* 4 October 1932 in *Ba-sa'ar*, Ketavim 12, ed. Eri Jabotinsky (Jerusalem 1959).

32. Vladimir Jabotinsky, 'The Rule of the Fist in the Yishuv', *Haynt* 28 October 1932; *Jewish Weekly* 4 November 1932.

33. *Betar* June 1933.

34. *The Revisionist* 1 July 1933.

35. Vladimir Jabotinsky, 'The Rule of the Fist in the Yishuv', *Haynt* 28 October 1932; *Jewish Weekly* 4 November 1932.

36. Vladimir Jabotinsky, 'National Arbitration', *Moment* 6 January 1933.

37. Vladimir Jabotinsky, 'Zion and Communism', *Rassvet* 22 May 1932; *Hadar* February-April 1941.

38. Vladimir Jabotinsky, *Jewish Morning Herald* 5 February 1933 in Joseph B. Schechtman, *The Jabotinsky Story: Fighter and Prophet 1923-1940* (London 1961) p.41.

39. Vladimir Jabotinsky, 'Zionist Fascism', *The Zionist* 25 June 1926.

40. See Robert O. Paxton's review of Ze'ev Sternhall's 'The Birth of Fascist Ideology' in the *New York Review of Books* 23 June 1994.

41. Leone Carpi, *L'Italia Del Popolo* 5 June 1919.

42. Vladimir Jabotinsky, Letter to Benito Mussolini, 16 July 1922, *Igrot 1918-1922* (Jerusalem 1997) pp.337-340.

43. Vladimir Jabotinsky, 'The Fate of Palestine and the Fate of the Mandate in the Perspective of the Altered Situation in the Mediterranean', *Jewish Call* October-November 1936,

44. *The Times* 12 October 1935.

45. *Doar Hayom* 21 February 1936.

46. Meir Michaelis, *Mussolini and the Jews* (Oxford 1978) pp.84-87.

47. Vladimir Jabotinsky, 'Italy', *Hayarden* 21 August 1936.

48. Vladimir Jabotinsky, *Haynt* 14 October 1932.

49. Vladimir Jabotinsky, Letter to J. Bartlett. 9 December 1938 Jabotinsky Archives.

50. Alain Dieckoff, *The Invention of a Nation: Zionist Thought and the Making of Modern Israel* (London 2003) pp.198-199.

51. Vladimir Jabotinsky, 'The Jewish State: The Way to Achieve that Goal', *Betar Monthly* 15 October 1931.

52. Ibid.

53. Ibid.

54. Vladimir Jabotinsky, 'The Idea of Betar', *Ba-Derech la-medina*, Ketavim 11, ed. Eri Jabotinsky (Jerusalem 1952-3) p.321.

55. Katie Fluxman, 'Why We Differ', in *The Legion* (Betar South Africa) 15 September 1934.

56. Joseph Klausner in L. Altman, 'Two Worlds', *Betar Monthly* 15 August 1931.

57. Gabriel Preil, 'Political and Cultural Zionism', *Betar Monthly* April 1932.

58. Vladimir Jabotinsky, 'Misdar', *Hadar* 30 March 1941.

59. Vladimir Jabotinsky, 'Shiva', *Evreiskaya zhizn* no. 6 June1904; *Hadar* November 1940.

60. Vladimir Jabotinsky, 'A Message from Jabotinsky', *Betar Monthly* April 1932.

61. Vladimir Jabotinsky, *Jewish Herald* 19 July 1940.

62. *Betar Monthly* 15 May 1931.

63. Ibid.

64. Vladimir Jabotinsky, 'National Sport', *Jewish Herald* 12 May 1939.

65. Vladimir Jabotinsky, 'The Idea of Betar', *Ba-Derech la-medina*, Ketavim 11, ed. Eri Jabotinsky (Jerusalem 1952-3) p.321. 'This is Betar' (South Africa 1952).

66. Vladimir Jabotinsky, 'Afn Pripitshek', *Haynt* 16 October 1931; *Jewish Herald* 12 September 1947.

67. *Betar Monthly* August 1931.

68. Interview with Yitzhak Shamir 25 July 2000.

69. Vladimir Jabotinsky, 'The Meaning of Preparedness', *Haynt* 1 April 1932.

70. Ibid.

71. Ibid.

72. Yehoshua Heschel Yeivin, 'Betar and the Revolution in Zionism', *Betar Monthly* 10 February 1932.

73. 'On the Activities of Keren Tel Chai in Palestine', Jabotinsky Archives.

74. Jeremiah Halperin, 'Ships to the Rescue', *Hadar* May-June 1940.

75. 'The Jewish Navigation League and Marine Department of Shilton Betar', *Jewish Call* January 1936.

76. 'Zionism and the Sea', *Jewish Call* July 1934.

8. MODELS FOR THE RADICALS

1. *Betar Monthly* Bulletin 15 May 1931.

2. *Betar Monthly* Bulletin 15 June1931.

3. Vladimir Jabotinsky, 'His Children and Ours: On Herzl's Children', *Haynt* 26 September 1930; *Hadar* February 1940.

4. Yehoshua Heschel Yeivin, *Doar Hayom* 7 November 1930.

5. Yitzhak Ben-Zvi, 'Why a Jewish Legion?', *Der Yiddisher Legioner* no.1 5 May 1918 in Yitzhak Ben-Zvi, *The Hebrew Battalions* (Jerusalem 1965) pp.18-19.

6. Theodor Herzl, *The Complete Diaries of Theodor Herzl* ed. Raphael Patai vol.4 (London 1960) pp.1596-1597.

7. Vladimir Jabotinsky, *Avtobiografia: Sippur Yamai*, Ketavim 1, ed. E. Jabotinsky (Jerusalem 1947) p.28.

8. Ibid. p.28.

9. Ibid. p.31.

10. Michael Stanislawski, *Zionism and the Fin de Siècle: Cosmopolitanism and Nationalism from Nordau to Jabotinsky* (London 2001) p.134.

11. Vladimir Jabotinsky, *Morgen Zhurnal* 15 January 1933 in Joseph B. Schectman, *The Jabotinsky Story: Rebel and Statesman 1880-1923* (New York 1956) p.41.

12. Michael Stanislawski, *Zionism and the Fin de Siècle: Cosmopolitanism and Nationalism from Nordau to Jabotinsky* (London 2001) pp.140-141.

13. Vladimir Jabotinsky, 'Rebel of Light', 1912 in *Uma V'Chevra*, Ketavim 9, ed. E. Jabotinsky (Jerusalem 1949-1950) pp.99-110.

14. Vladimir Jabotinsky, Letter to Victor Jacobson, 25 May 1915 *Igrot 1914-1918* (Jerusalem 1995) p.41.

15. Vladimir Jabotinsky, 'The Revolt of the Old Men', 1937 in *Uma V'Chevra*, Ketavim 9, ed. E. Jabotinsky (Jerusalem 1949-1950) pp.225-236.

16. Vladimir Jabotinsky, 'Crisis of the Proletariat', 1932 in Joseph Nedava, *Ekronot Munkhim L'Baiyot Ha-Sha-uh* (Tel Aviv 1981) p.34.

17. Maffeo Pantaleoni, 'Lutocrazia e bolshevismo giudaicos gretolano il fascismo', *La Vita Italiana* July 1921.

18. Vladimir Jabotinsky, *Avtobiografia: Sippur Yamai*, Ketavim 1, ed. E. Jabotinsky (Jerusalem 1947) p.29.

19. Marinetti's comments to a PEN conference in Dubrovnik, *Jewish Chronicle* 2 June 1933.

20. Renzo de Felice, *The Jews in Fascist Italy* (New York 2001) p.24.

21. Vladimir Jabotinsky, 'Eleventh Hour', *Jewish Herald* 3 February 1939.

22. Memo of Raffaele Guariglia, Section V, Oriental Affairs to Under-Secretary of

Foreign Affairs, Fulvio Suvich 4 November 1935 in Renzo de Felice, *The Jews in Fascist Italy* (New York 2001) pp.158-159.

23. Ibid. p.525.

24. Andrzej Nieuwazny, 'Napoleon and Polish Identity', *History Today* May 1998.

25. Adam Zamoyski, *Holy Madness: Romantics, Patriots and Revolutionaries 1776-1871* (London 1999) pp.388-389.

26. Józef Pilsudski, *The Memoirs of a Polish Revolutionary and Soldier* ed. Darsie Gillie (London 1933) p.186.

27. Józef Pilsudski, Letter to Feliks Perl in Andrej Garlicki, *Jósef Pilsudski* translated by John Coutouvidis (Aldershot 1995) p.59.

28. Vladimir Jabotinsky, *The Jewish War Front* (London 1940) pp.55-56.

29. Ibid. p.68.

30. Ibid. p.72.

31. Jerzy Tomaszewski, 'Anti-Semitism of Men and Anti-Semitism of Things: Inside Vladimir Jabotinsky's World of Ideas' in *The Jews in Poland* vol.2 ed. Slawomir Kapralski (Cracow 1999) pp.137-144.

32. *Jewish Chronicle* 17 November 1933.

33. Jerzy Tomaszewski, 'Antisemitism of Men and Antisemitism of Things: Inside Vladimir Jabotinsky's World of Ideas' in *The Jews in Poland* vol.2 ed. Slawomir Kapralski (Cracow 1999) p.114.

34. Joseph B. Schechtman, *The Jabotinsky Story: Rebel and Statesman 1880-1923* (New York 1956) pp.148-149.

35. Vladimir Jabotinsky, *Hayarden* 22 May 1936.

36. Vladimir Jabotinsky, *The Jewish War Front* (London 1940) pp.55-66.

37. Israel Eldad, *Ma'aser Rishon* (Tel Aviv 1976) pp.340-341.

38. Yaakov Shavit, 'Politics and Messianism: The Zionist Revisionist Movement and Polish Political Culture', *Studies in Zionism* vol.6 no.2 Autumn 1985 p.242.

39. Vladimir Jabotinsky, *Hadar* November 1940.

40. Uri Zvi Greenberg, 'Radiance', translated by David Aberbach in David Aberbach, 'Fanatic Heart: The Poetry of Uri Zvi Greenberg', *CCAR Journal: A Reform Jewish Quarterly* Spring 2003 p.23.

41. Interview with Yitzhak Shamir 25 July 2000.

42. S. Landman, 'The Lesson of Ireland', *The New Palestine* 10 February 1922.

43. Vladimir Jabotinsky, Letter to Shimon Bernstein, 4 May 1915 *Igrot 1914-1918* (Jerusalem 1995) p.26.

44. Vladimir Jabotinsky, Letter to Alexander Manuilov, 29 April 1916 *Igrot 1914-1918* (Jerusalem 1995) p.61.

45. Joseph Heller, 'Jabotinsky's Use of National Myths' in *Political Struggles in Literary Strategies: Studies in Contemporary Jewry* vol.12 ed. Ezra Mendelsohn (Oxford 1996) pp.189-191.

46. Vladimir Jabotinsky, 'Ireland', *Russkie vedomosti* 15 May 1916.

47. *Jewish Herald* 29 July 1938.

48. Vladimir Jabotinsky, 'Introduction to the Theory of Economy' 1938 in *Uma*

V'Chevra, Ketavim 9, ed. E. Jabotinsky (Jerusalem 1949-1950) p.206.

49. Vladimir Jabotinsky, 'On the Brink of the Precipice', *Jewish Herald* 17 December 1937.

50. Vladimir Jabotinsky, *Unzer Welt* 21 January 1938.

51. *Jewish Herald* 21 January 1938.

52. Robert Briscoe (with Alden Hatch), *For the Life of Me* (London 1958) p.264.

53. *Jewish Herald* 10 November 1939.

54. Vladimir Jabotinsky, 'Points from V. Jabotinsky's address at Dublin', 12 January 1938, Jabotinsky Archives.

55. David Levine, 'From an interview with Shoshana Raziel', 5 July 1966 in David Raziel, Yeshiva University Ph.D. thesis 1969 p.143.

56. Abba Achimeir, *Doar Hayom* 28 October 1930.

57. Yosef Katznelson, *Hanasich hashahor: Yosef Katznelson v' hatenuah haleumit b'shanot hashloshim* ed. Yosef Achimeir (Tel Aviv 1983) pp.270-276.

58. P. S. O'Hegarty, 'Ha'hitkomemut Bishnat 1916', in *Bamachteret* 5 (Shevat 5701 – January-February 1941) in *Lochamei Cherut Israel* vol.1 (Tel Aviv 1982) pp.53-56.

59. P. S. O'Hegarty, *The Victory of Sinn Fein: How It Won it and How It Used It* (Dublin 1924) pp.4-5.

60. Israel Scheib, *Hamedina* 17 February 1940; 23 February 1940.

61. Interview with Yitzhak Shamir 25 July 2000.

62. P. S. O'Hegarty, *The Victory of Sinn Fein: How It Won it and How It Used It* (Dublin 1924) p.138.

63. B. Ha'Cohen (Lubotsky), *Hamashkif* 17 May 1943.

64. Edmond Schechter, *Hamashkif* 31 March 1939; 9 April 1939.

9. ON TWO FRONTS

1. Statement by Vladimir Jabotinsky, World Union of Zionist Revisionists Circular Letter 132, August 1931.

2. Joseph B. Schechtman, *The Jabotinsky Story: Fighter and Prophet 1923-1940* (London 1961) pp.156-157.

3. *Jewish Chronicle* 2 October 1931.

4. Vladimir Jabotinsky, Letter to Eliahu Ben-Horin, 24 October 1931, Jabotinsky Archives.

5. *Jewish Chronicle* 11 September 1931.

6. *Jewish Chronicle* 18 December 1931.

7. Speech of Meir Grossman to the 5th All-Polish Zionist-Revisionist Conference on 27 December 1931, World Union of Zionist-Revisionists Executive Committee, Jabotinsky Archives.

8. Speech of Vladimir Jabotinsky to the 5th All-Polish Zionist-Revisionist Conference on 28 December 1931, World Union of Zionist-Revisionists Executive Committee; *Haynt* 30 December 1931.

9. *The Times* 6 January 1932.

10. Press CommuniquéExecutive Committee, World Union of Zionist Revisionists, 4 January 1932, Jabotinsky Archives.

11. Vladimir Jabotinsky, 'Disobedience', *Haynt* in the *Jewish Chronicle* 1 January 1932.

12. *Jewish Chronicle* 15 January 1932.

13. Report of T.H. Preston, Chargéd'Affaires, British Legation, Kovno, 14 November 1930 PRO CO 733 186.

14. H.M. Knatchbull-Hugessen, British Legation, Riga, Letter to Arthur Henderson 20 November 1930 PRO CO 733 186.

15. Vladimir Jabotinsky, Letter to Eugene Soskin, 3 February 1931 in Joseph B. Schechtman, *The Jabotinsky Story: Fighter and Prophet 1923-1940* (London 1961) p.436.

16. Vladimir Jabotinsky, Letter to Baruch Weinstein, 26 May 1932, Jabotinsky Archives.

17. Vladimir Jabotinsky, 'On Adventurism', *Haynt* 26 February 1932.

18. Yehoshua Heschel Yeivin, 'Mechulal Brit HaBiryonim' in Abba Achimeir, *The Man who Turned the Tide* ed. Joseph Nedava (Tel Aviv 1987) p.33.

19. Vladimir Jabotinsky, 'Brit Trumpeldor', *Rassvet* 3 February 1929.

20. Vladimir Jabotinsky, Letter to Yirmiyahu Halperin, 17 May 1928 *Igrot 1928-1929* (Jerusalem 2002) pp.72-73.

21. Vladimir Jabotinsky, Letter to Yirmiyahu Halperin, 25 November 1928 *Igrot 1928-1929* (Jerusalem 2002) pp.173-174.

22. Yirmiyahu Halperin, Letter to Vladimir Jabotinsky, 30 November 1928 MZ 3\1631\A, Jabotinsky Archives.

23. Vladimir Jabotinsky, Letter to Yirmiyahu Halperin, 26 April 1929 *Igrot 1928-1929* (Jerusalem 2002) p.250.

24. Vladimir Jabotinsky, Letter to the teachers at the Betar School for madrichim in Tel Aviv, 6 May 1929, *Igrot 1928-1929* (Jerusalem 2002) p.257.

25. Vladimir Jabotinsky, Letter to Menachem Arber 21 May 1929 *Igrot 1928-1929* (Jerusalem 2002) p.262.

26. Abba Achimeir, Letter to Vladimir Jabotinsky, 25 October 1928, Jabotinsky Archives.

27. Yirmiyahu Halperin, Letter to Abba Achimeir, 3 March 1929, Jabotinsky Archives.

28. Ibid.

29. Vladimir Jabotinsky, Letter to the teachers at the Betar School for madrichim in Tel Aviv, 6 May 1929 *Igrot 1928-1929* (Jerusalem 2002) p.257.

30. Yosef Zahavi, 'Revolutionary Zionism: From Brit HaBiryonim to Etzel' in *Hanasich hashahor: Yosef Katznelson v' hatenuah haleumit b'shanot hashloshim* ed. Yosef Achimeir (Tel Aviv 1983) p.293.

31. Abba Achimeir, 'Shall We Miss it?', *Doar Hayom* 25 September 1929.

32. Abba Achimeir, *Doar Hayom* 10 October 1928 in Abba Achimeir, *Revolutionary Zionism* (Tel Aviv 1965-6) p.21.

33. Joseph Heller, 'Monism of the Goal' or 'Monism of the Means'? The Conceptual and Political Debate between Ze'ev Jabotinsky and Abba Achimeir, 1928-1933', *Zion* 52 (Tel Aviv 1987) pp.327-334.

34. Yehoshua Heschel Yeivin, 'Betar and the Revolution in Zionism', *Betar Monthly* 10

February 1932.

35. Abba Achimeir, *Doar Hayom* 10 October 1928 in Abba Achimeir, *Revolutionary Zionism* (Tel Aviv 1965-6) p.21.

36. Joseph Klausner, *The New Palestine* 1 May 1931.

37. Abba Achimeir, *Ha'am* 19 July 1931.

38. Joseph Heller, 'Monism of the Goal' or 'Monism of the Means'? The Conceptual and Political Debate between Ze'ev Jabotinsky and Abba Achimeir, 1928-1933', *Zion* 52 (Tel Aviv 1987) pp.327-334

39. Vladimir Jabotinsky Speech on the Disturbances 29 August 1929 in *Neumim 1927-1940*, Ketavim 5, ed. E. Jabotinsky (Tel Aviv 1957-58) p.93.

40. Abba Achimeir *Doar Hayom* 4 October 1929.

41. Joseph Heller, 'Monism of the Goal' or 'Monism of the Means'? The Conceptual and Political Debate between Ze'ev Jabotinsky and Abba Achimeir, 1928-1933', *Zion* 52 (Tel Aviv 1987) pp.327-334.

42. Abba Achimeir, *Doar Hayom* 17 September 1930.

43. Oswald Spengler, Letter, December 1918, quoted in Alastair Hamilton, *The Appeal of Fascism: A Study of Intellectuals and Fascism 1919-1945* (London 1971) p.113.

44. Joseph Heller, 'Monism of the Goal' or 'Monism of the Means'? The Conceptual and Political Debate between Ze'ev Jabotinsky and Abba Achimeir, 1928-1933', *Zion* 52 (Tel Aviv 1987) pp.315-322.

45. Abba Achimeir, 'Where is Democracy Headed?', *Hapoel Hatzair* 27 August 1926 pp. 8-9 in Joseph Heller, 'Monism of the Goal' or 'Monism of the Means'? The Conceptual and Political Debate between Ze'ev Jabotinsky and Abba Achimeir, 1928-1933', *Zion* 52 (Tel Aviv 1987) pp.315-322

46. Ibid.

47. Ibid.

48. Abba Achimeir, *Doar Hayom* 10 October 1928 in Abba Achimeir, *Revolutionary Zionism* (Tel Aviv 1965-6) p.21.

49. Abba Achimeir, *Doar Hayom* 29 January 1929.

50. Ibid.

51. Abba Achimeir, *Doar Hayom* 10 October 1928 in Abba Achimeir, *Revolutionary Zionism* (Tel Aviv 1965-6) p.21.

52. Ibid.

53. *Hazit Ha'am* 2 August 1932.

54. Abba Achimeir, 'Where is Democracy Headed?', *Hapoel Hatzair* 27 August 1926 pp. 8-9 in Joseph Heller, 'Monism of the Goal' or 'Monism of the Means'? The Conceptual and Political Debate between Ze'ev Jabotinsky and Abba Achimeir, 1928-1933', *Zion* 52 (Tel Aviv 1987) pp.315-322.

55. Yosef Zahavi, 'Revolutionary Zionism: From Brit HaBiryonim to Etzel' in *Hanasich hashachor: Yosef Katznelson v' hatenuah haleumit b'shanot hashloshim* ed. Yosef Achimeir (Tel Aviv 1983) p.293.

56. Abba Achimeir, 'Yirmiyahu shel Russia', *Haboker* 31 January 1936.

57. Abba Achimeir, 'Chernov', *Hamashkif* 6 June 1943.

58. Abba Achimeir, 'The Octobrist Festival: Ten Years After', *Ha'aretz* 7 November 1927; 'If I am not for myself who will be for me', *Ha'aretz* 15 November 1927; 'The Creation of the Peace at Brest-Litovsk', *Ha'aretz* 23 November 1927.

59. Vladimir Jabotinsky, 'Zion and Communism', *Rassvet* 22 May 1932.

60. Joseph Nedava, 'Who were the Biryoni?', *Jewish Quarterly Review* vol.63 1972-3 p.317.

61. Tractate Gittin 56a, *Babylonian Talmud* in Joseph Nedava, 'Who were the Biryoni?', *Jewish Quarterly Review* vol. 63 1972-3 p.317.

62. Yehoshua Heschel Yeivin, 'Mechulal Brit HaBiryonim' in Abba Achimeir: *The Man who Turned the Tide* ed. Joseph Nedava (Tel Aviv 1987) p.34.

63. Abba Achimeir, Letter to the Youth, *Hazit Ha'am* 29 March 1932.

64. *Hazit Ha'am* 6 April 1932.

65. Yehoshua Heschel Yeivin, 'The Torah of Bar-Kochba', *Hazit Ha'am* 4 June 1932.

66. Yehoshua Heschel Yeivin, 'Mechulal Brit HaBiryonim', in Abba Achimeir: *The Man who Turned the Tide* ed. Joseph Nedava (Tel Aviv 1987) p.33.

67. *Hazit Ha'am* 12 February 1932.

68. Abba Achimeir, 'Letter to the Youth', *Hazit Ha'am* 29 March 1932.

69. Derek J. Penslar, 'The Foundations of the Twentieth Century: Herzlian Zionism' in *Israel Studies* vol.6 no.2, Summer 2001.

70. Vladimir Jabotinsky, Letter to Shlomo Gepstein, 10 December 1928 *Igrot 1928-1929* (Jerusalem 2002) p.178.

71. Abba Achimeir, Letter to Vladimir Jabotinsky, 25 October 1928 Jabotinsky Archives.

10. THE FALL AND RISE OF THE MAXIMALISTS

1. Joseph B. Schechtman and Yehuda Benari, *History of the Revisionist Movement* vol.1 (Tel Aviv 1970) pp.321-322.

2. Ibid. pp.323-324.

3. Ibid.

4. Joseph B. Schechtman, *The Jabotinsky Story: Fighter and Prophet 1923-1940* (New York 1961) pp.435-438.

5. Press communiqué Executive Committee of the World Union of Zionist Revisionists 4 January 1932, Jabotinsky Archives.

6. Vladimir Jabotinsky, 'On Adventurism', *Haynt* 26 February 1932; 'More on Adventurism', Haynt 29, 31 July 1932. See Shmuel Katz, *Lone Wolf* (New York 1996) p.1407.

7. Simon Schama, *Citizens: A Chronicle of the French Revolution* (New York 1989) p.604.

8. Vladimir Jabotinsky, written comments on a letter of the London secretariat to the Revisionist Centre in Tel Aviv, 4 April 1932, Jabotinsky Archives.

9. Vladimir Jabotinsky, Letter to the Executive Committee of the World Union of Zionist Revisionists, 16 January 1932, Jabotinsky Archives.

10. PRO CO 733/6819.

11. Vladimir Jabotinsky, Letter to the Executive Committee of the World Union of

Zionist Revisionists, 16 January 1932, Jabotinsky Archives.

12. Vladimir Jabotinsky, Letter to Leone Carpi, 7 October 1931, Jabotinsky Archives.

13. Vladimir Jabotinsky, Letter to Angelo Donati, 19 November 1931, Jabotinsky Archives.

14. Vladimir Jabotinsky, Letter to Benito Mussolini, 16 July 1922 *Igrot 1918-1922* (Jerusalem 1997) pp.337-340.

15. Leone Carpi, Letter to Benito Mussolini, 5 November 1931, Jabotinsky Archives.

16. Vladimir Jabotinsky, 'Zionist Fascism', *The Zionist* 25 June 1926.

17. Vladimir Jabotinsky, Letter to the Secretariat of the World Union of Zionist Revisionists, 12 April 1932, Jabotinsky Archives.

18. *Jewish Herald* 29 April 1938.

19. Vladimir Jabotinsky, Letter to the Secretariat of the World Union of Zionist Revisionists, 11 April 1932, Jabotinsky Archives.

20. *The Revisionist Bulletin* 25 May 1932.

21. *Hazit Ha'am* 4 March 1932.

22. Vladimir Jabotinsky, 'The Meaning of Preparedness', *Haynt* 1 April 1932.

23. Vladimir Jabotinsky, *Hazit Ha'am* 20 May 1932; 27 May 1932.

24. Vladimir Jabotinsky, Letter to Avraham Weinshall, 17 March 1932, Jabotinsky Archives.

25. Vladimir Jabotinsky, *Hazit Ha'am* 22 March 1932.

26. Wolfgang Von Weisl, 'The Eve of the New World War', *Hazit Ha'am* 29 March 1932.

27. Abba Achimeir *Hazit Ha'am* 29 April 1932 in Joseph Heller, 'Monism of the Goal' or 'Monism of the Means'? The Conceptual and Political Debate between Ze'ev Jabotinsky and Abba Achimeir, 1928-1933', *Zion* 52 (Tel Aviv 1987) pp.344-352.

28. Abba Sikra (Achimeir), *Hazit Ha'am* 15 July 1932.

29. *Hazit Ha'am* 9 August 1932.

30. Vladimir Jabotinsky, 'Grandpa Liberalism', *Haynt* 14 October 1932 in Israel Eldad, 'Jabotinsky Distorted', *The Jerusalem Quarterly* (1980) no.16 p.34.

31. Vladimir Jabotinsky, 'More on Adventurism', *Hazit Ha'am* 5 August 1932.

32. Ibid. in *The Political and Social Philosophy of Ze'ev Jabotinsky* ed. Mordechai Sarig (London 1999) p.117.

33. Ibid.

34. Vladimir Jabotinsky Letter to Yehoshua Heschel Yeivin, 9 August 1932, Jabotinsky Archives.

35. Ibid.

36. Vladimir Jabotinsky, Letter to the Commander of Betar in Eretz Israel, Tel Aviv, 7 July 1932, Jabotinsky Archives.

37. Vladimir Jabotinsky, 'If I Were Young in 1932', *Middle East and the West* 7 July 1958.

38. Vladimir Jabotinsky, Letter to David Ben-Gurion, 30 March 1935, in *The Political and Social Philosophy of Ze'ev Jabotinsky* ed. Mordechai Sarig (London 1999) pp.74-75.

39. Abba Sikra, 'Basle or Zimmerwald', *Hazit Ha'am* 15 July 1932.

40. Ibid.

41. Ibid.

42. *Hazit Ha'am* 9 August 1932.

43. *Hazit Ha'am* 29 July 1932.

44. Vladimir Jabotinsky, *Hazit Ha'am* 13 September 1932.

45. Vladimir Jabotinsky, *Neumim 1927-1940*, Ketavim 5, ed. E. Jabotinsky (Tel Aviv 1957-1958) pp.137-147.

46. Vladimir Jabotinsky, handwritten notes (in Russian) for his opening speech at the 5th Revisionist Conference in Vienna in August 1932. The many deletions of passages testify to Jabotinsky's determination to utilize the correct psychological language in order to forge a sense of unity rather than antagonize different factions. For example, one section crossed out contained the sentence 'there can be no peace with the Palestinian Arabs until they cease their opposition to Jewish colonization. Even within this, 'peace' is crossed out and replaced with 'compromise': Jabotinsky Archives.

47. Abba Achimeir, 'National Dictatorship in the Wider World', *Doar Hayom* 29 January 1930.

48. Isaiah 3:6.

49. *Hazit Ha'am* 13 September 1932.

50. A. Zir, 'An Evaluation of the Congress', *Hazit Ha'am* 20 September 1932.

51. Ibid.

52. *Hazit Ha'am* 20 September 1932.

53. Ibid.

54. Benyamin Eliav, 'Vina, Acco, Yerushalayim', *Abba Achimeir: The Man who Turned the Tide* ed. Yosef Nedava (Tel Aviv 1987) p.65.

55. A. Zir, 'An Evaluation of the Conference', *Hazit Ha'am* 20 September 1932.

56. Eliahu Ben-Horin, *Rassvet* 11 September 1932.

57. Wolfgang von Weisl, 'Manhig Ha'sikarikin', *Abba Achimeir: The Man who Turned the Tide* ed. Yosef Nedava (Tel Aviv 1987) p.41.

58. *Jewish Chronicle* 9 September 1932.

59. Benyamin Eliav, 'Vina, Acco, Yerushalayim', *Abba Achimeir: The Man who Turned the Tide* ed. Yosef Nedava (Tel Aviv 1987) p.65.

60. Ibid. Eliav quotes Jabotinsky's (incorrect) comparison of Charlemagne being succeeded by Pepin the Short.

61. Vladimir Jabotinsky, 'Leader', *Moment* 3 July 1934.

62. *Sefer Betar* vol.1 ed. Chaim Ben-Yerucham (Tel Aviv 1969) p.425.

63. Benyamin Eliav, 'Vina, Acco, Yerushalayim', *Abba Achimeir: the Man who Turned the Tide* ed. Yosef Nedava (Tel Aviv 1987) p.65.

64. Vladimir Jabotinsky, *Hazit Ha'am* 7 October 1932.

65. *The New Judea* August-September 1932.

66. Vladimir Jabotinsky, *Neumim 1927-1940*, Ketavim 5, ed. E. Jabotinsky (Tel Aviv 1957-1958) p.153.

67. Abba Achimeir, 'Romantic Realism or Realistic Romanticism' *Hazit Ha'am* 30 September 1932 in Joseph Heller, 'Monism of the Goal' or 'Monism of the Means'? The Conceptual and Political Debate between Ze'ev Jabotinsky and Abba Achimeir,

1928-1933', *Zion* 52 (Tel Aviv 1987) pp.315-369.

68. *Hazit Ha'am* 3 February 1933.

69. Abba Achimeir, 'The Shell and the Kernel', *Hazit Ha'am* 31 March 1933.

70. Vladimir Jabotinsky, 'Germany', *Hazit Ha'am* 24 February 1933.

71. Joseph B. Schechtman, *The Jabotinsky Story: Fighter and Prophet 1923-1940* (New York 1961) p.438.

72. Julius Freulich, 'The Roles of Betar', *Hazit Ha'am* 10 March 1933.

73. Vladimir Jabotinsky, Letter to Joel Pincus, 5 May 1938, Jabotinsky Archives.

74. Vladimir Jabotinsky, 'The Revisionist Movement and Germany', *Hazit Ha'am* 12 May 1933.

75. Yfaat Weiss, 'The Transfer Agreement and the Boycott Movement: A Jewish dilemma on the eve of the Holocaust', *Yad Vashem Studies* vol.26 (Jerusalem 1998) pp.129-171.

76. Vladimir Jabotinsky, Letter to the Editors of *Hazit Ha'am*, 17 May 1933 in Vladimir Jabotinsky, *Michtavim*, Ketavim 18, ed. E. Jabotinsky (Tel Aviv 1958) p.331.

77. *Hazit Ha'am* 19 May 1933.

78. Sir Arthur Wauchope, Letter to Sir Philip Cunliffe-Lister, 19 January 1935 PRO CO 7332662.

79. Vladimir Jabotinsky, 'At the Crossroads', *Moment* 15 June 1934.

80. Vladimir Jabotinsky, Letter to Sir Philip Cunliffe-Lister, 16 June 1934 PRO CO 7332661.

81. *Jewish Telegraphic Agency* 21 July 1934.

82. PRO CO 7332661.

83. *Jewish Chronicle* 29 September 1933.

84. *Jewish Telegraphic Agency* 17 December 1934.

85. *Jewish Telegraphic Agency* 24 July 1934.

86. Joseph B. Schechtman, *The Jabotinsky Story: Fighter and Prophet 1923-1940* (New York 1961) p.440.

87. Ibid. p.165.

88. *Jewish Chronicle* 25 November 1932.

89. *Hazit Ha'am* 10 March 1933.

90. *Hazit Ha'am* 17 March 1933.

91. *Haynt* 26 March 1933 in Joseph B. Schechtman, *The Jabotinsky Story: Fighter and Prophet 1923-1940* (New York 1961) p.175.

92. Press Release, World Union of Zionist-Revisionists 5 April 1933.

93. *Hazit Ha'am* 31 March 1933.

94. Abba Sikra, 'The Third Zionist Movement', *Hazit Ha'am* 28 March 1933.

11. RAZIEL, STERN AND BEGIN

1. A. Zir, 'A Review of the Conference', *Hazit Ha'am* 20 September 1932.

2. *Hazit Ha'am* 13 September 1932.

3. 'What Do the Maximalists Want?' *Hazit Ha'am* 7 April 1933.

4. Abba Achimeir, *Madrich Betar* September 1932.

5. Benno Lubotsky, *Madrich Betar* January 1933.

6. Shlomo Vardi, *Hamedina* 19 February 1933.

7. Benno Lubotsky, *Hamedina* 12 February 1933.

8. Max Bodenheimer, *Prelude to Israel: The Memoirs of M. I. Bodenheimer* ed. Henriette Hannah Bodenheimer (London 1963) p.314.

9. *Hazit Ha'am* 28 March 1933.

10. Menachem Begin, Speech, 25 March 1933, Netzivut Betar, Warsaw, May 1933.

11. *Sefer Betar* vol.2 ed. Chaim Ben-Yerucham, (Tel Aviv 1969) pp.441-445.

12. Menachem Begin, *Hamedina* 25 October 1934.

13. Menachem Begin, 'A Legend in His Lifetime', *Unzer Velt* 9 August 1935.

14. *Jewish Frontier* January 1935

15. Israel Scheib (Eldad), *Ma'aser Rishon* (Tel Aviv 1950) p.20.

16. Bulletin no.1, Union of Zionist-Revisionists, London January 1935.

17. *Hadar* November 1940.

18. Minutes of the Second World Conference of Betar, 6 January 1935, Jabotinsky Archives.

19. Eitan Haber, *Menachem Begin: The Legend and the Man* (New York 1978) pp.43-44.

20. *Hazit Ha'am* 28 March 1933.

21. *Davar* 25 February 1933.

22. Uri Zvi Greenberg, 'The Knife Wielding Messiah', *Hazit Ha'am* 4 August 1933.

23. Vladimir Jabotinsky, 'The Idea of Betar', *Ba-Derech la medina,* Ketavim 11, (Tel Aviv 1952-1953) pp.307-336.

24. Vladimir Jabotinsky, Letter to Hans Bloch in Joseph B. Schechtman, *The Jabotinsky Story: Fighter and Prophet 1923-1940* (London 1961) p.217.

25. *Jewish Chronicle* 22 June 1934.

26. Yehoshua Ofir, *Rishonei Etzel 1931-1940* (Tel Aviv 2002) pp.51-53.

27. Chaim Shalom Halevi, *Hametsuda* (Tel Aviv 1978) pp.13-14.

28. Joseph Heller, *The Stern Gang: Ideology, Politics and Terror 1940-1949* (London 1995) p.307 n.31.

29. Avraham Stern, 'Chayalim Almonim', *Hametsuda* Bet August 1932.

30. Avraham Stern, *Sefer HaShirim* (Jerusalem 1964) p.39.

31. Samuel I 16:18.

32. David Levine, Ph.D. thesis on David Raziel Yeshiva University 1969.

33. Yaakov Weinshal, *Ha-dam asher ba-saf: sipur chay'yov u-moto shel Yair – Avraham Stern* (Tel Aviv 1978) pp.64-69.

34. Interview with Shoshana Raziel, July 1966 in David Levine PhD thesis on David Raziel Yeshiva University 1969 p.143.

35. Testimony of Avraham Tehomi, first Commander of the Irgun, 1966 in David Levine, *David Raziel: The Man and the Legend* (Tel Aviv 1991).

36. Abba Achimeir, 'Alcazar and Restraint', *Hayarden* 6 November 1936.

37. Vladimir Jabotinsky, Letter to J. H. Thomas MP, Secretary of State for the Colonies 22 April 1936 PRO CO 733/037.

38. Joseph B. Schechtman, *The Jabotinsky Story: Fighter and Prophet 1923-1940* (London 1961) p.303.

39. Vladimir Jabotinsky, Letter to Jacob De Hass, August 31 1936; 15 September 1936, Jabotinsky Archives.

40. Joseph Heller, 'Ze'ev Jabotinsky and the Revisionist Revolt against Materialism: In Search of a World View', *Jewish History* vol.12 no.2 Fall 1998 pp.55-56.

41. *Eleventh Hour* 12 March 1937.

42. *Eleventh Hour* 24 October 1937.

43. Vladimir Jabotinsky, 'Ul tochnit He'evacuatzia', *Neumim 1927-1940*, Ketavim 5, ed. E. Jabotinsky (Tel Aviv 1957-1958) pp.197-212.

44. Hanoch (Howard) Rosenblum, 'The New Zionist Organization's Diplomatic Battle Against Partition 1936-1937', *Studies in Zionism* 11 (2) 1990 p.157.

45. *Jewish Telegraphic Agency* 18 July 1937.

46. *Eleventh Hour* 27 August 1937.

47. Vladimir Jabotinsky, *Hayarden* 12 July 1936.

48. Joseph B. Schechtman, *The Jabotinsky Story: Fighter and Prophet 1923-1940* (London 1961) p.447.

49. Interview with Shimshon Yunitchman 1957 in Joseph B. Schechtman, *The Jabotinsky Story: Fighter and Prophet 1923-1940* (London 1961) p.322.

50. Ibid. p.323.

51. Ibid. p.450.

52. Ibid. p.451.

53. *Eleventh Hour* 1 October 1937.

54. *Eleventh Hour* 24 September 1937.

55. Joseph Heller, *The Stern Gang: Ideology, Politics and Terror 1940-1949* (London 1995) pp.32-33. Heller believes that Frankel was drowned by fellow members of the Irgun.

56. Vladimir Jabotinsky, 'Eleventh Hour', *Jewish Herald* 3 February 1939.

57. *Palestine Post* 15 November 1937.

58. *Haboker* 17 November 1937.

59. Vladimir Jabotinsky, Speech at Shoreditch Town Hall, East London, 23 November 1937 *Zionews* 24 November 1937.

60. Shmuel Katz, *Lone Wolf: A Biography of Vladimir Ze'ev Jabotinsky* (New York 1996) p.1589.

61. Yaakov Weinshal, *Ha-dam asher ba-saf: sipur chay'yov u-moto shel Yair – Avraham Stern* (Tel Aviv 1978) p.110.

62. *Jewish Frontier* January 1935.

63. David Raziel, 'Active Defence' in David Levine, *David Raziel: The Man and the Legend* (Tel Aviv 1991) p.120.

64. On Uriel Halperin known later as the poet and Canaanite Yonatan Ratosh, see Joseph Heller, *The Stern Gang: Ideology, Politics and Terror 1940-1949* (London 1995) pp.34-37; Yaakov Shavit, *The New Hebrew Nation: A Study in Israeli Heresy and Fantasy* (London 1987) pp.30-36.

65. Uri Zvi Greenberg, *Sefer ha-kitrug ve-ha'emuna* Collected Works vol.3 (Jerusalem

1991).

66. Anita Shapira, *Land and Power: The Zionist Resort to Force 1881-1948* (Oxford 1992) pp.242-246.

12. THE CONFRONTATION

1. *Zionews* 28 February 1938.

2. J.M. Troutbeck, British Legation, Prague Letter to Anthony Eden, 14 February 1938 PRO Co 733/376/13.

3. *Le-Ma'an Ha-Moledet* 14 January 1938.

4. Vladimir Jabotinsky, *Unzer Welt* 17 December 1937.

5. *Medina Ivrit* 18 February 1938.

6. *Ha'am* 4 March 1938.

7. Yaakov Shavit, *The New Hebrew Nation: A Study in Israeli Heresy and Fantasy* (London 1987) p.36.

8. *Sefer Betar* vol.2 ed. Chaim Ben-Yerucham, (Tel Aviv 1969) p.711.

9. Ibid. p.716.

10. Ibid. pp.718-719.

11. Aharon Propes, 'After Prague', *Hamedina* 20 February 1938.

12. Menachem Begin, *Hamedina* 20 February 1938.

13. 'Palestine: The High Commissionership', memorandum by the Secretary of State for the Colonies 8 October 1937 CAB 24/271 CP 232 (37).

14. Ibid.

15. Vladimir Jabotinsky, Letter to Malcolm MacDonald, 3 June 1938, Jabotinsky Archives.

16. *Jewish Herald* 8 July 1938.

17. David Raziel, 'Those who die will redeem the Homeland', in David Levine, *David Raziel: The Man and the Legend* (Tel Aviv 1991) p.133.

18. Menachem Begin, *Hamedina* 29 July 1938.

19. Aharon Propes, *Hamedina* 29 July 1938.

20. Vladimir Jabotinsky, Letter to Kaplan, 13 August 1938, Jabotinsky Archives.

21. CID Report for the High Commissioner annex.1 secret no.2. Note on present position in regard to Revisionists, August 1938.

22. *Palestine Post* 13 September 1938.

23. Uriel Halperin, 'Proposals for the Third Conference of Betar, August 1938', Jabotinsky Archives.

24. Uriel Halperin, *Hamedina* 20 August 1938.

25. Hillel Seidman, *Menachem Begin* (New York 1990) p.134.

26. Aharon Propes, *Trybuna Narodawa* 9 September 1938.

27. Stenographic Notes of the Third World Conference of Betar, Warsaw 1938. The speeches of Begin and Jabotinsky are taken from the original handwritten notes, Jabotinsky Archives.

28. Ben Ami, 'Third Kinus' in *This is Betar South Africa 1952*.

29. Protocols of the Third World Conference of Betar (Bucharest 1940), Jabotinsky Archives.

30. Menachem Begin, unpublished reconstruction of his speech at the Third World Conference of Betar, Jabotinsky Archives. This was verified by Yechiel Kadishai as Begin's handwriting.

31. Interview with Menachem Begin, *Yediot Achranot* 24 October 1980.

32. Israel Scheib (Eldad), *Ma'aser Rishon* (Tel Aviv 1950) pp.21-22.

POSTSCRIPT

1. Broadcast of 'The Voice of Liberated Zion', 4 March 1939, in *Jewish Herald* 17 March 1939.

2. Vladimir Jabotinsky, Letter to Abraham Abrahams, 21 September 1938, Jabotinsky Archives.

3. Vladimir Jabotinsky, Letter to Michael Haskel, 25 September 1938, Jabotinsky Archives.

4. Mordechai Katz, 'The Essence of Betar', *Jewish Herald* 14 July 1939.

5. Joseph B. Schechtman, *The Jabotinsky Story: Fighter and Prophet 1923-1940* (London 1961) p.460.

6. Vladimir Jabotinsky, Letter to Solomon Jacobi, 16 March 1939, Jabotinsky Archives.

7. Sasson Sofer, *Begin: Anatomy of a Leadership* (Oxford 1988) p.247 n.13.

8. David Ben-Gurion, Letter to Eliahu Golomb, 12 September 1938, *Zionews* 7 November 1938.

9. *Hamedina* 3 April 1939.

10. Yaakov Weinshal, *Ha-dam asher ba-saf: sipur chay'yov u-moto shel Yair – Avraham Stern* (Tel Aviv 1978) p.115.

11. Menachem Begin, 'When the Enemy Threatens', *Hamedina* 21 April 1939.

12. Menachem Begin, 'Tertium Non Datur', *Hamedina* 28 April 1939.

13. Vladimir Jabotinsky, *Jewish Herald* 7 July 1939.

14. Vladimir Jabotinsky, 'Amen', *Moment* 9 July 1939; *Jewish Herald* 21 July 1939.

15. Sasson Sofer, *Begin: Anatomy of a Leadership* (Oxford 1988) p.26.

16. Vladimir Jabotinsky, Telegram to the Irgun, 24 June 1939 in David Niv, *Ma`arakhot ha-Irgun ha-Tseva'i ha-Le'umi: Me-haganah le-hat.kafah 1937-1939* part 2, (Tel Aviv 1965) p.239.

17. *The Times* 22 May 1939.

18. 'Reaction to the White Paper', the Irgun Zvai Leumi in Eretz Israel, June 1939, Jabotinsky Archives.

19. Ada Ushpiz, 'Letters from the Underground', *Ha'aretz* 22 January 1998.

20. Joseph Heller, *The Stern Gang: Ideology, Politics and Terror 1940-1949* (London 1995) p.92.

21. Vladimir Jabotinsky, *The Jewish War Front* (London 1940).

22. Vladimir Jabotinsky, Letter to Neville Chamberlain, 4 September 1939, PRO CO 733/401/75266 803.

23. Vladimir Jabotinsky, 'The ABC of the Jewish Army', *American Jewish Chronicle* 20 June 1940.

24. *Jewish Herald* 26 July 1940.

25. Joseph Heller, *The Stern Gang: Ideology, Politics and Terror 1940-1949* (London 1995) pp.134-136.

26. *Jewish Herald* 28 May 1948.

27. *Jewish Herald* 1 October 1948.

28. Menachem Begin, 'The Truth about the *Altalena*', Central Zionist Archives 21.387.

29. *Herut* 2 August 1948.

30. Menachem Begin, 'Ze'ev Jabotinsky', *Herut Hamoledet* 5 August 1948.

31. *Herut* 20 October 1948.

32. Yonathan Shapiro, *The Road to Power: The Herut Party in Israel* translated by Ralph Mandel (New York 1991) p.70.

33. Menachem Begin, 'The Two Crowns of Yair', *Jewish Herald* 20 January 1962.

34. Harry Hurwitz, *Menachem Begin* (Johannesburg 1977) pp.58-60.

35. Yonathan Shapiro, *The Road to Power: The Herut Party in Israel* translated by Ralph Mandel (New York 1991) pp.107-108.

BIBLIOGRAPHY

JOURNALS AND NEWSPAPERS

American Jewish Chronicle
Daily Express
Davar
Die Welt
East European Jewish Affairs
Ha'aretz
Haboker
Haynt
Igeret Lagolah
Jerusalem Quarterly
Jewish Chronicle
Jewish Frontier
Jewish History
Jewish Morning Herald
Jewish Quarterly Review
Jewish Telegraphic Agency
Jewish Weekly
Journal of Israeli History
L'Echo Sioniste
L'Italia Del Popolo
Le Peuple Juif
Middle East and the West
Morgen Zhurnal
New York Evening Post
New York Review of Books
Palestine Post
Patterns of Prejudice

Revista Italiana Di Sociologia
Soviet Jewish Affairs
Studies in Zionism
The New Judea
The New Palestine
The Times
Yad Vashem Studies
Yediot Aharanot
Zion

PUBLICATIONS ASSOCIATED WITH THE REVISIONISTS, BETAR AND THE IRGUN

Betar (New York 1933)
Betar Monthly (New York 1931-1932)
Di Tat (Warsaw 1938-1939)
Doar Hayom (Jerusalem 1928-1931)
Eleventh Hour (Johannesburg 1937)
Ha'am (Jerusalem 1931)
Ha'am (Tel Aviv 1938)
Hadar (New York 1937-1953)
Hamashkif (Tel Aviv 1938-1949)
Hamatarah (Tel Aviv 1933)
Hamedina (Warsaw 1934-1939)
Hametsuda (Palestine 1932-1933)
Herut (Tel Aviv 1948-1965)
Hayarden (Jerusalem, Tel Aviv 1934-1941)
Hazit Ha'am (Jerusalem, Tel Aviv 1932-1935)
Information Bulletin (London 1936-1938)
Jerozolima Wyzwolona (Warsaw 1938-1939)
Jewish Call (Shanghai 1933-1941)
Jewish Herald (Johannesburg 1937-1986)
Jewish Navigation (London 1936)
Jewish Standard (London 1940-1950)
Jewish Tribune (Johannesburg 1932-1933)
Le-Ma'an Ha-Moledet (Tel Aviv 1938)
Madrich Betar (Warsaw 1932-1935)
Medina Ivrit (Prague 1934-1939)
Moment (Warsaw 1910-1939)
Our Voice (New York 1934-1936)
Rassvet (Paris 1924-1934)
The Revisionist (New York 1933)

The Revisionist Bulletin (London 1929-1932)
The Zionist (New York 1926)
Trybuna Narodawa (Cracow 1934-1939)
Unzer Welt (Warsaw 1934-1939)
Zionews (London 1937-1939)
Zionews (New York 1940-1944)

ARCHIVES AND RESEARCH LIBRARIES

British Library, London
British Newspaper Library, London
Central Zionist Archives, Jerusalem
Herbert Samuel Archives, Oxford
Holocaust Museum, Washington
Jabotinsky Archives, Tel Aviv
Jewish National Library, Jerusalem
Library of Congress, Washington
National Archives (PRO) London
New York Public Library: Jewish Division

OFFICIAL RECORDS AND PUBLICATIONS

Haycraft Commission Command Paper 1540. (London 1921)
Churchill White Paper, Command Paper 1700, (London 1922)
Western or Wailing Wall in Jerusalem, Command Paper 3229, (London 1928)
Shaw Commission Command Paper 3530, (London 1930)
Evidence in Public Sessions of the Shaw Commission Colonial no. 48, (London 1930)
Shaw Commission. Evidence taken in camera. (London 2003)
Hope-Simpson Report, Command Paper 3686, (London 1930)
Passfield White Paper, Command Paper 3692, (London 1930)
Peel Commission Report, Command Paper 5457, (London 1937)
White Paper, Command Paper 6019, (London 1939)

PUBLISHED WORKS

Achimeir, Yosef, ed. *Hanasich hashachor: Yosef Katznelson v'hatenuah haleumit b'shanot hashloshim* (Tel Aviv 1983)
Akzin, Benjamin, *Mi Riga L'Yerushaliyim* (Jerusalem, 1989)
Avineri, Shlomo, *The Making of Modern Zionism* (London 1981)
Barzilay-Yegar, Dvorah, *Bayit Leumi La'am Hayehudi: Hamusag Bekhashiva – 1923* (Jerusalem 2004)

Begin, Menachem, *The Revolt* (London 1980)
 – *Mori, Ze'ev Zhabotinski* (Jerusalem 2001)
Bela, Moshe, *Olamo shel Zhabotinski* (Tel Aviv 1972)
Bellamy, Richard, *Modern Italian Social Theory: Ideology and Politics from Pareto to the Present* (Cambridge 1987)
Ben-Hur, Raphaella Bilski, *Every Individual a King* (Washington 1993)
Bentwich, Norman, *England in Palestine* (London 1932)
Bentwich, Helen, *Tidings from Zion: Letters from Jerusalem 1919-1931* ed. Jennifer Glynn (London 2000)
Ben-Yerucham, Chaim, ed. *Sefer Betar: Korot umekorot*, vol.1 (Tel Aviv 1964)
 – vol.2 (Tel Aviv 1969)
Berlin, Isaiah, *Against the Current: Essays in the History of Ideas* ed. Henry Hardy (London 1979)
 – *The Proper Study of Mankind* (London 1998)
Bernstein, Eduard, *Ferdinand Lassalle as a Social Reformer* (London 1893)
Biger, Gideon, *An Empire in the Holy Land: Historical Geography of the British Administration in Palestine 1917-1929* (Jerusalem 1994)
Bodenheimer, Max, *Prelude to Israel: The Memoirs of M.I. Bodenheimer* ed. Henriette Hannah Bodenheimer (London 1963)
Briscoe, Robert, (with Alden Hatch) *For the Life of Me* (London 1958)
Cohen Brandes, George Morris, *Ferdinand Lassalle* (London 1911)
Croce, Benedetto, *History of Europe in the Nineteenth Century*, translated from the Italian by Henry Furst, (London 1934)
Dieckhoff, Alain, *The Invention of a Nation: Zionist Thought and the Making of Modern Israel* (London 2003)
Dubnov, Simon, *Nationalism and History* (New York 1970)
Dugdale, Blanche, *Arthur James Balfour: First Earl of Balfour* vol.1 (London 1936)
Eliav, Binyamin, *Zikhronot min Hayamin* ed. Danny Rubinstein (Tel Aviv 1990)
de Felice, Renzo, *The Jews in Fascist Italy* (New York 2001)
Footman, David, *The Primrose Path: A Life of Ferdinand Lassalle* (London 1946)
Friedman, Saul S., *Pogromchik: The Assassination of Simon Petlura* (New York, 1976)
Garlicki, Andrej, *Jósef Pilsudski* translated by John Coutouvidis (Aldershot 1995)
Graetz, Michael, *The Jews in Nineteenth Century France: From the French Revolution to the Alliance Israélite Universelle* (Stanford 1996)
Graur, Mina, *HaItonut shel HaRevizionistit b'shanim 1925-1948* (Tel Aviv 2000)
Greenberg, Uri Zvi, *Sefer ha-kitrug ve-ha'emuna* Collected Works vol.3 (Jerusalem 1991)
Ha'am, Ahad, *Kol Kitvei Ahad Ha'am* (Jerusalem 1956)
Haber, Eitan, *Menachem Begin: The Legend and the Man* (New York 1978)
Hamilton, Mary Agnes, *Sidney and Beatrice Webb: A Study in Contemporary Biography* (London 1932)
Heller, Joseph, *The Stern Gang: Ideology, Politics and Terror 1940-1949* (London

1995)

von Herrnritt, Herrmann, *Die Nationalitaet als Rechtsbegriff* (Vienna 1899)
    – *Nationalitaet und Recht* (Vienna 1899)
Hertzberg, Arthur, *The Zionist Idea* (Philadelphia 1997)
Herzl, Theodor, *The Complete Diaries of Theodor Herzl* ed. Raphael Patai vol.1 (London 1960)
Hess, Moses, *Rome and Jerusalem* (New York 1918)
Hurwitz, Harry, *Menachem Begin* (Johannesburg 1977)
Hyamson, A.M, *Palestine under the Mandate* (London 1950)
Jabotinsky, Vladimir, *Feuilletons* (St. Petersburg 1913)
    – Introduction to *Chaim Nachman Bialik: Poems from the Hebrew* ed. L. V. Snowman (London 1924)
    – *Pocket Edition of Several Stories – Mostly Reactionary* (Paris 1925)
    – *The Jewish War Front* (London 1940)
    – *The Story of the Jewish Legion* translated by Shmuel Katz (New York 1945)
    – *Ktavim Tsionim Rishonim*, Ketavim 8, ed. E. Jabotinsky (Jerusalem 1949)
    – *Uma V'Chevra*, Ketavim 9, ed. E. Jabotinsky (Jerusalem 1949-1950)
    – *Ba-derech la-medina*, Ketavim 11, ed. E. Jabotinsky (Jerusalem 1952-1953)
    – *Felyetonim*, Ketavim 13, ed. E. Jabotinsky (Tel Aviv 1953-1954)
    – *Al Sifrut Ve-Omanut*, Ketavim 6, ed. Eri Jabotinsky (Jerusalem 1958)
    – *Zikhronot ben-dori*, Ketavim 15, ed. Eri Jabotinsky (Jerusalem 1958)
    – *Reshimot*, Ketavim 16 ed. Eri Jabotinsky (Tel Aviv 1958)
    – *Michtavim*, Ketavim 18, ed. Eri Jabotinsky (Jerusalem 1958)
    – *Avtobiografia: Sippur Yamai*, Ketavim 1, ed. E. Jabotinsky (Jerusalem 1958)
    – *Shirim*, Ketavim 2, ed. E. Jabotinsky (Jerusalem 1958)
    – *Neumim 1905-1926*, Ketavim 4, ed. Eri Jabotinsky (Jerusalem 1957-8)
    – *Neumim 1927-1940*, Ketavim 5, ed. Eri Jabotinsky (Jerusalem 1958)
    – *Ba-sa'ar*, Ketavim 12 ed. Eri Jabotinsky (Jerusalem 1959)
    – *Ekronot Munchim L'Baiyot Ha-Sha-uh* (Tel Aviv 1981) ed. Yosef Nedava
    – *Ha-Revizionizm Ha-Tsioni B'Hitgubshuto* (Tel Aviv 1985) ed. Yosef Nedava
    – *Igrot* vol.1 May 1898-July 1914 (Jerusalem 1992) ed. Daniel Carpi and Moshe Halevi
    – *Igrot* vol.2 September 1914-November 1918 (Jerusalem 1995) ed. Daniel Carpi and Moshe Halevi
    – *Igrot* vol.3 December 1918-August 1922 (Tel Aviv 1997) ed. Daniel Carpi and Moshe Halevi
    – *Igrot* vol.4 September 1922-December 1925 (Jerusalem 1998) ed. Daniel Carpi and Moshe Halevi
    – *Igrot* vol.5 January 1926-December 1927 (Jerusalem 2000) ed. Daniel Carpi and Moshe Halevi

– *Igrot* vol.6 January 1928-December 1929 (Jerusalem 2002) ed. Daniel Carpi and Moshe Halevi

– *The Political and Social Philosophy of Ze'ev Jabotinsky: Selected Writings* ed. Mordechai Sarig (London 1999)

Kaplan, Eran, *The Jewish Radical Right: Revisionist Zionism and its Ideological Legacy* (Wisconsin 2005)

Kapralski, Slawomir, ed. *The Jews in Poland* vol.2 (Cracow 1999)

Katz, Shmuel, *Lone Wolf: A Biography of Vladimir Ze'ev Jabotinsky* (New York 1996)

Kisch, F. H., *Palestine Diary* (London 1938)

Klausner, Joseph, *Menachem Ussishkin* (London 1944)

Kleiner, Israel, *From Nationalism to Universalism: Vladimir Ze'ev Jabotinsky and the Ukrainian Question* (Toronto and Edmonton 2000)

Kling, Simcha, *Joseph Klausner* (New York 1970)

Kobler, Franz, *Napoleon and the Jews* (Jerusalem 1975)

Labriola, Antonio, *Socialism and Philosophy* translated by Ernest Untermann (Chicago 1934)

Laqueur, Walter, *History of Zionism* (London 1972)

Laqueur, Walter, and Barry Rubin, *The Israel-Arab Reader: a Documentary History of the Middle East Conflict* (London 1984)

Levine, David, *David Raziel: The Man and the Legend* (Tel Aviv 1991)

MacDonald, J. Ramsay, *A Socialist in Palestine* (London 1922)

Mahler, Raphael, *A History of Modern Jewry 1780-1815* (London 1971)

Mazzini, Giuseppe, *Essays of Joseph Mazzini* edited William Clarke (London n.d.)

Meinertzhagen, Richard, *Middle East Diary 1917-1956* (London 1959)

Mendelsohn, Ezra, ed. *Literary Strategies: Studies in Contemporary Jewry* vol.12 (Oxford 1996)

Mendes-Flohr, Paul R., and Jehuda Reinharz, *The Jew in the Modern World: A Documentary History* (London 1995)

Michaelis, Meir, *Mussolini and the Jews* (Oxford 1978)

Mossek, M., *Palestine Immigration Policy under Sir Herbert Samuel* (London 1978)

Nedava, Yosef, ed. *Abba Achimeir: The Man who Turned the Tide* (Tel Aviv 1987

Niv, David, *Hairgun Hazvai Haleumi: Hahagana Haleumit* (Tel Aviv 1965)

Nordau, Max, *Zionism: Its History and Victims* (English Zionist Federation 1905)

– *The Meaning of History* (London 1910)

– *Fernbeben Zionistische Schriffen* (Berlin 1923)

– *Max Nordau to His People* introduction by Ben-Zion Netanyahu (New York 1944)

Nordau, Anna and Maxa, *Max Nordau* (New York 1943)

Ofir, Yehoshua, *Rishonei Etzel 1931-1940* (Tel Aviv 2002)

O'Hegarty, P. S., *The Victory of Sinn Fein: How it won it and how it used it* (Dublin 1924)

Pilsudski, Jósef, *The Memoirs of a Polish Revolutionary and Soldier* ed. Darsie Gillie

(London 1933)

Pundt, Alfred P., *Arndt and the National Awakening in Germany* (New York 1935)

Rabinowicz, Oscar K., *Vladimir Jabotinsky's Conception of a Nation* (New York 1946)

Reinharz, Jehuda, *Chaim Weizmann: The Making of a Statesman* (Oxford 1993)

Renner, Karl, *Der Kampf der österreichischen Nationalen um den Staat* (Vienna 1902)

Rousseau, Jean Jacques, *Confessions* Book 5 Oevres Completes (Paris 1995)

Rubenstein, Sondra Miller, *The Communist Movement in Palestine and Israel 1919-1984* (Boulder 1985)

Rubinstein, Amnon. *From Herzl to Rabin* (New York 2000)

Sachar, Howard M., *Dreamland: Europeans and Jews in the Aftermath of the Great War* (New York 2002)

Sacher, Harry, ed. *Zionism and the Jewish Future* (London 1916)

Said, Edward W., *Orientalism: Western Concepts of the Orient* (London 1995)

Samuel, Herbert, *Liberalism: An Attempt to State the Principles of Contemporary Liberalism in England* (London 1902)

  – *Memoirs* (London 1945)

  – *Creative Man* (London 1949)

Schama, Simon, *Citizens: A Chronicle of the French Revolution* (New York 1989)

Schechtman, Joseph B., *The Jabotinsky Story: Rebel and Statesman 1880-1923* (New York 1956)

  – *The Jabotinsky Story: Fighter and Prophet 1923-1940* (New York 1961)

  – and Yehuda Benari, *History of the Revisionist Movement* (Tel Aviv 1970)

Schirokauer, Arno, *Ferdinand Lassalle: The Power of Illusion and the Illusion of Power* (London 1931)

Shapira, Anita, *Land and Power: The Zionist Resort to Force 1881-1948* (Oxford 1992)

Shapiro, Yonathan, *The Road to Power: The Herut Party in Israel* (New York 1991)

Shavit, Yaacov, *The New Hebrew Nation: A Study in Israeli Heresy and Fantasy* (London 1987)

  – *Jabotinsky and the Revisionist Movement 1925-1948* (London 1988)

Sheib, Israel, (Eldad) *Ma'aser Rishon* (Tel Aviv 1950)

Smith, Sir George Adam, *The Historical Geography of the Holy Land, especially in relation to the History of Israel and the Early Church* (London 1891)

Sofer, Sasson, *Begin: An Anatomy of a Leadership* (Oxford 1988)

Stanislawski, Michael, *Zionism and the Fin de Siècle: Cosmopolitanism and Nationalism from Nordau to Jabotinsky* (Berkeley 2001)

Stern, Avraham, *Sefer HaShirim* (Jerusalem 1964)

Taggar, Yehuda, *The Mufti and Jerusalem and Palestine Arab Politics 1930-1937* (London 1986)

Talmon, J. L., *Israel Among the Nations* (London 1970)

de Tocqueville, Alexis, *On the State of Society in France before the Revolution of 1789* (London 1888)

Vital, David, *A People Apart: The Jews in Europe 1789-1939* (Oxford 1999)

Webb, Sidney and Beatrice, *The Letters of Sidney and Beatrice Webb* ed. Norman Mackenzie vol.3 *Pilgrimage 1912-1947* (Cambridge 1978)

Weinberg, David H., *Between Tradition and Modernity* (New York 1996)

Weinberg, Robert, *The Revolution of 1905 in Odessa* (Bloomington 1992)

Weinshal, Yaakov, *Ha-dam asher ba-saf: sipur chay'yov u-moto shel Yair – Avraham Stern* (Tel Aviv 1978)

Weitz, Yehiam, *From a Fighting Underground to a Political Party: The Creation of the Herut Movement 1947-1949* (Beer Sheba 2003)

Weizmann, Chaim, *Zionism and the Jewish Problem in Zionism and the Jewish Future* ed. Harry Sacher (London 1916)

   – *Trial and Error* (London 1949)

   – *The Letters and Papers of Chaim Weizmann;* Series A Letters; vol.10 July 1920-December 1921 (Jerusalem 1977)

   – Series A Letters vol.13 March 1926-July 1929

   – Series A Letters vol.14 July 1929-October 1930

Weizmann, Vera. *The Impossible Takes Longer* (New York 1967)

Zamoyski, Adam, *Holy Madness: Romantics, Patriots and Revolutionaries 1776-1871* (London 1999)

Zipperstein, Steven J., *Elusive Prophet: Ahad Ha'am and the Origins of Zionism* (London 1993)

INDEX